I0095947

A Responsive Technocracy?

EU politicisation and the consumer policies of the European Commission

Christian Rauh

ecpr PRESS

© Christian Rauh 2016

First published by the ECPR Press in 2016

The ECPR Press is the publishing imprint of the European Consortium for Political Research (ECPR), a scholarly association, which supports and encourages the training, research and cross-national co-operation of political scientists in institutions throughout Europe and beyond.

ECPR Press
Harbour House
Hythe Quay
Colchester
CO2 8JF
United Kingdom

All rights reserved. No part of this book may be reprinted or reproduced or utilised in any form or by any electronic, mechanical, or other means, now known or hereafter invented, including photocopying and recording, or in any information storage or retrieval system, without permission in writing from the publishers.

Typeset by Lapiz Digital Services

Printed and bound by Lightning Source

British Library Cataloguing in Publication Data

A catalogue record for this book is available from the British Library

HARDBACK ISBN: 978-1-785521-27-0
PAPERBACK ISBN: 978-1-785522-49-9
PDF ISBN: 978-1-785522-50-5
EPUB ISBN: 978-1-785522-51-2
KINDLE ISBN: 978-1-785522-52-9

www.ecpr.eu/ecprpress

ECPR Press Series Editors
Peter Kennealy (European University Institute)
Ian O'Flynn (Newcastle University)
Alexandra Segerberg (Stockholm University)
Laura Sudulich (University of Kent)

More in the ECPR Press Monographs series

Consultative Committees in the European Union: No Vote – No Influence?
(ISBN: 9781910259429)
Diana Panke, Christoph Hönnige and Julia Gollub

Why Centralisation? Concept, Theory and Comparative Evidence from
Sub-National Switzerland
(ISBN: 9781785521294)
Sean Mueller

Situating Governance
(ISBN: 9781907301681)
Antonino Palumbo

Democratic Reform and Consolidation: the Cases of Mexico and Turkey
(ISBN: 9781907301674)
Evren Celik Wiltse

Please visit http://www.ecpr.eu/ecprpress for information about new
publications.

To Ulla, Pauline and Jasper

Table of Contents

Abbreviations

ANEC	Association Européenne pour la Coordination de la Représentation des Consommateurs dans la Normalisation (European Association for the Coordination of Consumer Representation in Standardisation)
BEUC	Bureau Européen des Unions de Consommateurs (European Consumers' Organisation)
BSE	*Bovine spongiform encephalopathy* ('mad cow disease')
CE	Conformité Européenne (European Conformity)
CEN	Comité Européen de Normalisation (European Committee for Standardisation)
CENELEC	Comité Européen de Normalisation Électrotechnique (European Committee for Electrotechnical Standardisation)
CIAA	Confédération des Industries Agro-Alimentaires de l'UE (Confederation of the Food and Drink Industries of the EU, today: FoodDrinkEurope)
DG	Directorate-General (of the European Commission)
DG AGRI	Directorate-General Agriculture and Rural Development
DG ENTR	Directorate-General Enterprise and Industry
DG INFSO	Directorate-General Information Society and Media
DG JLS	Directorate-General Justice, Liberty, and Security
DG MARKT	Directorate-General Internal Market and Services
DG SANCO	Directorate-General Health and Consumer Protection
DG TREN	Directorate-General Transport and Energy
EB	Eurobarometer
EC	European Community
ECJ	European Court of Justice
ECTAA	European Travel Agents' and Tour Operators' Associations
EEC	European Economic Community
EP	European Parliament
EPTO	European Passenger Transport Operators
EU	European Union
EURO COOP	European Community of Consumer Cooperatives
EuroCommerce	Association of Commerce of the European Union
FAZ	*Frankfurter Allgemeine Zeitung*
GPSD	General product safety directive

ISC	Inter-service consultation
MEP	Member of the European Parliament
MS	Member state
NGO	Non-governmental organisation
QMV	Qualified majority voting
RAPEX	Rapid exchange of information system for dangerous non-food products
SEA	Single European Act
TEC	Treaty establishing the European Economic Community
TEU	Treaty on European Union
TFEU	Treaty on the functioning of the European Union

List of Figures and Tables

Figures

Tables

Acknowledgements

While all remaining errors and shortcomings are mine, the multi-annual research work that finally led to this book has benefitted enormously from the strong support of various people.

First and foremost, I wish to thank especially Miriam Hartlapp. My participation in her group on 'Position formation in the EU Commission' – funded by the Volkswagen Foundation and hosted by the WZB Berlin Social Science Centre Berlin – provided the resources necessary to generate the insights presented here. But much more important than resources, being part of Miriam's team offered challenging but always fruitful discussions that lastingly shaped my thinking on politics, on researching it and on quite a few other important things.

I am also thankful to Michael Zürn, who provided precious remarks and perspectives on the conceptualisation of my raw ideas. In addition, by granting early access to the productive debates in his 'Global Governance' department at the WZB he provided a stimulating environment for thinking about the politicisation of authority beyond the nation state which was, and is, a constant motivation to push my own work further.

In addition, the book builds on the direct or indirect support of various colleagues and friends. The thoughts presented here have been particularly sharpened in exchanges with Jacob Düringer, Pieter De Wilde, Dominic Höglinger, Liesbeth Hooghe, Deborah Mabbett, Julia Metz, Merlin Schaeffer, Waltraud Schelkle, and Gerald Schneider. And, on the one hand or the other, the book has been treated by the diligent proofreading of Barçın Uluışık.

But above all, I am indebted to my family and especially to my partner Ulla. Despite successfully handling at least equally challenging professional projects, she has always covered my back during the highs and lows of academic life. And she gave birth to our wonderful children Pauline and Jasper. Thank you.

Chapter One

Introduction

For large parts of its history, European integration has been an elite-driven project. Consecutive transfers of political powers to the supranational level and the resulting policy choices of European institutions were largely a matter of executive actors negotiating behind closed doors. For a long time, political elites could safely rely on a 'permissive consensus' among the wider publics, which were rather unified in their generalised support for the political unification of Europe (Lindberg and Scheingold 1970; Down and Wilson 2008).

But this permissive consensus eroded over time. The public referenda that defeated the European Constitution and the social unrest following the European Union's (EU) responses to the financial and currency crises are but two challenges to a purely executive mode of European integration (Statham and Trenz 2012; Rauh and Zürn 2014). Analysts are increasingly concerned with the extent to which European 'decision making has shifted from an insulated elite to mass politics' (Hooghe and Marks 2009: 13). Various recent works attest a growing *politicisation of European integration* (e.g. Hutter and Grande 2014; Risse 2014; De Wilde and Zürn 2012; Statham and Trenz 2012; Zürn 2006). Following the seminal definition of De Wilde (2011: 560, emphasis added), politicisation refers to a 'polarization of opinions, interests or values, and the extent to which they are *publicly* advanced towards the process of policy formulation within the European Union'. It is not the fact that the supranational decisions are highly political that is decisive here – this has been the case since the infancy of European integration. Politicisation rather refers to the increasing body of empirical evidence suggesting that European integration no longer proceeds outside the wider public's main field of vision.

Supranational decision making is more and more visible in public media (Boomgaarden *et al.* 2010; Sifft *et al.* 2007; Peters *et al.* 2005). This media visibility reacts systematically to specific European events (De Vreese *et al.* 2006; De Vreese 2003: chapter 3) and increases particularly in those areas where most national competences have been transferred to the supranational level (Koopmans 2007; Koopmans and Erbe 2004). Also contemporary public opinion is neither unified nor generally supportive of European integration, but rather responds systematically to political decisions at the supranational level (Toshkov 2011; Ecker-Ehrhardt and Weßels 2010; Down and Wilson 2008; Eichenberg and Dalton 2007; Franklin and Wlezien 1997). And the public is not only watching; it also feeds its evaluations back into the political process. Contrasting the 'second-order' perspective (Reif and Schmitt 1980), voters progressively consider European elections and referenda as relevant political choices in their own right

(Lubbers 2008; Garry *et al.* 2005; Koepke and Ringe 2006; Ferrara and Weishaupt 2004). More intriguingly, the public relevance of supranational decision making transcends purely European ballots, and enters the domestic electoral arena as well (Hutter and Grande 2014; Adam and Maier 2011; Hooghe and Marks 2009; Kriesi 2007; Steenbergen *et al.* 2007; Marks *et al.* 2007; Netjes and Binnema 2007; Ray 2007; Tillman 2004). The emergence of Eurosceptic parties in almost every EU member state (Taggart and Szczerbiak 2002), a number of 'Europrotests' (Uba and Uggla 2011; Della Porta and Caiani 2007; Imig and Tarrow 2001), and indications of a changing cleavage structure (Teney *et al.* 2014; Kriesi *et al.* 2012) underline that politicisation challenges the well-practised elite-driven paths to the 'ever-closer union' that the Treaty of Rome envisioned.

Politicisation thus has a prominent place in core debates about European integration. Scholars stressing national identities see a 'constraining dissensus' emerging (Hooghe and Marks 2009) that cannot be fully absorbed by the current EU institutions (Bartolini 2006a). Even more blatantly, intergovernmental accounts perceive insulation from short-term political pressures as a necessary condition for the output-driven cooperation of nation states in Europe (Majone 2005, 2000; Moravcsik 2002, 1998). In these views, it is actually the de-politicisation of transnational challenges – achieved through quiet-running intergovernmental bargains and the delegation of regulatory powers to insulated technocracies – that enables credible commitments to lasting cooperative policy solutions. Seen from this angle, public politicisation is a significant peril that threatens to undermine the very decision-making efficiency that has motivated European integration in the first place.

Others, in contrast, emphasise the opportunities that politicisation provides for European integration. Early neo-functionalists already anticipated the 'widening of the audience [...] interested and active in integration', but ultimately expected 'a shift in actor expectations and loyalty towards the new regional center' in response (Schmitter 1969: 165–6). In fact, the politicisation of European integration we have observed in the recent decade not only addressed intergovernmental conflict lines, but rather entailed the articulation of direct demands from the European public towards the supranational level (Zürn 2006). For those who argue that insulated policy making in Brussels challenges 'even the "thinnest" theories of democracy' (Follesdal and Hix 2006), public visibility and contestation promise to make the preferences of the wider public audible in the EU's political system (Hix and Bartolini 2006; Mair 2005; Magnette 2001b, 2001a). While national and supranational executives care predominantly about economic competitiveness, the wider public prefers a market-flanking policy that 'protects them from the vagaries of capitalist markets' (Hooghe 2003: 296; see also Dehousse and Monceau 2009). In such a setting of deviating public and elite preferences, an insulated decision-making system is prone to bias. The absence of public control provides specialised interests with structural lobbying advantages that can lead to capture 'with the consequence that regulatory outcomes favour the narrow "few" at the expense of society as a whole' (Mattli and Woods 2009: 12; see also Posner 1974; Stigler 1971; Olson 1965/1971). Seen from this angle, politicisation helps to overcome the democratic deficits of the EU and enhances the responsiveness of supranational governance to a wider set of societal interests.

Taken together, we have considerable evidence on an increasing politicisation of European issues on the one hand, and far-reaching expectations regarding its effects on the procedures and trajectories of European integration on the other. But while the scholarly community has invested intensively in the question whether European integration is and should be politicised, there is remarkably little empirical research on the actual consequences of public politicisation at the supranational level. It is exactly this gap that the present book aims to address. Does the public politicisation of European integration affect the intricacies of supranational decision making at all? Do supranational elites really adapt their choices if they 'must look over their shoulders when negotiating European issues' (Hooghe and Marks 2009: 5)? And if so, do their reactions indicate declining decision-making efficiency or enhanced democratic responsiveness?

To provide a hard test of the supposed politicisation effects, this book concentrates on the day-to-day *policy making of the European Commission* in Brussels. While the two other legislative actors of the EU – the Council of Ministers and the European Parliament (EP) – dispose of at least indirect delegation chains to the European public (e.g. Tallberg and Johansson 2008; Hobolt and Høyland 2011), the Commission is the most detached and most technocratic player in the European polity. By design, it is supposed to be insulated from short-term public pressures (e.g. Majone 2002; Nugent 2000; Radaelli 1999b; Featherstone 1994; Haas 1958/1968). However, at the same time, the European Commission holds the monopoly of legislative initiative in the EU. This renders the Commission an extraordinarily powerful administration with significant influence over the actual contents of binding European law (e.g. Pollack 1997a; Tsebelis and Garrett 2000). In other words, the European Commission itself embodies the tensions between technocratic, insulated decision making and democratically responsive supranational governance (Tsakatika 2005; Christiansen 1997). If public politicisation of European integration matters at this central institutional anchor point, we face a strong indication that it matters for the substance and procedures of supranational decision making in the EU as a whole.

The book furthermore concentrates on *European consumer policy* – an issue area comprised of all policy measures that aim to protect the end user of products or services against risks and disadvantages in economic life (Weatherill 2005; Cseres 2005; Mitropoulos 1997). This policy field is intrinsically linked to the original mission and the political agenda-setting powers of the European Commission (Micklitz *et al.* 2004). On the one hand, national consumer protection laws create barriers for producers or providers of services willing to trade across national borders. Such national laws thus threaten to undermine the aspired efficiency of the internal market that the Commission is expected to achieve. On the other hand, increasing cross-border trade in goods and services means that the economic interests, safety and health of consumers can no longer be effectively protected at the national level alone. In a European market, consumer risks often originate outside particular nation states, which eventually raises societal demand for supranational re-regulation of consumer protection. Against this two-sided pressure, it is unsurprising that consumer policy has been one of the fastest growing supranational policy fields in recent decades (Kurpas *et al.* 2008), which, however, attracts little interest in the political science community. What is more, the policy area is particularly suited to study politicisation effects. Consumer protection measures usually entail costs for very specific producer interests, but spread benefits over the diffuse mass of consumers. This distribution of narrowly concentrated costs and wildly dispersed benefits render the policy area exceptionally vulnerable to collective action failures and regulatory capture (Strünck 2006: chapter 2; Trumbull 2006: 45–6; Pollack 1997a; Young 1997). If the politicisation of European integration indeed has the power to counterbalance biases of insulated decision making, this should be observable in the consumer policies proposed by the European Commission.

Within these cornerstones, the book's major argument holds that public evaluation of the Commission's policies gains a greater weight under higher levels of general EU politicisation. The more supranational decision making is publicly visible and contested, the more actual policy choices at the supranational level will matter for the public's overall stance on further authority transfers to the EU. As an organisation with an interest in retaining supranational regulatory competences, the Commission will thus try to generate widely dispersed policy benefits during high politicisation periods. In consumer policy, this should be manifested in legal provisions that alter the existing distribution of rights among producers and consumers to the advantage of the latter. Yet devising outwardly consumer-friendly policies comes at a political cost. Such positions alienate the traditional stakeholders of the Commission, most notably the member state governments and the producers operating across borders. In addition, public attention is selective over time and over regulatory issues. A high level of general EU politicisation will thus affect the Commission's position only if the wider public simultaneously also cares about the more specific issues that a particular Commission initiative covers: only then, the Commission faces the risk that its policy choices affect the public's general evaluation of European integration. In a nutshell, this book claims that a sufficiently politicised context of European integration, in combination with a high degree of contemporaneous issue salience, leads to policy proposals from the European Commission that explicitly redistribute rights from the narrowly concentrated set of producer interests to the widespread mass of European consumers.

Chapter Two proposes a politicisation indicator that combines media visibility of the EU, polarisation of public opinion on EU membership and public mobilisation on European issues. These data suggest that the politicisation of European integration has increased systematically since 1991, while also being subject to significant short-term fluctuations. Against this background, Chapter Three first reviews the Commission's institutional set-up and seminal explanations for its policy choices and then derives a theoretical model of Commission responses to an increasingly politicised context. This model is then translated to the context of European consumer policy, which results in testable hypotheses on the Commission's policy choices under varying levels of politicisation and issue salience.

Chapters Four–Six then present systematic case studies on seventeen consumer policy initiatives from the European Commission under the Prodi and Barroso presidencies between 1999 and 2008. Structured along three major subfields of European consumer policy – contractual consumer rights, product regulation, and food safety – the three chapters show whether and how politicisation and issue salience matter to the Commission's preferred distribution of regulatory benefits. They draw on encompassing documentation of the internal process and external stakeholder positions as well as on forty-one semi-structured interviews with the directly involved Commission officials. Reconstructing the multi-annual policy formulation processes by combining this with the indicators for politicisation and issue salience generates novel insights on how the public visibility and contestation of European issues affects existing conflict lines and the intricacies of decision making within Europe's central agenda setter.

Pulling the case study findings together, Chapter Seven finally presents a comparative perspective on consumer policy formulation in the European Commission. Co-variation across and within the analysed processes underlines that the European Commission is indeed sensitive to the political context of legislative drafting and, most notably, to the public politicisation of European integration. However, the findings also show that this effect is severely constrained. First, the anticipated preferences of national governments in the Council effectively limit the Commission's responsiveness to wider public interest across almost all cases. Second, policy positions providing enhanced consumer protection stir partially strong turf conflicts among individual Directorates-General (DGs) of the European Commission. And third, respective legislative initiatives often profoundly challenge extant and deeply entrenched supranational policy solutions.

In the light of these results, Chapter Seven concludes on the opportunities and risks of public politicisation. The book's findings underline that enhanced public visibility and contestation of European issues indeed open up a leeway in which Brussels' policies can be reconnected to widely shared preferences among the European citizenry. Nonetheless, the scrutinised cases also underscore that this comes at the cost of more thorny and legally less consistent decision-making procedures within the Commission. Whether the democracy-enhancing or the efficiency-undermining effects will prevail ultimately depends on adequate institutional responses to the public politicisation of European integration: the policy formulation process analysed in this book imply that the European Commission is not yet fully able to absorb societal conflict lines and lacks institutional incentives to systematically channel them into the decision-making machinery of the EU.

Chapter Two

The Public Politicisation of European Integration

Before analysing whether and how the European Commission responds to the politicisation of European integration, we need a clearer picture of this phenomenon. During the infancy of the European Community (EC) after World War II, the integration process was by and large an exclusive affair of national and European executives as well as economic leaders. These elites hardly had to fear something like widespread politicisation as they could safely rely on a 'permissive consensus' among the wider citizenry (Lindberg and Scheingold 1970: especially chapters 3 and 8). During the 1950s and 1960s, citizens of the European Community founding states did not see much immediate relevance of European integration to their daily lives, and were diffusely supportive of economic coordination at the supranational level. Tacit approval among the wider publics and a correspondingly low mobilisation potential did not constrain political integration beyond the nation state. Rather, pooling and delegation of national powers in the EC were mainly driven by the interactions of the directly involved and largely freehandedly operating political elites (ibid. 250).

But even in these early days of European integration, observers did not expect the permissive consensus to be projected indefinitely into the future. Lindberg and Scheingold (1970: 277–8) themselves warned that 'the level of support or its relationship to the political process would be significantly altered' if the supranational polity was 'to broaden its scope or increase its institutional capacities markedly'. Likewise, neo-functionalists argued that the accumulation of powers at the supranational level would eventually lead to a politicisation of European integration (Schmitter 1969: 165–6). The expansion of supranational competences into more salient policy domains was expected to increase 'the controversiality of joint decision making' leading to 'a widening of the audience or clientele interested and active in integration' (ibid.). Similar claims can be found in recent sociological theory of international relations. Here, scholars argue that the accumulation of political authority beyond the nation state triggers increasing societal demands for the public justification of decision making in the inter- and supranational realm (Zürn *et al.* 2012). Since more and more national powers have been delegated to EU institutions, or were pooled in majority votes among European governments in the meantime (Biesenbender 2011; Börzel 2005), these perspectives lead us to expect that European integration has become much more politicised among the wider citizenry since its inception. In this spirit, recent integration theory claims that the permissive consensus is increasingly superseded by a 'constraining dissensus' in the publics of the European member states (Hooghe and Marks 2009).

Nevertheless, we should not too hastily conclude that European integration has finally and fully entered the realm of mass politics, or that politicisation is a stable background condition of policy making in Brussels. Even proponents of enhanced public contestation on supranational matters admit that politicisation has been subject to significant short-term swings in the recent history of the integration process. Widespread politicisation of supranational matters still seems to depend on favourable opportunity structures: for example, it is created by specific events such as the referenda or elections (De Wilde and Zürn 2012; Rauh and Zürn 2014).

Other accounts even doubt that European decision making resonates among the wider publics on a sustained basis at all. Scholars in this vein argue that the politicisation of European integration among ordinary citizens is of temporal nature at best, or even maintain that the EU still operates 'in areas where most citizens remain "rationally ignorant"' (Moravcsik 2002, 2006). European competences are seen as far too technical and far too irrelevant for the daily grind of ordinary citizens who would thus deliberately remain uninterested and inactive. Contestation would be limited to narrow societal segments that are directly affected by specific regulatory powers. Concerning the wider publics, these perspectives assume that European integration still enjoys a broad acceptance that is based on its welfare-enhancing orientation and its expertise-driven procedures. Authors in this vein believe that the 'permissive consensus' is by and large intact, and even promote the active de-politicisation of European decisions to maintain the technocratic basis on which the political unification of Europe has prospered so far (Hurrelmann 2007; Bartolini 2006a; Majone 2000). From these more sceptical perspectives, the politicisation of European integration is a very contained short-term phenomenon, but is hardly subject to an increasing long-term trend.

So, is the public politicisation of European affairs a rather constant background condition of contemporary policy making in the European Commission, or is it mainly limited to particular short-term episodes? This chapter sheds light on this question, and aims to disentangle the short-term and long-term dynamics in the politicisation of European integration among the wider citizenry. It reviews prominent approaches in the recent literature and proposes a time-consistent operationalisation along three major components of politicisation: public visibility, polarisation of public opinion, and public mobilisation on European issues. These conceptual choices enable a continuous, monthly measurement of the aggregate politicisation potential that European integration has unfolded in the six founding states of the EC between 1990 and 2009. A composite index shows that public politicisation is indeed subject to a robust long-term trend. However, this long-term tendency is mainly driven by the polarisation of public opinion while the public visibility of European integration and active mobilisation on supranational matters exhibit more stationary patterns with contained short-term bursts. These patterns suggest that the European Commission nowadays faces a much stronger politicisation potential of European integration than during its founding days, which, however, is still subject to significant variation in the short term.

2.1 Where, how and when to measure the politicisation of European integration?

Most generally, politicisation refers to 'the demand for, or the act of, transporting an issue into the field of politics' (Schmidt 2004, author's translation). This rather generic meaning accounts for the prominence of the concept, but for empirical comparisons it often remains underspecified. Yet several scholars have recently invested heavily in rendering the concept operational, although they focus on different societal arenas.

In the realm of international relations, Zürn *et al.* claim that politicisation occurs in a broad range of societal arenas, and define it 'as growing public awareness of international institutions and increased public mobilisation of competing political preferences regarding institutions' policies or procedures' (Zürn *et al.* 2012: 71). This definition rests on two major insights. First, politicisation is more than just a synonym for declining support of inter- or supranational governance. Both resistance to specific international institutions *and* the formulation of pro-active demands for more or other international policies are expressions of politicisation (see also Ecker-Ehrhardt 2012). Second, politicised and de-politicised elements of international authority can be delineated by drawing on discourse and systems theory (see also Zürn 2013). International authority enters the political sphere only where its collectively binding decisions are publicly communicated and contested. In contrast to authority that is only exercised in intergovernmental negotiations, technocratic agencies, or specialised expert fora, politicisation means that inter- and supranational decisions are pulled into the public spotlight so that those societal interests without a reserved place at the negotiation table can also have a say.

In a similar spirit, Statham and Trenz (2012: 3) argue that 'politicization is distinct from conflicts and bargaining that remain behind closed doors within institutions, and between governments, because it is publicly visible'. In their view, politicisation means that supranational issues become subject to debates and controversies in the public sphere. For Statham and Trenz, the most important societal arena to capture politicisation is thus the mass media, because it is where disagreement about supranational issues is conveyed to the wider public. While they share an empirical focus on mass-mediated debates, the politicisation concept employed by Hutter and Grande (2014) concentrates more narrowly on conflict among political parties that compete for votes in the national electoral arena. For them, politicisation of European affairs is a combination of how salient respective issues are for parties during election campaigns, how strongly partisan actors differ on these issues, and how many different actors take part in the corresponding mass-mediated debates. Other authors share this party-based focus and analyse how European affairs are politicised by partisan factions in national parliamentary debates (Wendler 2013; De Wilde 2014; Rauh 2015).

Yet again, others warn that a sole concentration on such highly institutionalised arenas of political competition in EU member states is insufficient to understand whether politicisation affects the democratic quality of supranational decision making. Particularly, Hurrelmann *et al.* (2015) emphasise that we also have to take the broader citizenry into account. In their view, European integration can be considered politicised only if and when different aspects of the political unification of Europe are raised by ordinary citizens as a relevant object of – or factor in – the collective decision-making process (ibid. 2). Studying selected citizen focus groups in 2010, they find that some EU-related topics – most notably the benefits and costs of their home countries' EU membership, and the democratic legitimacy of the EU – have achieved at least a moderate saliency in ordinary citizens' minds.

Finally, De Wilde's (2011) extensive review finds that the recent European integration literature uses the politicisation concept to denote various political conflicts that involve different cleavages and take place in several societal and institutional arenas of European multi-level governance. Yet by pointing to interdependencies between the various settings in which politicisation plays out, De Wilde carves out that we observe an encompassing process. He identifies two overarching features common to all applications (ibid. 566). First, all approaches using the concept are driven by a societal understanding of politics. Rather than focussing solely on the actions of supranational executives, politicisation research addresses the active involvement of a wider set of societal actors ranging from political parties, over mass media and social movements, which is implicitly or explicitly expected to resonate among the wider citizenry. Second, politicisation takes place at the 'input' side of supranational governance. It involves the formulation of demands and partially competitive claims making in the public sphere. Along these lines, the present book sides with De Wilde's definition of politicisation as 'an increase in polarization of opinions, interests or values and the extent to which they are publicly advanced towards the process of policy formulation within the European Union' (De Wilde 2011: 560).

In this light, an intensified and widened contestation within institutionalised arenas of different governance levels in Europe is one – yet not the most decisive – element of politicisation. The normative hopes attached to the politicisation concept rather hinge on the degree to which such institutionalised contestation has the potential to resonate among the wider publics. Politicisation will only lead to enhanced deliberation and improved democratic representation if domestic and supranational decision makers actually 'must look over their shoulders when negotiating European issues' (Hooghe and Marks 2009: 5). The endeavour to analyse whether politicisation provides a meaningful constraint for policy making by the European Commission, thus leading to a clear answer to *where to measure politicisation*: the key question for our purposes here is whether the often elite-driven conflicts on European integration unfold resonating potential among the wider citizenry of Europe.

Despite disagreements on the societal arena in which politicisation should be captured best, contemporary literature entails a remarkable agreement on *how* to capture it. Clearly, none of the discussed approaches uses politicisation as 'just another variable', but all of them treat it as a multi-dimensional concept (Zürn *et al.* 2012: 72). More specifically, the reviewed literature converges to three core components of politicisation.

The first one is *visibility* and refers to the extent to which different aspects of European integration are actually perceivable by the wider public. The early work of Schmitter (1969: 165) speaks of an 'audience' in this regard. For De Wilde (2011: 568), politicisation requires that the public is 'able to follow the proceedings of the debate'. Statham and Trenz (Statham and Trenz 2012:3) argue that politicisation is distinct from elite conflicts about European integration 'because it is publicly visible'. Likewise, Hutter and Grande (2014: 1003–4) take the level of salience attributed to European issues in mass-mediated debates as a necessary condition for politicisation. Hurrelmann *et al.* (2015) emphasise citizen knowledge about, and 'discursive saliency' of, EU affairs as a key criterion. And finally, Zürn *et al.* (2012: 74) consider the 'widespread societal awareness of international institutions' as a central element of politicisation processes. From all of these perspectives, then, politicisation increases with the degree to which issues of European integration are visible among the wider public.

The second politicisation component is the *polarisation* of opinions and positions on issues of European integration. Hurrelmann *et al.* (2015: 3) point to the 'extent of conflict'. Statham and Trenz (2012: 3) make 'controversies' a defining element of their politicisation concept, thereby siding with the early hypothesis of Schmitter (1969: 165), who refers to 'controversiality' of joint decision making in Europe. Hutter and Grande (2014) argue that 'actors need to put forward differing positions' if one refers to politicisation. Zürn *et al.* (2012: 74) also base their conceptualisation on 'diverging demands' and 'competing preferences'. In De Wilde's (2011: 567) words, an 'issue can only become politicized, when there are at least two different opinions on the subject'. For our purposes here, accordingly, politicisation increases with the degree to which opinions on European integration among the wider citizenry differ or even become polarised.

The third and final component figuring in virtually all conceptualisations of politicisation is *mobilisation*, meaning the extent to which deviating opinions and positions are actually voiced in the political process. Schmitter (1969: 165) writes about 'the audience or clientele [becoming] active in integration' while De Wilde's (2011: 560) definition entails that 'opinions, interests or values [...] are publicly advanced'. Similarly, the politicisation concept put forward by Zürn *et al.* (2012: 74) requires that 'competing preferences are uttered in the public realm'. Hutter and Grande (2014) focus on Schattschneider's idea of the 'expansion of conflict', which they operationalise as the number of different actors actively participating in public debates about Europe. And for Hurrelmann, Gora, and Wagner (2015: 2), politicisation implies that issues of European integration are actively 'raised' as relevant factors in collective decision-making processes. For our purposes, then, politicisation increases with the degree to which different actors among the wider citizenry actually mobilise on issues of European integration.

In sum, the recent literature provides a rather clear-cut answer on *how to measure the politicisation of European integration*: politicisation is understood here as a combination of increasing public visibility of European affairs, a growing polarisation of public opinions on questions of European integration, and an active mobilisation on supranational questions.

This finally leaves the question of *when to measure the extent of politicisation*. Two core issues have to be considered in this regard. First, the question of whether politicisation is driven by long-term trends or presents a contained short-term phenomenon implies that we need a rather continuous measurement that is not biased towards specific events or episodes of European integration. Second, as highlighted in the introduction, the normative relevance of the question of whether and to what degree European integration is actually politicised in the wider public lies in the fact that the supranational institutions have acquired a tremendous level of political authority over the course of European integration, which in turn has triggered debates about their democratic quality (Zürn 2006). The time period in which politicisation is measured should thus cover major steps of competence transfers from the European nation states to the supranational centre. The majority of scholars interested in different aspects of politicisation consider the 1992 Treaty of Maastricht as the most relevant watershed in this regard. This particular step of European integration ultimately pushed supranational decision making into the realm of 'high politics', set off an increasing parliamentarisation but also vibrant debates on the democratic deficit, triggered diversification of public opinion on the EU, and caused a boom of lobbying activities from varying segments of the European society in Brussels (see for example Featherstone 1994; Hooghe and Marks 1999; Majone 2002; Broscheid and Coen 2003; Eichenberg and Dalton 2007; Jolly 2007; Down and Wilson 2008). Accordingly, the question of whether politicisation is subject to long-term trends or only peaks around certain key events requires us to cover the period of the Maastricht negotiations as a major point of comparison.

In summary, this brief survey of the recent literature clarifies the first empirical task for the purposes of the book: establishing whether the politicisation of European integration among the wider citizenry is a stable background condition – or a fluctuating variable – for Commission policy making means asking for continuous, time-consistent indicators for the public visibility of European matters, the polarisation of public opinion on European integration, and the public mobilisation on European affairs among the wider European citizenry since the early 1990s.

2.2 The core components of public politicisation in cross-temporal perspective

Clearly, this is an ambitious empirical task, and three scope limitations have to be acknowledged. First, the present analysis covers the six founding states of the EC; that is, Belgium, France, Germany, Italy, Luxemburg and the Netherlands. Resource-intense data collection, as well as strongly varying data availability over all current EU member states, made this necessary. Yet against pragmatic constraints the EU-6 provide the best possible sample for studying the temporal dynamics of EU politicisation. These states have a common history of integration, and were subject to supranational authority for the same amount of time, which provides comparable starting points for the public discourse. Second, the interest here lies in consistently tracking the extent of public politicisation over time. This book neither digs into cross-national differences in levels, contents or cleavage structures, nor does it address whether the observed politicisation is horizontal or vertical in nature. Recent research on such questions made significant progress (e.g. Kriesi 2007; Adam and Pfetsch 2009; Koopmans and Erbe 2004; Peters *et al.* 2005) but must remain limited to a smaller number of measuring points in time. Third, the indicators developed here cover a twenty-two-year period from 1990 to 2011 in monthly intervals. Against limited data availability for early periods of European integration, this includes reasonably varying levels of EU authority, and allows the analysis of long-term trends as well as short-term swings.

The public visibility of European integration

Starting with the first component of politicisation – public visibility – the operationalisation focuses on mass media data. In line with the various approaches to politicisation discussed above, this rests on the assumption that mass media provide the major channel through which European citizens can perceive the process and products of European integration at all. In addition, communication research shows that media data pick up the dynamics of interest particularly well. First, commercial media are hardly neutral transmitters of factual EU activity but are generally biased towards stories with a higher news value; that is, those issues for which editors believe that public salience actually exists (cf. Epstein and Segal 2000: 73). Second, public media provide the main stage for political actors wanting to highlight diverging positions on European matters (Gerhards *et al.* 2009; Koopmans 2007). And third, political and technocratic elites themselves use mass media to infer public moods (Van Noije *et al.* 2008; Van Belle *et al.* 2004). Thus, media content is highly relevant for assessing how visible European matters are among the wider public.

More specifically, I concentrate on the EU's prominence in major quality newspapers. These outlets encompass the most frequent and most elaborated discourses on European policies, politics and polity (Pfetsch *et al.* 2008; Sifft *et al.* 2007). The outreach of television news or specific tabloids may be greater in some countries and conclusions from the quality press would be biased upwards if we were to judge on any absolute level of visibility. Yet we are mainly interested in time-consistency here, and relying on national opinion leaders provides the most sensitive indicator for the likelihood that specific issues and events of European integration are visible among the wider citizenry at all.

But the existence of cognitive limits and issue competition in the broader public must be acknowledged. We can meaningfully assess the EU's visibility only in relation to a rough estimation of all other issues on the public agenda (Princen 2009). Accordingly, the indicator presents the monthly number of articles that contain at least one reference to the EC or EU expressed as a share of the

Figure 2.1: Public visibility of European integration

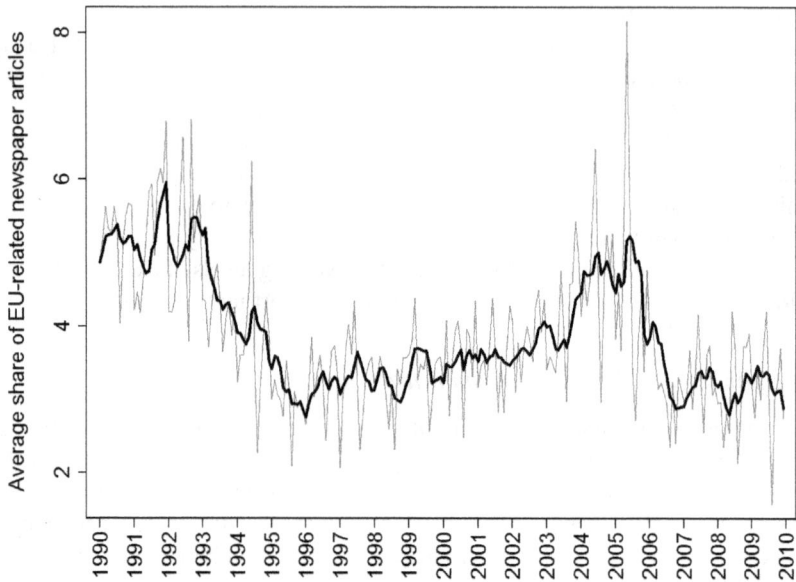

Note: The grey line presents the average monthly share of EC/EU related articles in five major European newspapers (see text for details); the black line plots the respective six-month moving average.

overall monthly number of articles published in the newspapers under analysis. At least one quality newspaper per country is digitally available for the whole investigation period except for Luxemburg, where all three major newspapers keep only paper-based archives prior to 2007. For the average visibility values plotted in Figure 2.1, data from *L'Echo* (Belgium), *Frankfurter Allgemeine Zeitung* (Germany), *Le Monde* (France), *Corriere della Sera* (Italy) and *NRC Handelsblad* (the Netherlands) have been combined.[1]

This first *politicisation* component apparently shows no consistent trend over time. As indicated by the grey line, its monthly values are rather volatile and reflect that August and December are traditionally the months with lower levels of political activity in Brussels. The six-month moving average (black line) is also not subject to a consistent trend, but rather offers a range of change points between 1990 and 2009. As expected in most of the literature on EU

1. Data from *L'Echo* and *Corriere della Sera* were directly accessed via the digital archives available at the newspapers' websites. Data from *Le Monde* and *NRC* were available via LexisNexis, and the *Frankfurter Allgemeine Zeitung* was accessed via the newspaper's portal for university libraries. Search strings and individual time series are available upon request.

politicisation, the preparation and adoption as well as the thorny ratification period of the Maastricht Treaty between 1990 and 1993 exhibit comparatively high – if not the highest – levels of public visibility for European integration. Yet afterwards, our visibility indicator declines, except for a local peak marking the June 1994 elections to the EP. This downward movement reverts, however, in 1996 when political discussions about the Treaty of Amsterdam took off and were later concluded with the treaty adoption in June 1997. From there, the smoothed indicator indicates steady positive increases, but on a comparatively small scale. With the first draft for a European constitution in mid-2003, the debates about Eastern enlargement in the same period, and the accession of ten new member states and the EP election in early 2004, this changes, and the visibility of European integration increases markedly. The average levels stay on this high plateau in the following two years, which also contain the strongest visibility peak around the constitutional referenda in the Netherlands and France in summer 2005. Yet when Merkel and Sarkozy announced a 'reflection phase' after the failure of the constitutional project, the EU's newspaper visibility also drops noticeably.

The discussions on the Lisbon Treaty halt, but do not revert, this trend. With some scattered local maxima marking the adoption of the Lisbon Treaty, its thorny ratification in Ireland, and the EP election in 2009, the data stagnate at a level of roughly 3 per cent of newspaper articles with EU references. Taken together, thus, these visibility data point to a short-term burst around major events of European integration, but do not directly speak of for a consistently positive trend towards enhanced politicisation.

The polarisation of public opinion on European integration

Turning to the second component – the polarisation of public opinion on European integration – extant politicisation research provides sophisticated empirical models, but respective data collections are often limited to smaller sections of states and time (e.g. Ecker-Ehrhardt 2012). The only EU-related data that have the necessary scope and consistency in both time and geographical coverage are the biannual Eurobarometer series with their seminal 'membership' item (Franklin and Wlezien 1997). For each wave, a multi-stage, random samples of roughly 1,000 respondents from each member state population aged fifteen and over are asked to indicate whether they consider their country's EU membership as 'a good thing, a bad thing, or neither good nor bad'.

This is a widely used measure of public support for European integration, since a country's EU membership is the most 'existential fact' of the integration process itself (Eichenberg and Dalton 2007: 133). The measure also bears the advantage that it asks for a broad instrumental assessment that is related to – but does itself not measure – support for individual EU policies or competences (Lubbers and Scheepers 2005). In other words, this indicator taps a cumulative assessment on all matters of European integration and captures the tipping points in individual opinions on European integration as a whole. I assembled the respective raw data on an individual level from the EU-6 states and all relevant Eurobarometer surveys during the investigation period.[2]

On the whole, these data indicate a slight decline in the mean levels of EU support between 1990 and 2009.[3] Yet public support and politicisation are quite different concepts. As outlined above, politicisation does not necessarily mean opposition to the EU, but finds expression in demands for more integration or particular policies as well (Zürn *et al.* 2012). What is decisive is not the opinions themselves, but the fact that opinions differ. Theoretically, the same mean level of EU support might be brought about by a broad societal consensus, or by an intense debate among two or several poles among the European public. Technically speaking, we are, at this point, not primarily interested in the mean levels of opposition or support, but in their distribution among the European public (Down and Wilson 2008: especially 7). Asking for polarisation as a central politicisation component requires us to ask how diverse public opinion is, how far it spreads across the opinion spectrum, and to what extent European citizens cluster around differing preferences for or against European integration.

A good measure of dispersion is the variance in the distribution of individual opinions; that is, the squared average deviation from the mean level of public EU support. The higher the variance, the higher is the likelihood that two randomly selected individuals differ in their opinion on the EU. Accordingly, I calculated the variance of public support for EU membership across each of the EU-6 states in each Eurobarometer half-year.[4] However, variance is not fully sufficient to capture polarisation, as this measure ignores whether opinions are clustered. Variance is

---

2. The data sets are provided by GESIS Mannheim and can be identified by their catalogue numbers. Starting from the Mannheim Trend File (ZA3521) that ends in 2002, I combined data on each respondent's support for their country's EU membership, as well as the relevant weight variables. The membership item is part in one spring and one autumn wave per year, each sampling roughly 1,000 respondents per member state. The relevant waves were EB 58.1 (ZA3693), EB 59.1 (ZA3904), EB 60.1 (ZA3938), EB 61 (ZA4056), EB 62 (ZA4229), EB 63.4 (ZA4411), EB 64.2 (ZA4414), EB 65.2 (ZA4506), EB 66.1 (ZA4526), EB 67.2 (ZA4530), EB 68.1 (ZA4565), EB 69.2 (ZA4744), EB 70.1 (ZA4819), EB 71.1 (ZA4971), EB 71.3 (ZA4973), EB 72.4 (ZA4994), EB 73.4 (ZA5234), and EB 75.3 (ZA5481). Unfortunately, the European Commission dropped the item from the autumn surveys in 2010 and 2011 so that only the spring data are available for these two years. For the EU-6 during 1990–2011, the combined data set contains 440,359 individual-level observations, of which 323,032 have valid values on the membership variable. Missing values and in particular the 'don't know' category have not been considered here. Recent research indicates that the latter category contains both actually ambivalent and indifferent respondents (see Stoeckel 2013; Van Ingelgom 2013). I appreciate the support of Meinhard Moschner (GESIS) and Ulrich Kohler (WZB) in identifying the relevant data sets and their hints on the weighting procedures.

3. The item on EU membership ranges from 1 'good thing', over 2 'neither nor', to 3 'bad thing'. Throughout the investigation period (1990–2009), the average of the nationally weighted means is 1.44 with a cross-temporal standard deviation of 0.08. The mean level changes from 1.26 in the second half of 1990 to 1.61 in the second half of 2011.

4. For a half-year and an EU-6 state given by $\sigma^2 = \sum_i (x_i - \bar{x})^2 / N - 1$ where x_i is the weighted value for individual i on the membership item, and N denotes the number of individuals in the respective national sample.

affected by both the extremity of individual opinions and the proportion of individuals holding deviant opinions. Consider the example of an extreme societal consensus in which all individuals hold the same opinion at one extreme position. If one individual changes his or her opinion to the other end of the spectrum, variance increases quickly. The problem is that the same increase in variance may occur if a larger number of individuals change their opinion only modestly. A single-peaked distribution with a few extremist outliers can hold the same variance as a distribution with two equally large poles (DiMaggio *et al.* 1996: 695). The latter case, however, provides a stronger indication for politicisation because it is more relevant if European integration is contested in the breadth of European societies rather than at the fringes only.

Figure 2.2: Polarisation in public opinion on European integration

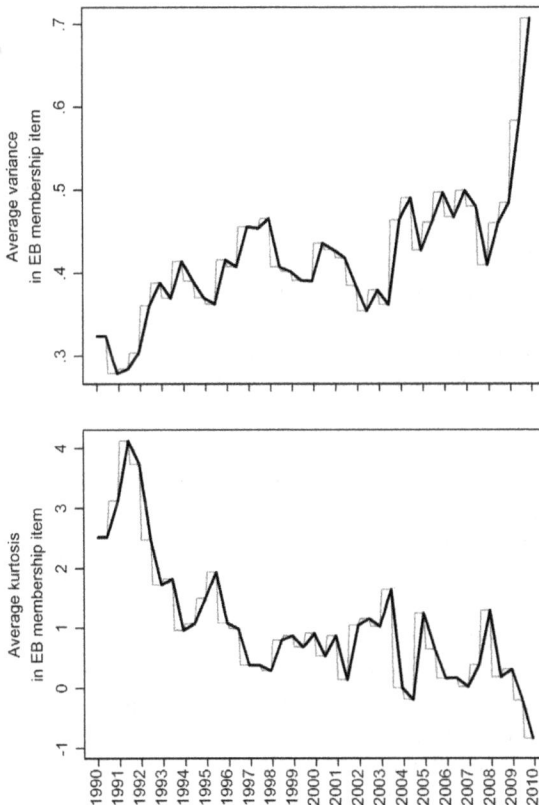

Note: Grey lines present the EU-6 average of variance and kurtosis in the distribution of individuals on the seminal Eurobarometer (EB) membership item (see main text for details). Data are only available biannually and are interpolated for the half-year in which the respective survey wave was fielded. Black lines plot the respective six-month moving average.

Public opinion scholars have taken up this idea, and complement the spread of opinion with its modality (DiMaggio *et al.* 1996: 694; Down and Wilson 2008: 32). They point to the fourth moment, *kurtosis*, which captures the 'peakedness' of distributions. If public opinion is rather consensual and exhibits a single mode, kurtosis values are strongly positive. They decline when the distribution flattens out, and reach zero if the curvature of a normal distribution is reached. A value of –1.2 indicates an equal distribution of opinions among the public (in our case identical group sizes for supporters, opponents and citizens indifferent towards EU membership) and even lower levels indicate increasing bipolarity that would be perfect for a value of –2 (indicating a population equally split into supporters and opponents of European integration in our case). Complementing the spread of public opinion, higher kurtosis values indicate that an increase in variance is the result of infrequent extreme opinions, as opposed to frequent modestly sized deviations from the mean opinion. I accordingly calculated the kurtosis of public EU support across each member state in each Eurobarometer half-year.[5] Figure 2.2 plots the EU averages of the two complementary polarisation measures.

Both indicators of opinion polarisation apparently co-vary to a considerable degree ($r = -0.85$), which has also been shown for earlier periods and other samples of EU member states (Down and Wilson 2008: especially 45–7). This indicates that the increasing variance in public opinion in fact represents modest movements of a large number of individuals rather than the emergence of only a few extreme changes in individual positions. In other words, public opinion on European integration diverges in the breadth of the societies in the EU-6 states. Note, however, that the data 'only' indicate that public opinion moves towards polarisation, but is far from being polarised already. The kurtosis values suggest that the distribution is still far from being bimodal, but they show that the distribution on this cumulative measure of public EU support has flattened out significantly over time.

Overall, this relative view of public opinion polarisation is consistent with the expectation of a positive politicisation trend, paralleling the increasing delegation and pooling of political authority in Brussels. Starting from a strongly peaked distribution skewed towards public support during the Maastricht period, public opinion becomes increasingly dispersed after this major treaty had been negotiated in 1991 and 1992. This move towards polarisation is only interrupted briefly after the elections to the freshly empowered EP in 1994. After the Amsterdam Treaty in 1997, the measures stagnate and public opinion becomes even slightly more consensual again after the adoption of the Nice Treaty in early 2001. Yet with the onset of the constitutional process and the Eastern enlargement looming in 2003, variance and the flatness in the distributions of individual opinions on EU membership increase markedly, leading to lower average and much more volatile

---

5. Technically, the average kurtosis for a given half-year is $k = \dfrac{\sum\left(x_i - \bar{x}\right)^4}{N\sigma^4} - 3$ where σ is the variance, x_i is the weighted value for individual i on the membership item, and N denotes the number of individuals in the respective national sample.

levels of polarisation in the period 2005–8. During the ratification period of the Lisbon Treaty, and also during the parliamentary elections in 2009, we see a strong increase in the variance of public opinions on EU membership, while the kurtosis values imply that the spread of public opinions has now also become flatter than a standard normal distribution. Taken together, thus, our polarisation indicators indeed speak for a long-term trend towards a higher contestation potential of European integration among the wider citizenry.

Public mobilisation on European affairs

We can now turn to mobilisation as the third and final component of politicisation. This directs our attention to a time-consistent measure of the relative extent to which differing opinions on European integration are actually voiced in the public realm. The politicisation literature discussed above most often emphasises partisan competition within the EU member states in this regard (Hutter and Grande 2014). But for the purposes of assessing the politicisation potential in the wider European public that the European Commission faces, relying on domestic partisan competition as the only indicator for mobilisation on European issues in the wider public has three shortcomings. First, parties have different strategic incentives to make European issues salient (Netjes and Binnema 2007) and their emphasis of European issues may not directly reflect the mobilisation potential in the wider public. Second, and related to that, cueing on European affairs between parties and their voters is a reciprocal process, as it is hard to infer public moods directly from partisan action (Steenbergen *et al.* 2007). And third, from the perspective of the European Commission, domestic partisan conflicts might be less important, particularly since partisan conflict lines are comparatively less relevant within the institution itself (Hartlapp *et al.* 2014; Wonka 2008a). Mobilisation of European issues in partisan competition raises many relevant questions in its own right, but for consistently assessing the politicisation potential that the Commission faces among the wider public, it is only of limited value.

Others have instead suggested analysing the extent to which organised societal interests reorient their activities towards the regional centre, for example, by establishing offices in Brussels (cf. Zürn *et al.* 2012: 74–5). However, for studying politicisation among the wider public, two operational challenges ensue. First, one would need to distinguish interest groups according to their purpose. To capture public politicisation – particularly if one thinks about it in democratic terms – it should make a difference whether one deals with promoters of wider societal interest, or with specialised interests such as business groups. Second, one would need a time-consistent registry along which the interests thus classified could be tracked at reasonably small intervals. Unfortunately, the available data sources are insufficient on both of these dimensions (Berkhout and Lowery 2010).

Both party- and interest groups-based measures for the mobilisation potential of European affairs entail a bias towards conflict among elites that does not directly reflect mobilisation potential among the wider citizenry. For our purposes here,

Figure 2.3: Public mobilisation on European issues

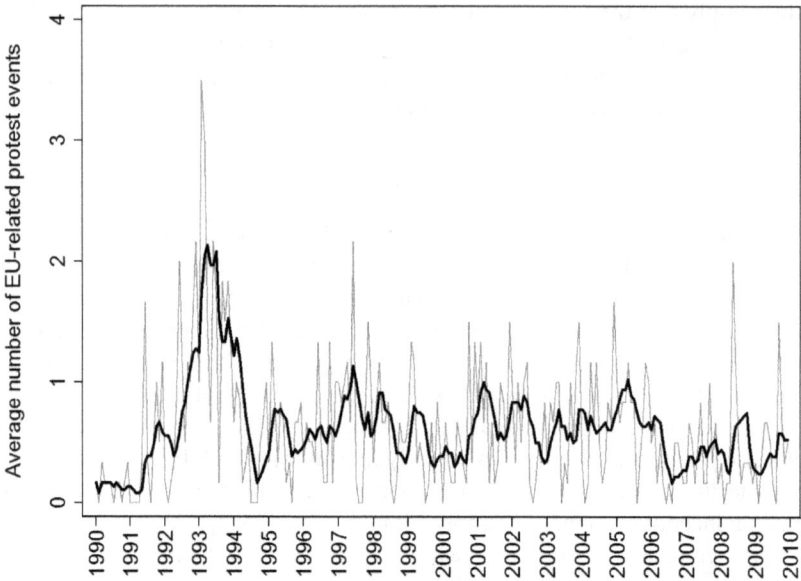

Note: The grey line presents the monthly EU-6 average of 'Europrotests' (see main text for details). The black line plots the respective six-month moving average.

I thus rather consider how frequently European citizens themselves mobilise for or against the EU directly. To this end, the most prominent concept is the so-called *Europrotest* (Imig and Tarrow 2001). Europrotests are defined as 'all incidences of contentious claims making to which the EU or one of its agencies is in some way either the source, the direct target, or the indirect target of protests and the actors come from at least one member state' (ibid. 32, see also Uba and Uggla 2011). Note that this includes both opposition and political demands on the EU. Compared to party positions or interest groups, the cross-temporal frequency of Europrotests is much more demanding in terms of mobilisation among the wider citizenry. Active and publicly visible protests – be they manifestations, strikes, blockades, or even more violent actions – involve higher individual costs than casting a ballot or delegating interest representation. Europrotests arguably involve a sufficient number of individuals for whom matters of European integration are of a very high salience, be it because they hold extreme positions or have particular stakes in EU policies. With a view to measuring the broader concept of politicisation, Europrotests thus present a rather demanding indicator of the extent to which varying opinions on European integration are mobilised politically.

For our endeavour of gaining a glimpse of the cross-temporal variation of politicisation during the investigation period, the frequency of Europrotests proves useful. A consistent measure of mobilisation's most demanding expression gives us some leverage in discussing trends over time. Luckily, Katrin Uba and Fredrik Uggla have extended the seminal work of Imig and Tarrow, and have kindly provided their monthly counts of Europrotests between 1992 and 2007.[6] In order to cover my investigation period completely, I employed their coding scheme (see Uba and Uggla 2011: especially 391–3) and extended the data collection to also include the period 1990–1, as well as 2008–11. The procedure involves identifying relevant news articles and wire copies by searching for common occurrences of different EC/EU and protest descriptors. The wealth of resulting documents is then individually screened, compared to the Europrotest definition, and coded accordingly. Since these data collection efforts are comparatively high – just for the year 2008 approximately 3,200 documents had to be screened – I refrained from coding all subcategories of Europrotests in the original research.[7]

Figure 2.3 shows the average number of Europrotests in the EU-6 states. As suspected, Europrotests are a very demanding form of mobilisation: the overall numbers are low, with an average of less than one Europrotest per month in most of the EU-6 states, and the monthly EU-6 averages (grey line) are very volatile.[8]

The long-term development of this mobilisation indicator does not exhibit a consistent trend, but points to rather contained short-term bursts. As for the public visibility of EU affairs, the Maastricht period in particular between 1991 and 1993 catches the eye immediately. Especially during the Treaty's ratification period in early 1993, we observe more than two Europrotests per month and member state. A closer look into the underlying data highlights that this peak is essentially driven by protests of French farmers, but mobilisation activity also increases particularly in Belgium and Germany during these months. Although at a comparatively lower level, the adoption of the Amsterdam Treaty in mid-1997 is also accompanied by a wave of public protests, this time mainly concentrated in Italy, France and Belgium. Another local maximum can be observed around the ratification of the Nice Treaty during 2001, which fell together with the apex of the anti-globalisation movement that also addressed the EU directly in the streets of Brussels. Also during the introduction of the Euro and discussions on reform of the European agricultural policy in 2002, protest numbers increase slightly. Finally, a minor peak is observed during the ratification (and failure) of

---

6. Again, this is a media-based measure that most likely suffers from selection bias towards the largest, most disruptive or spectacular Europrotest (Ortiz *et al.* 2005). However, this bias should not affect the time consistency of the indicator, which is of greatest importance here.

7. While I could access almost all sources mentioned by Uba and Uggla (2011: note 3), I had to substitute the US American Reuters with Agence France-Presse (AFP) which is the largest European news agency. To ensure consistency, I tested the inter-coder agreement by also coding the period from January to June 1992, and comparing it to the original data, which led to an acceptable Cronbach alpha of 0.76.

8. The data cover 898 Europrotests in the EU-6 for the 240 months between 1990 and 2009. The majority occurred in France (361), followed by Belgium, which hosts the unofficial EU capital (267). Further down the line, we find Germany (112), Italy (ninty-six), and then the Netherlands (thirty-three), as well as Luxemburg (twenty-nine).

the EU constitution in 2005, when not only the constitution itself but also the liberal impetus of the EU services directive was publicly contested in the streets of various EU-6 states. Yet afterwards, the level of contentious claims made towards Europe in the streets of the EU-6 drops markedly. Taken together, thus, our mobilisation indicator peaks around major events of European integration, but these bursts in the most demanding form of mobilisation do not exhibit consistent trends and remain limited to very contained periods.

2.3 A composite politicisation index

So what do the three core components tell us about the temporal nature of the public politicisation of European integration? The individual time series highlight that conclusions on the public politicisation of European integration faced by the European Commission have to be reached with caution: the dynamics of its different components among the wider European citizenry vary strongly.

The public visibility and mobilisation indicators exhibit declining tendencies at first sight. This, however, is strongly leveraged by the Maastricht period in 1992–3 and vanishes almost completely once this specific period is controlled for. Public mobilisation on European matters shows a rather stable mean with scattered, monthly peaks afterwards. The public visibility of European integration increases only slowly between 1994 and 2003, but witnesses another pronounced peak in the years 2004–5 when EP elections, the Eastern enlargement, and the failure of the constitution followed closely upon each other. Afterwards, visibility drops again. Thus, the first two components seem to support the view that the public politicisation of European integration is a contained short-term phenomenon driven by specific events.

But the two indicators for opinion polarisation contrast this strongly and exhibit a consistent trend towards an enhanced politicisation potential among the wider public. Major increases can be observed after 1992 and 2008, and the almost monotone rise of the deviation and the polarity in the public attitudes towards the EU is only marginally interrupted after 2001, but returns to a positive trend in mid-2004 and again to an even more impressive growth rate in 2009. This politicisation component thus supports those accounts that expect that increasing supranational authority to be directly reflected in a growing public politicisation potential of governance beyond the nation state.

Taken together, the individual politicisation components do not conclusively tell us whether we observe a positive trend or only contained periods of contention. Yet the empirical discussion so far points to at least loose cross-correlations among the three components. It is also not hard to speculate on various interdependencies among the visibility of the EU, the polarisation of respective public opinions, and the mobilisation addressing supranational politics. Citizens receiving more information on the EU are arguably more likely to develop a differentiated opinion which, in turn, raises their disposition for active mobilisation. Yet these interdependencies are far from unidirectional. More aggregate mobilisation, for example, will most probably lead to a more differentiated public opinion and to more visibility at the same time. A more differentiated public opinion provides an enhanced sound board in which news about the EU and mobilisation efforts can resonate widely.

For the book's central question of whether and how the European Commission responds to the politicisation of European integration, such interdependencies are only of secondary interest, however. What we need to provide with respect to the core research question are comparisons of the *state or level* of politicisation across those points in time at which the Commission takes different, comparable policy choices. To this end, it is plausible to assume that, from the perspective of Brussels, visibility, polarisation and mobilisation are perceived as independent expressions of politicisation at any given point in time. From the hallways of the Commission's main offices, an increase in media reporting, a differentiating public opinion, or an increasing number of protests directed to the EU all signal that the potential for a public contestation of supranational powers has increased. From this perspective, then, the adequate measurement for the state of politicisation at a single point in time is an *additive index* that summarises the three components in an unbiased way.

Figure 2.4: A composite index for the public politicisation of European integration

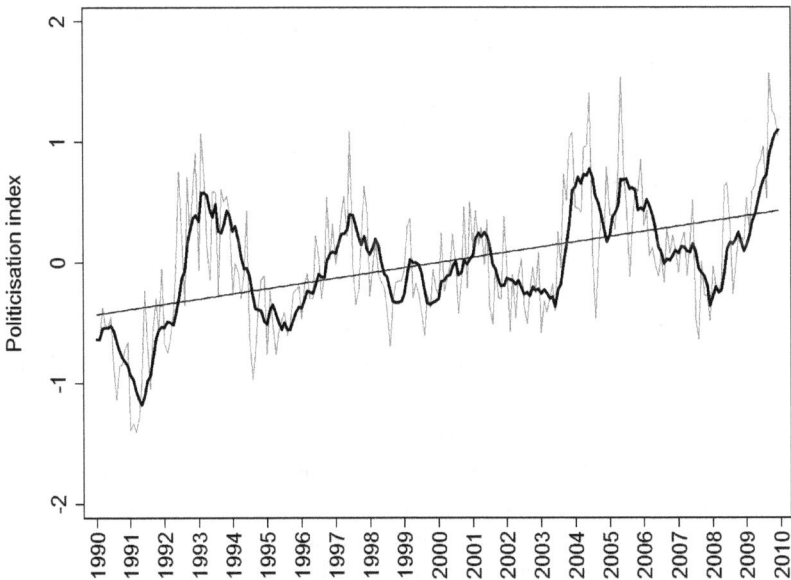

Note: The grey line presents the monthly index value, the black line its six-month moving average (see main text for details). The straight black line, in addition, provides a time trend estimated by a simple ordinary least squares regression (see Appendix A for details).

In technical terms, we face the difficulty that the three components are measured on different scales. Simply adding those up would increase the weight of those components that have a greater numerical variation. Since there is no theoretical reason as to whether visibility, polarisation or mobilisation is most relevant to the overall level of politicisation, such an implicit weighting is to be avoided. Thus, the monthly values of the visibility, opinion variance and kurtosis, as well as mobilisation, have been z-standardised into four generic time series that fluctuate around their investigation period mean (as indicated by 0) with a standard deviation of 1. Averaging across the individual components thus forces them to a common scale, and adds up to a composite index of politicisation that itself has an expectancy of zero. While this generic index, plotted in Figure 2.4, cannot be interpreted in absolute terms, it enables us to draw relative conclusions *within* the period covered here, for example, on the question whether politicisation was higher in December 1990 as compared to December 2009.

As compared to anecdotal evidence or a focus on specific components, this index provides a truly time-consistent perspective along which we can compare the relative politicisation potential of European integration among the wider citizenry of Europe between January 1990 and December 2009. From this perspective, the overall politicisation of European integration in the wider public is indeed subject to short-term swings driven by varying levels of visibility and mobilisation which, however, do not offset the positive long-term trend that is driven by an increasingly diverging public opinion.

A simple trend line calculated by an ordinary least squares regression illustrates this (Figure 2.4). Additional analyses of the politicisation index in Appendix A furthermore show that this trend line is not leveraged by individual events. Rather, once individual treaty revisions or EP elections are controlled for, the slope of the trend line becomes even more pronounced. Regarding short-term fluctuations around this long-term trend, the descriptive regressions in Appendix A confirm the visual inspections above: politicisation levels peak particularly during EU treaty ratifications and EP elections while the particular effects differ across the individual events that occurred during the period studied here.

2.4 Conclusion: Long-term growth and short-term variation in public EU politicisation

This chapter has set out with the question of whether the politicisation of European integration is nowadays a constant background condition of contemporary Commission policy making, or whether it is a contained short-term phenomenon only. Based on a survey of the respective conceptual literature and a detailed analysis of the major components of politicisation derived from this literature – public visibility, polarisation and mobilisation – the truth seems to lie somewhere in the middle.

Driven mainly by diverging public opinion on EU membership as the most existential fact of the political unification of Europe, the European Commission today faces indeed much higher levels of politicisation compared with earlier periods of European integration. While the Maastricht Treaty turns out as a watershed of politicisation among the wider citizenry as expected, later episodes of contention reach similar values on the politicisation index developed here. They even excel the politicisation levels observed during Maastricht, in particular, during the years 2004 and 2005, in which a hitherto unseen enlargement of the Union, European elections and the political efforts to achieve a European Constitution occurred together. Likewise, after the comparatively quiet adoption of the Lisbon Treaty in 2008, the politicisation measure reaches unseen heights during the year 2009.[9] Even when controlling for individual events of European integration, this positive trend towards an enhanced politicisation potential among the wider citizenry remains robust.

Yet there still is remarkable variation around this trend line in the short-term. While the Commission nowadays faces much higher levels of politicisation on average, we also observe periods in which the composite indicators decline again, mainly due to variation in public visibility or mobilisation on European issues in the streets. In a constrained form, then, the politicisation of European integration may also serve as a variable for policy making in the European Commission, which possibly opens a leeway for strategic considerations. Whether and how we can expect the Commission to respond to these patterns of public politicisation is a key question of the next chapter.

---

9. Note that this period marks only the onset of the financial and later sovereign debt crisis in Europe, which has pushed visibility, polarisation and mobilisation even further in all contemporary EU member states. For a respective extension of the indicators developed here that also includes 2010 and 2011, see Rauh and Zürn (2014).

Chapter Three

Politicisation and Consumer Policy Formulation in the European Commission

The European Commission is at the heart of the EU's political system. Besides its significant powers in overseeing compliance with the Union's treaties, in implementing community policies, and in representing the EU on the international stage, its most distinguished feature is its monopoly in initiating European legislation. In most areas, neither the Council nor the EP can enact binding law without a legislative proposal from the Commission.[1] Along this institutional feature, Europe's central bureaucracy controls significant agenda-setting powers, which provide it with high leverage in influencing the contents of supranational policies (see for example Tsebelis and Garrett 2000; Schmidt 2000; Princen 2009).

Broad strands of the literature on supranational decision making in the EU assume that the Commission exploits these powers, not the least to its own benefit (most explicitly, e.g. Franchino 2007; Cram 1997; Pollack 1994). Also the argument on the Commission's policy responses to enhanced politicisation of European integration developed in this chapter rests on the assumption that the 'utility function of the Commission is positively related to the scope of its competences' (Majone 1996: 95). In line with the classical theory of bureaucracy (e.g. Downs 1966/1967: chapter III; see also Tullock 1987), the Commission is expected to strive for more competences where regulatory powers are particularly attractive, given tight budgetary constraints and the ever simmering question of subsidiarity (cf. Dunleavy 2000).

This is clearly a simplifying assumption, given that the Commission is made up of individual officials with varying attitudes and preferences (Kassim *et al.* 2013). However, attitudinal research also shows that Commission officials tend to assess their organisational environment along rational calculations (Bauer 2012) and seem to realise that the public politicisation of European integration challenges the transfer of national competences to the supranational level (Bes 2014). Against this background, it should be noted that theoretical model developed here also

---

1. In some policy areas, the Commission shares the right of initiative with the Council. In addition, one of the major innovations of the Treaty of Lisbon was to extend the public's right to ask the Commission to come forward with proposals from the Parliament and the Council (Article 225, 241 and 11 TFEU, respectively). Under the European Citizens' Initiative, one million citizens who are nationals of a significant number of member states can ask the Commission to submit a proposal. Both of these more recent rules curtail the Commission's monopoly of initiating legislation in some policy areas, but they still rely on Europe's central agenda setter when it comes to formulating the actual contents of the respective policies. Without doubt, then, no other body determines the substance of EU legislative proposals in the way that the Commission does.

works if we relax this assumption and only expect that Commission officials will usually hold a preference to retain at least the current supranational competences of the organisation they work in – be it from competence-seeking, problem-solving or even ideological motives (see also Hartlapp *et al.* 2014: chapter 12). How, then, should we expect a thus conceptualised European Commission to respond to the long-term increases and short-term fluctuations in politicisation uncovered in the preceding chapter?

3.1 Commission policy making under varying levels of EU politicisation – a theoretical model

On the most abstract level, the increasing politicisation of European integration challenges the Commission with new legitimacy demands (Zürn 2006; Hooghe and Marks 2006a, 2009). The more the broad public becomes alert to supranational decisions and the more it ascribes relevance to them, the more the Commission's exercise of power comes under public scrutiny. And the more the Commission's authority is publicly questioned, the more it is rational for a competence-seeking organisation to care about the broad acceptability of its policies. Otherwise, the Commission jeopardises the further transfer of national competences to the European level, as the 2005 referenda and the accompanying debates on the services directive in France and the Netherlands have forcefully demonstrated. But how can the Commission influence the public's evaluation of the legitimacy of supranational competences?[2]

Following the seminal distinction of input and output legitimacy (Scharpf 1999a; Krapohl 2007), we must first acknowledge that the input-oriented route – that is, legitimation through increasing participation of the public – appears more or less blocked at the moment. The history of the European Constitution, its mitigated version in the form of the Lisbon Treaty, and the conflict-laden attempts of a more or less direct election of the Commission president in the EP elections in 2014, have underlined once more that further democratisation and a more direct bonding of Commission action to public preferences can hardly be expected in the near future. Likewise, a more differentiated and systematised

---

2.   Note that I use the term 'legitimacy' here as a descriptive rather than a normative concept (cf. Peter 2010; Tsakatika 2005; Zürn 2004). Following the Weberian conceptualisation, the legitimacy of a political order such as the EU is understood as a subjective belief in the acceptability of that political order (Weber 1925/1978). In other words, legitimacy is considered as an empirical social fact, and refers to the degree to which those governed accept the authority of the political order even if it contradicts their individual preferences at times. This empirical understanding is intentionally distinct from normative conceptualisations of legitimacy, which address the (moral) rightfulness of political authority against theoretically chosen benchmarks and justifications. While the choice of such benchmarks can indeed be politically relevant as discussed further below, this book does not intend to judge whether the Commission should live up to a particular normative benchmark. Furthermore, legitimacy is related but not equal to political support for an authority (cf. Easton 1975: 450–3). While the absence of legitimacy as defined here implies the absence of political support, the fact that those governed accept an authority does not necessarily imply that they also support it when being faced with a choice.

participation of societal interests, which some authors understand as throughput legitimacy (e.g. Holzhacker 2007), is strongly limited in its potential to signal enhanced involvement possibilities to a diffuse European public. By its very nature, European policy formulation operates at a highly aggregated level so that the inclusion of societal interests works only through rather detached umbrella organisations or mass surveys limited either in depth or in representativeness.

Thus, mainly the output route remains. Indeed, the political science literature largely agrees that the European Commission derives its legitimacy from the added value its decisions produce for its stakeholders (e.g. Majone 1996; Menon and Weatherill 2002; Moravcsik 2002; Tsakatika 2005) – a seminal feature of only indirectly accountable bureaucracies (Downs 1966/1967; Tullock 1987). So, who are the Commission's major stakeholders?

Most strands of integration theory or the literature on the 'regulatory state' see the purpose of delegating competences to a supranational bureaucracy in solving coordination problems among nation states. While increasing interdependencies and expected gains motivate international cooperation, the strongly varying preferences of individual governments and free-riding incentives aggravate credible national commitments to cooperative policies. Against these problems of high search costs and incomplete contracting, the Commission was designed as an institution with policy formulation and monitoring powers (e.g. Haas 1958/1968; Featherstone 1994; Pollack 1997a; Moravcsik 1998; Tallberg 2002; Franchino 2007). Since the 1957 Treaty of Rome, cooperation within the EC has strongly focused on the stimulation of economic growth through the creation of a common market (Jabko 2006). Along this line, the Commission is often seen to mainly push a liberalisation agenda through removing, overruling or harmonising all national policies that were perceived as barriers to trade (e.g. Scharpf 1999a).

If one adds public politicisation to the picture, however, this source of output legitimacy is insufficient at best. It follows the model of 'executive multilateralism' and predominantly rests in the relationship of national governments and the Commission, whereas politicisation, as defined in the preceding chapter, entails the articulation of direct political expectations or demands from the European public towards the supranational level (Zürn 2013). Whereas the institutional design of the Commission hinges on the idea of insulating its decisions against political pressure and relies mainly on the assent of national executives, widespread politicisation invariably makes the European public a much more direct stakeholder of supranational decisions in Europe.

Yet the pursuit of economic growth through an increasingly integrated European market is hardly suitable for demonstrating the immediate added value of supranational decisions to this very public. While gains from increasingly open markets take time to materialise and can often only be demonstrated by counterfactual arguments, the immediate political costs of liberalisation are instantaneously visible to the diffuse public. The *plombier polonaise* that figured prominently in the French debate on the services directive serves as a prominent example for the clash between the long-term desirability of economic cooperation and negative distributive effects for broadly vested societal interests in the short term. Seen this way, the newly emerging need to generate output legitimacy vis-à-vis a broad public requires the Commission to be able to demonstrate more immediate benefits of the policies it devises (cf. Ecker-Ehrhardt and Weßels 2010). Yet becoming responsive to political pressure may undermine the Commission's ability to find cooperative policies that instil consensus among its traditional stakeholders; that is, the member state governments. Therefore, politicisation is often seen as a significant peril to political progress in Europe (Hurrelmann 2007; Bartolini 2006b; Majone 2005, 2002; Moravcsik 2004). From this perspective, we would expect that politicisation drastically decreases the Commission's room for manoeuvre in devising European policy.

In contrast to this expectation, however, there is also reason to believe that politicisation has enabling rather than constraining effects for a competence-seeking Commission. The emergence of the public as a mindful stakeholder with political expectations and demands on European integration can also provide a basis for expanding regulatory competences. The Commission may use such demands to identify and to justify additional cooperation in previously disintegrated domains. In this line, neo-functionalist theory expects more public political involvement in European integration to lead to a 'manifest redefinition of mutual objectives' (Schmitter 1969: 166; cf. Hooghe and Marks 2006b). But even where such bold expectations do not hold, politicisation may allow the Commission to claim that more public interest regulation is a necessary side payment to secure the gains flowing from purely economic cooperation. Along these lines, a broad empirical literature shows how the Commission has successfully acted as a political entrepreneur and exploited changing political contexts to establish its own competences in new policy areas (e.g. Cram 1997; Simpson 2000; Moravcsik 1999). Hence, to the extent that the organisation can reconcile the goal of economic cooperation among nation states with more immediate political interests of the public, politicisation can also have enabling effects for the Commission.

But how do these contradicting expectations actually impinge on the Commission's policy positions? To answer this question, it is required to shift our perspective from the general politicisation of European integration to the individual policy choices that the Commission faces. At this level, we cannot presuppose *per se* that the general politicisation of European integration has enabling or constraining effects. It would be wrong to assume that a politicised context allows the Commission to seek the production of immediate and widely dispersed political benefits in each and every initiative. Serving only widespread interests of the public might contradict the original *raison d'être* of the Commission as an independent market regulator, which, in turn, would alienate its more traditional stakeholders, most notably national governments. For a competence-seeking actor that aims to increase its output legitimacy vis-à-vis *all* of its stakeholders, this results in a trade-off. Hence, while politicisation provides the Commission with political incentives to appeal to the diffuse public, this comes at a political cost for each individual legislative initiative. Expressed differently, a politicised context of European integration is a necessary condition for the production of immediate, widely dispersed political benefits by the Commission, but it is not sufficient to explain such policy choices.

Rather, the effect of politicisation on individual position formation processes should depend on the Commission's anticipation whether this particular initiative will actually influence the public's overall evaluation of supranational powers. Yet from a broad body of public opinion research, we know that the public hardly follows each and every proceeding on the political agenda. Rather, cognitive boundaries and information costs lead to a selective public attention that varies over time – particularly on issues exceeding the domestic domain (see for example Downs 1972; Aldrich *et al.* 1989; Zaller 1992; Stimson 1999; Burstein 2003; Soroka 2003; Oppermann 2010).

It follows that some Commission initiatives may fly safely below the public radar, while others may touch issues that the public currently cares about. But only with regard to the latter can the Commission gain or lose in terms of its output legitimacy vis-à-vis the public. Therefore, the general context of politicisation will only exhibit the hypothesised effects if the Commission receives signals that the legislative initiative in question is relevant to the broad public at the time it is drafted or proposed. The *contemporaneous public salience* of the issues to be regulated – that is, the degree to which the issues are easily understandable and visible among the broader public (Mahoney 2008; Epstein and Segal 2000) – is a decisive variable moderating the link between politicisation and the policy output of the Commission.

Along these lines, Figure 3.1 summarises the theoretical model, which describes a feedback loop of politicisation. The general 'polarization of opinions, interests or values and the extent to which they are publicly advanced towards the process of policy formulation within the European Union' (De Wilde 2011: 560, *see* also Chapter Two in this volume) render the European public a stakeholder that is relevant to the Commission's future growth of competences. For the Commission, this creates a basic incentive to serve immediate, widespread public interests with its policies (a). Yet at the level of individual policy initiatives, this link is moderated by the degree of public salience attached to the regulated issues at the time of policy formulation (b). The basic model is driven by two not directly observable strategic considerations of the Commission. In publicly salient domains, the Commission can be reasonably sure that its policy position is perceived by the public (c). And if this is the case, the public's evaluation of the particular initiative in question should feed back into the general political evaluation of overall decision making in the EU (d). To put it in a nutshell, the overall politicisation of supranational powers provides the Commission with incentives to be responsive to immediate public interest which, however, should become mainly relevant with the public salience of the individual issues at stake in a given policy proposal.

The alert reader might notice that this central argument contains a good deal of endogeneity in at least two respects. First, the concepts of general EU politicisation and contemporaneous salience of specific policy initiatives are not perfectly disjoint, but are rather nested. The general EU politicisation can be understood as a response to the sum of individual supranational decisions (Zürn *et al.* 2007) so that

Figure 3.1: Theoretical model

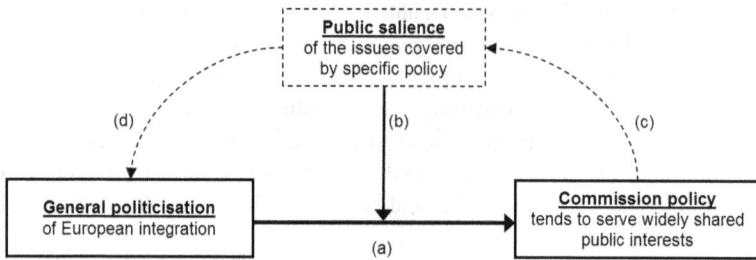

```
                          ┌─────────────────────────────┐
                          │       Public salience       │
                  - - - - │    of the issues covered    │◄- - - -
              /           │      by specific policy     │          \
            /             └─────────────────────────────┘            \
      (d) /                            │ (b)                         \ (c)
        /                              │                              \
       ▼                               ▼                               
┌──────────────────────┐                         ┌──────────────────────────┐
│ General politicisation │────────────────────────▶│     Commission policy     │
│ of European integration│           (a)           │ tends to serve widely shared│
└──────────────────────┘                         │     public interests      │
                                                  └──────────────────────────┘
```

salience is nothing other than politicisation on a much smaller scale. And indeed, long-term perspectives on the politicisation of European integration assume a cumulative process, and thus closely resemble the traditional political science concept of political support and opposition (De Wilde 2011: 565–6; Weßels 2007; Zürn *et al.* 2007; Easton 1975). Initially, only specific policies related to European integration were contested. The more this was the case, however, the more the respective politics and even the polity itself became subject to debate. However, while a broad range of evidence supports this long-term perspective, it does not disqualify the model proposed here. By centring the perspective on individual legislative acts and corresponding policy choices, the context condition of a *general* politicisation of European integration and the *specific* contemporaneous issue salience can be kept analytically separate (see also below).

Second, endogeneity may occur at the level of individual initiatives because, in principle, the Commission can manipulate public salience even *during* policy formulation. For example, the Commission can try to push an issue up the public agenda by publishing specific studies or by widely circulating consultation documents. It may even try to exploit the press more directly. And indeed, if the Commission acts as a policy entrepreneur as outlined in theoretical terms above, then we should expect it to do so if it serves the aim of competence enhancement. While this creates a sort of short circuit in the model summarised in Figure 3.1, it does not contradict the expectation that the salience of a proposal is the decisive variable to render an influence of the legitimacy demands emerging from politicisation possible. Rather, it is a confirmation of this expectation, if the Commission adapts its position *after* the salience of the initiative in question has been successfully increased. In any case, the possibility of such short circuits highlights that an empirical evaluation of the model needs to take the process of policy formulation into account.

To sum up, this theoretical section argues that a competence-seeking Commission in an increasingly politicised European integration context faces strong incentives to generate widely dispersed public benefits if the respective policy issue to be regulated shows a high degree of contemporaneous public salience. To render this rather abstract expectation empirically tractable, the following section introduces European consumer policy as a highly suitable testing ground for this argument. By discussing the key features of this supranational policy field, we can formulate more precise expectations of the Commission's position before we turn to the institutional features of the policy formulation process within the European Commission.

3.2 European consumer policy and the choice variable of the Commission

For the purposes of this book, consumer policy comprises all policy measures that aim at protecting the end user of products or services against risks and disadvantages in economic life (Weatherill 2005; Cseres 2005; Mitropoulos 1997). Rules in this policy area may cover specific consumer market transactions (e.g. rules on contract terms), prescriptions of information provision and labelling (e.g. rules on food ingredient lists), or even particular product standards and respective liabilities (e.g. rules on product safety). In the seminal classification of Lowi (1964), the paramount majority of consumer policy decisions falls into the category of regulatory policy where governmental intervention is based on authoritative rules stated in general terms. Since such universally applicable rules invariably reduce or expand the alternatives of private actors, devising consumer policies confronts the regulator with the decision of 'who will be indulged and who deprived' (ibid. 690–1).

In essence, consumer policy regulates the relationship between consumption and production in the marketplace, and is 'about government intervention in the contractual relationship between the consumer and the producer to ensure that the private interests of consumers are met' (Trumbull 2006: 14).[3] Considering the political demands for such intervention by both affected societal groups, the heterogeneous and diffuse nature of consumer interests initially allows us to expect little political clout vis-à-vis producers. While the almost 500 million European citizens may in principle benefit from regulatory interventions that promote their position in the marketplace, none of them can be excluded once such measures are enacted and, thus, none of them has individual incentives to actively support decisions in this vein. In this light, consumer policy serves as a prime example for collective action problems since Mancur Olson's (1965/1971) seminal work on the subject (see also Pollack 1997b). Indeed, the comparatively low number of producers has much stronger incentives to lobby the Commission, for example, by offering industry information the Commission cannot gather on its own. This distribution of narrowly concentrated costs and widely dispersed benefits should therefore increase the political weight of producers interested in trading across borders in Europe (Beyers 2008; Dür 2008; Eising 2007; Broscheid and Coen 2003).

---

3. I use the concept of producers here to capture producers and retailers of goods as well as service providers.

However, classical regulation theory argues that this imbalance in consumer and producer power can be overcome by entrepreneurial politics on part of the regulator (Wagner 1966; Wilson 1980; Frohlich *et al.* 1971; see also Posner 1974; or Kingdon 1984). As the entrepreneur metaphor suggests, the regulator will provide consumer-friendly positions as long as they can privately gain by doing so. If the observed politicisation allows the Commission to seek greater output legitimacy among the broad, generalised public as theorised above, the production of immediate and widely dispersed benefits are a priced resource (cf. Klüver 2010; Meyer 2009; Strünck 2006). The argument developed in the preceding section thus leads to the expectation that a Commission proposal becomes more consumer-friendly once the regulated issue area is subject to high public salience. But how does serving immediate, widespread public interest in consumer policies relate to the Commission's traditional focus on the creation of a common market?

This question requires a closer look on the policy choices the Commission faces. From a purely economic perspective, consumer policies are justified where they remedy *market failures* that otherwise preclude consumers from reaping the benefits of the full choice offered in a perfect market. Accordingly, regulatory interventions are meant to create a level playing field between demand and supply so as to reach allocative efficiency. In this view, consumer policy is in fact competition policy, and it aims at maximising the total welfare generated in the market place (e.g. Cseres 2005). Such a position in consumer policy is perfectly consistent with the traditional market-making approach of the Commission. Obviously, differing national consumer protection regimes can be regarded as barriers to trade. Producers offering products or services across borders in particular face costs in adapting to the different national rules and regulations. As such, national governments can, in principle, exploit consumer protection legislation as a non-tariff trade barrier shielding the national market against international competition. Relying solely on this reasoning, in turn, provides the European Commission with a justification to act based on the respective articles in the EU treaties (especially Article 95 EC, see Micklitz *et al.* 2004). Thus, the Commission could fulfil its basic task of market creation by legislatively establishing the lowest common denominator of the differing national regimes. Such a policy position would alienate the traditional stakeholders – that is, the member state governments and cross-nationally operating producers – the least, and constitutes the rational strategy for the Commission in the absence of public salience.[4] In analytical terms, thus, the market failure rationale and its focus on consumer choice are perfectly consistent with the long-term goal of market creation, and thus represents the benchmark position for the Commission's consumer policies in this study.

---

4. Note, in this view, that consumer policy almost always involves the setting of product- but not process-related standards in the seminal distinction of Scharpf (1999b; see also Vogel 1995). Thus, outright Council opposition to such liberalising Commission proposals need not be expected, because member states do not have to fear a regulatory competition 'downwards' – since products in consumer markets do not only compete on price but also on quality (as affected by national consumer protection rules).

Nevertheless, cross-border trade barriers are not the only economically relevant failure of consumer markets. For example, the unequal distribution of information between producers and consumers is another prominent cause of inefficient market outcomes (Akerlof 1970) that the Commission could tackle when pursuing its long-term goal of market making. And, in fact, since Maastricht, the European treaties entail a clear, albeit legally weak, basis for European standards going beyond purely negative integration at a 'high level of consumer protection' (Article 153 TEC, Micklitz *et al.* 2004).

However, any Commission policy moving beyond the benchmark of a lowest common denominator among national regimes makes a focus on the distribution of political benefits immediately relevant. On the one hand, even pure economic theory itself does not argue that remedies to market failures are neutral in distributional terms. While corrective measures may ultimately target the Pareto frontier, any move in this direction will advantage some market participants and disadvantage others (e.g. Mabbett 2010; Hooghe and Marks 2006b). In any case, correcting market failures entails costs for those producers or consumers that had earned rents in the previously failing market. So, even if the regulator is able to devise policies that are efficient in the purely economic sense, this will generate a distinct pattern of support and opposition among the affected segments of society, given that the respective policy is visible to all affected groups. In political economy terms, this shifts the emphasis away from total welfare considerations, and directs attention to the welfare of individual stakeholder groups. To the extent that the regulator is disproportionately dependent on the beneficiaries of a particular regulatory initiative, this 'politicization of market failure' moves the political outcome away from the equilibrium that a perfectly unfettered market would have produced (Buchanan and Vanberg 1988).

But even beyond that, the market failure justification for consumer policies is often criticised for considering regulation only as a second best solution to pure market outcomes, thereby assuming that all other political justifications are essentially arbitrary (Prosser 2006; McVea 2005; Janning 2004). Critics in this vein argue that a more political perspective should not only focus on consumer choice in the market, but should rather emphasise consumer rights (see also Micklitz and Weatherill 1993). These normatively oriented approaches point out that consumer policies can be, and have empirically been, used to pursue other socially defendable goals apart from market functioning. Examples are tackling public health issues, the stimulation of demand in specific product or service sectors, or rewarding particularly ethical commercial practices (cf. Strünck 2006: chapter 4; Janning 2004). In this view, consumer policy can as well be subsumed under what the debate in the United States (US) debate on the regulatory state has termed 'social regulation'. Distinct from economic regulation that is directed at unbiased competition, social regulation focuses on 'the externalities and social impact of economic activity' (Williams and Matheny 1984: 430) and the corresponding 'socially acceptable levels of risk' (Reagan 1987: 18). While this literature recognises the fuzziness of the borderline between economic and social regulation, the latter can be identified through its focus on particular problems or functions rather than on particular industries, while it strives for aims that cannot be achieved by increased competition alone. Based on these considerations, a regulator may also conceptualise consumer policy as a distinct form of social policy that is based on a rationale of *redistribution* (e.g. Schelkle and Mabett 2010: especially 2). Of course, regulatory policies do not involve direct redistribution of funds, but this rationale is directed at the intentional reallocation of rights in ways that strengthen a presumably weaker party.

So far, *market failure* and *redistribution* have been presented as largely normative justifications which, for some consumer policies, might result in observationally equivalent positions.[5] While the above argument on Commission behaviour under increasing politicisation may allow us to expect an increasing use of redistribution arguments, for our purposes here this political rhetoric is only relevant as long as it empirically results in substantially different policy proposals. In abstract terms, once we have passed a certain level of regulatory consumer protection, proposals that are based on a redistributive justification should differ from those based on a market failure justification. A *market failure* proposal would stop where economically efficient markets are reached, a *redistribution* proposal might go well beyond, if the politically desirable distribution of rights in society is not yet achieved.

In fact, the chosen justifications should lead to substantially differing policies since they are directed at protecting different types of consumers (Cseres 2005: 320 pp.). On the one hand, policy positions based on the market failure justification should follow a *laissez-faire* model, which is directed at a fully sovereign consumer. Where the regulator assumes that consumers are able to define their needs and translate these to rational purchase decisions, competition policy and information disclosure are sufficient tools to protect or, to express it differently, to enable this market participant. Any further regulatory intervention beyond this criterion, in contrast, distorts the market by raising production and transaction costs for producers. This may even drive some producers out of the market, and ultimately results in an economically suboptimal market equilibrium.

On the other hand, the logic of redistribution leads to an *interventionist* model of consumer policy. This model is grounded in the assumption that the consumer is a structurally weaker market participant in markets that are obscured by product differentiation and the multiplicity of packaging, advertising and distribution. Against this assumption, consumer policies aim to restore the balance between consumers and producers. Accordingly, the respective regulatory measures are conceived as being a zero-sum conflict between these societal groups, which can only be overcome by mandatory rules intervening in support of the consumer.

---

5.   This is most obvious as regards information failure. Regulatory intervention prescribing producer information duties can be justified by informationally inefficient markets, or it can be based on the political will to alter the distribution of rights among producers and consumers in society. Without further analysis, the respectively chosen justification tells us little about the actual level of consumer protection that the Commission will propose.

Table 3.1: Ideal-type consumer policy models

	Laissez-faire model	Interventionist model
Long-term goals	Remedy market failures	Redistribute rights
Basic assumptions	Free competitive markets result in best terms for consumers	Free competitive markets produce an imbalance of economic power between producers and consumers
Addressed consumer	Average rational, reasonably circumspect and information-seeking consumer	Weak, vulnerable and overburdened consumer
Policy goals	Enable consumer sovereignty	Restore balance of consumers and producers
Policy tools	Mutual recognition, beyond only competition law or disclosure of information, no intervention in transaction and product standards	Mandatory rules on information provision and labelling, prescription of transaction substances, for example by standard terms and conditions, strong intervention in product standards
Short-term costs and benefits	Cross-border producers gain through market access	Producers face costs from bearing additional responsibilities
	Immediate consumer benefits only scarcely visible	Consumer protection and empowerment can be easily communicated

Source: Author, partially adopted from Cseres (2005: 322).

These ideal-type models – summarised in Table 3.1 – thus differ in their relation to the traditional Commission approach to market creation in Europe, but also with regard to the political costs and benefits they offer in the short term. Where consumer policy regulates for the rationally and reasonably circumspect consumer as in the *laissez-faire* model, it can be easily argued that removing trade barriers increases consumer welfare by allowing greater choice, more market efficiency and lower prices. However, where protection of the weakest consumers is considered, as in the *interventionist* model, more complexity in open markets and less familiar products even threatens consumer welfare (Mabbett 2010), providing a political rationale for taming rather than freeing market forces.

Regarding the political spoils the Commission can distribute, the *laissez-faire* model increases market access, pleasing especially producers interested in cross-border trade. While policies under this model would not necessarily hurt consumers, they also fail to allow the Commission to communicate immediately visible benefits to the wider public. As noted earlier, the benefits of free markets unfold in the long term and can only be measured along counterfactual arguments. Thus, the *laissez-faire* model offers little opportunity to generate increased public legitimacy for European Commission competences. In contrast, the *interventionist* model concentrates all costs of consumer market risks on the producer side, while the Commission can easily claim to have protected and empowered each and every citizen. Given the context of politicisation and the public salience of this particular initiative, such a distribution of political costs and benefits raises the appeal of the interventionist approach for the Commission – even though this approach might contradict its traditional way of creating the common market and thereby risks alienating more traditional stakeholders.

In this view, consumer policy provides an ideal testing ground for the broader question of whether politicisation of European integration has indeed the potential to skew regulatory outcomes towards serving the immediate interests of a diffuse European public. The policy area is closely related to the goal of creating undistorted markets in Europe, but it also provides short-term political incentives for market intervention going beyond a logic based on mere competition.

Of course, the ideal-type models drawn up here are not perfectly exclusive, but rather present extreme points of a continuum on which the Commission can place its consumer policy proposals. However, they illustrate that the key political choice variable that the Commission faces in this policy area is the distribution of rights and duties between the societal groups of producers and consumers. Essentially, the Commission has to decide for each legislative initiative on how the costs of risks and externalities created in European markets are distributed among these two societal segments.

Where the respective policy proposal regulates market transactions, the Commission may either employ the principles of *caveat emptor* (let the buyer beware) or *caveat venditor* (let the seller beware), or it may choose any distribution of responsibilities in between. Where the initiative concerns the provision of information, the Commission could leave responsibility for gathering the relevant product information to the consumer, it could require the mandatory provision of only some key features, or it could force producers to label their products comprehensively. Additionally, where product safety is concerned, the Commission could draft a proposal that lets consumers bear all product risk, it could propose certain minimum standards, or it could demand from producers that each and every risk is eliminated before market access is granted. In other words, the Commission has to decide to what extent it regulates and restricts producer activity to produce immediately visible benefits for the diffuse mass of European consumers.

Arguably, the Commission does not take such decisions in a regulatory vacuum. Besides a probably existing legal status quo at the European level, there certainly are national consumer policy regimes that differ in their degree of interventionism on particular questions of consumer policy (see for example the concise comparison of the French and German regimes offered by Trumbull 2006). While existing rules may limit the number of politically attractive or politically viable policy options (see also below), they do not deprive the Commission of a

Figure 3.2: The Commission's consumer policy choice variable – allocating rights between producers and consumers

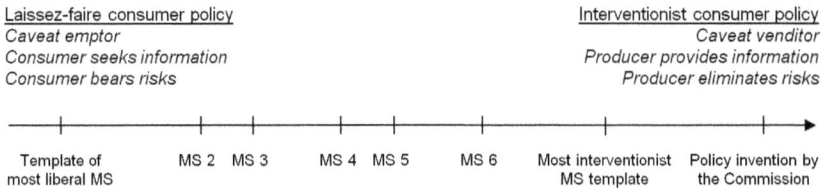

Laissez-faire consumer policy
Caveat emptor
Consumer seeks information
Consumer bears risks

Interventionist consumer policy
Caveat venditor
Producer provides information
Producer eliminates risks

| Template of most liberal MS | MS 2 MS 3 | MS 4 MS 5 | MS 6 | Most interventionist MS template | Policy invention by the Commission |

Note: MS = member state.

choice on allocating rights among producers and consumers within the given room for manoeuvre. What is more, the existence of national regimes offers relevant regulatory templates for tackling particular consumer policy issues. Combining the features of European consumer policy we have derived so far, Figure 3.2 summarises the Commission's choice variable in a stylised context of seven member states.

This conception provides the *major dependent variable in the empirical analyses of this book*, and allows us to specify the original hypothesis further. As long as the Commission has no incentive to demonstrate the immediate benefits of its policies to the European public, its consumer policies will boil down to the least intrusive way of harmonising differences in national regimes. Mutual recognition, country of origin, or some form of minimum harmonisation will be proposed, in line with the goal of creating an internal market. But in the context of an increasingly politicised process of European integration, this position will change if the respective decision involves issues that are immediately salient to European citizens. In this case, we expect the Commission to propose a much more interventionist position that immediately affects the balance of producer and consumer interests to the advantage of the latter. The Commission will either transfer extant solutions from more interventionist member states to the European level or, if the preferences of other EU actors allow it (see below), will even offer regulatory innovations for the benefit of consumers. For European consumer policy, thus, the claim that politicisation increases the Commission's responsiveness to short-term political demands boils down to the following hypothesis:

If the overall context of European integration is sufficiently politicised, and if the regulated issue area shows a high degree of contemporaneous public salience, Commission initiatives in the field of consumer policy will entail more interventionist positions.

While this hypothesis provides us with some empirical leverage to test the theoretical claims, Section 3.1 has emphasised that a procedural view on policy formulation is warranted. And, in fact, the institutional decision of the policy formulation process within the European Commission holds several other factors that might attenuate or even counter the proposed explanation for European Commission positioning in consumer policy. These factors are discussed, in turn, to derive more precise empirical implications and to sketch possible alternative explanations.

3.3 Policy formulation processes inside the Commission

So far, the theoretical discussion has treated the European Commission as a monolithic political actor with a common interest of pleasing stakeholder demands in order to increase its own policy competences. However, while the unitary actor assumption has dominated the literature, more recent research highlights that the multi-staged, multi-actor nature of policy formulation in the Commission is highly relevant to explaining the resulting policy positions (Hartlapp *et al.* 2013, 2014). In fact, the relationship between a politicised context of European integration, the public salience of a particular consumer policy and the degree of interventionism the Commission proposes might be attenuated by the process of internal decision making.

Policy formulation in the lead Directorate-General

Let us thus first concentrate on policy formulation within one of the Commission Directorates-General (DGs). In the Commission department that holds the 'lead' on a particular initiative, typically middle-ranking *fonctionnaires* are responsible for the legislative proposal. While they perform major tasks such as communication with external stakeholders or writing legislative drafts, policy formulation involves differing degrees of vertical coordination. This can involve the Director-General and the Directors of the different divisions within a DG. Likewise, the Commissioner and his personal political counsellors on sectoral issues – the so-called Cabinet – can take part in drawing up the position. Alongside the official procedures, the administrative and political leadership of the DG performs mainly management functions, and serves as a gatekeeper in controlling what is presented as an official department position (Commission of the European Communities 1995). If the theoretical mechanism linking a politicised context and the salience of a proposal to the final Commission position applies, we should be able to observe certain implications for this drafting process within the lead department.

Initially, salient and non-salient proposals should differ with the *internal actors that dominate the policy formulation process* (De Wilde 2011: 562; Radaelli 1999a; Wilson 1980: 366ff). Given that highly visible proposals are exploited to demonstrate the immediate benefits for consumers, the respective drafting processes will involve the administrative and political hierarchy to a greater extent than non-salient proposals. On the one hand, the political level of the Commission has incentives to direct its scarce resources to these drafting processes because these actors will have to defend the contents to the public. In addition to this responsibility, politicians can possibly reap individual benefits by representing publicly attractive positions (Wonka 2008a). Thus, for salient issues, the political leaders of a DG will invest more time in controlling their administration. On the other hand, the administrative leadership of the involved DGs has the function of reconciling the competing political and technocratic demands, and present the final position as 'both technically and politically defensible' (Gormley 1986: esp. 605). The more a regulated issue area is publicly salient, the more necessary will be the mediation of technocratic and political considerations, thereby also increasing the involvement of administrative leaders. Especially in a politicised context, thus, proposal salience will draw the higher echelons of the Commission's internal hierarchy to the drafting table, making it more likely that the Commission's policy position directly aims at serving immediate public interests in these cases.

Moreover, if the theoretical mechanism applies, we should expect differences in the *time horizon* governing drafting processes (e.g. Tholoniat 2009; Shapiro 2008). If salience is low and drafting aims at market efficiency rather than at producing immediate public benefits, we expect a less rushed policy formulation process than for highly salient proposals. One reason is the issue attention cycle (e.g. Downs 1972), as well as the unsteady public attention mentioned earlier. If salience of the issue area is already high during drafting, the DG needs to demonstrate the widely dispersed benefits of its output before public attention declines again. Such pressure will most probably be transmitted by the greater involvement of the political level. In contrast, a low salience proposal where the Commission works – comparatively unobserved – aiming at market efficiency and a stable compromise among member states will require much more expertise, research and strategic anticipation, and thus more time.

The latter directly points to the stakeholder contacts that a DG organises during drafting. Regarding the *pattern of consultation*, one initially suspects that under more salient proposals the drafting DG will increase its contact with public interest groups and consumer representatives at the expense of other stakeholders, such as producers (Beyers 2008; Pollack 1997b; Gormley 1986). This is one strategy that the Commission can use to signal an open ear to the public interest, and to evaluate which particular policy options are attractive to the diffuse mass of consumers. Yet, this is not necessarily the only rational strategy if the theory on the link between politicisation, issue salience, and the Commission's position in consumer policies holds. If the drafting DG already plans to produce a proposal that leans towards immediate public benefit, broad consultation during the production of the proposal can also be a political asset in defending the final position, as it shields against allegations of political bias.

In other words, access to consultation procedures does not equal actual influence. Essentially, thus, the pattern of consulted groups does not provide us with empirical leverage to evaluate the major hypothesis. However, the actual responsiveness to the different stakeholders is more meaningful in this regard. As implied by the major argument, under more salient proposals, the drafting DG should tend to take the demands of public interest and consumer groups on board while it should disproportionately decline the demands of producers. In contrast, the theoretical framework leads us to expect that, under less salient proposals, the DG's position should mirror external demands in a more balanced, or even a producer friendly manner (Mahoney 2007).

In sum, stronger involvement of the political and administrative hierarchy, shorter time horizons, and increased responsiveness to public interest groups provide three observable process implications of the postulated theoretical model. Beyond policy formulation in the lead department, however, a second element of internal drafting processes challenges the assumed direct relationship between a proposal's salience, and the degree of intervention in the consumer policy proposed by the Commission. This element is the need for coordination across Commission departments.

Coordination across Commission Directorates-General

As a rule, the lead department has to collaborate with a number of other DGs on a partly formalised basis before the final legislative initiative can be presented by the Commission as a whole (Hartlapp *et al.* 2013; Spence 2006). This institutional feature is particularly relevant for European consumer policy, because the field touches upon the mandates of several DGs within the Commission. In fact, these organisational overlaps mirror quite neatly the tension between *laissez-faire* and more interventionist models of regulation in European consumer policy.

Basically, European consumer policy measures are most often drafted by DG for Health and Consumers (SANCO), which started as a minor Commission service, but holds a mandate for health and consumer policy since 1999 (Guigner 2004). In terms of legislative output, DG SANCO has been one of the most strongly growing DGs in the Commission during the last decades (cf. Kurpas *et al.* 2008), and, in 2007, its political leadership was split. From there on, the Commission had a Commissioner solely responsible for consumer policies – a post that was filled by Meglena Kuneva from Bulgaria.

However, historically, many legislative proposals touching upon consumer issues were developed in the DG for Internal Market and Services (MARKT), which is directly responsible for the free movement of goods and services in the internal market. Consumer policy measures also cut across the mandate of the DG for Enterprise and Industry (ENTR), which holds the responsibility for common enterprise and industry policies. Likewise, the mandates of DGs with a more sectoral orientation like the DG for Agriculture and Rural Development (AGRI), the DG for Energy and Transport (TREN), or the DG for Information Society and Media (INFSO) are affected if individual regulatory issues interfere with relationship of consumer and producer interests in these specific sectors. However, the traditional policies of these DGs did not directly target the consumer as a specific stakeholder, but rather aimed at liberalisation and the creation of Europe's internal market. Accordingly, these overlaps of internal competences should have implications for the theoretical model linking politicisation, issue salience, and the interventionism in the aggregate position finally taken by the Commission as a whole.

The model above started with the assumption of a competence-seeking Commission, and it is reasonable that this assumption similarly applies to its individual departments (cf. Christiansen 2001, 1997; Harcourt 1998; Cram 1997). The different Commission services are thus expected to defend their existing scope of competences, and will try to broaden it where possible. More precisely, they will do so with their existing responsibilities as a starting point. Commission services are not fully free to pick any policy arbitrarily, but they need to justify their policy position along their initial *raison d'être*, along the existing policies and instruments they already control, and along the stakeholder relationships they have developed in the past. In other words, I assume that their preferences are functionally motivated (cf. Meier 1989). This allows us to expect that a certain element of bureaucratic politics – that is, the prevalence of 'turf' conflicts (Nugent 2000) – is eminent in consumer policy formation, and must thus be part of the explanation of the final Commission position.

Moreover, we must expect that the salience of an individual initiative affects this internal conflict potential (cf. Radaelli 1999a). Consider firstly the case of a low salience proposal drafted by the consumer policy DG SANCO. The preceding sections imply that we should expect a *laissez-faire* proposal in this case because the Commission only serves the legitimacy demands of its traditional stakeholders. Without the need to demonstrate immediate benefits to the broader public, SANCO will stick to the status quo of market-making policies simply because it will raise the least opposition among cross-nationally operating producers and member states while it still broadens the competences of SANCO in managing and (partly) enforcing an additional piece of law in the respective issue area. In terms of internal interaction, such a proposal also entails the advantage for DG SANCO that this position will stir the least conflict among the competing services within the Commission. While some turf issues may not be avoided, a liberal consumer policy of SANCO will at least not challenge the contents of the likewise liberal policies DGs like MARKT and ENTR have traditionally pursued.

Nonetheless, the picture changes if the public salience of the initiative rises. As argued above, legitimacy demands from the public make more interventionist consumer policies more easily defendable outside the Commission. This provides SANCO with an incentive to increase its competence even beyond a pure market regulation by proposing an interventionist consumer policy that moves additional capacities to the supranational level. Consider food policy as an illustration here. A proposal along the *laissez-faire* model would, for example, prescribe mutual recognition of the respectively regulated foods. But, if a Europe-wide scandal surrounding the respective food arises, SANCO can go beyond that, and can more easily justify moving certain functions of product or producer controls under its own auspices, thereby making stricter producer standards applicable all over the EU. Internally, however, such more interventionist drafts would result in opposition from those DGs that have historically regulated for and gained their support from producer interests, such as DG MARKT and DG ENTR. Against these considerations, we would expect more internal conflict under an increased salience of a consumer policy initiative.

But does the intensity of internal conflict rise with issue salience in an unconstrained manner? The answer is clearly 'no', because the theoretical mechanism provides a countervailing logic as well. Recall that the argument on issue salience is dependent on the general politicisation of European integration. It has been argued in Section 3.1 that politicisation serves as a necessary condition for a Commission incentive to serve immediate and widely dispersed public interests. This expectation is grounded in the observation that politicisation confronts the Commission *as a whole* with the danger of stalemate in European integration if the legitimacy of Commission output vis-à-vis the broad public cannot be maintained. But if stops and backlashes in a further transfer of national competences to the supranational level happen to hamper the overall growth of the Commission, this would also create a constraint on each DG's ability to expand its individual competences. From this perspective, the generation of immediate output legitimacy for overall Commission initiatives should be a common interest for all internal actors, according to our assumptions. And such common interest should at least partly trump internal conflict. Particularly in highly salient initiatives in a strongly politicised context, this consideration may decrease the opposition of DGs defending the more liberal status quo.

Thus, our general theoretical framework implies a curvilinear relationship between an initiative's salience and the level of internal conflict. With rising salience, incentives for more interventionist policies of some DGs will increase, leading to opposition of market-oriented DGs. Yet, this opposition will be much more cautious if the public is sufficiently aware of the initiative or the issues it covers. In addition, the more overall European decision making is politicised, the more this caution should be pronounced, because this context condition moves the common interests of all internal actors in a positive public image of the European Commission to the fore. A higher degree of politicisation will thus attenuate the effect of proposal salience on internal conflict. Figure 3.3 summarises these theoretical expectations.

In theoretical terms, these considerations provide an additional micro-foundation to the hypothesised mechanism in which politicisation is a necessary condition that can only sufficiently explain the Commission's interventionism in conjunction with issue salience. The more politicised the context of supranational decision making is, the less intense will internal opposition be, and the more easily can interventionist consumer policies be asserted within the Commission. However, even in a context of stable, high politicisation, these considerations emphasise that the hypothesised relationship of an initiative's salience and the interventionism of Commission consumer policies cannot be linear. The moderating and mediating effects of internal conflict rather imply that a certain, politicisation-dependent threshold of public salience is required in order to form a final Commission position that actually promotes immediate public interests. Below such a threshold, internal opposition would cancel out the interventionism targeted by some DGs.

In sum, all this points to the fact that any fair empirical test of the relationship of politicisation, issue salience and position taking must consider the dynamics of

Figure 3.3: Inter-DG conflict and issue salience under varying levels of EU politicisation

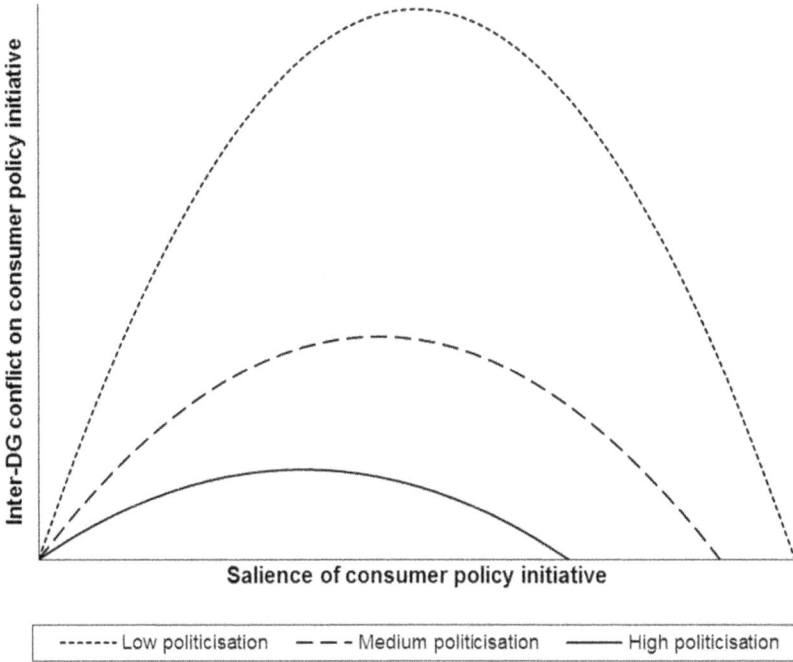

internal Commission interaction as a relevant source of additional explanations. While the expectation on a curvilinear relationship between salience and internal conflict does not provide precise thresholds so far, the subsequent comparison of seventeen consumer policy drafting processes should allow initial empirical insights in this regard.

3.4 Alternative explanations for Commission positioning in consumer policy

The process-based perspective has refined the theoretical mechanism linking politicisation, issue salience, and the degree of intervention in Commission consumer policies. However, while the discussion has focussed on the major input factors of interest for the purposes of this book, this does not imply that the proposed theoretical model is a deterministic one, or that the only alternative is the null hypothesis of inertia, under which the Commission simply does not react to the changed context. Of course, position formation in the European Commission is subject to a range of other factors too numerous to be adequately discussed here (but see Hartlapp *et al.* 2014: esp. Chs. 2 and 12). This, once more, warrants an open eye for the detailed process of position formation on the individual policies. Yet, to enhance the power of the research design developed further below, this section briefly discusses some of the more prominent alternative explanations and their empirical implications for Commission position formation in consumer policy.

Anticipation of member state and EP preferences

The theory proposed here predicts that individual Commission actors will proactively serve and exploit the public interest in order to safeguard the scope for further competence gains. Initially, this entrepreneurial perspective contrasts with a prominent view that perceives the Commission merely as an agent of national governments, willingly satisfying the preferences of its major principals (Bailer 2006; Moravcsik 1999). And, in fact, it cannot be denied that a Commission proposal is only the starting point of European legislative decision making. Thus, most proposals are constrained insofar as they need to survive majority decisions in the EP and, most importantly, in the Council subsequently. But can we thus infer that the Commission position is sufficiently explained by anticipating the preferences that govern inter-institutional decision making?

I argue that this is not the case. While the agency view proves useful in refining the major argument, it does not provide a sufficient, fully sketched counter-explanation. Even if the Commission can perfectly anticipate the preferences of the inter-institutional players – which would require considerable and empirically observable efforts during drafting – this will hardly result in only one feasible policy initiative for a given consumer issue. Even if the feasible policy space is constrained by the preferences of individual member states (or parliamentary factions for that matter), the Commission will still face a choice on the degree of interventionism it proposes.

Consider the hypothetical case in Figure 3.4 as an illustration of this argument. For simplicity, we assume a stylised Council consisting of seven member states (MS), five of which are sufficient to reach a qualified majority needed to adopt consumer policy proposals of the Commission (cf. Tsebelis and Garrett 2000). These member states differ in the degree of their support for interventionism in the regulation of the particular consumer issue at hand. In addition, we assume that the issue is not regulated at the European level yet – that is, the *EU SQ* equals zero – and that the member state governments have Euclidean preferences – that is, the utility of the policy proposal declines symmetrically around the indicated ideal points.

In this simplified setting, the Commission could, for example, propose a consumer policy that only mildly intervenes in the market, comes with a distribution of rights favourable to producers, and roughly equals the extant regime of the least interventionist member state (*CP1*). Under our assumptions, such a proposal would easily find the necessary five/seven majority as it makes every Council member better off as compared to the European status quo. However, in the same

Figure 3.4: Consumer interventionism and political feasibility in a stylised seven-member Council

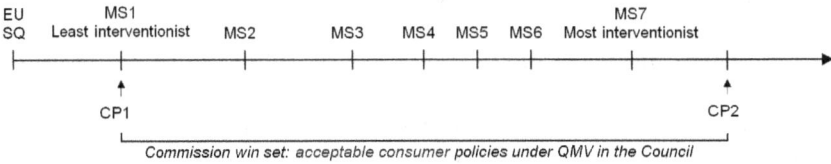

Note: EU SQ refers to the legislative status quo at the EU level, while CP1 and CP2 signify two different consumer policy options with higher degrees of interventionism. MS1–MS7 denote different member state preferences, while QMV refers to qualified majority voting in the Council.

setting of member state preferences, the Commission could propose a much more interventionist consumer policy that goes even beyond the regime of the most interventionist member state (*CP2*). Still, this Commission proposal is acceptable to a Council majority of five out of seven members: *MS3* would be indifferent as compared to the *EU SQ*, while it would make members 4 to 7 significantly better off. One and the same preference setting in the Council thus allows the Commission to choose any degree of interventionism within the win set, spanned by the extreme *laissez-faire* proposal (*CP1*) and the most interventionist of the feasible consumer policies (*CP2*).

Of course, this is a highly simplified setting with strong assumptions. Nevertheless, even if we relax the assumptions of Euclidian preferences and the absence of relevant European regulation, the win set arguably scales down – which, however, does not change the fact that, under most preference settings, it will remain *a set of feasible policies*. So even if the Commission can anticipate preferences perfectly, it still faces the choice of how to distribute rights between consumers and producers – a choice that should be mediated by politicisation and the salience of the respective proposal. However, while the agency view does not counter the mechanism proposed in this thesis, we can expect that it constrains it. To account for this complementary explanation of the Commission's policy choices, we have to consider the extent to which the Commission anticipates the preferences of external institutional EU actors when drafting consumer policies.

The nationality and partisanship of the responsible Commissioners

While the agency approach thus provides an additional refinement for the salience-based argument, other prominent approaches more straightforwardly dissent from the explanation proposed in this book. Rather than anchoring their arguments in the institutional self-interest of the Commission and its sub-organisations, a range of studies focuses on the characteristics of individual Commissioners as relevant factors in explaining Commission and DG positions. Scholars in this vein suggest either socialisation effects or delegation chains between the Commissioners and the national governments appointing them. According to this view, national as well as partisan interests, rather than legitimacy demands, should influence the content of Commission proposals (e.g. Wonka 2008a; Wonka 2007; Thomson 2008; see also Döring 2007; Smith 2003).

As former Commissioners have until now only rarely taken up national political careers after their Brussels term, it remains debatable whether delegation chains actually work in European politics. In addition, one can doubt that individual Commissioners have sufficient power and resources to fully steer the long-term, multi-stage and multi-actor drafting processes within the Commission (Hartlapp *et al.* 2013). Ultimately, however, these are empirical questions, and the approaches provide clear empirical implications contrasting the argument on politicisation and issue salience. If arguments on Commissioner characteristics actually hold, we should observe Commissioner involvement throughout the drafting processes of the scrutinised consumer policies. Furthermore, the degree of interventionism in the proposed consumer policies should rather vary with the home country and/or the party membership of the responsible Commissioner rather than with the salience of individual initiatives. In other words, the degree of interventionism in consumer policy proposals (and the level of conflict within the Commission) should vary with the political leadership of the responsible DGs, but not within the terms of office of the respective Commissioners.

Consumer policy as industry protection

Another alternative explanation for the Commission position is related more to the particular policy area. When it comes to explaining the level of regulatory consumer protection, a 'productionist view' is often taken (Trumbull 2006: 167). According to this assumption, high standards are in fact driven by industry interests (cf. also Vogel 1995; Young and Holmes 2006). From this perspective, which is essentially based on the structural advantages of producers lobbying for regulation, consumer policy does not primarily protect consumers; it rather protects industries. The idea is that codifying extant practices in the domestic market place creates entry barriers for external producers, thereby reducing pressures from international competition. In contrast with the politicisation/salience argument proposed here, such approaches do not consider the distribution of rights between producers and consumers as the relevant choice variable for the Commission, but look at the distribution of market access between European and international producers. Interventionist consumer policies would thus not be a means to please legitimacy demands from the broader public, but would serve to make the EU a trading bloc in line with the interests of European producers.

The plausibility of this argument can be doubted on a theoretical level. Given the prevalence of strong differences in the consumer protection regimes of European member states, one can hardly assume a common interest for a particular level of consumer protection among European producers. Rather, the Commission should face producer interests varying along national lines. If these differing interests have explanatory power as to the Commission's position in drawing up consumer policy initiatives, the argument hardly differs from the anticipation of national preferences and the nationality of individual Commissioners discussed above. But again, the question of whether they are the legitimacy demands of the broader public in highly salient initiatives or the interests of producers that drive Commission position formation is, in fact, an empirical one.

One observable implication of the productionist view is that the Commission should be responsive to voiced producer interests during drafting, regardless of the public salience of a given initiative. Another implication is that we should expect the Commission's sub-organisation for external trade (DG TRADE) to be actively involved in consumer policy formulation. These implications should help distinguish the productionist view from the politicisation and salience-based argument proposed here.

3.5 Summary of the argument and its observable implications

This book argues that the politicisation of European integration observed in Chapter Two confronts the European Commission with new legitimacy demands voiced by the broader European public. Against this background, the Commission is faced with a trade-off in pursuing either its traditional policy of market liberalisation in Europe, or the creation of immediate and widely dispersed benefits, when formulating policy choices that are fed into the legislative process of the EU. Assuming a competence-seeking motivation, we developed the expectation that the Commission's decisions in a politicised context tip towards the latter if the respective legislative initiative is contemporaneously salient to the broader public.

This general argument is broken down to the area of consumer policy, where regulatory decisions of the Commission predominantly affect the distribution of rights among consumers and producers. The historical goal of market creation more neatly fits to a *laissez-faire* model of consumer policy, whereas creating immediate benefits for the broader public can be more easily achieved by an *interventionist* model, entailing a distribution of rights favourable to the diffuse consumer interests at the expense of the more narrowly concentrated producer interest. Accordingly, it is hypothesised that non-salient initiatives in the policy field will tend to the liberal-market end of the continuum, while salient initiatives will exhibit a much higher degree of interventionism.

From this central hypothesis, four additional empirical implications regarding the process of policy formulation have been derived. First, in a politicised context, more salient initiatives draw the higher hierarchical levels in the Commission into policy formulation. Second, under such salient proposals, the time horizon of the drafting process should be significantly shorter. Third, independent of the actual pattern of consultation, the drafting unit should be more responsive to those demands voiced by the public interest or consumer groups. Fourth, and finally, we would expect a curvilinear relationship between the salience of the proposal and conflict within the Commission, which implies a certain threshold of salience above which the final Commission position shifts towards more interventionist positions.

Table 3.2: Summary of hypotheses and observable implications

Central hypotheses: The degree of interventionism in Commission consumer policy proposals...	Observable implications – outcome: Commission proposals...	Observable implications – process: Drafting processes...
The politicisation argument		
...rises when the politicisation of European decision-making combines with the public salience of the respectively regulated issue area.	...in salient areas, are based on templates from the member states with the most paternalistic CP regimes or even contains policy innovations distributing further rights to the consumer. ...in salient areas, mirror the voiced demands of consumer associations. ...in non-salient areas, are based on mutual recognition or harmonise at the level of less interventionist member state regimes and conform more to the voiced demands of producer interests.	...involve the administrative and political hierarchy more in salient initiatives. ...are significantly shorter and more rushed, the more the initiative is salient. ...are more responsive to the demands of consumer associations, the more the initiative is salient. ...will exhibit an increasing level of inter-DG conflict with rising salience, which will decline again above a certain, politicisation-dependent threshold.
Prominent alternative explanations		
...depends on the political feasibility in the Council and in the Parliament.	...mirror the demands of national governments or EP fractions that are particular powerful or decisive in the given preference setting.	...largely revolve around the evaluation of national and parliamentary interests rather than around consumer or producer interests.
...depends on the national interest of the responsible Commissioner's home country.	...effectively correspond with the national templates of the Commissioners' home countries.	...involve Commissioners heavily throughout their whole duration.
...depends on the partisan interests of the responsible Commissioner's party affiliation.	...effectively correspond with the ideological template of the Commissioner's partisanship.	...involve Commissioners heavily throughout their whole duration.
...mirrors producer interests in protection against international competition.	...effectively correspond with producer demands voiced regarding the respective initiative.	...are mostly responsive to the demands of producer associations and to nationally voiced interest.

Beyond the major argument of this book, the anticipation of the inter-institutional process, the characteristics of individual Commissioners and the productionist view on consumer policies have been discussed as possible alternative explanations for the degree of interventionism by the Commission in consumer policies. Table 3.2 summarises the hypotheses and the empirical implications that drive the analyses of the Commission's individual policy choices presented in the subsequent chapters.

3.6 Empirical strategy

How can these propositions then be evaluated empirically? The theory states a causal chain from general politicisation of European integration and the salience of specific regulatory issues to the characteristics of the drafting process and the resulting interventionism contained in consumer policies proposed by the European Commission. Accordingly, the relevant *unit of analysis* is the Commission drafting process for an individual European consumer policy proposal.

Yet consumer policy itself did not exist as an individually circumscribable competence of the EU before the Treaty of Maastricht in 1992 (see Weatherill 2005: chapter 1), and was strengthened with a specific treaty base only in Amsterdam in 1997 (Article 153, cf. Micklitz *et al.* 2004). This was reflected in a small Commission service (DG XXIV) from 1995 onwards, but resulted in a fully-fledged DG with legislative competences only after Commission President Prodi moved significant personnel resources and the relevant legal competences for food and product safety to this DG (known since then as DG SANCO, cf. Guigner 2004). In order to avoid basing conclusions on the adolescent phase of the Commission's consumer policy department, the *investigation period* starts with the inauguration of the Prodi Commission in September 1999. As an end point, November 2008 is chosen. This marks both the end of the first Barroso Commission and the outset of the research project at hand. In other words, the *universe of relevant cases* comprises all Commission proposals for binding EU law in consumer policy during two complete Commission terms (1999–2008).[6]

The sampling strategy, described in greater detail in Appendix B, identifies 247 respective proposals in the EU's EUR-Lex database. Because of the need to study policy formulation processes, in the absence of readily accessible data on internal drafting by the Commission,[7] and given the information-intensive measurement of the Commission's interventionism (see below), this population was systematically broken down further. The final sample ensures variation in the major independent variables and alternative explanations, allows for an analysis

---

6. Covering two full Commission terms, in addition, provides controllable variation over Commissioners and Commission presidents as one possible confounding influence on the Commission's policy choices.

7. Both the principle of collegiality and strategic advantages in inter-institutional negotiations incentivise the Commission as a whole to restrict the systematic access to such information (Wonka 2008a, see also the 'transparency' regulation (EC) 1049/2001.

Table 3.3: Sample of legislative drafting processes in consumer policy (1999–2008)

ID	Proposal no.	Adoption	Legislative content	Lead DG	Procedure	Subfield
1	COM(2000)139	29 March 2000	General product safety	SANCO	Oral	P
2	COM(2000)222	8 May 2000	Food supplements	SANCO	Written	F
3	COM(2000)392	12 July 2000	Universal service and users' rights relating to electronic communications networks and services	INFSO	Oral	T
4	COM(2001)546	2 October 2001	Sales promotions in the Internal Market	MARKT	Oral	T
5	COM(2001)784	21 December 2001	Air passenger rights	TREN	Written	T
6	COM(2002)443	11 September 2002	Consumer credit	SANCO	Written	T
7	COM(2003)356	18 June 2003	Unfair business-to-consumer commercial practices in the internal market	SANCO	Oral	T
8	COM(2003)424	16 July 2003	Nutrition and health claims made on foods	SANCO	Oral	F
9	COM(2003)671	10 November 2003	Adding vitamins, minerals and certain other substances to foods	SANCO	Written	F
10	COM(2005)457	11 October 2005	Placing pyrotechnic articles on the market	ENTR	Written	P
11	COM(2006)428	28 July 2006	Food additives	SANCO	Written	F
12	COM(2007)53	14 February 2007	Common framework for the marketing of products	ENTR	Written	P

Table 3.3 *(continued)*

ID	Proposal no.	Adoption	Legislative content	Lead DG	Procedure	Subfield
13	COM(2008)9	25 January 2008	Safety of toys	ENTR	Written	P
14	COM(2008)40	30 January 2008	Providing food information to consumers	SANCO	Oral	F
15	COM(2008)614	8 October 2008	Consumer rights	SANCO	Oral	T
16	COM(2008)816	4 December 2008	Rights of passengers when travelling by sea and inland waterways	TREN	Written	T
17	COM(2008)817	4 December 2008	Rights of passengers on bus and coach transport	TREN	Written	T

of within-case variation (cf. Hall 2008), focuses on cases with comparable legal scope, and is small enough to enable a 'structured focused comparison' using the derived hypotheses and observable implications (George 1979). In other words, the sampling approach exploits all available information *ex ante* so as to enable a 'plausibility probe' of the theoretical propositions that allows a meaningful dialogue between the parsimonious theory and a complex empirical reality (Eckstein 1975: 108–13; George 1979; Pahre 2005). Table 3.3 lists the seventeen finally selected cases.

This sample can be further divided along the types of consumer risk and disadvantage the respective policy measure touches upon. First, the largest group of eight cases covers economic consumer risks in specific contractual market transactions (*T*). In these cases, Commission initiatives propose to equip the consumer with varying degrees of rights in interactions with economic providers of products or services. Prime examples in this regard are the proposed Unfair Commercial Practices Directive in June 2003 and the Consumer Rights Directive in October 2008. Second, a group of five Commission initiatives covers particular safety risks associated with retail products or services (*P*). Here, the Commission's policy choices propose a particular distribution of product safety risks among producers and consumers. Prime examples are the proposed General Product Safety Directive (GPSD) in March 2000 or the Toy Safety Directive in January 2008. Thirdly, a set of five acts concerns health risks associated with the consumption of food products (*F*). Here, respective Commission proposals entail a certain distribution of risk bearing among food consumers and food producers. Prime examples are the proposed Food Supplements Directive of May 2000 or the initiative for a Food Additives Regulation in July 2006.

These classes of risk – contractual, product safety and health risks – affect consumers at an increasingly fundamental level. In line with the seminal hierarchy of human needs (Maslow 1943), individuals should prefer harm to their economic status in contractual interactions to harm to their external health from unsafe products which, in turn, would be preferable to any harm to their internal health touched upon by food regulations. In other words, these three issue areas have differing baseline likelihoods of becoming salient to the European public. It is far easier to create a damaging news story about health risks in food than about economic risks in consumer contracts. Less technically speaking, at any given moment, we could expect public attention to be higher for issues related to harmful food, followed by issues about harmful retail products, followed by issues concerning economic risk to consumers (cf. Hood *et al.* 2004: especially chapter 6). For a theoretical model that links politicisation to Commission policy output via public salience, these differing baseline likelihoods may act as another moderating variable. Controlling for this possibility by analysing the respective cases subsequently in three separate chapters adds an additional layer of comparison that provides further empirical leverage for the purposes of this book.

Beyond the cross-temporal variation in the politicisation of European integration uncovered in Chapter Two, an empirical evaluation of the theoretical model then also requires measurements for issue salience and interventionism in the Commission's final position. *Salience* refers to the significance and importance that the public ascribes to an issue relative to others (Franklin and Wlezien 1997; Wlezien 2005; Oppermann and Viehrig 2008; Oppermann 2010; see also Gormley 1986; Mahoney 2007). It captures the attention or the relative prominence the public devotes to a particular topic at a given point in time.

The operationalisation of this concept faces three challenges. The first one is the breadth or the specificity of the issues in question. For example, judgements may differ depending on whether one asks about the salience of consumer product safety in general, the salience of toy safety, or the salience of specific chemical substances in particular baby toys. Each consumer policy proposal may affect a myriad of different issues with varying breadth and specificity so that measurement of the related issue salience(s) presupposes an in-depth analysis of policy formulation. Accordingly, a qualitative analysis of the legal texts, stakeholder positions and related documentation is needed to uncover the issues in which we can establish the theoretically relevant level of salience. Yet this hampers systematic comparison and clashes with a second challenge in operationalising issue salience, which lies in disentangling the contemporaneous public salience our argument requires from the retrospective salience that might be inferred from in-depth research into policy formulation. Certain issues may appear to have been salient only with hindsight, but what we need to know is whether 'the actors [...] thought the issue [...] was salient at the time they were resolving it, regardless of whether analysts now view it as salient' (Epstein and

Segal 2000: 72).[8] Experts engaged in policy formulation – be it the drafting Commission officials themselves or interest group representatives – will consider these issues as 'truly consequential', which is often mixed with judgements on their public salience (ibid. 79). In other words, in-depth research on issues needs to be complemented by a somewhat more objective measure of contemporaneous public salience. The third challenge, then, lies in finding relevant data that can track variation in contemporaneous public salience over time.

Against these challenges, the book's empirical strategy for operationalising issue salience rests on three cornerstones (see Appendix C for details). First, following broad traditions of political science and organisation research, issue salience is captured by the frequencies with which the respective issues figure in public media (see for example Lodge 2011; Oppermann and Viehrig 2008; Mahoney 2007; Van Belle *et al.* 2004; or Kemp 1984). This rests on the assumption that issues to which the public is likely to pay more attention are reflected in more frequent news media reporting (Franklin and Wlezien 1997: 350), and it avoids a retrospective bias, since only truly contemporary information drives the time series (Epstein and Segal 2000).[9] Second, an automated analysis of legal documentation and stakeholder position papers retrieves a set of keywords for each of the three policy subfields identified above – the economic risks of consumers in market transactions, the risks related to the safety of consumer products and the health risks related to the consumption of food – and then assesses the relative frequency with which they figure in four major European newspapers between 1999 and 2008.[10] These time series, presented individually in the three subsequent chapters, gives us a broad indication of how the salience of each of the three subfields varied over time. Third, and finally, I complement these broad time series with salience measures for the more specific issues that each of the seventeen proposals under analysis covers. After an initial analysis of the legal text and accompanying stakeholder positions, I assess how specific instances regulated by the envisaged Commission proposal figured in the press during the process of policy formulation within the Commission. For example, the specific issue salience measure for the proposal on air passenger rights (case no. 5 in Table 3.3; *see* Chapter 4.3 in this

---

8. This risk of retrospective bias is particularly real in studying Commission proposals because these proposals usually mark the onset of intense political negotiations in the EP or the Council of Ministers. The negotiations may highlight the importance of particular political issues that were not thought to be relevant at the time of drafting within the European Commission.

9. Debates on 'mediatisation' or 'priming' show that public opinion itself is at least partially influenced by the topics and respective valences that modern media and their editors select (e.g. Meyer 2009; Van Noije *et al.* 2008; Kiousis 2004; Soroka 2003). But even if this holds true, high levels of media reporting indicate high contemporaneous public salience (cf. Oppermann 2010), and thus mirror the cross-temporal variation we are interested in here. In addition, using media data assumes that contemporaneous salience means roughly the same thing to media editors as it does to political actors in the Commission. However, given that both types of actors 'make this calculation at about the same time, within the same political context, this assumption does not seem a particularly onerous one' (Epstein and Segal 2000: 73).

10. For greater detail on the broad and specific newspaper search strings, please see Appendix C.

volume) assesses whether the overbooking practice of airline companies made news when the proposal was drafted between 1999 and 2001. Taken together, these combined measures allow comparative conclusions on the contemporaneous public attention devoted to the issue that the Commission aimed to regulate.

The theoretical model, then, finally requires an operationalisation of the major dependent variable, that is, the consumer policy *interventionism* in the seventeen legislative initiatives of the European Commission. Arguably, there is no objective or politically unbiased measure of this concept (cf. Janning 2004). Rather, as outlined in Chapter 3.2, the degree of interventionism an observer sees in a particular rule critically hinges on their *a priori* assumptions on the relative powers of producers and consumers. Yet this is an essentially political question that the book at hand cannot and does not seek to answer. Rather than striving for an absolute judgement on whether the Commission's proposals fail to meet normatively justified standards of intervention, my interest here lies in a relative measure along which the different Commission proposals under analysis can be compared.

Since the Commission does not make its choices in a regulatory vacuum, the political context of each drafting process provides a number of anchor points for a relative evaluation of the chosen distribution of rights among producers and consumers. Most importantly, either there is an extant regulatory status quo for a particular problem in EU law, or the European Commission can at least observe the regulatory solutions that exist in member states. Furthermore, consumer and producer groups themselves voice regulatory demands indicating which options are at all conceivable. Each of these political demands or extant regulatory solutions provides a particular distribution of rights that empirically favours either consumers or producers. For each regulatory issue, thus, we can define a continuum of possible choices that ranges from the least interventionist solution – the solution burdening the consumer with most risks – to the most interventionist option – the option shifting most risks to the producer side. Setting the final Commission position in relation to these extreme points reveals whether the proposal must be considered as a *laissez-faire* or as an *interventionist* solution.

Of course, each of the proposals in Table 3.3 affects varying numbers of different specific issues. For a fair and politically unbiased judgement on the Commission's consumer policy interventionism, each proposal is thus decomposed into a manageable set of key provisions, meaning sets of articles which distribute logically linked rights among consumers and producers. For each of these provisions, I then locate the degree of interventionism based on (1) stakeholder demands and possible policy options for the respective provision, (2) the options contained in the final legal text, and (3) a comparison of these options with the respective regulatory status quo. In other words, the operationalisation of the key dependent variable captures whether the Commission proposal undermines, exceeds or simply reinforces the regulatory distribution of rights among consumers and producers that existed at the time of drafting. While this operationalisation requires a detailed and rather technical perspective at times, the qualitative judgements summarised in the individual case studies and

Appendix E are reproducible so that we can distinguish political rhetoric from substantial interventionism.

Beyond mere correspondence between the input (EU politicisation and issue salience) and output variables (consumer interventionism), the theory section has derived a range of process implications from the major model which increase the leverage of our *medium-N* set-up. Following the approach that Peter Hall (2008) has dubbed 'systematic process analysis' (also known as 'process tracing', see George and Bennett 2005: especially chapter 10), each drafting process in the Commission is reconstructed along the specific observable implications derived above. Process tracing, in addition, provides additional control over the chronology of the individual events that make up the final policy choice, and enables us to ensure temporal sequence as one condition of causality. More importantly, it explicitly allows for the within-case variation that may be highly relevant to theory refinement. Without having to determine the point in drafting time at which politicisation and/or salience must be present *a priori*, we remain sufficiently flexible and allow for the possibility that politicisation, issue salience and the envisaged distribution of rights among consumers and producers co-vary during policy formulation. Along these lines, the subsequent empirical chapters will reconstruct the drafting processes for each of the selected Commission proposals structured along the major output hypothesis, as well as the four process implications (cf. Table 3.2).

A range of different data sources had to be combined, particularly so because public access to information on internal Commission dynamics is severely restricted.[11] In such a context, expert interviews can maximise the amount of available information (Littig 2008). Obviously, those officials that took part in the seventeen legislative drafting processes are the most knowledgeable individuals in this regard. Since I was not interested in making inferences on Commission officials themselves, but on the sample of legislative proposals, I relied on a non-probability sampling strategy of identifying relevant interviewees in the Commission. It was based on (1) the officials' formal positions and (2) reputational information gained during initial research (Tansey 2007; Aberbach and Rockman 2002; Goldstein 2002). Furthermore, in order to cross-validate individual interviewee information, I spoke to several contacts for each case, scattering sources across six different DGs and four hierarchy levels (cf. Berry 2002, see Appendix D for further information).[12]

This information was complemented by written information as far as possible. While some interviewees granted access to internal process documentation, such

---

11. Both the principle of collegiality that governs Commission decision making as well as the strategic advantages of a common position in inter-institutional negotiations incentivise the organisations as a whole to restrict systematic access to such information (Wonka 2008a, see also the exceptions in the so-called 'transparency' regulation (EC) 1049/2001.

12. Note that anonymity was assured to interviewees so that information gained through interviews is marked only by the sequential interview and then the paragraph number generated in the broader project context (such as COM166:22 or COM002:83 etc.). See also Appendix D.

as preliminary draft proposals, I filed a systematic, formal request for document access with the Secretariat-General of the Commission after the interview phase was finished, and it was granted for some documents.[13] In addition, a broad range of secondary sources was available for reconstructing the drafting processes. Referenced individually in the case studies, these sources involve (1) published Commission documents such as discussion papers, consultation documents, press releases, impact assessments, as well as the final proposal itself, (2) stakeholder documents such as position papers of interest groups, and (3) contemporary coverage by press agencies such as Agence Europe and by the newspapers also used in the index construction above.

Taken together, this material provides the necessary tools to study whether and how the politicisation of European integration affects the process and products of policy formulation in Europe's central agenda setter. Along these lines, Chapters Four–Six will now take a closer look at the drafting process of individual consumer policies.

---

13. Access appears to have been denied particularly for those proposals where the interviews indicated differing policy positions within the Commission. All refusals of document access were based on the exception in Article 4(3) of the 'transparency' regulation (EC) 1049/2001, which reads: 'Access to a document containing opinions for internal use as part of deliberations and preliminary consultations within the institution concerned shall be refused even after the decision has been taken if disclosure of the document would seriously undermine the institution's decision-making process, unless there is an overriding public interest in disclosure.'

Chapter Four

Economic and Contractual Consumer Rights

If we let consumer outcomes be the guiding standard for policy decisions in a host of areas, including the Internal Market, we will hit two birds with one stone: efficient resource allocation and competitiveness on the one hand, and increased consumer satisfaction and therefore increased legitimacy for the EU on the other.

Meglena Kuneva, European Commissioner for
Consumer Affairs Speech in Berlin, 26 February 2007

This chapter focuses on the first subfield of consumer policy, which deals with business-to-consumer transactions and the corresponding economic interests of consumers. Economic consumer interests have played an important role in European integration, which is frequently justified by enhanced market efficiency offering a wider choice, lower prices and higher quality to consumers. In that sense, some consider the creation of the internal market as a consumer policy of the 'hidden type' (Weatherill 2005: 5), in which economic consumer interests are primarily served by means of European competition policy (Cseres 2005: especially 153). Yet as the ideal-type models in Chapter Three have highlighted, consumer policy may go well beyond mere questions of market efficiency and develop a much more interventionist thrust that is explicitly geared towards protecting the consumer.

In the same vein, consumer policy can set itself apart from contract law. While contract law aims to insure the market participant's expectations by enforcing bilateral agreements, it is usually designed on the basis of mutual balance rather than of protecting a structurally weaker party. In addition, contract law runs on voluntariness and on the *caveat emptor* principle, under which the buyer is responsible for judging the quality of the respective good (Cseres 2005: 154–5). Both competition policy and contract law are thus related to consumer policy, but do not circumscribe the full set of regulatory choices the Commission may make in this area.

In fact, the historical development of supranational consumer policy competences can be read as a story of emancipation from their competition policy and contract law roots. The Treaty of Rome did not contain a specific legal basis for an economic consumer policy, but mentions the consumer only as a potential beneficiary of Europe's agricultural and competition policies (Cseres 2005: 194). Whereas the European Council concluded some resolutions in parallel with the consumerist movement in the early 1970s, it also clarified therein that there were no supranational competences on the matter. Additionally, although the Commission tried to create a 'new impetus for consumer protection policy' with a policy paper in 1986, national governments trimmed its approach by emphasising that supranational policy should not be about 'consumer rights' but solely about 'consumer choice' (Weatherill 2005: 6–9).

Nevertheless, Jacques Delors' internal market programme and the Single European Act (SEA) provided a new momentum for the supranational protection of economic consumer rights. Questions of economic consumer protection were invariably touched on 'as part of the Commission's efforts to remove technical obstacles to trade' (Pollack 1997b: 583). On the one hand, the Commission could justify consumer policy efforts by lacking cross-border market access for producers. The European Court of Justice's (ECJ) 1979 judgement in *Cassis de Dijon* strongly confined national regulatory barriers to trade, but also allowed them if they demonstrably served the 'fairness of commercial transactions or the defence of the consumer' (Weatherill 2005: 44ff.; also Stuyck 2000: 390). Member states tried extensively to exploit this leeway, which was facilitated by strong variations across national consumer protection regimes. Common law countries, like the United Kingdom (UK), focused primarily on competition law, while Germany, for example, also had general contract terms in place. The French solution went further and emphasised consumer information and consumer-oriented contract law, whereas the Nordic countries had well-developed consumer protection laws established (Cseres 2005: 195).

On the other hand, the internal market programme addressed market access not only from the producers' point of view, but also from that of consumers. It was argued that Community measures should also create the trust that consumers needed to trade across borders. Accordingly, a European consumer policy regime on the basis of 'minimum harmonisation' was pursued – which was supposed to create certain baseline standards of protection, without necessarily undermining higher national standards.

From both producer- and consumer-oriented perspectives, the Commission anchored all subsequent consumer policy initiatives in its internal market competences, most notably those in Article 95 of the SEA. This entailed the strategic advantage that such acts required only a qualified majority in the Council (Cseres 2005: 196–8). Along these lines, the first supranational regulations in the issue area covered very specific market transactions with immediate cross-border relevance, such as the package travel directive (Directive 90/314/EEC, see also Rischkowsky 2007).

Paralleling these formal ventures into the issue area, the Commission acted as a 'policy entrepreneur' by ensuring that stakeholder demand for supranational consumer protection was audible in Brussels (Pollack 1997b). As early as 1961, it invited national consumer associations and advised them that 'the general interests of consumers in the common market are not represented to the same extent as those of producers' (Commissioner Mansholt cited in Young 1997: 158). The European umbrella of national consumer associations, BEUC (*Bureau Européen des Unions de Consommateurs*), was founded only two months later, and established a secretariat in Brussels in 1973. Beyond providing advice and political incentives, the Commission actively sponsors consumer associations such as BEUC and EURO COOP even today by bearing more than one-third of their operational budget (ibid. 165ff.).[1]

Both the increasingly fragmented legal system and demands from pressure groups may explain the 'breakthrough' that the Maastricht Treaty presented in 1992 for the supranational protection of consumers (Weatherill 2005: 15–8; also: Cseres 2005: 198–9). The treaty text recognised supranational consumer protection as an internal market policy and a supporting measure for national consumer protection. Regarding the latter, the Treaty contained a consumer protection title that was not tied directly to the imperative of market integration (Article 129a), but limited Commission action to supporting, supplementing and monitoring policies (Micklitz *et al.* 2004: 375).

Five years later, the Treaty of Amsterdam pushed supranational consumer policy even further. The EU's new treaty base made the protection of health, safety and the economic interests of consumers a specific purpose of Community policy. Having specified this, consumer information, education and organisation were no longer considered only as 'interests' but were now denoted as 'rights'. Furthermore, the consumer protection title (now Article 153) was widened by including a horizontal clause according to which a high level of protection should be a consideration in all Community initiatives (Cseres 2005: 200).

Hence, roughly two years before start of the period under investigation in this book, these treaty revisions opened a leeway for Commission initiatives, targeting the consumer as a specific party in market transactions. However, while such initiatives allow more interventionist Commission positions, they do not provide a guarantee in this regard (Micklitz *et al.* 2004; see also Micklitz and Weatherill 1993). Article 153 has an explicitly confined scope enabling only supplementary action which, in addition, must find the agreement of a unanimous Council. Commission officials actively dodged this hurdle, and none of the major Commission initiatives in consumer policy was based on Article 153, but they still relied on the internal market provisions under Article 95 (COM112:105, 141). Yet while these provisions basically allow Commission action in consumer policy, a 1998 ECJ judgement had clarified that consumer protection alone is an insufficient justification in the absence of actual trade barriers.[2] In other words, a market-making motivation must be discernible in any Commission proposal under Article 95. With a view to our theoretical model, thus, extant EU treaties provide a leeway for Commission proposals that tend towards interventionist models, while a narrow reading may also lead to a 'triumph of market freedom over market regulation' (Micklitz *et al.* 2004: 375). Basically, the Commission

---

1. BEUC, the main consumer representation in Europe, received 46 per cent of its funding from the EU budget in 2010 (http://www.beuc.org/Content/Default.asp?PageID=2144, accessed 8 August 2011).

2. Case C-376/98, *Germany v. Parliament and Council* on tobacco advertising (cf. Micklitz *et al.* 2004: 375).

faces the choice between a liberal or an interventionist approach as implied by our major dependent variable (cf. Strünck 2006: 125). But are there organisational incentives to go beyond a mere *laissez-faire* model of the supranational protection of economic consumer rights?

In fact, the formal emancipation of consumer policy from its competition policy roots was also mirrored by institutional differentiation within the Commission itself (Rischkowsky 2007: 30ff.; Weatherill 2005: 17–18). While it started off as a minor unit in the predecessor of DG Competition in 1968 (DG IV), consumer policy responsibility was combined with environmental affairs between 1981 and 1989 (DG XI). Later, it was outsourced to a single standing service which, however, did not have the status of a fully-fledged DG: it 'suffer[ed] from a low budget and vulnerability to the policy concerns of more powerful DGs, such as AGRI [agriculture] and MARKT [internal market]' (Weatherill 2005: 17). Only in 1995 did it officially become a DG (XXIV) under the ambitious political leadership of Commissioner Emma Bonino from Italy. The new service pushed the involvement of consumer pressure groups significantly, but internally it was not yet on an equal footing with the more traditional legislative DGs. Today's administrative strength was reached only when DG XXIV became DG SANCO in 1999 and was replenished with significant manpower from DG ENTR and DG AGRI in the wake of the BSE (*bovine spongiform encephalopathy*) crisis (Guigner 2004, see also Chapter Six in this volume).

Taken together, as of 1999, all ingredients for the politics hypothesised in Chapter Three were present in the field of economic and contractual consumer rights. The Commission had a legal justification for respective acts: it faced a choice between liberal and interventionist policies, and there was an internal proponent of enhanced consumer protection which, however, still had to develop its competences against more traditional departments of the European Commission.

In addition, the major independent variables – politicisation of European integration (*see* Chapter Two in this volume) as well as the public salience of economic and contractual consumer rights – varied strongly during the investigation period. Figure 4.1 shows the respective salience timeline and the adoption dates of the Commission proposals in this subfield of consumer policy. The specific contents of this press coverage are discussed in the individual case histories below, but on this aggregate measure we initially see that the Commission proposal on user rights in electronic communications (case 3) was adopted and also drafted in a period when the salience of the broader issue area was comparatively low and fluctuated around the investigation period mean. The same holds for the proposal on sales promotions (case 4), despite the fact that it was finalised by the Commission when the six-month salience trend slowly started to increase. The Commission proposal on air passenger rights (case 5) was finalised only two months later, also at a level of general issue salience not far above the mean.

Figure 4.1: Public salience of the issue area 'economic and contractual consumer rights'

Note: Figures provide the average percentage share of newspaper articles with issue-area specific keyword combinations (*see* Chapter 3.6 and Appendix C in this volume for details). The grey curve presents monthly values while the bold curve indicates the six-month moving average. Horizontal lines indicate the investigation period mean +/−1 one standard deviation. Vertical lines mark the adoption months of sampled Commission proposals in the issue area.

When the proposed directive on consumer credit (case 6) was tabled by the Commission another nine months later, the salience of economic and contractual consumer rights had risen further and lingered at a comparatively high level. This holds true for the proposal on unfair commercial practices (case 7), the adoption of which coincides with a major leap in reporting on the policy issue in question. This proposal as well as its discussions in the Council and the Parliament accounts for the increased public salience of economic consumer risks subsequently, but after approximately three years of high issue salience, the relative prominence of this policy subfield declines dramatically so that the proposals on general consumer rights (15), as well as on bus and maritime passenger rights (16 and 17), are drafted and finalised at a level of issue salience that systematically undercuts the mean by one standard deviation.

But do these variations matter for policy drafting within the Commission? Does interventionism in the Commission's position on economic consumer protection vary at all? Does it actually increase under higher levels of politicisation and issue salience, or do alternative explanations carry greater weight? To dig into these questions, the following pages separately analyse each of the eight sampled cases that fall into the issue area of economic and contractual consumer rights.[3]

4.1 Universal service and users' rights in electronic communications

The first sampled case in the issue area is an initiative for a directive on universal service and users' rights in electronic communication networks and services. It was formally adopted by the Commission on 12 June 2000 (Commission of the European Communities 2000h), and it refers to a sector in which the supranational protection of economic consumer interests was hitherto considered as a matter of competition policy only. In EU member states, electronic communications and especially telephony had traditionally been offered by either state-owned companies or providers benefitting from regulatory monopolies (Waverman and Sirel 1997). Yet with a set of European laws initiated by the Commission during the early 1990s, the sector was formally liberalised in 1998 despite sustained opposition from some national governments (Kiessling and Blondel 1998). To give an example, in a dispute on financing universal service obligations, the Commission had brought France before the ECJ only three months before the proposal at hand was adopted (Smith 2000b).

Against the background of national intervention in the sector, the Commission proposal came as part of the 2000 'Telecoms Package', which entails four further directives aiming at enhanced competition in the formally liberalised telecommunications market. At the time, hopes for the electronic communication markets were rising high. Related industries attracted enormous investments, which later turned into the 'dot-com bubble', and in March 2000 the EU's Lisbon strategy emphasised electronic communications in its endeavour to make Europe 'the most competitive and dynamic knowledge-based economy in the world' (European Council 2000).

It was thus not surprising that most proposals in the Telecoms Package came with a rather explicit industry focus. However, the particular proposal at hand chiefly targets the end users of electronic communication services and grants basic services and rights to all consumers.[4] Despite its consumer focus, the text was not prepared by the Commission's newly established consumer policy DG (SANCO), but was drafted in the specialised DG for Information Society and Media (INFSO).

---

3. The subsequent summaries of the process-tracing efforts concentrate solely on the explanations and factors derived in Chapter Three (*see* especially Table 3.2). For other factors of internal position formation and more encompassing presentations of the individual drafting processes, the reader may refer to Rauh (2012: Chapters Four–Six) or Hartlapp *et al.* (2014: chapter 7).

4. Unlike other consumer policies, the state-driven history of the sector accounts for the fact that the proposal does not directly regulate consumer or producer behaviour, but rather defines the rights and duties of the traditionally responsible national regulatory agencies (NRAs), who then implement the distribution of rights between service providers and consumers.

An analysis of the proposal's legal text (Commission of the European Communities 2000h) reveals four sets of provisions that affect the distribution of rights among producers and consumers.[5] While the extent of universal service obligations varied in European member states, the issue area was already covered by European law. In the earlier liberalisation of the sector, Directive 98/10/EC confined the playing field for 'universal service for telecommunications in a competitive environment'. This document provides a baseline for a relative judgement on the Commission's consumer policy interventionism in the case at hand. Against this regulatory status quo, three out of the four key provisions actually redistribute certain rights to the consumer side.

First, the general principles and scope provisions clearly extend user rights in Europe as compared to the old directive. Beyond mentioning only affordable prices, the proposal now also allows national intervention in 'circumstances in which [...] consumers' needs are not satisfactorily met' (Article 1). And, while Directive 98/10/EC covered only fixed telephone services, national regulators now also need to ensure user access to fax services and especially to data rates sufficient for internet usage. Combined with obligatory directory services and enhanced service choices for disabled and socially needy users, these instances provide some qualitative moves towards increased user rights in Europe.

Second, the proposal allows national authorities to intervene with provider freedom if it serves the affordability of communication services for the user. Generally, providers may not charge for facilities that are unnecessary to the universal services outlined above and must make specific expenditure-control facilities available. These include itemised billing, selective barring of outgoing calls free of charge (e.g. 0190 numbers), prepayment systems, phased payments of connection fees, and staged reactions to the non-payment of bills. Service providers may only disconnect users after 'due warning', and must maintain specific connections such as emergency numbers at all times. Beyond that, providers must publish a certain set of service quality indicators while national regulators may set respective performance benchmarks for related issues such as the fault repair time. Such measures were not foreseen in the earlier directive so that this key provision also represents at least a slight intervention in favour of consumer interests.

Third, the proposal contains encompassing rules on consumer contracts in electronic communications. While appearing quite detailed and consumer-friendly, a systematic comparison to the old directive shows that only free user access to emergency numbers and a guaranteed number portability when changing contracts are additional consumer protection measures in the new proposal.

Fourth, and finally, a set of provisions on retail price controls is marginally relevant to the distribution of rights among producers and consumers. Given the often monopolist structure of national telecoms markets, such measures had previously been common practice to protect consumers against excessive prices.

---

5. For an overview of the key provisions analysed and the basis for comparison in each analysed policy proposal, see Appendix E.

The proposal specifies that national regulatory agencies can maintain existing tariff obligations, but only if a periodical analysis confirms that their national market is 'not effectively competitive'. This periodical review was not foreseen in the existing Directive 98/10/EC, and this key provision can be interpreted as a move towards a more liberalised market since it implies consecutively less authoritarian intervention in setting consumer retail prices.

In combination, the relative positioning of these four sets of provisions affecting consumer and producer rights shows that, while this proposal still focuses on instilling competition in electronic communications, it also provides some moves towards more consumer policy interventionism in the sector. Can these policy choices be explained by the influence of EU politicisation and issue salience that the model predicts?

During the initial stages of the drafting process in early 1999, the general politicisation of European integration saw a local peak, which can be traced to the resignation of the Santer Commission in March, EP elections in June and the Berlin Council in July, which prompted massive farmer protests against reforms of the agricultural budget (*see* Figure 2.4 in Chapter Two in this volume). While EU politicisation dropped markedly afterwards, the indicator again entered an upward trend at the beginning of 2000. This trend particularly reflects the public visibility of discussions surrounding the conclusion of the Lisbon agenda and the preparations of the Biarritz Council in October aiming at the conclusion of the Charter of Fundamental Rights. However, compared to the politicisation peaks around Maastricht and Amsterdam in the years before the policy-making process, the particular politicisation levels observed during drafting were only intermediate, yet on average slightly higher than in the years from 1990 until 1999.

The aggregate salience indicator (see Figure 4.1) exhibits an upward trend during the drafting period. Rising throughout 1999, we can observe a single temporally confined peak in the autumn. Yet the long-term trend stayed at mean levels until the adoption of the proposal. Delving into the media data that feed this indicator highlights that economic consumer rights were discussed at the time in relation to e-commerce, not least because of a parallel European directive concluded by the Council and an EU–US 'safe harbour' agreement allowing transfer of customer-related data. These topics, however, account only for an average contemporaneous salience level, and touch the issues of the proposal under analysis only at the fringes. Yet the topic of universal service in electronic communications itself was visible on the public agenda. A more specific search[6] revealed newspaper articles discussing guaranteed user services in liberalised and liberalising countries such as the US, Spain, Italy and Poland (e.g. Zafra 1999; Betts 1999; Lerner 2000). Newspaper reports also covered the alleged market

---

6. The search required that a respective article contained 'universal service' *and* one of 'telecoms', 'electronic communications' or 'telecommunications'. For the German, French and Spanish newspapers, the respective translations used by the Commission have been employed. The *Financial Times* contained nineteen hits for the period 1 January 1999–12 July 2000, the *Frankfurter Allgemeine Zeitung* (*FAZ*) had ten, *Le Figaro* five, and *El País* fifteen.

distortions emerging from the French system of financing universal service obligations (e.g. Le Gales and Renault 1999; Owen 2000; Iskander 2000), which ultimately led to the Commission's infringement proceeding against France (*FAZ* 2000c). Furthermore, the drafting was paralleled by direct newspaper reports on the plans for the proposal analysed here – at least since the Commission's early consultation efforts from 1999 onwards (e.g. Hargreaves 1999; Bär-Bouyssière 1999; *FAZ* 2000e). Taken together, the aggregate indicator and the visibility of the narrower issues signal medium to high levels of contemporaneous issue salience which, in addition, increase slightly during drafting. So, did these context factors affect the policy choices within DG INFSO?

The two officials explicitly responsible for the universal service proposal (COM127:15) pursued a 'twofold' ambition by intending that 'basic telecom services should be provided throughout Europe', and that 'basic consumer protection guarantees [...] are provided there as well' (COM128:33). In other words, the unit 'tried to highlight that there was a new political importance for users' rights' (COM127:151). In the broader development of liberalising the European telecoms market, the proposed regulation was seen as 'an intermediate point on the way to competitiveness. And if you are going to regulate progressively less and less, then you have to empower consumers in the marketplace' (ibid.). Clearly, consumer protection was seen as 'the other side of liberalisation' (COM128:43).

The first formal consultation in November 1999 had communicated this decision to re-regulate universal service with an emphasis on user interests.[7] However, since the 'universal service directive was by no means a totally new piece of legislation' (COM127:41), the officials also planned a certain amount of 'carry over' from the start, and the responsiveness to consumer concerns voiced in the consultation did not go so far as to 'rethink basic aspects' (COM127:47). Deviating too much from the extant directive was also not possible because officials were 'working against the clock', as their hierarchy was pushing for particular consultation and publication dates (COM127:281). This pressure was coming from the parallel Lisbon strategy, which was adopted four months before the proposal and aimed explicitly at exploiting telecommunications as a means to stimulate economic growth in Europe. Grasping this political momentum by a timely adoption of the package was immensely important for the political leadership of DG INFSO, because it gave them a head start into the legislative activities of the Prodi Commission.

In this light, it should also be noted that DG INFSO largely avoided consultation with other Commission departments up until the inter-service consultation (ISC) formally required it three months before the adoption of the proposal (COM127:219). The most important interlocutors within the Commission were DG COMP (for Competition) and DG SANCO. In fact, there were heavy turf

---

7. The original communication (COM[1999]539) is no longer available online, but its summary indicates that both issues were already part of the consultation from the start. See: http://europa. eu/legislation_summaries/internal_market/single_market_services/l24216_en.htm (accessed 24 November 2010).

conflicts with DG COMP, which, however, did not revolve around consumer policy interventionism but rather addressed the correct treaty base and the formal responsibilities within the Commission (Hartlapp *et al*. 2014: 167). Conflicts with DG SANCO, in contrast, were much less pronounced – arguably so, because this only recently established department had less internal weight than the historically powerful DG COMP.

Nevertheless, the consumer policy service demanded from INFSO 'what you would expect them to be interested in the light of their so-called constituencies' (COM127:85). This, for example, concerned the extended scope of universal service obligations outlined above. INFSO willingly extended universal services beyond mere fixed telephony, but did so more out of the aim to stimulate growth in the sector and to make the regulation 'technology neutral' (COM114:41). Yet the consumer side demanded much more. While they saw the factual inclusion of dial-up internet as 'progress', consumer associations wished to add 'a satisfactory speed' as an additional condition (BEUC 2000c: 3; Commission of the European Communities 2000d: 15). Internally, DG SANCO pushed along this line and demanded the inclusion of broadband internet into the universal service definition. INFSO, however, 'saw no justification for that' in economic terms (COM127:51). In fact, broadband access was hardly prevalent in Europe, and defining it as a universal service obligation would have created enormous costs among service providers. Such an interventionist move was also not backed politically. In the 1999 consultation, industry stakeholders and, most notably, member state governments considered the current scope of universal service as sufficient (Commission of the European Communities 2000d: 14–5).

Yet a clause in the finally adopted proposal that foresees a period review of the scope of universal services offered a compromise solution between the contending industry and consumer interests. It satisfied most user groups which saw it as 'an essential tool [...] to combat social exclusion' in the future (Commission of the European Communities 2000d: 14– 15). In this clause, consumer associations demanded that the review proposed by INFSO should consider social demands as well (BEUC 2000c: 5) – a concern that DG INFSO conceded only during the late stages of drafting.[8]

Nonetheless, INFSO's drive to regulatory consumer protection was less developed when it comes to the specific rules for national imposition of universal service obligations. One of the most controversial issues was governmental compensation and the financing of universal service. In its ideal position, INFSO considered that such interventions would not be necessary at all in a liberalised European market. However, 'some member states' were of a different opinion, and INFSO grudgingly adopted their position (Commission of the European Communities 2000d). Most likely, France – being subject to a contemporaneous infringement procedure – was in opposition here. But while the anticipation of dissenting votes in the Council affected position formation on this matter, the

---

8. Apparently, the phrasing that the review should be undertaken with a view to social developments was not part of INFSO working drafts as of spring 2000 (cf. BEUC 2000b: 10).

Commission sustained the pressure and announced its intention 'to scrutinise such schemes closely to ensure that they are justified, transparent and appropriate' (ibid. 25).

Another controversial issue concerned the interests of disabled consumers, on which DG SANCO in particular was 'extremely insistent'. SANCO internally asked for guarantees that disabled persons could enjoy universal services to the same extent as non-disabled users. For INFSO, however, this 'guarantee of result' would have involved too much market intervention, turning universal service into a maximum, rather than a minimum standard (COM127:93). During negotiations paralleling the ISC in spring 2000, they went for a 'compromise' between consumer and producer interests, by prescribing at least an equivalent level of access (COM127:103).

Also with regard to defining affordability of universal services, consumer associations would have liked to go beyond what is in the proposal. They demanded to include the cost of living, while the proposal itself considered only telecommunication prices and income. Similarly, the provisions on governmental interventions in tariffs did not go far enough in their view: instead of only allowing member states to enact common tariffs throughout their territory they should be obliged to do so. Likewise, *allowing* member states to enforce special tariffs for needy persons was considered insufficient – from the perspective of consumer associations, the national level should be obliged to do so (BEUC 2000c: 3–4). INFSO had tested the waters on this issue already as the 1999 consultation proposed to draw up guidelines on affordability assessment – a soft-law approach that would not alienate national governments too quickly. However, stakeholder and national responses appear to have been mixed in this regard (Commission of the European Communities 2000d: 15), so that INFSO backed off during the position formation process.

In contrast, INFSO's proposal to enable governmental oversight on the quality of communication services found support among national regulators despite provider opposition (Commission of the European Communities 2000d: 17). Finally, the general rules on the control-of-expenditure mechanisms were very much welcomed by the consumer associations. Clearly, some higher demands with regard to non-payment abounded (BEUC 2000c: 4), but in the light of industry opposition, DG INFSO's position again presented some middle ground between consumers and producers.

Finally, contractual consumer rights were simply transferred from extant directives, on unfair contract terms and on consumer protection in distance contracts (Commission of the European Communities 2000h: 13). For consumer associations, this extant general regime was insufficient, and they added a range of demands that the proposal did not fulfil (BEUC 2000c: 6–7). However, in not taking these demands on board and relying solely on what was already available at the European level, INFSO took the least controversial and the least work-intensive way of position formation. On the one hand, giving in to these consumer demands would have meant creating precedents in an ongoing turf battle on commercial practices between DG MARKT and DG SANCO (see below); on the other, it would have lengthened the position formation process because of the need to translate the additional consumer demands into legally viable provisions. Against the hierarchy's time pressure and an ongoing turf war in the Commission, this additional level of consumer protection was sacrificed.

In contrast, the issue of number portability and its extension to mobile services was very much welcomed by consumer associations as it 'is essential to competition' (BEUC 2000c: 9). Indeed, number portability was emphasised by the Commission as one of the key consumer attainments of the proposal (cf. Commission of the European Communities 2000b). However, the solution in the proposal was considered suboptimal on the consumer side. First, portability should not have to be requested by consumers but should be the standard. Second, it should be free of charge, because otherwise service providers would set the price for portability at a level that would effectively present itself as a deterrent to switching providers (BEUC 2000c: 9). Generally, this consumer position was also maintained by national regulators in the 1999 consultation, where particularly those regulators that already had portability in place argued that it was 'working effectively' (Commission of the European Communities 2000d: 17). In contrast, most mobile operators opposed it, arguing that implementation costs would be substantial, while new entrant companies and operators already facing national number portability rules were in favour of introducing the obligation at the European level (ibid.). The position INFSO took followed the views of consumers, national authorities, and some of the operators by making the obligation European, but also catered to the interest of opposing operators by allowing charges for portable numbers, and by making portability subject to consumer requests.

In sum, this compromise solution neatly mirrors the stance that the lead department INFSO had exhibited throughout proposal formulation. Essentially, also this consumer-oriented part of the telecoms package served mainly to push the liberalisation agenda in an economically promising sector, of which INFSO wanted to remain in charge. Delineating universal service and users' rights at the European level mainly serves to remove the justification for sustained national intervention in the sector. Against this background, INFSO took a relatively liberal stance on those key provisions that dealt with direct government intervention in the market (e.g. on financing obligations and retail price controls). Yet the general belief that consumer empowerment was a necessary condition for successful liberalisation affected those provisions that dealt more directly with the relationship of consumers with service providers, for example, with regard to contractual consumer rights. In sum, however, DG INFSO raised protection only slightly, and did so only as long as it served the liberalisation of the sector.

As such, the individual case provides only minor hints with regard to the theoretical model developed in Chapter Three. Consumer policy had not been fully emancipated from competition policy in the sector the proposal covers. But the case's limited value is also due to observing only intermediate levels of politicisation, which provides little analytical leverage. Some within-case variation is interesting, however. Major concessions to the consumer side, especially with regard to the review clause on the scope of universal service provisions, occurred only late during drafting when both general politicisation of European integration and issue salience exhibited rising trends. Yet this variation in INFSO's position is arguably only part of the story.

Clearly, drafting was rushed, and both administrative and political hierarchies had their take on the drafting process. However, rather than immediate public salience, this can be traced more to the political momentum that the parallel Lisbon strategy had triggered. Likewise, internal conflict had other roots than the interventionism in INFSO's position. It was rather grounded in a solid turf conflict with DG COMP, and some minor demands for protection from DG SANCO. Finally, responsiveness to consumer associations was consistently subordinated to the aim of competition enhancement.

Even when INFSO wanted to go further in the name of the consumer – for example, with regard to special tariffs for needy persons – position formation was confined by anticipated member state opposition. Yet INFSO did not confine position formation only with regard to consumer protection, but also with hindsight to increased liberalisation, as the issue of producer compensation for universal service obligations shows. Clearly, approaches explaining position formation through anticipated political feasibility in the Council bear relevance for the case at hand.

4.2 Sales promotions in the internal market

Rather than being grounded in the peculiarities of a specific sector, the next sampled case proposes a general regulation on cross-border sales promotions, which covers price reductions, free gifts, coupons and vouchers, promotional contests and the like (Commission of the European Communities 2001a). Dealing directly with producer activities directed at changing consumers' purchase decisions, the measure is clearly a consumer policy issue. But also this case was not drafted by the uprising consumer policy DG SANCO. Rather, DG MARKT was responsible for the proposal adopted in October 2001.

By 1996, DG MARKT had published a stakeholder consultation on the broader area of 'Commercial communications in the internal market' (European Commission 1996), which was followed up by a communication in March 1998 (European Commission 1998). MARKT's strategy on commercial communications was not necessarily targeted at supranational legislation from the start, but was meant to analyse whether and, if so, which national measures hampered 'the development of efficient cross-border marketing strategies of European industry' (ibid. 7).

The backdrop of this approach was formal producer complaints that gave rise to a range of cases before the ECJ (for an overview, see European Commission 1996: 5–8). Essentially, relevant ECJ rulings render commercial communications subject to mutual recognition. But case law also highlights that certain national restrictions are justified if they are proportionate and serve certain other public policy objectives upheld in the Treaties. Given the sheer number of producer complaints, DG MARKT argued that a more systematic review of national legislation was necessary, and proposed an assessment methodology oriented along the lines of the extant ECJ jurisprudence. This can be understood as an early commitment to treat national legislation in the area first and foremost as a trade barrier in the internal market.

Yet since the ECJ case law had allowed certain exemptions, DG MARKT required local knowledge to assess the relevant national laws. To this end, a group of national experts was inaugurated in 1998, which started to scrutinise national laws on sales promotions as a first specific area of commercial communications. Drafting officials claim that only the initial results of this group in late 1998 highlighted that a European law was necessary, thus giving rise to the drafting process analysed here (COM133:29).

Within the investigation period thus defined, starting in late 1998 we can attest intermediate levels of general EU politicisation up until mid-2000. Yet the politicisation indicator developed in Chapter Two exhibits a constant rise during the first half of 2001, which led to a pronounced local peak in July of the same year. Anti-globalisation protests addressing the EU resulted in the unfortunate climax of violent protests accompanying an EU Council meeting in Gothenburg during June. Also, more specific policies such as the handling of BSE and the food-and-mouth disease, defence matters, as well as fishery and transport policies, drew European citizens into the streets at this time. Besides, the EU was also visible in the media because of the Treaty of Nice and the failed Irish referendum in June 2001. Despite the fact that politicisation started to decline again in the second half of 2001, we can safely say that the final stages of drafting this particular proposal occurred at a time when the EU faced a strong public challenge.

This, however, is not true of the salience of the specific issues at stake in the proposal under analysis. As noted earlier, the aggregate public salience indicator reached intermediate levels during 2000, but the timeline shows a clear decline until mid-2001. For the last three months before proposal adoption, the indicator rises moderately, and arrives at its investigation period mean in October 2001 when the sales promotion proposal was finally adopted. The underlying media data show that this minor increase was again driven largely by a range of editorials on the protection of consumer data and also, to a lesser extent, by the Council adoption of the E-Commerce Directive during September, as well as by an EU proposal on banking fees in Europe.

The narrower issue of sales promotions, in contrast, was virtually absent from media reports.[9] Between January 1999 and the adoption of the proposal in October 2001, only one article from the sample of four quality daily European newspapers

---

9. The specific newspaper research required that both 'sales promotions' and 'consumer' were contained in the title or body of the article and covered the period 1 January 1999–2 October 2001. As usual, the respective translations employed by the Commission were used for the German, French and Spanish newspapers. Adding 'consumer' as a second search term was necessary since the German term 'Verkaufsförderung' has a range of different meanings that inflated the number of hits. Search results for the other newspapers were not affected by this decision so that the following number of hits resulted: *Financial Times*:zero; *Frankfurter Allgemeine Zeitung*: ten, *Le Figaro*: zero; *El País*: zero. Even among the ten *FAZ* hits, 'Verkaufsförderung' and 'Verbraucher' co-occurred nine times, although the articles did not involve the issues covered by the proposal in any way.

covered the issue area directly. In the light of this one late article, public attention to the specific issues covered by the proposal must be considered low.

Thus, while rising politicisation towards the end of drafting should have created the Commission's demand for visible initiatives that served widespread public interest, the low and partly declining salience levels of contractual consumer rights and sales promotions in particular signalled that the case at hand was hardly a useful weapon in demonstrating output legitimacy to the public. But what policy choices did the Commission, and in particular DG MARKT, make on the proposal?

To analyse the relative degree of interventionism in the Commission proposal (Commission of the European Communities 2001a), it has to be compared to the different national rules since no comparable supranational law existed. The ECJ cases driving the 1996 Green Paper (European Commission 1996: 5–8) refer to restrictions in Luxembourg, the Netherlands, France, Italy, Portugal, Greece, Belgium and particularly Germany. In addition, the later report of the group of national experts indicated also some restrictions on sales promotions in the more liberal countries such as the UK (European Commission 2001a: especially Section 1). Against this background, the legal text of the 2001 Commission proposal contains four sets of provisions that directly affect the extant distribution of rights among producers and consumers.

The first key provision actually bans all national rules that present general prohibitions of sales promotions, prescribe limitations on their value, prohibit them beyond seasonal sales or stipulate any prior authorisation procedures (Article 3). Given that some countries largely prohibited discounts (e.g. Denmark or Greece), that some member states confined the value of sales promotions (e.g. France) and that some national regimes limited most promotions to specific seasonal sales (e.g. Germany and Belgium), this particular provision clearly enhances the freedom of business operators. This is further underlined by the provision that all remaining national rules are subject to mutual recognition in the EU's internal market. Arguably, this empowers sellers from less interventionist countries of origin to circumvent extant or future national restrictions. According to the analytic report of the expert group, some of the thus banned national rules are justified under competition concerns, but many of them were passed to protect national consumers against undue incentives (cf. European Commission 2001a: Sections 1–2). Insofar, the Commission position on this first key provision undermines many of the much more interventionist regimes and thus corresponds more to a *laissez-faire* model of consumer policy.

The second set of key provisions, in contrast, harmonises specific consumer protection rules at the supranational level (KP4.2). Article 4 of the proposal refers to an encompassing and partly far-reaching annex that defines information obligations for sellers and promoters. The particular rules differ for discounts, free gifts and coupons, and are too numerous to be listed here. But comparing them to the legal status quo as given by the expert group report (European Commission 2001a: Section 1) reveals that this provision extends certain information rules that existed in only some national regimes also to those countries that had previously been unregulated. Since the resulting net effect is more information for consumers through increased producer obligations, this provision points more towards the interventionist end of the consumer policy spectrum. In a similar vein, the proposal enhances the protection of children and adolescents by banning promotional activities that collect data from children, contain possibly harmful gifts or use alcoholic beverages as a promotional tool.

Finally, a third set of key provisions facilitates cross-border redress for consumers affected by faulty sales promotions (Article 6; KP4.3). Beyond revealing their identity, it obliges producers to respond to complaints, and requires that announced helplines, codes of conduct and dispute resolution schemes are truly backed in practice. While these rules are clearly consumer-friendly, they merely specify certain information requirements that were already regulated in the annex. The rules on redress mechanisms, furthermore, corresponded mainly to prohibitions of misleading advertising that existed in almost all national regimes. In sum, these particular provisions enhance legal clarity, but do not present a deviation from the distributive status quo.

With one decidedly liberal, one slightly interventionist, and one indifferent set of key provisions, the classification of the proposal on our dependent variable is rather clear. The most interventionist key provision of the proposal requires hardly anything beyond mere information requirements that are also present in *laissez-faire* regimes of consumer policy (cf. Chapter Three). But quite a few extant national regimes were passed on the assumption that sales promotions create undue incentives, seducing consumers into non-rational purchase decisions, corresponding more to the interventionist end of the policy spectrum. Yet the first key provision of the proposal under analysis either prohibits such regimes or undermines them by mutual recognition. Relative to what existed previously in European states, thus, the overall Commission proposal is much more congruent with a market-making, rather than with an interventionist model of consumer policy. In this way, Article 1 of the proposal indeed defines the 'proper functioning of the internal market' as the sole objective. How did this policy choice come about?

The proposal content was developed under the auspices of the MARKT unit responsible for the free movement of services. When asked what prompted them to tackle the area, drafting officials emphasised the formal complaints by individual companies with their unit that go back to 1992 (COM79:29). Among others, a Dutch compact disc club had tried to enter the German market with a 'three for the price of one' offer. This, however, was forbidden by the German *Rabattgesetz*, and the producer complaint resulted in a formal infringement procedure paralleling the legislative drafting process (COM133:33). In 1998, a reasoned opinion was sent and, failing to react, Germany was referred to the ECJ in 1999 (Commission of the European Communities 1998). The major argument of the drafting officials was that the German provisions discriminated against foreign competitors wanting to build a client base in the German market (Commission of the European Communities 1999).

This parallel process highlights that the decision to tackle sales promotions as a sole internal market issue had been taken very early by the officials themselves.

Neither the involvement of the line hierarchy nor of the political leadership – that is, the liberal Dutch Commissioner Bolkestein or his independent predecessor from Italy, Mario Monti – was mentioned. Rather, the position formation process happened to '95% at least' at the administrative level of DG MARKT (COM133:132).

Following the 1996 Green Paper and the 1998 communication, the MARKT unit contacted the permanent national representations in Brussels, and each of the then fifteen member states delegated one or two officials from the national ministry of economics or equivalents to an expert group with the task of evaluating national restrictions on sales communications (COM133:54, see also European Commission 2001a: Section 5). The decision that this group should first focus on sales promotions was driven by German opposition to the parallel infringement procedure. The Commission officials thought that restrictions on sales promotions were only prevalent in Germany making this issue an 'easy' one to start with. Rather than preparing a legislative draft, MARKT officials hoped to create a 'fourteen governments against Germany' situation in the expert group that would make this single member state unilaterally change its legislation, or at least accept mutual recognition. (COM133:29).

However, this idea was not viable. First, the expert group uncovered restrictions on sales promotions in almost all member states (COM133:57). Second, it provided MARKT officials with further information on 'public interest' justifications of national laws. In sum, the work of the expert group resulted in twenty-five different types of sales promotion legislation and, based on the assessment methodology already developed in the 1996 Green Paper (European Commission 1996), categorised them either as non-proportionate and trade-inhibiting, as justified and proportionate in the national context, or as justified and proportionate for the European public interest. This threefold classification laid the cornerstone for the later proposal as the officials decided along these lines whether the specific rules should be prohibited, should fall under mutual recognition or should be harmonised at the European level.

Against this decisive role of national experts, one could assume that the policy choices of DG MARKT were driven by the anticipation of Council positions. A closer look, however, shows that MARKT did not sacrifice its market-making endeavour to such strategic considerations. Initially, the narrowly pre-specified assessment procedure constrained the representatives of the national ministries by requiring them to identify all national restrictions on these issues, asking them to outline their justifications (cf. European Commission 1998: 8–9; 2001a). Based on this, these experts together made up the list of twenty-five sales promotion restrictions, and went on to apply the 'proportionality test' as defined by MARKT's assessment methodology to each category (European Commission 2001a). This procedure minimised information asymmetries among national experts, and between the experts and the MARKT officials, while leaving little room for guarding particular national interests. Rather, the MARKT officials had designed a procedure that produced local knowledge without challenging the overall aim of trade creation.

MARKT's approach to proportionality testing also goes back to ECJ judgements on cross-border service provision. In several instances, the Court had upheld the principle of proportionality, meaning that 'requirements imposed on the providers of services must be appropriate to ensure achievement of the intended aim and must not go beyond what is necessary in order to achieve that objective' (e.g. in European Court of Justice 1991: para. 15; or European Court of Justice 1995: para. 45). MARKT's interpretation was that 'it must not be possible to obtain the same result by a less restrictive rule' (European Commission 1996: 7). Again, this early commitment, and the strict reliance on European case law in designing the assessment procedure indicate that the expert group would be unlikely to change MARKT's overall liberalising position.

An even stronger piece of evidence opposing the view of a nationally driven expert group is the final report in March 2001, roughly seven months before proposal adoption. This report signalled sustained member state opposition to the Commission's market-making endeavour. Belgium, for example, argued that mutual recognition in sales promotions 'is likely to lead to deregulation that is detrimental to the general objectives of protecting consumers' (European Commission 2001a: Section 2, p. 21). Germany, likewise, announced that 'there are no plans at present to discuss amendments to the legal provisions governing discounts' and 'reject[ed] the move towards mutual recognition at Community level' (ibid. 22). Similarly, Denmark, Greece and Portugal opposed, while a number of other countries sided with, the French position of 'yes, subject to certain rules' at the European level. These countries (e.g. Luxembourg and the Netherlands) argued that at least minimum harmonisation would be necessary, and proposed transferring their regulatory status quo to the supranational level. However, as the preceding section has shown, MARKT's final position imposed general bans, prescribed mutual recognition and harmonised only information requirements. Compared to the scattered landscape of member state demands, the anticipation of national preferences seems not to haven driven MARKT's position to any significant degree.

This lack of response to national concerns also raised doubts within more central Commission departments. During ISC, the Legal Service (DG SJ) doubted whether a regulation – which would be immediately binding on member states – was really the most suitable instrument for the proposal at hand. The SJ suspected that such a strict instrument would not be enforceable vis-à-vis national governments, and preferred the form of a directive, which is based on national transposition measures. MARKT officials, however, defied this concern and argued that a single regulation would create much less red tape for industry than individual transpositions in fifteen European states. Politically, MARKT's position was very much backed because, in the wake of the Lisbon strategy's emphasis on European competiveness, a high-level group was developing a 'better regulation' strategy for the Commission at the time (COM79:58).

In contrast to MARKT's sheer stubbornness in the face of member state opposition, the responsible unit had provided a valuable contact point for industry stakeholders ever since the initial producer complaints. The predominant majority of responses to the 1996 Green Paper came from 'users' of sales promotions such as producers or sellers, as well as from providers of commercial communication services such as advertising agencies. To a lesser extent, the 'receivers' of sales promotions, such as consumer associations, responded to DG MARKT's consultation (European Commission 1998: 3). Besides the formal consultation, feedback from the industry was also 'regular' during the later stages of policy formulation. This spurred further input on particular national rules with trade-inhibiting effects, and MARKT's endeavour to liberalise the area yielded 'an enormous, a very, very positive response from the industry' (COM133:156).

Yet this is not to say that consumer representatives had no take on the Commission proposal. In the 1996 consultation, BEUC had demanded that consumer concerns should be made an explicit part of the proposed assessment scheme, and MARKT did so by at least mentioning transparency as a relevant consumer right in the revised procedure (European Commission 1998; 2001a: Section 3). Later, this directly fed into the harmonisation of information requirements at the European level. Similarly, the rules on children's protection and redress systems meet the demands of consumer associations voiced in the Green Paper consultation.

Nevertheless, the consumer umbrella association was rather unsatisfied with MARKT's final position and its own abilities to exert influence (BEUC 2002c). For one thing, the recognition of only economic consumer interests was unsatisfying for BEUC, which claimed that 'transparency cannot be the only means of protection' (ibid. 6). The general argument is that there are a range of other vulnerable groups, the protection of which could be a justifiable aim of national and supranational regulation. Under MARKT's position, any further restrictions would be ruled out, however.[10] Further, BEUC explicitly notes a lack of access to the position formation process of DG MARKT (ibid. 5). While consumer interests were heard in the 1996 consultation, the subsequent evaluation of national rules took place without their representation in the expert group. But apart from MARKT's rather selective responsiveness to external interests, why were consumer interests not asserted in the internal coordination with the respective Commission DG?

In fact, MARKT's *laissez-faire* approach led to a heated internal battle with DG SANCO. SANCO was preparing its own inroad into the area of cross-border producer-to-consumer interactions at the time. Discussed further below, the consumer policy DG had started to draft a directive on unfair commercial practices while MARKT was finalising the proposal analysed here. Since sales promotions were only one of the commercial practices SANCO's unfinished proposal should cover, the consumer policy DG claimed that MARKT regulated on their 'turf' (COM79:55). What is more, both DGs pursued strongly varying conceptualisations. While SANCO's policy line focused on 'business-to-consumer

---

10. Note that the consumer organisation did not oppose harmonisation per se. Indeed, consumers had protested especially against the protectionist effects of the German *Rabattgesetz*, which effectively limited consumer choice and price competition. However, they emphasised that harmonising to the lowest common denominator could not be the solution (BEUC 2002c: 2).

relationships', MARKT's proposal was at least equally motivated by fighting unfair cross-border competition among producers (COM79:51). These were 'two different approaches' where SANCO worked for 'harmonisation' while MARKT worked 'on the basis of mutual recognition' (COM91:143–51). Accordingly, SANCO considered MARKT's position internally as 'too liberal' (COM79:35). But the drafting officials defended their 'business angle', and considered their assessment procedure as a superior technocratic solution to the problem. SANCO, by contrast, was perceived as 'praying for different constituencies' following the 'political drive' of Commissioner Byrne, who wanted to have a strong 'consumer protection proposal' to establish the legislative capacities of his own DG (COM79:72).

The argument that turf interests – rather than actual consumer concerns – drove SANCO's position is underlined by the shortage of attempts to change the actual content of the sales promotion proposal. Of course, the drafting officials in DG MARKT knew that something was coming up and SANCO officials were invited to some of the expert group meetings early on. But those on the MARKT side could recall neither the participation nor the input of SANCO officials in this early stage of drafting (COM79:47 and 37). After SANCO announced a Green Paper for 2001, MARKT organised a bilateral meeting in addition which, however, involved 'no consultation on the provisions' (COM113:92).

However, when the formal ISC was launched in early 2001, SANCO suddenly provided extensive comments and thereby hit the brakes on the formal process (COM133:92). Because 'they were not ready with their Green Paper [...] they kept this proposal hostage so that it was proposed at the same time' (COM113:96). This strategy worked out indeed: both MARKT's sales promotions proposal and SANCO's Green Paper on EU consumer protection were discussed and adopted at the same meeting of the College of Commissioners on 2 October 2001 (Secretariat-General 2001: 12). Therefore, rather than trying to change the substance of MARKT's liberal proposal, SANCO ensured that the outside world could see that there were two options on the table on how to regulate consumer rights supranationally in the future.[11]

So, what do the procedural observations tell us about the theoretical considerations in Chapter Three? Basically, the liberal thrust of the sales promotion proposal is consistent with the theoretical model: Under high levels of politicisation that combine with only low levels of issue salience, we should expect liberalising proposals. Beyond the expected outcome, the process hypotheses on lacking responsiveness to consumer demands, limited involvement of the political level

---

11. With the benefit of hindsight, this paid off: both the sales promotion proposal and SANCO's later proposal on unfair commercial practices were ultimately handled by the same committee of the EP. The parliamentarians preferred the higher level of consumer protection under SANCO's proposal, adopted it, and simply left sales promotion on the table without discussing it further. When the 2005 drive for simplification of European legislation came (European Commission 2005b), DG Enterprise and the Secretariat-General 'searched for victims', and the sales promotion was finally withdrawn (COM79:64). What is more, MARKT's broader strategy on commercial communications ended with this single failed proposal.

in non-salient initiatives, and a process duration driven by extensive fact-finding procedures are also in line with the proposed model.

However, the particular history of the drafting process raises doubts on whether MARKT's positions would have changed if the high politicisation levels during the late stages of drafting had met high levels of issue salience. MARKT had committed to a mission of liberalisation early on, and leaving this path would have entailed the danger of surrendering the issue area to the up-and-coming DG SANCO. In fact, MARKT's position on sales promotions can be seen as clinging to its original organisational purpose, namely the removal of trade barriers in Europe's internal market. Shifting emphasis to public interest justifications would have made MARKT's approach simply superfluous since SANCO started to occupy the field from that perspective. Even if they are justified technocratically, specific policy choices may simply reflect internal turf considerations.

Regarding the hypotheses on Commissioner nationality and partisanship, evidence is mixed in the case at hand. The Dutch Commissioner, Bolkestein, came from a liberal party (the VVD) and a national background in which sales promotions were comparatively mildly regulated, but, given that the process appears to have been steered from the administrative level, this had little influence.

4.3 Air passenger rights

Chronologically, the subsequent case in the sample is a proposal for a supranational regulation of air passenger rights (Commission of the European Communities 2001b), an area that had hitherto been covered only by Regulation (EEC) 295/91 on common rules for a denied-boarding compensation system. Also here, the broader policy context was the formal liberalisation of the respective economic sector.

Coming into effect in April 1997, EU law allowed each European air carrier to operate freely from and within any member state. The demise of the formerly ubiquitous nationality barriers in the air transport market quickly unfolded an enormous economic impact. Six new European airlines emerged immediately, and frequency and capacity, as well as the number of routes within Europe, have increased steadily ever since (Morrell 1998; European Commission 2007).

Beyond its efforts to liberalise international air transport (Rauh and Schneider 2013), DG TREN also had ideas of re-regulating the air transport market within Europe. Just after formal liberalisation in 1997, the transport policy department proposed an amendment to the existing European law on air passenger rights which, however, was rejected by the Council.[12] But DG TREN pursued its regulatory plans further by an information campaign on existing air passenger rights in the Union (Commission of the European Communities 2000e: 6). This was complemented

---

12. This rejection had nothing to do with consumer protection, but was due to a conflict about its application to Gibraltar airport: Gibraltar is officially a British overseas territory with a strategically important Royal Navy base, but Spain has never accepted British sovereignty there (Commission of the European Communities 2001b: 2–3; cf. also Cohen 1999).

by envisaged legislative plans in the 2001 White Paper on transport policy, which declaredly aimed to 'refocus Europe's transport policy on the demands and needs of its citizens' (COM33:140, BEUC 2002a: 2–3).

This drafting period – defined by the Council's failure with the initial proposal in November 1998 and the final proposal adoption in December 2001 – largely coincides with the two cases discussed above, and the trends in the relevant indicators for the independent variables in the theoretical model of this book can be quickly summarised: with regard to the general EU politicisation, we can attest a minor peak in 1999, intermediate levels up until mid-2000, and a constant rise during the first half of 2001 with a pronounced local peak in July (cf. also Chapter Two in this volume). The drafting process thus started with intermediate levels of EU politicisation, then experienced a clear slump, and was finalised in a period when legitimacy of European integration was outwardly challenged.

The general public salience of economic and contractual consumer rights (see Figure 4.1) rose somewhat during 1999, declined again until July 2001, and then sharply rose to and exceeded mean levels in the two months before proposal adoption. Issues driving the indicator during this time concern the protection of shoppers' data as well as EU initiatives on e-commerce and banking fees. However, zooming in on the issue of overbooked, cancelled or delayed flights, specific newspaper searches also show a comparatively high level of public visibility.[13] Of course, the terrorist attacks of September 2001 and the resulting difficulties in air transport account for the enormous quantity of reporting on flight delays and cancellations shortly before the proposal was adopted. But reporting on the issue area was already rather high during the first two years of drafting. On the one hand, a huge number of respective newspaper reports covered pilot strikes – for example, in Spain during spring 1999, in the US and France during summer 2000 and in Germany during spring 2001. On the other hand, there is a large number of articles discussing how air transport liberalisation in Europe affected air passengers. Overbooking, as well as delay and cancellations, was an important topic in these reports (e.g. Done 2000; Scherer 1999).[14] Yet even independently of liberalisation, bad customer treatment by airlines made news at the time (e.g. Bray 1999; *Financial Times* 1999; Aissaoui and Ducros 2001; *FAZ* 2001b). And, also DG TREN's information campaign of 2000, as well as its actual

13. The underlying newspaper search covered the period 1 January 1999–21 December 2001, and required that the article's text fulfils the following conditions: (air travel OR air transport OR airline*) AND (passenger* OR customer*) AND (overbook* OR cancel* OR delay*). This resulted in 139 hits in the *Financial Times*, eighty-seven in the *Frankfurter Allgemeine Zeitung*, fifty-two in *Le Figaro*, and 233 in *El País*.

14. At the time of policy formulation, denied-boarding was a common form of yield management in the airline business. While overbooking often occurs because of operational reasons like delayed connecting flights, for example, so-called 'no-show' passengers were another reason (cf. Commission of the European Communities 2001b: 3–4). Specific ticket models or the speculations of selling agents make it possible that a range of passengers simply does not show up. Airlines, in response, try to forecast these no-shows for each flight, and then consciously overbook it accordingly. If such a forecast is wrong, however, some passengers actually present for their flight may be denied boarding.

legislative plans, attracted strong media attention well before the proposal was adopted (see for example Skapinker 1999; Prades 1999; Cohen 1999; Jolley 2000; Smith 2000a; Pozzi 2000; *FAZ* 2000b, 2001d, 2001a). In sum, there was sustained public visibility of the issues involved at the time that the proposal analysed here was being prepared by DG TREN.

In this light, the proposal itself was likely to resonate among the broader European public, providing a valuable tool to enhance the output legitimacy of European decision making. Additionally, given that European decision making was publicly contested in the first half of 1999 and, to an even greater extent, from summer 2000 onwards, the Commission also had incentives to exploit the proposal to that end. Accordingly, the theoretical model lets us expect a rather interventionist proposal. And indeed, comparing the legal text of the proposal (Commission of the European Communities 2001b) to the extant European status quo entailed in Regulation (EEC) 295/91 actually yields four sets of key provisions that clearly redistribute rights from the air transport operators to the passenger.

First, the scope of the regulation is clearly widened. It addresses all passengers starting from an airport within an EU member state as before, but now also includes passengers who use a Community carrier to fly from a third country into the EU.[15] The groups of addressees thus defined are protected by the proposed law if they are *denied boarding*, as in the old regulation, but now also if their *flight is cancelled* for reasons within the responsibility of the air carrier or subcontractors, or if their *flight is delayed*. Accordingly, the Commission proposes to enhance both the number of potential beneficiaries of protection as well as the instances under which such protection is warranted. On the idealised consumer policy continuum, this clearly points towards the more interventionist end of policy choices.

Second, although denied boarding was regulated at the supranational level before, the proposed rules on such instances point towards a stricter and more passenger-friendly system. The proposal prescribes a so-called 'volunteer system', which was only mentioned in the earlier regulation: if boarding denials are necessary, carrier representatives have to ask for volunteers wanting to surrender their reservation in exchange for individually negotiated benefits; if no agreement can be reached, denied passengers are entitled to immediate compensation and assistance. Compensation rates are fixed at €750 per flight for distances under 3,500 kilometres, and at €1,500 for all longer flights, which means that compensation rates more than quadrupled those in the extant regulation.[16] If the passengers accept re-routing resulting in a delay of less than two hours, they are still entitled to a 50 per cent compensation rate. Air transport operators

---

15. The Concept of a Community carrier was established during the first liberalisation efforts in 1992. It refers to all airlines that are more than 50 per cent owned and controlled by nationals of EU member states. Thus, for example, a flight operated by Air France – owned predominantly by French and Dutch nationals – from Washington to Brussels is covered by the proposed law. However, according to the proposal, passengers on such flights enjoy European rights only if they do not benefit from compensation and assistance in the third country.

16. This is true, given that that extant compensation rates were 150 and 350 ECU, respectively, and that ECU and euros were exchanged at a rate of 1:1 in 1999.

must additionally offer a choice between (1) reimbursement of the travel cost, including reimbursement for missed connections and associated costs later in the journey, and the cost of a return flight to the original point of departure at the earliest opportunity, (2) re-routing 'under comparable transport conditions' to the final destination at the earliest opportunity, or (3) re-routing at a later date at the passenger's convenience. The old regulation did not cover return or connecting flights. Furthermore, the new proposal allowed denied passengers awaiting a later flight meals, refreshments and hotel accommodation, where necessary, free of charge. Clearly, with regard to denied boarding, the proposed regime enhances consumer rights significantly at the expense of operators.

This also holds for a third key provision. Passenger rights in the case of cancellation or delay had not been covered by the regulatory status quo before. In the case of flight cancellation, the operator now has to make 'every effort' to contact the affected passengers before check-in and to negotiate the conditions under which they are willing to surrender their reservations (Article 10). 'At the very least' the carrier has to offer the choice between reimbursement (including return flights), re-routing at the earliest opportunity, or re-routing at the next possible date at the passenger's convenience. All passengers that could not be reached before and that show up at check-in shall be offered compensation, assistance and care, as in the case of denied boarding. These producer duties can only be circumvented for cancellations for which 'the air carrier or tour operator can prove that it was done solely because of exceptional circumstances beyond its responsibility'. Operator duties are similar for long delays; that is, if the passenger has to wait two hours in the case of short flights or four hours in the case of long flights. In these cases, the passenger immediately has the right to assistance as specified above. Basically, they are again offered the choice between reimbursement and the different re-routing options. This right already applies if the operator 'expects a flight to be delayed' for the specified time limits. Furthermore, for disabled persons and for unaccompanied children, the right to care (meals and refreshments) applies as soon as a delay of at least two hours is expected. By these rules, the proposal basically extends the enhanced protection against denied boarding to instances of cancellations and delays, which provides another indication of a more interventionist model of consumer policy choices.

Lastly, passenger protection is underlined by a range of implementation and enforcement rules (Article 4, 14–15) that were not as clearly specified in the extant law. Air transport operators have to make the above defined rights part of the contract, and none of them may be waived or derogated by specific clauses. Passengers now have to be informed about their rights at the check-in desk[17] and by leaflets if denials, cancellations, or delays occur. This again exceeds the existing provisions in Regulation 91/295. Unlike the old regulation, furthermore,

---

17. The prescribed sign for check-in counters reads 'If you are denied boarding or if your flight is cancelled or delayed for at least two hours, ask at the check-in counter or boarding gate for the text stating your rights, particularly with regard to compensation and assistance' (Article 14).

the proposal now contains additional obligations for member state authorities to enforce the foreseen regime by penalties for infringements, among other things.

This summary of the decisive provisions[18] highlights that the proposal has a clearly subjective focus on passengers, not only in absolute terms by establishing solely rights for passengers and solely duties for carriers, but also in relative terms when compared to the level of passenger protection in the older regulation. Analysis of the legal text thus, in fact, reflects the declared aim of the DG TREN officials 'to assure that the consumer [gets] full benefits from the liberalisation from the internal market' (COM33:128). But how did this interventionist position come about during drafting?

As early as 1998, the officials were aware that something had to be done about overbooking in air transport. In fact, the issue 'was all the time in the media' and, since 'the Commission is always listening', this was 'the first source of information' stimulating the renewed drafting efforts (COM33:136). Within DG TREN, one desk official was largely responsible but actively kept the administrative hierarchy informed throughout the whole process (COM33:374). Along that route, the political leadership of DG TREN – at the time Commissioner Loyola De Palacio from the Spanish Partido Popular – was also aware of policy formulation. The drafting unit described policy formulation as a 'feedback process' in which the administrative level holds 'a lot of possible, different initiatives', and matches these options with 'priorities at the political level' and the 'political momentum' it senses from its stakeholder contacts and media reception (COM33:164; also COM33:176 and 136).

Both the political leadership and external stakeholders were involved very early in the unit's legislative strategy. Already in January 2000, a consultation document was sent to carriers, passengers, and airport representatives (Commission of the European Communities 2000c: 2) that covered operator duties in the case of denied boarding and flight cancellation (Commission of the European Communities 2000e: 8–9). Sixteen air carriers and respective associations, three travel agent representations, one airport association and twelve national authorities, as well as twelve consumer organisations and eleven disabled people's unions, responded to this early consultation (ibid. Annex II). Based on this broad input, DG TREN already identified most of the issues that became part of the proposal later, and also included the contested area of delayed flights (ibid. 9).

Following this consultation exercise, the drafting unit prepared an official Commission Communication to Council and Parliament in late June 2000. In presenting the Communication to the public, Commissioner de Palacio (DG TREN) highlighted that 'although many fares have fallen, passengers [...] feel defenceless when they are victims of overbooking or suffer serious delays. It is time for the Community to respond and to strengthen the protection of passengers' (Commission of the European Communities 2000a). What is more,

---

18. The review clause (Article 19), the repeal of extant regulation (Article 20), and the entry into force provision (Article 21) have not been considered in the above discussion of the proposal's legal text.

the Communication was presented together with the DG SANCO Commissioner for consumer policy, Byrne. The communication triggered a formal Council resolution in October 2000 (Council of the European Union 2000) as well as a report by the EP in June 2001 (European Parliament 2001).

This drafting history highlights three elements of DG TREN's strategy. First, a clearly subjective focus on passengers prevailed throughout the whole process. Second, using the information campaign, a rather broad consultation, and by throwing in the political weight of two Commissioners, the officials ensured as much publicity as possible during the drafting process. Third, issuing its ideas as a formal communication in summer 2000, DG TREN ensured that both the Council and the EP had to deliver a formal response. This was a clear signal for the political feasibility of an interventionist approach and – given that the public was apprehensive of the respective issues at the time – it functioned as a kind of insurance for DG TREN in this regard.

Essentially, air transport was chosen as the first area of passenger rights regulation because 'the Community has advanced much further in creating a single market for air transport than for transport by road and rail' (Commission of the European Communities 2000e: 8). Being well aware that liberalisation had been 'about advantages for the industry', the drafting officials took the perspective of 'the consumer's right to benefit' (COM33:124). From an industry point of view, DG TREN's regulatory job was done with the liberalisation in 1997, but not from the perspective of the consumer.

Formally, acting for consumers – 'which in air transport means passengers' (Commission of the European Communities 2000e: 7) – was justified by the freshly enacted consumer protection article in the Treaty of Amsterdam. With its horizontal clause, this article presented the legal justification for turning European transport policy in the consumer's direction (see also Council of the European Union 2000). The broader political context abetted a passenger-friendly approach as well. Drafting officials mentioned the Lisbon idea of 'putting citizens at the heart of the internal market', and 'translate[d] this big political guideline into concrete measures [...] in the transport sector' (COM33:176). Accordingly, the proposal 'is a European regulation which is sort of very close to the citizen' (COM33:174).

But politically even more importantly, the decision to tackle air passengers first was triggered by contemporaneous public pressure: on the one hand, there was the salience of the issue of overbooking signalled by media reports; on the other, consumer organisations in particular filed complaints on air transport with DG TREN. Public pressure was said to have been high because 'air passengers tend to be urban people with a certain revenue level. So that makes them more likely to complain than other kinds of passengers'. It was also mentioned that Brussels' legislators, particularly Members of the European Parliament (MEPs), were all frequent air passengers themselves, which made position taking comparatively easy (COM33:176). In this political context, the consultation in early 2000 delivered enough stakeholder support to decide 'that the regulation of 1991 was not enough and that it was time to review it' (COM33:136 and 146).

Clearly, more compensation for denied boarding, as well as for cancellation and delays, was not in the interest of the airline industry. In fact, airline associations would have preferred voluntary agreements at best (Commission of the European Communities 2000e: 9). The Commission actually allowed such a self-regulatory solution in the June 2000 Communication, but threatened a legislative proposal if carriers did not manage to draw up a satisfactory measure by April 2001 (Commission of the European Communities 2000e:15–16, 17–18). This ultimatum was backed by national governments through the Council's response (Council of the European Union 2000), and the European airline associations managed to put together an agreement with only one month's delay.[19]

However, for the Commission this agreement did not go far enough as it entailed no rules on compensation in the case of denied boarding or cancellation (COM33:302, Commission of the European Communities 2001b: 2). The EP report in mid-2001, roughly six months before proposal adoption, agreed with this hard-line position, and encouraged the Commission to go forward with legislative drafting (European Parliament 2001: 7). Since the official ISC was launched only two months later, the responsible TREN unit apparently already had a legislative text in the drawer.

Counting on the strategic support of the EP was a systematic element in drafting the air passenger rights regulation. Comparing the different legislative texts one can see, for example, that international flights coming into the EU entered the Commission's position only in response to amendments the EP had made to the preceding proposal in 1998. In covering such flights, the Commission almost exhausted its territorial competence (BEUC 2002a: 5), and one can assume that TREN needed the support of the Parliament to demand such a far-reaching provision from the Council. Similarly, the Parliament had already backed the inclusion of cancellations in 1998 (cf. European Parliament 2001: 7–8).

The inclusion of delayed flights also found EP support (European Parliament 2001: 7), but was only communicated in June 2000 after the stakeholder consultation (Commission of the European Communities 2000e: 3). The support from the EP fits the public pressure impulse rather well because the issue of delays was one of the most common forms of passenger discomfort in air transport at the time. National governments also signalled their support for this scope extension in the absence of a voluntary agreement (Council of the European Union 2000: especially priority 3), and thus opened up the necessary room for manoeuvre that enabled TREN to include it in the formal proposal.

This anticipated political support was in fact necessary because the inclusion of delays was one of the most heavily contested provisions. Consumers welcomed it, and only regretted that the strict compensations for cancellations and denials were not transferred to delays as well (BEUC 2002a: 10). Airlines, in contrast, fiercely opposed the provisions, arguing that 'in Europe's heavily congested airspace it

---

19. See: http://ec.europa.eu/transport/air_portal/passenger_rights/doc/2001/commitment_airlines_en.pdf (accessed 6 April 2010).

is not easy to establish who is to blame for late departures' (Commission of the European Communities 2000e: 9; Odell 2000). Although DG TREN originally sided with consumers and planned compensation obligations also for delays, it was considered 'legally impossible' to find a solution because 'identification of the cause of a delay may be difficult, particularly when it is an effect of earlier delays'. To this extent, even in cases that were not caused by *force majeure*, a carrier would have to pay the passenger without being able to collect the burden from the actually responsible party (Commission of the European Communities 2000e: 17).

While this would have violated basic principles of European law, TREN was much less hesitant on compensations for denied boarding and cancelled flights. Following its media prominence, the officials started with the declared aim of limiting the practice of overbooking to the smallest possible amount. In order to calculate respective compensation rates, the officials asked airlines for revenue data, but the airlines were unwilling to obey (Commission of the European Communities 2001b: 5). TREN reacted viciously and more than quadrupled the compensation rates as compared to the extant regulation. Consumer associations were 'pleased' (BEUC 2002a: 8).

Consumer associations also welcomed the rather far-reaching obligations for national authorities that the Commission proposal prescribed (Commission of the European Communities 2001b: 8), but considered an even more sophisticated enforcement and complaint handling-system was needed (BEUC 2002a: 11). It has to be noted, however, that TREN refrained from further elaboration because DG SANCO was already working on a more general law on cross-border enforcement of policies. By the means of cross-reference, this broader piece later also covered redress for air passengers (cf. Karsten 2007: 126).

This highlights the closeness of the proposal to the original policy mandate of DG SANCO. Yet despite overlapping 'turfs' in regulating for the consumer, the DG TREN officials recalled nothing but 'synergies' with their SANCO colleagues (COM33:230). While some information was exchanged informally, SANCO appears not to have pressed for particular points (COM33:234). As noted earlier, SANCO's Commissioner also helped in defending the June 2000 Communication publicly. This lack of conflict also carried through until the final stages of drafting, so that the formal ISC went 'smoothly' without additional coordination at the political level (COM33:242).[20] In fact, the proposal was finally adopted in December 2001 by a written procedure only.

In terms of the outcome, thus, the case of air passenger rights is fully consistent with the major hypothesis scrutinised in this book. Intermediate to extraordinary levels of EU politicisation combined with a sustained and comparatively high contemporaneous public interest in the regulated issue area, which then resulted

---

20. Note, however, that this information must be taken with a pinch of salt. At the time of writing, DG TREN had not responded to the formal request for ISC documentation. Drafting officials also mentioned some interaction with DG MARKT, but made no substantial statement on either the content or the quality of this interaction.

in a policy position that is clearly oriented towards the interventionist model of consumer policy.

Also the within-case variation and the process observations are in line with theoretical expectations. Contemporaneous issue salience explained the timing of the proposal as it accounted for a quick restart of drafting after the 1998 failure. Public salience also accounted for making air transport the first transport mode for which passenger rights were re-regulated. And salience also accounted for some of the substantial positions in the proposal, particularly with regard to the high compensation rates, making overbooking a prohibitively costly practice for transport operators.

Most interestingly, once the decision for a renewed initiative was taken, the drafting department engaged rather actively in sustaining public visibility of the regulated issue. Yet the actual public commitment to a formal drafting process came only with the Communication in summer 2000, when the politicisation of European decision making exceeded its mean levels, and two Commissioners publicly backed the initiative. While the industry managed to agree on a voluntary agreement on denied boarding – the only issue that had been supranationally regulated at all – the Commission showed its teeth in spring 2001 and went for a much more encompassing proposal. This happened at a time when European decision making was publicly challenged to an unprecedented degree. Thus, also with regard to the timeline, the Commission's and especially DG TREN's strategy conforms to the theoretical model.

Likewise, the process hypotheses on political involvement and on time period, as well as on responsiveness to consumer interests, are in line with the model. Commissioners jumped on the bandwagon when intermediate levels of politicisation were reached, legislative drafting became more rushed during these late stages of drafting, and TREN's positions conformed much more to the consumer rather than to the industry's demands emerging from the broad consultation.

Yet the fourth process hypothesis is not in line. Given the high degree of interventionism entailed in TREN's position, we would have expected stronger opposition from more industry-prone DGs such as MARKT (internal market) or ENTR (enterprise and industry). However, they were strikingly absent. In the last stages of drafting, the theoretical model would explain this by the high degree of politicisation that instils a common interest for politically beneficial proposals among all internal actors. However, the drafting period also experienced a slump in politicisation in late 1999 and early 2000, in which the drafting officials also did not recall any conflictual interactions within the Commission. It stands to reason that TREN's clear sectoral competence insulated them; however, without further evidence, this question cannot be answered conclusively. For the consumer policy DG, in contrast, outright support during drafting is documented. Arguably, they could be satisfied with the TREN proposal because it was consistent with their upcoming proposals on unfair commercial practices (see below). Against these drafting processes and the battle they led against DG MARKT at the time, SANCO arguably had few resources to engage further in TREN's drafting efforts.

Beyond politicisation and issue salience, considerations of political feasibility in the later inter-institutional process informed the lead DG's policy position. For sensitive issues such as the inclusion of flights into and out of EU territory or the addition of delays, the drafting officials proactively sought the political support of the Council and the Parliament. By publishing a formal Communication at a time when both EU politicisation and issue salience were high, the Commission could treat this as credible commitment from other institutional EU actors.

Alternative explanations seem to be of little relevance for the process studied here. On the one hand, the interventionist position can hardly be explained by Commissioner de Palacio's membership of a conservative party, nor do national interests appear to have played a role in the case in general. On the other hand, the productionist view is not furthered by the case at hand as the interventionist outcome was pursued in the face of opposition from virtually all 'producers' in the air transport sector.

4.4 Consumer credit

Roughly one year after the air passenger rights proposal, on 11 September 2002, the European Commission adopted a proposal for a directive on consumer credit (Commission of the European Communities 2002b), addressing a changing but growing segment of the internal market. While people in the 1970s and 1980s lived in a 'cash society', private credit had become the 'lubricant of economic life' (COM89:31). Financial instruments such as product-related credits, credit cards, and the overdraft facilities of private accounts had spread quickly and fuelled private consumption (COM119:197). At the time of proposal adoption, consumer credit amounted to 7 per cent of the EU-15 GDP, and exhibited a growing tendency (Commission of the European Communities 2002b: 3).

The area was already loosely covered by European law, but the extant directive 87/102/EEC on consumer credit as well as its 1990 and 1998 amendments were minimum harmonisation measures. In other words, the extant regime allowed European member states to enact more stringent rules (Commission of the European Communities 2002b: 2–5), and a myriad of differing consumer credit regulations persisted in Europe.

Given the immense economic importance of this market and its fragmented nature, DG MARKT, which was responsible for financial services in the Santer Commission, tackled the issue area early on. A Green Paper in 1996 as well as a follow-up in 1997 highlighted the need to support cross-border credit provision by regulatory means. While MARKT had the lead at the time, the predecessor of the consumer policy DG had already participated in sketching the early policy outlines. Including the consumer perspective made sense from an internal market perspective: not only creditors but also borrowers should operate across borders to stimulate growth (Commission of the European Communities 1997). Along these lines, MARKT and SANCO (DG XV and XXIV at the time) together proposed a directive on distance marketing of consumer financial services in 1998, which was signed by the Council and the Parliament in the same month that the consumer credit proposal was adopted by the Commission. Against this cooperative history in the regulation of consumer financial services, the early Prodi Commission surprisingly decided in 1999 that DG SANCO should draft the consumer credit regulation unilaterally (COM119:17).

The actual drafting process of the consumer credit proposal again partly overlapped with the preceding cases. In the above discussions, we have learned that EU politicisation was on the rise in early 2000, stagnated at intermediate levels in the second half-year, and jumped to unknown heights during 2001. But in autumn 2001, the multi-dimensional indicator developed in Chapter Two declined and reached a sub-standard plateau in 2002 where it stayed until the consumer credit proposal was adopted in September 2002 (see also Chapter Two in this volume).

The salience indicator for the issue area (see above) exhibits the opposite movement. After a slight rise in late 1999, it remained at medium levels throughout 2000 and declined again until summer 2001. From there on it rose, exceeded its investigation period mean in late 2001, and consistently and distinctly ranged above that threshold afterwards. In fact, one month before the proposal was adopted, the indicator reached the highest value observed in the investigation period so far. The underlying media data highlight a range of topics that drove public visibility in 2002. While the press reported on some earlier Commission proposals in the area, such as distance marketing in financial services and sales promotions, the biggest overarching issue in the sample of relevant news reports was online shopping and the related security of credit cards (e.g. Bembaron 2001b).

This alone already points to the narrow issue area of consumer credit, and a more specific search algorithm indicates that there was in fact sustained public visibility.[21] Much of the rather intense newspaper reporting emerges from the relevance of consumer credit to economic growth – often aggregate figures on consumer credit are taken as an indicator for domestic demand and economic activity (e.g. *FAZ* 2000d; Oualalou 2000). However, consumer over-indebtedness and the aggressive marketing strategies of credit agencies also find frequent press attention (e.g. *FAZ* 2000a; Aissaoui 2002; Quioc 2001; Bembaron 2001a). In that sense, it is not too surprising that newspapers reported on the MARKT and SANCO initiative on distance marketing in financial services (e.g. *FAZ* 2002a). But also the drafting process covered here also gave rise to early newspaper reports (e.g. *FAZ* 2002b), particularly in summer 2002 when a preliminary draft proposal was leaked to the press (Guerrera 2002a).

---

21. The underlying search required that 'consumer credit' occurred in the respective article and covered the drafting period as of 1 September 1999 to the proposal adoption on 11 September 2002. This resulted in 337 hits in the *Financial Times*, 211 in *Le Figaro*, 106 in the *Frankfurter Allgemeine Zeitung* and thirty-two in *El País*. Two modifications apply. First, in the Spanish case the technical term 'credito al consumo' is rarely used, which accounts for the comparatively low number of hits. A less specific search relying on 'consumidores' and 'credito' retrieves many more articles on the issue area, but also irrelevant results so that I stick with reporting only the comparative results here. Second, the Commission translation used an inadequate technical term in its French proposal title. Rather than using 'crédit aux consommateurs' as employed by the Commission, I searched for 'crédit à la consommation', which is the more conventional French term referring to consumer credit.

In sum, this contemporaneous salience highlights that the Commission could have been fairly sure that the envisaged proposal on consumer credit would be visible to the broader European public. In fact, the officials involved considered it to be 'a very political file' (COM119:171) with 'a big public appeal' (COM119:171). Given the explicit peak of EU politicisation during 2001 – emerging mainly from a protest wave but also from EU visibility due to the introduction of the Euro – there were thus clear incentives at the time to demonstrate regulation for widespread public interest with an interventionist proposal. Yet this prediction has to be taken with a pinch of salt, since the politicisation did not stay at consistently high levels throughout the drafting process. In late 1999, as well as throughout 2002, the short-term variation in politicisation was comparatively low so that the theoretical model makes no unambiguous prediction, except that we would expect particular commitments to interventionism in the middle of the drafting process. So, what policy choices did SANCO actually make?

With thirty-eight articles and eighty-nine pages, the proposal is a rather lengthy and complex initiative (Commission of the European Communities 2002b). In comparing the encompassing contents to the extant Directive 87/102/EEC and the manifold national rules, I grouped them into six sets of provisions that distribute rights among consumers and creditors.

First, this is the scope and the approach of the proposed policy choices. Compared to the former directive, the proposal also covers surety agreements, all credits independent of the amount and also advances on a current account or overdraft facilities, as well as other forms of short-term consumer credit that had been excluded before. Only credits granted for the purchase of immovable property (mortgage credits) are explicitly excluded. National governments should not enact further provisions or derogations on these matters, and are explicitly requested to take measures against creditors who try to avoid consumer protection by basing themselves in non-member countries. In other words, the Commission chooses a total harmonisation approach centred on the consumer's country of origin, while the extant directive was based on minimum harmonisation and made no reference to the applicable territorial law. By centring law on the consumer, the Commission's choice at least limits creditors' opportunities to deviate towards less restrictive non-EU states, and thus enhances consumer protection.

A second set of highly relevant provisions concerns the general creditor obligations prior to the conclusion of a credit agreement. The proposal clarifies various creditor obligations for information provision during advertising and negotiation. Compared to the status quo, these rules piece together various obligations from the more interventionist member state regimes (cf. Commission of the European Communities 2002b: 11–13). Further, the proposal prohibits any off-premise negotiation of credit agreements, which were possible in all EU member states except the UK, Belgium, and Luxembourg before. Most importantly, Article 9 generally prescribes the principle of responsible lending. This provision states that a creditor must be assumed 'to have previously assessed, by any means at his disposal, whether the consumer and, where appropriate, the guarantor can reasonably be expected to discharge their obligations under the agreement'.

Basically, the creditor can be made responsible if the consumer fails to fulfil the contract. This far-reaching position was not part of the extant directive, nor was it an element in extant national regimes. Only in the Netherlands and in Belgium had 'similar or comparable' legislation been in place (ibid. 15). Hauling the principle of responsible lending to the supranational level and making it applicable in all fifteen member states must be considered as a highly interventionist policy choice.

The third set of decisive provisions on the characteristics of consumer contracts speaks a similar language. Beyond banning a range of hitherto unregulated contract terms now considered 'unfair', these rules grant the consumer with a general right of withdrawal for fourteen calendar days after the agreement. Only a few national regimes had foreseen such cooling-off periods and all of them were shorter than the proposed fourteen days. Regarding various enhanced information requirements for the contract, particularly the costs of credit to the consumer as expressed by the annual percentage rate (APR), catch the eye. The APR expresses the yearly consumer cost of borrowing as a share of the total amount of credit. The proposal prescribes the exact calculation to be used, and exhaustively defines the elements that have to be considered. Among a range of possibly hidden costs, the proposal also requires the inclusion of third-party costs such as notary fees or even insurance premiums. In advertising and contracting, thus, creditors must also disclose costs going beyond their control. In addition, the Commission proposal neatly prescribes what assumptions are allowed in APR calculation, and requires the consumer to be informed about applied assumptions, for example on the expected duration of the credit agreement. While the 1990 amendment to the original directive of 1987 had already included an APR formula (Directive 1990/88/EC Annex II), the proposal at hand is much more detailed with regard to cost elements and employed assumptions (cf. also Commission of the European Communities 2002b: 17–18). Again, the regulator intervenes in creditor freedom so as to aid consumers.

A fourth set of key provisions regulates unforeseen terminations of the credit agreement. The Commission generally entitles the consumer to fully or partially discharge his obligations before the time fixed in the credit agreement. The creditor may claim indemnity for early repayment, which has to be 'fair and objective'. Regarding possible consumer default, the proposal prohibits creditors from enacting 'disproportionate measures' in recovering due amounts. Creditors must send a default notice providing consumers with 'a reasonable period of time' before the creditor can demand immediate payment and/or resolution of the credit agreement. These duties may only be circumvented in demonstrable cases of fraud if the customer's actions breach the terms of the credit agreement. Further, the creditor may not suspend consumer drawdowns 'unless he justifies his decision', and is required to provide consumers with a detailed statement of account free of charge. These rules are completely new and were not part of the extant European directive. Given that they contain solely requirements on the creditor in the case of non-compliance by the consumer, they again underline a rather interventionist stance.

The same is true of recovery or repossession of defaulted consumer credits. Creditors may repossess financed goods only if the consumer has given their explicit consent or if they have repaid less than one-third of the total amount of credit. In all other cases, repossession requires judicial procedures. Compared to the extant directive, the proposal additionally protects those consumers who have already repaid a third of the overall credit. Similar legislation had earlier been in place only in Belgium, Ireland, the Netherlands, Luxembourg and the UK (Commission of the European Communities 2002b: 25). The proposal goes further, as creditors or debt collection agencies, in addition, may not claim any fees or indemnities from the consumer unless they have been part of the initial credit agreement. Besides, it bans a large range of credit recovery practices that might be detrimental to the consumer such as documents pretending to come from a judicial authority, incorrect information, inscriptions about debt on envelopes, or physical and psychological harassment. Like some of the earlier provisions in the proposal, these recovery rules are also completely new, thus further increasing the level of consumer protection at the EU level.

A fifth set of key provisions covers consumer rights vis-à-vis third parties. These rules ensure that the consumer has the same means of legal defence against credit insurers and debt collection agencies, to name two. More importantly, they regulate joint and several liability where credits are directly linked to the purchase of goods or services. If a supplier of goods or services acts as a credit intermediary, both the supplier and the creditor are jointly and severally liable for defects in products or services bought on credit. Particularly in this regard, consumer rights are strengthened. The extant directive limited consumer liability rights to a closely specified list of circumstances that basically amounted to cases where the creditor and the supplier had a sort of 'exclusive link', or where 'subsidiary liability' applied. Only the UK had prescribed that a credit card company could be held liable for any good purchased with the card. Extending this principle to the whole of Europe moves the Commission position clearly towards a very interventionist model of consumer policy.

The final set of key provisions contains various enforcement rules. Besides some enhanced data production in now obligatory consumer credit databases (Commission of the European Communities 2002b: 14–15), the proposal now also makes member states responsible for registering and monitoring creditors, for enacting penalties on infringements and for collecting consumer complaints, providing advice and establishing out-of-court redress procedures.

Drawing all these complex rules and their relative positioning vis-à-vis extant regimes together, the 2002 Commission proposal on consumer credit tends most clearly to the ideal type of an interventionist consumer policy. It contains obligations almost entirely on the 'producer's' side of the credit business. By the selective transfer of rules from the more restrictive member states, the proposal clearly tries to push European regulation towards a highly consumer-friendly position. Are these choices driven by the high levels of salience and politicisation during the middle and the end of the drafting process?

While the start of the drafting process during autumn 1999 coincided with the Prodi Commission and the new Commissioner for consumer policy, David Byrne, coming into office, the basic impulse for the proposal emerged at the administrative level. Drafting started with an 'internal discussion' in the unit, which then was 'trying to convince [the] political hierarchy that there was a need for a new directive' (COM89:44). Before turning to the political level, however, the drafting unit had to invest some time and resources, since '[t]echnically it was very difficult, a complicated issue' (COM111:194). Consumer credit was a highly, but diversely regulated issue area rooted in 'different regulatory traditions' such as the common law in the UK and the code civil in France (COM89:37). 'Making a single European rule' out of the 'different paths' to consumer protection was 'hideously difficult' (COM89:44).

All in all, the 'work was well-advanced' when the personal cabinet of Commissioner Byrne was 'presented with a draft' (COM111:149). While no exact information on the timing is available, the intense preparations at the service level required some time which allows us to assume that the political level was involved in summer 2000 at the earliest. The responsible cabinet member first discussed the officials' ideas with the then head of cabinet, who had previously held the same position in DG MARKT. With his agreement, the 'main content' was brought before the Commissioner to discuss 'where the political points lie' (ibid.); and the Commissioner agreed to go forward. In fact, besides the ongoing food scandals (cf. Chapter Six in this volume) and the preparation of the unfair commercial practices initiative (see below), the consumer credit proposal was seen as 'one of the major consumer proposals' for the Commission at the time (COM111:198).

Having this political backing, the drafting unit went public during summer 2001 when the general politicisation of EU decision making had reached a high point. On 8 June 2001, they issued a discussion paper outlining their ideas on extending the scope to more modern forms of credit, information and contract rules, arrangements on credit defaults, and 'fairer' sharing of responsibility among producers and consumers (COM89:70). This paper was followed by separate meetings with member state representatives, business associations from the credit sector and consumer representatives, during July 2001 (COM119:88, Commission of the European Communities 2002b: 3 and 4–5). While there was a 'clear desire' from the consumer associations (COM111:80), meetings with the industry showed a 'unanimous' opposition to the scope extensions, data protection provisions, the APR calculation, and most of all to the principle of responsible lending. In response to this outright industry disagreement, 'further consultation was entirely avoided' by DG SANCO (ESBG 2003: 2–3), so that 'the industry felt that it had been very much disregarded in the process' (COM119:88).

But the basic decision leading to these rifts with the industry had been taken earlier. In fact, the drafting SANCO officials did not have the 'average consumer' in mind when developing their ideas, but rather set out to protect the 'weak consumer' with their legislative proposal (COM89:82). In other words, drafting was based on the assumption that the consumer taking credit was not able to fully capture the implications of credit agreements, and thus needed to be protected against the banking or retail industry's exploitation of that very fact (COM89:86). This was not the least informed by an 'ongoing debate' on 'behavioural economics', which was a 'buzz word' at the time, and challenged the assumption of the consumer as a fully rational market participant (COM89:82). It resulted in the 'ambition of the 2002 project [...] to create a very comprehensive, very exhaustive consumer credit regulation which would be burdensome for industry' (COM89:46). Against this background, the drafting officials modelled the proposal around the 'Belgian law' – which appears to have been one of the most restrictive regimes – knowing well that this 'triggered all sorts of opposition' (ibid.). And the industry opposed furiously. The retail sector argued that the proposal contradicts 'the principle [...] that the [European Community] Consumer Protection legislation has to be measured against the [...] consumer of average intelligence, reasonably well informed and reasonably circumspect' (EuroCommerce 2003a: 2). The political level of SANCO tried to appease by arguing that the proposal harmonised the conditions of consumer credit mainly in order to achieve free circulation of credits and consumers in the internal market (COM111:74).

In fact, this reasoning was exactly the justification on which the traditionally responsible DG MARKT wanted to regulate the sector. In their view, 'financial services regulation in general had been aimed at really opening up a cross-border banking market' (COM119:39). They had a range of informal contacts with banks facing trade barriers, but 'couldn't get those companies to actually introduce formal complaints', because they were afraid to ruin their relationships with the national 'supervisory authorities' (COM119:43). So DG MARKT officials 'had more an ear [...] for the banking sector' (COM111:96), which turned to lobbying DG MARKT after SANCO refused any further consultation (COM119:88). In this line, MARKT considered SANCO's ideas as 'too interventionist' (COM119:100), and the initial set-up was clear: while MARKT considered the 'benefits of the internal market', SANCO considered 'the benefits of enhanced consumer protection' (COM119:35). This internal line of conflict carried through to every individual provision in the proposal.

With regard to the scope conditions, DG MARKT 'was very vigilant' on mortgage credits (COM119:119). In fact, DG MARKT and DG SANCO had together published a recommendation for better consumer information on home loans – the usual model of mortgage credits. But in SANCO's unilaterally published discussion paper only three months later, mortgage credits were suddenly mentioned as an element of the consumer credit proposal (European Commission 2001b: 6–7), an arguably strategic move that took MARKT officials completely by surprise (COM119:123). However, they argued that the 'consumer credit market was [...] less than a fifth of the size the mortgage credit market; the conditions around it were very different' (COM119:119). MARKT was actually successful in this battle as 'it was quickly decided not to judge mortgage credit' (COM89:86). Explaining this loss, SANCO officials noted that 'banks have huge power in the member states', and lobbied heavily against reorganising the national mortgage systems (COM111:70). Obviously, anticipating Council opposition had played a role here.

Consumer associations were disappointed about this exclusion, but strongly welcomed the other scope extensions (BEUC 2002b: 3–4; cf. also EURO COOP 2003b). The banking industry, by contrast, strongly opposed tighter regulation of smaller credit lines and threatened that 'the burden of such obligations would lead lenders avoiding the offer of credit lines on current accounts and overdrafts' (ESBG 2003: 4–6). Likewise, the retail sector feared 'additional costs' from the inclusion of 'small loans' (EuroCommerce 2003a: 4).

However, conflict on the scope extensions was marginal compared with conflict on the principle of responsible lending. Consumer associations cheered and reinforced that '[t]he lender is generally best placed to appreciate the repayment ability of the consumer and to evaluate the risk of default' (BEUC 2002b: 9). In contrast, the idea put the industry in a state of shock because the 'legally uncertain and vague terms [...] threaten[ed] to lead towards a considerable increase of litigation against credit providers in the event of consumers' default'. Such obligations were seen as 'neither realistic nor feasible because it is the consumer's and only the consumer's prerogative to take a decision concerning the purpose of the credit thereby defining the total amount of credit needed' (ESBG 2003: 7–9).

Mirroring these conflicts among external stakeholders, the principle of responsible lending also triggered the strongest arguments within the Commission. In fact, it was seen as the watershed provision, as it unambiguously answered the question whether one regulates in the interest of the consumer or in the interest of the internal market (COM89:80). Being asked how internal opposition from DG MARKT on this matter could be overcome, SANCO officials claimed to have had better arguments in the light of data on increasing over-indebtedness and press reports on individuals stuck in the credit carousel (COM89:70–118, COM119:197). But the issue was blocked in the formal ISC, and was individually negotiated by the cabinets of Commissioners Byrne and Bolkestein, so that 'in the end it [was] a political decision' (COM89:119).

Another controversial issue was the ban on negotiating consumer credit off business premises. This ban was not really in line with the directive on distance marketing of financial services, which MARKT and SANCO had proposed together in 1998. While this common proposal had allowed the conclusion of financial agreements via phone, the face-to-face marketing of consumer credits would be forbidden under the proposal at hand. This inconsistency highlights SANCO's unilateral approach to consumer protection and it stirred further discussions with MARKT officials (COM119:15 and 84). Yet the directive – which was negotiated with the Council at the time – left other footprints on the consumer credit proposal. The fourteen-day withdrawal period was actually transferred from there, which was 'very much welcomed' on the consumer side (BEUC 2002b:12). The industry, however, considered it 'inappropriate' to prescribe identical consumer rights for distance marketing and face-to-face agreements (ESBG 2003: 10).

The calculating and presentation of credit costs to the consumer were also attacked heavily by the banking industry (COM89:30). As noted above, the proposal also requires creditors to include third party costs in APR calculation. SANCO's respective reasoning is highly interesting: the minimum clause of the extant directive had allowed a broader set of cost bases in the member states. Accordingly, the new directive should include these broader sets, because otherwise market fragmentation cannot be overcome (cf. Commission of the European Communities 2002b: 5–6). While this is a classical market-making argument at first sight, it differs in an interesting respect because it takes the regimes with the highest level of consumer protection as the relevant benchmark. As visible in certain other elements of the proposal as well, SANCO was trying 'to reach convergence of legislation but at a high level – not at the smallest common denominator' (COM111:104). Unsurprisingly, DG MARKT disagreed, defended mutual recognition (COM119:59), and argued for a 'narrow sort of box of cost elements' in APR calculation 'along industry lines' (COM89:82, see ESBG 2003: 2–3, 10).

Likewise, SANCO's suggestion of proposing joint and several liability for goods bought on credit was highly contested. Also here the drafting officials considered only consumer protection benefits and picked the most stringent rule they could find among those in the member states. In fact, joint and several liability rules are largely transferred from Section 75 of the UK Consumer Credit Act (COM89:37, COM89:41). But since creditor liability was considered 'totally outlandish' in other European member states, the industry 'strongly opposed' it (ESBG 2003: 12), and DG MARKT initially opposed the idea as well (COM119:62). However, DG MARKT's political leadership finally gave in because Section 75 'was something very popular in the UK' so that 'no self-respecting politician was going to come around and change that'. Here, MARKT's leaders acknowledged that it would be a 'very difficult position for the Commission […] to say […] you are going to have to withdraw your protection from your consumers' (COM119:62). In other words, DG MARKT's political leadership backed down because it anticipated a politically detrimental reception of the resulting policy choice.

But all in all, DG SANCO's highly interventionist position faced a rather controversial coordination process within the Commission. By November 2001, the responsible directors in each DG had exchanged formal letters (COM119:127) and the proposal later 'had lots of problems' in the ISC (COM111: 124 and 149). In fact, DG MARKT fed a sixteen-page list of amendments into the coordination system, which was seen as 'pretty exceptional' (COM119:71). Besides MARKT, 'also DG Enterprise, a few other DGs, and the SecGen' voiced objections regarding 'the balance of the approach' (COM111:150). Accordingly, the cabinet of SANCO's Commissioner, David Byrne, took over, engaged in individual negotiations and 'arbitrations' with the cabinets of the blocking DGs, built coalitions and ultimately achieved the withdrawal of 'all suspended opinions' (COM111:142). At that stage, the political counsellors of Commission President Prodi had become relevant players 'because if you want to launch it into written procedure you need the agreement of the President' (COM111:154). In the end, these political negotiations led to a legislative text that entailed almost all of SANCO's original ideas (COM111:132).

To sum up, SANCO's straightforward consumer focus on financial services emerged from a scientific paradigm, as well as from the need (and the political will) to delineate its own competences from DG MARKT, which had traditionally regulated financial services along mutual recognition (COM89:90, COM119:139). However, the extremity of SANCO's position, as well as the fact that it passed despite outraged external and internal opposition, can hardly be explained without a consideration of the political context.

Against the sustained public visibility of consumer credit, SANCO's political leadership agreed on an interventionist approach to policy formulation during 2000 when the general politicisation of European decision making was set to rise again. Moreover, just when politicisation had arrived at unprecedented heights during mid-2001, SANCO published a discussion paper and publicly committed to the most controversial issues, such as responsible lending and the inclusion of mortgage credit. This happened with the agreement of SANCO's political leaders, and despite predictable opposition from other departments.

In line with incentives emerging from the politicised context and a salient regulatory issue, SANCO had publicly committed to a re-regulation of creditor–consumer relationships to the benefit of the latter. As predicted by one of the process hypotheses, this led to a rather controversial drafting process. However, in the light of having just experienced a strongly politicised period, internal opposition could be partly overcome due to the fear of publishing a proposal with a bad message to consumers. Where this logic did not apply, internal opposition was overcome with the help of the most central political institution within the Commission; that is, the President and his cabinet. In both respects, the common Commission interest of organisational well-being seems to have trumped conflict between the consumer and internal market fiefdoms.

Also with regard to other process hypotheses, the theoretical model performs rather well in the consumer credit case. Not only do the proposal's provisions conform more to consumer demands, the lead department actually barred the producer side almost completely from the policy formulation process. As we would expect it for salient initiatives, the administrative and political hierarchy was involved throughout the process, while the political level was actually responsible for finalising the proposal. Furthermore, despite the immense complexity of variations in national consumer credit regimes, a drafting time of exactly three years also seems to be fairly short.

However, in contrast to the other cases discussed so far, the political feasibility explanation has little relevance to the drafting process at hand. National governments were heard once in summer 2001, but no interviewee mentioned that national preferences had constrained policy formulation. And, as we have seen, while a range of national regimes provided role models for individual rules, these were always the positive outliers in terms of consumer protection, which does not necessarily speak to an attempt to find a majority position in the Council. Since the Council (along with some parliamentarians) had voiced opposition to total harmonisation, the drafting officials also considered some of the rules as 'too revolutionary' in hindsight (COM89:114, also 134).

Likewise, there is little direct evidence that individual Commissioners' characteristics had any causal role. One may claim that the opposition of DG

MARKT was driven by the infamously liberal Commissioner Bolkestein. Nevertheless, concessions by DG MARKT occurred only at the late stages of drafting when the cabinet of this Commissioner was directly involved in drafting. Similarly, 'trading up' hypotheses can be declined for in this case: virtually all SANCO's policy choices faced outright industry opposition. In sum, turf considerations, in combination with politicisation and issue salience, seem to best explain the observed process and its highly interventionist outcome.

4.5 Unfair commercial practices

Nine months after the consumer credit proposal, the Commission adopted another high-scale SANCO draft on 18 June 2003. The proposal for a directive on unfair commercial practices (Commission of the European Communities 2003b) claimed a much broader scope than the other cases discussed so far. Rather than covering specific sectors or particular commercial practices, it establishes a 'framework directive' regulating all pre-contractual business-to-consumer transactions, regardless of the products or services supplied.

The proposed framework touched a range of existing acts on either specific aspects of commercial practices – most prominently the misleading advertising directive – or specific products or services, for example, the timeshare directive. Like most extant consumer policies at the time, these directives set minimum standards, meaning 'that 15 sets of different requirements (soon to be 25) operate[d] in practice' (Commission of the European Communities 2003a: 6). So the regulatory status quo was a complex mixture of European minimum standards and more protective national rules.

Contrasting with the minimum harmonisation approach, another relevant piece of European legislation, was the E-Commerce Directive that had been proposed by DG MARKT in 1998 and became law in May 2000. Although limited to electronic commerce, it also regulated a broad range of commercial practices such as information requirements, commercial communications and contract conclusions in online trade. This initiative did not harmonise national regulations: its defining element was a country-of-origin principle according to which service providers are subject to the legislation of the member state in which they are established. With respect to consumer protection, e-commerce businesses were thus free to choose the member state regime that entailed the most favourable distribution of rights and duties. Beyond e-commerce, we have also seen earlier that DG MARKT had planned to liberalise business-to-consumer transactions further, particularly as regards commercial communications (*see* Chapter 4.2 in this volume). We have also seen that SANCO's plans for the area were not very welcome in DG MARKT, a conflict that culminated particularly in the parallel adoption of the sales promotions proposal and SANCO's Green Paper on consumer protection. In fact, this Green Book was SANCO's first publication on the proposal scrutinised here.

During the corresponding drafting period in 2001–3, we saw that the general politicisation of EU matters peaked markedly in late summer of 2001, but declined afterwards. In fact, public contestation on and visibility of EU matters fell far below their mean levels and stayed there until the first half of 2003, when the unfair commercial practices proposal was adopted (cf. Chapter Two in this volume). In contrast, it was also pointed out above that the public salience of consumer rights in market interactions exhibited the opposite trend (*see* chapter introduction above). Staying below its mean during 2001, the broad salience indicator rose in early 2002 and, despite some variation, stayed well beyond its average levels until finalisation of the proposal discussed here. Public visibility during 2002 was driven by media coverage of online shopping, as well as on the EU initiatives on distance marketing in financial services and the sales promotion proposal discussed above (e.g. Norman 2002). During 2003, the media data underlying the indicator also picked up a growing number of consumer banking issues (e.g. Jenkins 2003) – not least because of reporting on consumer credit regulation (e.g. Croft 2003) – while media attention regarding online shopping and advertising issues was sustained (e.g. McCartney 2003). Searches limited to reports on particular commercial practices and market participants covered by the present proposal also indicate some visibility.[22] All newspapers reported on specific cases involving misleading or even deceptive commercial practices (e.g. *FAZ* 2001c; Azumendi 2001; Sigaud 2002). The biggest overarching issues concerning commercial practices, however, were specific sales promotions, as well as the respective MARKT proposal that has been discussed above (e.g. *El País* 2001; *FAZ* 2002c; Guerrera 2002b). Besides, at least the British and the German press reported early on the unfair commercial practices proposal and discussed it mainly from the perspective of business concerns (Hargreaves 2001; Guerrara 2003; *FAZ* 2003b).

Based on this information, one must attest the comparatively high contemporaneous salience of unfair commercial practices which, in addition, exhibited a rising trend during the drafting process. However, politicisation experienced a pronounced peak at the beginning of the process, but ranged at a markedly low level afterwards. Against this combination of independent variables, the theoretical framework proposes little interventionism in the final proposal. If anything, the theorised political incentives for interventionism emerging from high politicisation and high issue salience should have been present only during early drafting in 2001.

The Commission's policy choice can be analysed by comparing four sets of key provisions to the scattered regulatory landscape of extant European and national laws. This concerns first the scope and harmonisation approach of the proposal. It covers all commercial practices before and after transactions, except where they affect health and safety aspects governed by other national or European rules. Likewise, specific regulations on commercial practice regulations, where the proposed directive on consumer credit or the proposed regulation on sales promotions (see above) are explicitly mentioned, are also exempted. These rules

---

22. The narrow search required that an article mentions 'unfair', 'misleading', or 'aggressive' and 'consumer*' as well as 'retailer', 'seller' or 'advertiser'. This resulted in 100 *Financial Times* hits, thirty-two in the *Frankfurter Allgemeine Zeitung*, twenty-three in *Le Figaro*, and eleven in *El País*.

appear initially favourable from the perspective of the European consumer, as they lay the foundation for a more encompassing consumer protection framework at the European level. Yet Article 4 also presents an internal market clause by prescribing that traders shall only comply with the laws of the member state in which they are established. At the same time, it prohibits member states from restricting the free movement of goods or services 'for reasons falling within the field approximated by this Directive'. Under the extant commercial practice directives, in contrast, minimum clauses enabled national provisions with a higher level of consumer protection and national governments could enact rules for practices not previously covered by European law. Thus, the first set of rules in the proposal presents a significant expansion of European competences in the area of consumer protection, but also effectively limits the level of authoritarian consumer protection that national governments can provide.

The second set of key provisions establishes particular rules for business-to-consumer interaction. On the one hand, it bans a list of practices generally considered unfair, such as pyramid promotional schemes, inertia selling and false claims on the time-dependent availability of products. A range of these practices was not previously regulated in many member states (Schmedes 2007: 288; Commission of the European Communities 2003a: 7), which seems to push the key provision into an interventionist direction. Nonetheless, the rules also present a general ban of unfair commercial practices by defining a legal test based on three conditions. Condition one states that an unfair practice must contradict the requirements of 'professional diligence'. Condition two requires that the 'average consumer' has to be considered as the benchmark in assessing the fairness of a commercial practice. As inherited from ECJ case law,[23] the '"average consumer" means the consumer who is reasonably well informed and reasonably observant and circumspect' (Commission of the European Communities 2003b: p. 9 and Article 2(b)). Condition three prescribes that an unfair commercial practice must 'materially distort or is likely to materially distort' the average consumer's decision with regard to purchasing the respective product or service.

By relying on the ECJ's rationalist conception of the consumer, the proposal deviates from the more restrictive national jurisprudence. For example, a 2000 judgement of the Belgian *Cour de Cassation* set the benchmark as the 'least attentive consumer who accepts without criticism the representations made to him and who is not in a position to see through the traps, exaggerations and manipulative silences'. Showing the same tendency, the highest German court described the average consumer as a 'casual observer' rather than a highly attentive individual (Commission of the European Communities 2003a: 8). This obviously contrasts with the well informed and circumspect consumer the Commission assumes in deciding which business practices are unfair. The effect of this choice for the distribution of rights and risk among producers and consumers becomes

---

23. See, for example, Case C-315/92, *Verband Sozialer Wettbewerb e.V v. Clinique Labatories SNC and Estée Lauder Cosmetics GmbH* (1994) ECR I-317 or Case C-210/96, *Gut Springheide GmbH v. Oberkreisdirektor des Kreises Steinfurt* (1998) ECR I-4657.

easily visible if we assume that consumers are distributed along the dimension of rationality in purchase decisions. If the legislator takes the least rational individual in this distribution as the benchmark, then all consumers receive legal protection. If the consumer of average attention is chosen as a benchmark, however, then it is willingly accepted that the lower half of the distribution of consumers may make inappropriate decisions in response to trader practices. We cannot compare all national regimes in greater detail here, but against the above-mentioned judgements, the Commission takes a rather liberal stance here so that the conclusion on this set of rules remains mixed.

A third set of key provisions defines and bans two specific forms of unfair commercial practices. First, misleading practices, which cause the average consumer to take a decision they would not have taken in the light of correct facts, are prohibited. Respective trader duties include the advertising and also the presentation of the product. Among other things, marketing a product on its intended similarity with other products – for example, selling a mobile phone that looks like an iPhone – or misleading omissions fall under the banned practices. The extant misleading advertising directive (Council Directive 84/450/EEC as amended by Directive 97/55/EC), in contrast, was less specific and did not refer as explicitly to the average consumer or respective ECJ jurisprudence. In addition, it contained an explicit minimum clause that allowed national governments to adopt 'provisions with a view to ensuring more extensive protection for consumers, persons carrying on a trade, business, craft or profession, and the general public'. As the proposed law repeals this extant directive, the Commission's choice here tends more towards a *laissez-faire* model of consumer policy. In contrast, the proposal also bans aggressive commercial practices, which was not previously an explicit part of supranational law. Assuming again an average consumer, an evaluation of aggressiveness should take into account the timing, nature and persistence of the trader's actions, the use of threatening or abusive language, the exploitation of known misfortunes or circumstances that impair the consumer's judgement, the existence of disproportionate and non-contractual barriers, or any threat to take action that cannot be taken legally. While it stands to reason that such practices were forbidden in most EU member states before, at the supranational level, this is an increase in consumer protection. Again, this set of key provisions takes a middle ground between *laissez-faire* and interventionist approaches to consumer policy.

The fourth and final set of key provisions entails enforcement rules. National implementation laws should enable legal action against illegal commercial practices by equipping the respective courts or administrative authorities with the power to cease or prohibit the unfair commercial practice in question, to require traders to substantiate their factual claims and to consider factual claims as inaccurate if the evidence demanded is insufficient. Furthermore, effective, proportionate and deterring penalties must be enacted. However, besides the option of independent complaint-handling mechanisms for existing codes of conduct, these rules equal the provisions in the extant EU directives, so that we cannot attest any change in the interventionism the Commission proposes in this regard.

This rather inconclusive perspective holds for the overall proposal. On the one hand, it broadens the scope of the EU's consumer protection regime on market transactions. On the other hand, however, it removes national powers for further protection and sets a benchmark for future evaluation of commercial practices that undermines more protective national jurisprudence. Given that the 'average consumer' thereby confines all future court decisions as well as further regulations, the final judgement tips more towards the *laissez-faire* side of the dependent variable scrutinised here. But what drove DG SANCO towards this choice?

Despite DG MARKT's attempts to occupy the regulation of business-to-consumer transactions, DG SANCO was formally responsible for managing most of the extant supranational laws in the area (COM91:97 and 110). With the inception of the Prodi Commission in 1999, a team of officials who considered themselves as 'newcomers' to the policy field were assigned to these laws, and realised that there were 'different rules on the same topic in the different directives [...] without any real sense behind it other than they were adopted at different periods of time'. Against this background, the drafting effort 'really was meant to clean up and also to find an instrument that would survive a little bit longer' (COM91:111).

The 'basic ideas' thus came from the experience of these officials in managing extant regulations and the resulting interference with the 'policy community' of interested stakeholders (COM112:95). But while the unit appears to have been the agenda setter, the idea of a unifying framework directive met 'no contradiction' at the political level (COM91:114). Directly at the beginning of drafting in 2001, the unit drew up a scoping paper that provided an initial overview of the legal situation in the member states, to inform SANCO's hierarchy 'what the outcome may be' (COM91:179). This put some 'political drive' behind the desk officials' approach, as Commissioner Byrne was very interested in a highly visible consumer policy proposal underlining his competences in the area (COM79:62). And indeed, particularly due to the horizontal nature of the envisaged initiative, his cabinet perceived the unfair commercial practices regulation as a rather important proposal for Byrne's term in office (COM111:98).

But despite its political attractiveness, all officials were well aware that it was going to be 'quite [a] controversial project' (COM91:103). While the industry had very much welcomed DG MARKT's 2001 sales promotions proposal, the business side had major doubts when it became known that SANCO was going for a more encompassing directive. As early as spring 2001, an alliance of fourteen business lobbying groups – among them publishers, advertisers and television companies – had directly approached Commission President Romano Prodi, arguing that too strict an initiative could have a significant impact on the competitiveness of the European economy (Hargreaves 2001). British industry particularly feared that SANCO was 'fencing them in', and reacted with 'tough resistance' from the start (COM91:103).

In this light, drafting officials realised that 'if [they] do not have as many facts and basic data on the table as possible this will never, never fly' (ibid.). Early producer opposition led officials to back their policy choices with as much empirical information as possible. On the one hand, this was translated into a broad study on national regulations conducted under the leadership of two German law professors (Schulze and Schulte-Nölke 2003). On the other hand, the drafting unit started to involve all stakeholders very early by issuing a broad public consultation. As we have seen earlier, SANCO officials blocked MARKT's sales promotion proposal until this consultation, in the form of the 'Green Paper on Consumer Protection', was ready for publication in October 2001. While being open as regards regulatory details, this consultation identified 'a framework directive containing a general duty in relation to unfair commercial practice as a possible basis for reform' (European Commission 2001c).

This move was particularly important in terms of gaining support from national governments. Much to the delight of DG SANCO, 'a majority of Member states [...] supported reform on the basis of a framework directive' (Commission of the European Communities 2003b: 2). Besides, even after this basic consent, SANCO involved national representatives intensively. This happened through a panel of national experts and two informal ministerial meetings (Commission of the European Communities 2003a: 22). Having garnered the agreement of national governments, the officials drew up another policy paper in June 2002, which summarised the earlier consultation and focused less on whether there should be a framework at all, but rather discussed the substantial content of such a framework (Commission of the European Communities 2002a; Schmedes 2007: 300).

Furthermore, SANCO tried to legitimise its approach by a Flash Eurobarometer surveying 16,129 consumers and 2,899 businesses.[24] Ultimately, all this stakeholder information was summarised in an 'extended impact assessment' (COM112:165, Commission of the European Communities 2003a: 2). These efforts underline that DG SANCO engaged very strongly in consensus building in the policy community. While '[s]ome stakeholders made strident criticism of the initiative in its early stages [...] many others have reviewed their position as the Commission's proposed approach has been clarified' (Commission of the European Communities 2003b: 7; see also Commission of the European Communities 2003a: 23). Yet much of this engagement was concerned with information collection, and especially with convincing the stakeholders that a framework directive was necessary at all. In fact, the history of stakeholder consultation highlights that the exact degree of interventionism the Commission would propose was left open until the first policy paper in June 2002 (Commission of the European Communities 2002a).

But how did the exact policy choices come about? The intense turf dispute with DG MARKT, as well as the early industry opposition, confronted the drafting unit with the challenge of producing a strong consumer policy proposal that would be attractive to their political hierarchy, while the same time avoiding more 'ideological battles' among external and internal stakeholders (COM112:285). They met this challenge by reframing consumer policy as one 'dimension of the internal market' in which 'specific legal barriers caused by the fragmented

---

24. See the report: http://ec.europa.eu/consumers/cons_int/safe_shop/fair_bus_pract/green_pap_ comm/studies/eb57-fb128_final_report_en.pdf (accessed 11 May 2010).

regulation of unfair commercial practices cause cost, complexity and uncertainty for firms *and* a lack of consumer confidence in cross-border transactions' (Commission of the European Communities 2003a: 3–4, emphasis added). In other words, SANCO argued that market functioning, rather than protection against unfair practices, was the most important concern from a consumer point of view. The major challenge for consumers, in that perspective, is not possible deception by traders but access to foreign markets. Accordingly, the proposal was solely based on Article 95 (internal market) of the EU Treaty, and does not, even in the recitals, mention Article 153, which demands a high level of consumer protection. Consumer associations strongly regret this as it signals a renunciation from the aim of increased protection (BEUC 2004b: 4).

This perspective is carried through particularly to the scope provisions of the proposal. If one wants to achieve greater 'consumer confidence', the expansion of the scope is a logical step because it is 'uncertainty which [...] deters consumers from buying cross-border' and the 'patchwork of regulation is extremely difficult to explain to consumers' (Commission of the European Communities 2003a: 8). While consumer associations basically welcomed this 'safety net' approach, they argued that confidence could be built especially through a tight regime for after-sales services and complaint-handling mechanisms (BEUC 2004b). Initially, the Commission DG had foreseen such a regime as part of its parallel proposal on consumer enforcement agencies. However, stakeholder responses to this issue in the 2002 policy paper stressed that 'costs to business were out of proportion to the consumer benefits'. Along that argument, SANCO simply decided that the same general principles should cover the pre- and after-sale stages rather than hammering out a specific set of requirements that would 'compel [...] companies to provide after sales service' (AE 2003b; Commission of the European Communities 2003a: 12, 23). While siding with the consumer demand in the early periods of drafting, SANCO muted its aims at the later stages.

Likewise, the idea that market access is the only interest shared by consumers and producers informed the unique harmonisation approach that combines a country-of-origin principle with a supranational re-regulation of protective rules that member states may not exceed. The 'internal market clause' eased life for businesses and underscored the horizontal nature to which SANCO aspired, while the 'maximum harmonisation element' aims to generate consumer confidence by prescribing a general and easily understandable level of protection. However, consumer associations saw this as 'a double-edged sword': Country-of-origin might undermine national protection rules that are not harmonised by the proposal, while maximum harmonisation depends heavily on the actual level of protection in the remaining provisions. Consumer representatives feared that this 'may inevitably end up being a compromise' in the Council (EURO COOP 2003a; Commission of the European Communities 2003a: 23), which would be 'a step back on protection' if existing national exemptions were no longer allowed (BEUC 2004b: especially 5–6, 8–10). But while the harmonisation rules were 'politically a demanding proposal' (COM112:77), the internal market clause was a gift for industry: they argued that it supports small and medium enterprises, raises consumer confidence, stimulates competitiveness and is thus perfectly consistent with the broader Lisbon strategy (AE 2004b; UNICE 2003).

A similar pattern of support and opposition can be observed for the particular rules on trader practices. In their 2001 Green Paper, SANCO officials already announced that a general producer duty of fair trading practices would be an element of the proposal, without, however, providing any detail as to how far such a duty would go. However, the final proposal contents itself with only banning unfair commercial practices. Again, the consumer policy interventionism in SANCO's position declined during the drafting process. Consumer associations would have welcomed a general duty for fair trading and considered the finally proposed ban 'not sufficiently wide in scope', if compared to the much broader producer duties under the law of Nordic EU member states (BEUC 2004b). Business representation, in contrast, argued against the general duty because a 'too vague and free standing status may easily lead to divergent national interpretation running counter to the primary objective of harmonisation and legal certainty' (UNICE 2003: 7–8). In the final proposal, SANCO obviously sided with the industry argument (cf. Commission of the European Communities 2003a: 23).

Much more contestation, however, focused on the rationalist conception of the average benchmark consumer. Consumer associations were shocked by the conscious choice of the ECJ approach, and argued that it deviates from implicit conceptualisations in extant directives (BEUC 2004b: 7–8; EURO COOP 2003a). Nevertheless, the SANCO officials, fully well aware that their choice was the 'most important trade-off in the proposal', considered the focus on the rational consumer rather than on the 'more credulous' one 'as a balance [...] struck between the need to protect the most vulnerable consumers and the freedom of business'. This is a rather business-friendly position, particularly if compared to the 'weak consumer' justification that the officials drafting the consumer credit rules had chosen (see above).

Similarly, SANCO reduced the interventionism in its policy choices during drafting with regard to misleading omissions. Instead of principally requiring the trader not to omit any material information, as in the final proposal, the initial idea was to enact a much more detailed regime of information particulars that must be disclosed. Again, the evaluation of trader costs versus increases in consumer confidence let SANCO decide to go for the less restrictive and more principle-based approach (Commission of the European Communities 2003a: 12). Likewise, SANCO attenuated its approach with regard to enforcement rules. Here, the original idea had been to automatically consider non-compliance with voluntary codes of conduct as a misleading commercial practice. However, following the 'strong response' in the 2002 business survey, SANCO abandoned this idea to the delight of small businesses, and in opposition to consumer demands (Commission of the European Communities 2003a: 12; UNICE 2003: 6; EURO COOP 2003a: 3).

Unfortunately, there is not sufficient information about how far these moves towards a more liberal model were influenced by the internal conflict with DG

MARKT.[25] However, after the battle on the parallel publication of SANCO's Green Book and MARKT's sales promotion proposal, the drafting officials knew that this 'was not going to be an easy ride' internally, and informed their political hierarchy about internal obstacles early on (COM91:290). While the main negotiators were the cabinets of Commissioners Byrne and Bolkestein (COM91:127–30), we also know that the industry at least tried to engage the cabinet of Commission President Prodi, as well as DG ENTR, as early as 2001 (Guerrara 2003; Hargreaves 2001). In sum, internal conflict potential seems to have been high at least at the onset of the drafting process.

With regard to the major theoretical model hinging on politicisation and salience, particularly the within-case variation in SANCO's position is highly interesting. During summer and autumn 2001, when rather high levels of politicisation met at least intermediate levels of issue salience, SANCO at least alluded a more interventionist approach by proposing a general producer duty for fair trading in the Green Paper. When politicisation declined in 2002, this was watered down to banning only more narrowly confined unfair practices which, in addition, took a fully rational consumer as a benchmark. While early business outrage in 2001 made SANCO cautious in committing to further substantial positions in the Green Book, we have seen that more interventionist ideas on the after-sales regime or on binding codes of conduct were also attenuated with declining EU politicisation among the European public. These moves towards a market emphasis in the position took place despite rising issue salience levels – suggesting that salience alone does not account for interventionism, but that its combination with a generally politicised climate is necessary.

Consistency with the major argument is also seen in the Commission's responsiveness towards external interests. While stakeholder consultations were exceptionally broad and encompassing, SANCO's decision to concentrate on consumer confidence rather than consumer protection ironically led to higher responsiveness vis-à-vis business interests: producer arguments were always based on increased market access while the claims of consumer representatives were more concerned with the political protection that consumers enjoyed in the different member states. Thus, the consumer demands fitted SANCO's approach less, particularly during the final, less politicised stages.

Yet again, the room for SANCO's choice between a *laissez-faire* model and a more interventionist approach was confined by national interest as uncovered in the early consultation phase. Particularly after the early producer opposition, the drafting unit invested intensively in engaging representatives from national governments up to ministerial level. Clearly, political feasibility in the Council yielded a highly relevant complementary explanation for the outcome at hand. No evidence, in contrast, could be found as regards Commissioner nationality and partisanship. This is especially evident in the comparative perspective: both the

---

25. Access to the internal coordination documents was denied in this case, as it 'would seriously undermine the institution's decision-making process' (Article 4(3) of 'transparency' regulation (EC) 1049/2001.

highly interventionist consumer credit proposal and the much more market-oriented commercial practices case were adopted under the same Commissioner. Obviously, variables changing over time can explain this change in the lead DG's position rather than its political leadership.

4.6 Directive on consumer rights

After the framework on commercial practices, the Commission published no new initiatives on economic and contractual consumer rights for quite some time.[26] But the DG SANCO unit responsible for the unfair commercial practices proposal actually already started work on the next encompassing consumer policy framework as early as winter 2003 (COM93:66). This was a proposal for a directive on consumer rights that was adopted after oral debate in the College on 8 October 2008 (Commission of the European Communities 2008d). While the unfair commercial practices proposal had covered trader actions in initiating a contract, the consumer rights proposal targeted the actual form and the obligations in such contracts.

Such a broad and large-scale consumer policy proposal nicely fitted the political guidelines of the new Commission President Barroso, who entered office in 2004. He set out with the idea of a 'clearly visible [...] Europe for citizens' (COM120:197), and also the Commission's single market review of November 2007 emphasises 'better results for consumers' (Commission of the European Communities 2008d: 3). Commission officials noted that 'Barroso [...] placed a premium on everything which appeared to provide direct advantage to citizens' (COM93:208). When the accession of Bulgaria and Romania in 2007 required two new Commissioner posts, consumer policy was emphasised even more by a split in DG SANCO's political leadership: the Cypriot Márkos Kyprianoú kept responsibility for health and food policy while the new Bulgarian Commissioner Meglena Kuneva became solely responsible for 'consumer protection'.

During this drafting period spanning from 2003 to 2008, the independent variables of the major model also show interesting movement. The low-level stagnation of general EU politicisation we have observed above came to an abrupt end in summer 2003. Our indicator (Chapter Two) exhibits a steep, monotone increase that results in maximum politicisation in July 2004. The enormous leap of public visibility driving the indicator reflects challenges to the structure of supranational authority in Europe. On the one hand, a draft constitution was presented in June 2003, which led to intergovernmental conflict and a failed agreement during a Brussels Council meeting in December. All this happened in the shadow of the huge Eastern enlargement that finally took place in May 2004. Public EU visibility was pushed even further by upcoming discussions on the

---

26. One interesting exception is the roaming regulation proposed by DG INFSO as document COM(2008)580 in September 2008. Note that this proposal was not flagged as a consumer policy measure in the PreLex database, and was thus not picked up by the sampling procedure developed in Appendix B.

future Commission president and no less by parliamentary elections in June 2004. Our polarisation measures (see Figure 2.2) suggest that these developments had a polarising effect on public opinion in the EU: its variance increased, while the distribution flattened out during late 2003 and early 2004.

Although the political climate cooled down moderately in late 2004, the first half of 2005 saw further increases and another pronounced peak of politicisation. This time, the indicator is mainly driven by widespread union protests against the liberalisation of services by the EU, British manifestations supporting the maintenance of the UK's budget rebate, and especially national mobilisation against the draft constitution. The constitution's ratification process met particularly heavy press coverage, which amounts for high visibility peaking with the failed referenda in France and the Netherlands in May and June 2005. In the wake of these failures, media interest was sustained for a while, but overall politicisation declined slowly, a movement that was only disrupted by a minor plateau in late 2006 reflecting rekindled discussions on reforming the EU's treaty base. After a drop throughout 2007 and early 2008, the indicator excels its mean only in summer 2008 when the international financial crisis moved EU responses into the spotlight. In sum, the first three years of the analysed drafting process in particular saw extraordinarily high levels of EU politicisation, which, however, declined in between and resurfaced only in the very final stages of policy formulation.

With regard to the issue area's public salience (see Figure 4.1), we see an explicit peak of the indicator between 2003 and 2004. This public visibility was partly driven by the former unfair commercial practices proposal (e.g. Friedrich 2004; *FAZ* 2004a), but especially by a re-sparked interest in financial consumer services and intense reporting on the privacy of online bank customers and shoppers. These topics also account for the indicator's plateau during 2005 when media reporting shifted increasingly to copyright infringements and online fraud. But in 2006, the public visibility of the broader issue area declined rapidly and fell to one standard deviation below the mean, where it stayed throughout the adoption of the proposal under analysis in October 2008.

Since the proposal was highly relevant for online shopping, the increased public awareness in the first two years of drafting can indeed be deemed relevant. More specific newspaper searches[27] indicate reporting on a range of topics such as consumer withdrawal rights (*FAZ* 2007j; Molina 2008), which were most often linked especially to online shopping (e.g. *FAZ* 2004c, 2005b; Collet 2006;

---

27. Finding a suitable algorithm in this regard was aggravated, since the issue area is rather broad and its most defining terms cover other economical topics as well. Against this background, I went for a rather restrictive approach in this case, and retrieved only articles from the period 1 January 2003–8 October 2008 that fulfilled the following condition: the article body had to contain consumer* AND (purchase* OR sale* OR retail*) AND (distance* OR doorstep* OR online* OR payment* OR delivery* OR contract*) AND (withdrawal* OR return* OR warranty*). After some trials, I additionally excluded articles that contained either 'investment' or 'stock' from the *Financial Times*, as this removed a range of irrelevant articles in this newspaper. The resulting hits were distributed as follows: *Financial Times* (159), *El País* (seventy-five), *Frankfurter Allgemeine Zeitung* (fifty-five), and *Le Figaro* (fifty).

Kutschke 2007; Sanz 2007). But newspapers also covered general developments in the European consumer policy regime (e.g. Bünder 2004; *FAZ* 2007b) and especially the 2007 Green Paper on consumer protection, which prepared the proposal (e.g. Friedrich 2007; Bounds 2007, see also below). And finally, Commissioner Kuneva advertised the proposal intensively during 2007 and 2008 until shortly before it was adopted (Carbajosa 2007; Appel *et al.* 2008; Tait 2008a, 2008b).

Both the broad indicator and the specific searches indicate that issue salience was especially high during the first three years of drafting, while some public visibility was sustained until the proposal's final adoption. Taken together with the particularly high politicisation levels during the first two years, the theoretical model leads to the expectation of a rather interventionist proposal. In a dynamic perspective, however, we would expect that interventionist positions prevailed, particularly at the onset of drafting and possibly during the last six to nine months of drafting.

But let's have a look at the outcome first. Here, we compare the rather complex legal text (Commission of the European Communities 2008d) with four directives on off-premises contracts (Directive 85/577/EEC), distance contracts (97/7/EEC), unfair contract terms (93/13/EEC) and consumer sales and guarantees (Directive 1999/44/EEC) and the partially more protective national rules.[28] This comparison is structured along six key provisions that distribute rights and duties among producers and consumers.

The first set relevant set of key provisions concerns the scope and harmonisation approach of the proposal. Compared to the regulatory status quo, monetary thresholds no longer apply, solicited trader visits are covered, and traders that do not regularly engage in distance marketing have to abide by the new law as well. These scope extensions present a move towards a more encompassing regulatory approach. Also in terms of harmonisation, the proposal is clearer than its predecessors. In contrast to the minimum clauses in the four extant directives, Article 4 prohibits national governments directly from introducing 'more or less stringent provisions to ensure a different level of consumer protection'. The impossibility of national 'upwards' deviations might be bad news for consumer protection, but its overall effect must be evaluated in conjunction with the more specific policy choices in the Commission proposal.

Regarding such specific rules, the proposal entails an encompassing set of pre-contractual information obligations for traders. It covers product characteristics; trader identity and contact details; prices including all taxes; all arrangements on payment, delivery, and complaint handling policy; the consumer's withdrawal rights; all information on after-sales services and commercial guarantees, as well as the contract duration. Moreover, it includes an explicit ban on hidden

---

28. DG SANCO published a table comparing certain articles of the proposal to respective national provisions. Where no further reference is made, this table is the main source for comparative statements regarding the member states. It can be accessed via: http://ec.europa.eu/consumers/rights/docs/comparative_table_en.pdf (accessed 24 February 2010).

charges – if a trader did not disclose all price-relevant information, the consumer is not required to pay. Particularly in respect of banning hidden charges – a rule that did not exist in national laws in such an explicit form – this set of obligatory information moves the Commission position towards a more interventionist model of consumer policy.

Even more trader obligations are established for off-premise and distance contracts concluded by hawkers or through online offers. In such cases, traders must additionally provide the consumer with a standardised withdrawal form containing full information on withdrawal rights and procedures. Also, the trader is made fully responsible for informing the consumer about all conceivable means of terminating the respective contract (e.g. relevant codes of conduct, dispute settlement mechanisms, and so on) in plain and intelligible language. While the extant distance contract directive (97/7/EC) contained similar requirements on trader information, the scope of the extant off-premise directive (85/577/EEC) is significantly exceeded. Neither directive, in addition prescribed a withdrawal form or required the trader to instruct the consumer about their rights. This demand for consumer 'education' was also not present in any national regime, so the withdrawal rules move the Commission position in an interventionist direction.

In addition, withdrawal rights under off-premise and distance contracts are specified even further. The consumer has the right to withdraw within fourteen days without any justification. Extant EU directives set the cooling-off period to seven days only, and most national regimes prescribed less than fourteen days (among others, Austria, Belgium, France, the Netherlands and the UK), while Malta and Slovenia demanded fifteen. Thus, the Commission position is oriented along the more protective regimes, and the very idea of a cooling-off period speaks against the assumption of a fully rational consumer that usually underlies *laissez-faire* models. To be fair, however, one has to note that the withdrawal rules for distance contracts also held something for traders. Five of the twenty-five member states (Germany, Estonia, Finland, Greece and Spain) had previously imposed the costs for returning goods on traders, while the current proposal requires consumers to pay. However, in the light of increased information requirements and a significantly extended standard period for most member states, the net effect of the withdrawal rules is more protection for European consumers.

A fourth set of relevant rules covers trader obligations after the conclusion of sales contracts. The trader must generally accomplish the delivery of goods within thirty days, and the risk of loss or damage passes to the consumer only upon reception. In European legislation, delivery had previously been unregulated, while the proposed time period was the same in almost all member states except in French and German contract law, which stipulate that contracts must be performed immediately unless the wording in the contract specifies otherwise. Regarding the 'passing of risk', most member states' rules would not be changed, while in Italy the transport risk was borne by the consumer. France and Spain, in addition, had a mixed regime, which advantaged traders in the case of *force majeure*.

Traders are also obliged to deliver goods in conformity with the contract, meaning that they fit earlier advertising or exhibited models, that they are suitable for the normal and indicated purposes and that they show the qualities of comparable goods. Having remained unregulated at the European level before, these rules largely mirror the status quo in the member states. Only Spain, Denmark and Finland also included provisions on proper packaging so that by and large the conformity rules leave the extant distribution of rights among producers and consumers intact.

Traders are generally liable for non-conforming products and consumers are entitled to repair or replacement, to a reduced price, or they even may rescind the contract – all free of any cost. However, the Commission proposes an 'order of remedies': The trader may choose whether to replace or to repair the product, and price reduction is only possible if he has proven that replacement or repair is unlawful, impossible or disproportionate. Neither in extant supranational law nor in most national regimes had such remedies been conclusively regulated before. In Slovenia, Greece, Lithuania and Portugal, consumers could freely choose any of the options, so that no order of remedies existed. An unequivocal statement on the Commission position's degree of interventionism is hard to make, while undermining five national regimes was obviously not the most interventionist option. In sum, some of the proposed rules on the trader's after-sales obligations enhance the regulatory status quo while they undermine it in others so that the judgement on this particular set of key provisions must remain indifferent.

An equally cautious statement applies for the fifth set of rules, which cover legal and commercial guarantees. The proposal prescribes that the trader is generally liable for two years under sales contracts, and this period restarts if a product is replaced. If any further commercial guarantees are provided and advertised, they are binding on the trader and must be drafted in plain and intelligible language while specifying the exact conditions. While these rules appear favourable to the consumer on first sight, the generalised two-year period undermines the status quo in the UK and Ireland (six years), Sweden (three years) and Hungary, Denmark and Germany where longer periods existed for specific product groups. In contrast, a renewed guarantee for replaced goods is the status quo only in Denmark, while it increases consumer protection compared to the regimes of all remaining member states. As difficult as it may be to reach a concluding judgement on the relative interventionism in these rules, the reduction of general guarantee periods in six out of twenty-five countries slightly inclines towards benefits for traders.

The sixth and final set of relevant key provisions covers the specifications of contract terms. Contract terms are generally prohibited if they 'cause a significant imbalance in the parties' rights and obligations'. All agreements require plain, intelligible and legible language and can only be concluded with the 'expressed consent' of consumers. This may initially appear self-evident, but it is particularly relevant in internet shopping as it outlaws pre-ticked boxes in online masks for contract conclusion. The proposal also contains a complete ban of inertia selling: that is, automatic contract conclusion in the absence of consumer resistance. In addition, two annexes define a broad range of specifically unfair and thus forbidden contract terms. In case of doubt, national authorities may judge on unregulated contract terms only by applying 'the interpretation most favourable to the consumer' (Article 36). Compared to the existing directive on unfair contract terms (1993/13/EC), these rules clearly extend the status quo. While the general ban was already in the 1993 directive, the list of unfair terms is wider, and in particular the ban on inertia selling, as well as expressed consumer consent, are regulatory innovations. The latter rule also did not exist in any member state before so that the Commission position on these key provisions clearly tends towards the interventionist end of the available policy options.

Yet summarising the analysis of the legal text across the six identified key provisions shows a moderately indifferent Commission position. Especially on the conclusion of and the withdrawal from online contracts, the proposal brings about a net gain of consumer protection. Also as regards pre-contractual information, consumer rights in any transaction are strengthened. Nevertheless, the analysis also uncovered some concessions to traders, such as those regarding guarantees or liability for defective goods. While the Commission does not choose the lowest common denominator of national regimes in these instances, it undermines the most protective solutions that were available in the regulatory landscape. In conjunction with the chosen overall harmonisation approach that prohibits any further national deviations, however, this has a liberalising effect. A final judgement on interventionism thus points to an intermediate level, placing the proposal at hand somewhere between the cases of consumer credit and unfair commercial practices. How did this intermediate position come about?

Drafting was handled by the very same team that had formulated the unfair commercial practices proposal (COM93:164). As the first framework directive based on full harmonisation, this initiative served as a role model both in terms of product and process (Commission of the European Communities 2008d: 7). Building on their broad experience and their manifold stakeholder contacts since 1999, officials at the administrative level provided the initial impulse for this successor proposal (COM93:74). The early ideas were developed quite silently during 2003 – not the least since unfair commercial practices attracted most stakeholder attention (COM120:33). As in the case of the earlier initiative, the drafting unit decided to build a broad 'knowledge base' first (COM120:117). After consulting the administrative hierarchy on which policy options should be reviewed (COM93:40), the unit tendered a study on the implementation of eight extant directives. The project began in 2004, was coordinated by the same German academics that had provided scientific input on unfair commercial practices, and was finished only in February 2008 with an extensive comparative legal analysis (Commission of the European Communities 2008d: 7).[29]

But the major political momentum built up early in 2005, when the Barroso Commission entered office. From then on, the regulatory plans were handled more openly, and the drafting process was subject to more 'political steer' (COM120:49). At that stage, the consumer rights initiative was already seen as a 'major legislative instrument' (COM93:48), as 'a sort of higher level piece of legislation [...] much

---

29. The study itself is available at: http://ec.europa.eu/consumers/rights/docs/consumer_law_ compendium_comparative_analysis_en_final.pdf (accessed 26 February 2010).

more politicised' (COM80:57), and, accordingly, as a 'politically weighty and sensitive proposal' (COM118:87). Also, the lower ranking officials knew 'that it attracts lots of attention'. On the one hand, they quickly came 'under huge pressure of interests from different business groups'; on the other, 'from the very beginning [they] knew that the proposal was important [...] because it touches an important element of citizens' life' (COM120:145).

In that context, 'the Commissioner decided first that [they] should go for a Green Paper' (COM120:49). So, just as for the unfair commercial practices proposal, the new political leadership of DG SANCO also chose to back the initiative using the broadest possible consultation procedure. The Green Paper on the 'review of the consumer acquis' was published in February 2007. It triggered 'over 300 responses from consumer and business associations, member states, the European Parliament, the European Economic and Social Committee, and other stakeholders such as academics or lawyers' (Commission of the European Communities 2008c: 1).

Beyond this broad consultation, SANCO tested the terrain with more specific discussion papers that were complemented by a business survey and a series of stakeholder workshops (Commission of the European Communities 2008d: 4), as well as by a 2008 Eurobarometer survey on consumer and retailer attitudes (Commission of the European Communities 2008c: 1). In addition, an 'extremely huge number of bilateral meetings' between Commission officials and interest representatives took place throughout the process (COM120:49). In the light of the proposal's political weight, the drafting officials considered it 'quite important [...] that the external stakeholders feel included'. They 'wanted to have the impact assessment as broad as possible and wanted to talk to as many people as possible' (COM120:109). But to which stakeholder demands has SANCO actually been responsive during the process?

The official's starting point was similar to the reasoning that had also prevailed in the case of unfair commercial practices. So, again, the approach was based on questions of market access and pursued the 'twinned objectives' of reducing business reluctance to trade cross-border *and* of enhancing consumer confidence in such transactions (COM93:46, COM120:37, cf. Commission of the European Communities 2008c; 2007b: 7–8). Both objectives first and foremost required the consolidation of extant EU law into 'more horizontally framed legal principles' (COM80:47).

This technocratic reasoning was directly translated into the 'full harmonisation' approach (COM120:41; KP16.1), which became the most contested provision both within and beyond the Commission. Internally, DG MARKT unsurprisingly favoured a mutual recognition clause (COM93:100, COM118:103, COM28:28), and argued that this was the only reliable insurance for liberalisation (COM118:113). For consumer transactions, this would have meant that the law in the trader's jurisdiction would apply in cross-border transactions. The DG for Justice, Liberty and Security (JLS), which was responsible for an even broader supranational inroad to contract law at the time, argued for exactly the opposite. JLS had itself proposed a country-of-origin provision for the Rome I regulation in

2005, but, during the corresponding Council negotiations, this principle was turned round. The final law in 2008 contained a country-of-destination principle meaning that the law of the consumer's place of residence was relevant (Commission of the European Communities 2008c: 6). JLS now also defended this member state verdict in the internal discussions on the consumer rights proposal so as not to endanger the ongoing development of European contract law by creating legal inconsistencies (COM93:108). The legal service supported JLS in this regard (COM80:83, COM118:99). Again, interest in a larger parallel programme for increasing supranational competences turned turf considerations into 'issues of legal principle related to the hierarchy of norms and the functioning of the single market' (COM80:83).

The formally responsible DG SANCO, however, opted for the middle ground between the competing MARKT and JLS positions. For one, SANCO considered MARKT's more liberal approach 'a less good regime from the consumer's point of view' (COM93:120). This perspective was indeed informed by the broader contemporaneous politicisation of Europe's approach to market making. 'Looking at the baggage and the history of things like the services directive [...] and debates that have been happening in Europe over the last four or five years [...], they made the call that a single market clause would not politically fly' (COM118:103). In other words, the approach to harmonisation 'became then more a question of politics rather than policy' (COM93:108), and further liberalisation was seen as a 'non-starter' (COM93:120). In this political context, SANCO's 2007 Green Paper had argued strongly against an internal market clause (Commission of the European Communities 2007b: 10–11), and garnered strong support from the EP, from all but five member states (DG Health and Consumer Protection 2007: 11), and also from consumer associations (Commission of the European Communities 2008c: 6).

SANCO, however, did not fully accept the JLS position either. Fully relying on the law of the targeted country would have contradicted their twinned objectives of enhancing market access for traders. Business interests lobbied strongly against this idea because they would have to adapt to twenty-seven different legal systems in the worst case (COM93:50). In between the two extreme approaches to harmonising consumer rights, the SANCO officials finally 'came to the conclusion that the only way [they] can create a common set of rules and a uniform feeling of [consumer] confidence was targeted maximum harmonisation' (COM93:58). This position did not only serve business interests. The drafting officials also did not expect that a complete country-of-destination principle would be politically feasible in the Council (COM93:108). Additionally, given that the respective Rome I regulation just had become law, an additional proposal prescribing this principle would hardly have been necessary from the member states' point of view. In other words, simply following the JLS' approach had risked losing the basic justification for separate regulation of consumer contracts under the auspices of DG SANCO.

The resulting compromise made neither business stakeholders nor consumer associations really happy. While business argued for the internal market clause, consumers considered full harmonisation as 'a crime against subsidiarity', and would have preferred the status quo that allowed national deviations for more protection (COM80:69, DG Health and Consumer Protection 2007: 10; BEUC 2009). Since both external and internal interests differed so much on the question of harmonisation, the issue remained debated throughout the whole process. SANCO's compromise position was only asserted during the very late stages, when both the administrative leaders as well as the political cabinets of the involved services negotiated bilaterally (COM118:95, COM80:89, COM93:136).

Besides the conflict about the harmonisation approach, the summary of the public consultation provides some valuable hints on SANCO's policy choices on other key provisions. While businesses opposed the extended cooling-off period if the traders failed to fully inform the consumer, both consumer associations and national authorities favoured the solution that is also entailed in the final proposal (DG Health and Consumer Protection 2007: 13–14). Furthermore, businesses demanded that derogations from the regulated contract terms might be negotiated individually, while consumer groups opposed this. The consultation highlighted that most member states aligned with the business position in this regard (DG Health and Consumer Protection 2007: 12), and the proposal followed this majority.

Against this pattern, it stands to reason that political feasibility in the Council constrained SANCO's approach for more consumer protection. This is also underlined with regard to the lists of unfair contract terms. Businesses preferred the indicative lists in the old directives, which served only to guide judges without being legally binding. SANCO's Green Paper, however, offered a stricter solution, of complementing this 'grey' list with a 'black' one. Here, the majority of national governments was in favour of the more protective solution (DG Health and Consumer Protection 2007: 12–13), which finally also became part of the 2008 proposal. Similarly, the consultation revealed that a majority of eighteen out of twenty-five member states supported the general introduction of a fourteen-day cooling-off period (ibid. 76). SANCO adopted this view, and backed it further by consumer studies and surveys (COM28:5, Commission of the European Communities 2008c: 2).

In the same vein, setting the length of guarantee periods (KP16.5) was said to have been 'a question of pitching' the varying national approaches whilst ensuring 'a high level of protection' (COM93:228). Here, SANCO apparently preferred more than the two-year period the proposal ended up with, but its plans were surrendered in the final political negotiations within the Commission, where particularly DG ENTR opposed them (COM71:37).

Concessions in the final internal negotiations could hardly be avoided. During the endgame, SANCO's consumer policy, Commissioner Meglena Kuneva, pushed hard for a timely adoption of the proposal (COM120:53). In order to enhance its visibility, she tried to have it read in the EP before the elections of summer 2009 (COM93:224). SANCO officials considered this a 'clever idea'. However, despite an informal commitment from the relevant committee, the Parliament did not start negotiations before the election, and the drafting officials were disappointed that the proposal did not get 'as much air time and publicity as [they had] expected' (COM93:216).

Nevertheless, surrounding the formal adoption, Commissioner Kuneva actively promoted the proposal in public. Besides the interviews mentioned already, and accounts in a range of national newspapers (e.g. Appel *et al*. 2008; Carbajosa 2007), she advertised its benefits for European citizens in a range of speeches that mainly sold key deviations from the regulatory status quo in the name of the consumer (e.g. Kuneva 2007, 2008b). It was vital that 'the consumer very clearly gains', and the European citizens should know that the Commission proposal brings 'tough new rules on delivery', an 'end to hidden charges', a 'ban on default pre-ticked boxes', a 'major crackdown on pressure selling' and a 'new see through clause' for them (Kuneva 2008a). Doubtless such strong public commitments account for the fact that, despite strong internal conflict, the proposal was finally adopted with the unanimous support of all Commissioners in the College (AE 2008c).

Kuneva's bold and outwardly consumer-friendly promotion of the proposal highlights that the public reception of the proposal indeed mattered during drafting. The change from Márkos Kyprianoú, a Cypriot centrist, to Meglena Kuneva from a Bulgarian liberal party 'did not have much of an impact policy-wise because [...] the incoming Commissioner shared the vision of the previous one' (COM120:125). But having a Commissioner solely responsible for consumer policy upgraded the drafting official's efforts politically because 'the proposal became extremely important for her and [...] she was able to devote much time and media attention to what [they] do' (COM120:129, COM93:74). Backing diffuse societal interest by clear-cut political mandates within the Commission may thus support a nexus between public salience and specific policy choices.

That salience together with a general politicisation of EU affairs might substantially influence the Commission's position is also neatly underlined by the consumer rights drafting process: business and DG MARKT pressures to liberalise the area further with a mutual recognition clause were explicitly defied in the face of public protest about the services directive, which had also driven the Dutch and French referendum failures during 2005. This fundamental decision by the drafting SANCO officials ultimately resulted in responsiveness to consumer interests on a range of smaller issues.

As predicted by the model, the encompassing and, on average, interventionist position of DG SANCO nevertheless stirred internal conflict with DG MARKT and, to a lesser extent, also with DG ENTR. However, political negotiations in the final phase of drafting – when politicisation rose again – were nevertheless able to generate unanimous support. This indicates at least some common political interest across DGs, despite rifts on specific policy positions. Also, it points to the involvement of political and administrative hierarchies that – as expected in theory – occurred early and constantly throughout the process.

Yet the case also shows the limits of the theoretical argument. Taking approximately five years, the drafting process was not as rushed as the theoretical model would have led us to expect. Rather the opposite is true; particularly because SANCO officials knew that the initiative was politically sensitive, they engaged in extraordinary consultation efforts to have a majority of stakeholders included and to back their approach by as many facts as possible. Avoiding allegations of partisanship might actually prolong drafting in a politicised context.

More importantly, the comparative analysis of the legal text highlights that the Commission finally took an only mildly interventionist stance on the question of how to redistribute rights among consumers and traders. Given the immense levels of EU politicisation at the beginning and during the finalisation of the proposal, combined with the comparatively high and sustained salience of online trade, this outcome does not fully meet the theoretical predictions. There is too little empirical material to track whether interventionism was downscaled during drafting, in line with fading public attention to EU matters and specific contractual consumer issues. Nevertheless, the available evidence on this case indicates that SANCO's initial drive towards more interventionist positions was effectively constrained by political feasibility considerations. On individual provisions, SANCO tended to follow the Council majority, as signalled by the Green Paper consultation in 2007.

4.7 Passenger rights on bus, coach and maritime transport

In December 2008, the Commission adopted two additional passenger rights proposals covering transport by bus and coach, as well as by sea and inland waterways (Commission of the European Communities 2008h, 2008f). Both proposals were drafted in parallel by the same DG TREN unit that wrote the 2001 air passenger rights initiative discussed above (see Chapter 4.3 in this volume). Since this original passenger rights initiative ultimately became EU law in 2004, supranational passenger protection was quickly developed further. In several formal communications, DG TREN repeatedly announced that 'passenger rights will certainly be one of the priorities for Community action over the next few years', by extending them to other modes of transport (e.g. Commission of the European Communities 2004). Therefore, it was no surprise that the Commission proposed an instrument on rail passengers in 2004, which Council and Parliament accepted in October 2007.

Compared to air and rail transport, bus transport presented a more 'atomised' market with a relatively large number of enterprises serving low-income and geographically isolated customers (Commission of the European Communities 2008a: 4). The maritime transport sector was even smaller, but it played an important role in most member states, all of which had regions where boats or ferries were the only viable transport solution (Commission of the European Communities 2008f: 2–3). Both markets, in addition, were already formally liberalised in 1992, long before the rail and air transport sectors. Accordingly, a supranational passenger rights regime was a logical step in DG TREN's legislative programme, and was initiated with a formal communication on 'strengthening passenger rights within the European Union' (COM33:226, Commission of the European Communities 2005c).

Hence, the drafting period from February 2005 to December 2008 largely overlaps with the consumer rights initiative discussed earlier. The first year of drafting saw a severe politicisation of European matters mainly driven by the failed ratification of the Draft Constitution (cf. Figure 2.4). Levels remained much above average until mid-2006, declined afterwards, and turned round in early 2008. Moving up again, they stayed around the 1990–2010 mean from July 2008 until the proposal was adopted.

In contrast, the broad-based salience measure (see Figure 4.1) declined during 2006 to rather low levels, which remained unchanged until the end of the investigation period. Yet even these low levels involved hardly any attention to bus or maritime transport passenger rights. Also the more specific newspaper searches underline this finding.[30] Only two reports on bus transport safety could be found, but they made no reference to the rights of affected passengers (Pardellas 2005; *FAZ* 2008). Where passenger rights were mentioned at all, the respective reports mainly revolved around public transport strikes in the UK, France and Spain (e.g. Chayet 2008; *El País* 2008). Only in Germany were there reports on passenger rights, but they almost completely dealt with rail rather than with bus or maritime transport (*FAZ* 2005a; Schwenn 2005). Maritime passenger rights were in fact only mentioned once (Menéndez 2008). With this scarce press coverage, the issue area was hardly visible to the European public. So, while the degree of politicisation arguably maintained the hypothesised Commission's incentives to provide an interventionist proposal to the public – particularly at the beginning or the end of the process – the low salience levels should have signalled a low likelihood that the proposals would be a suitable vehicle to demonstrate the Commission's consumer protection efforts. Especially compared to the air passenger rights proposal, the theoretical framework thus predicts a much less interventionist Commission position.

Surprisingly, however, analysing the five sets of provisions, which, in one way or another, distribute rights among consumers (passengers) and producers (bus or maritime carriers), indicates a rather interventionist stance in the 2008 Commission proposals. The first of these sets covers contractual consumer rights and the information obligations of the carriers. Here the proposal posits that carriers may not discriminate against passengers according to their nationality or place of residence, and may not waive any of the remaining passenger rights referred to the proposal. In contrast, 'conditions that are more favourable to the passenger' are explicitly allowed. No European fall-back option existed in this regard, and – according to later consultation documents – these consumer-friendly rules were not explicitly regulated in most member states. Moreover, the carrier has a range of duties to actively inform the passenger about the rights generated by the proposal before and during service provision. Furthermore, operators have to provide a 'reasoned opinion' within twenty days of consumer complaints. Comparable but

---

30. The algorithm required that newspaper reports fulfil the following condition: (bus OR coach OR ferry) and (passenger* OR traveller* OR consumer*) AND (liabilit* OR delay* OR cancellation* OR complaint* OR protection) AND (keyword: transport). This was given for forty-six articles in *El País*, thirty-nine in the *Financial Times* and *Le Figaro*, as well as twenty-six in the *Frankfurter Allgemeine Zeitung*.

voluntary complaint handling systems were previously in place in Germany, Spain and the UK, while little to no regulation existed in a number of other member states (European Commission 2006b: 24). Further, for bus and coach transport, there was a regulation on information provision which, however, was less general than the duty proposed here (Commission of the European Communities 2008h: 3). Against these backdrops, the first set of proposal provisions offers increased protection for passengers.

A second set of key provisions concerns the liability of transport providers in the case of accidents. Since liability for maritime transport was already covered by other international agreements,[31] these rules concern only bus and coach transport. Here, carriers are generally liable for all accidents related to the operation of the bus or coach service. Apart from a compensation cap at €220,000 – the so-called non-contestable limit – the proposal defines a range of passenger 'damages'; for example, death and other injuries, that must always be compensated. A range of detailed payment requirements and explicit assistance measures for passengers or their family members are specified. Furthermore, the bus or coach operator is made explicitly liable for lost or damaged luggage. Before these proposed provisions, bus and coach passengers were not covered by any European liability regulation (European Commission 2006b: 8). Also in the few national liability regimes, the set of 'damages' covered by the rules, and the maximum monetary thresholds were much less encompassing (European Commission 2006b: 30–1). Thus, also this set of key provisions must be seen as a further step towards increased protection of the consumer side of the transport market.

This leads to the provisions for passenger rights in cases of cancellations or delays. Where services are cancelled or delayed by more than three hours, the passenger must be offered alternative transport services even if this involves another operator. Passengers who decline have the right of reimbursement of the ticket price. Beyond that, the passenger is entitled to additional compensation to the value of the ticket price if the carrier fully fails in providing alternatives. For maritime transport, compensation rights are carried even further: for delays below 120 minutes, the passenger is entitled to 25 per cent of the ticket price, and to 50 per cent for anything beyond this timeframe. In addition, passengers are to be offered meals and refreshments if a delay of more than sixty minutes occurs. Finally, if the delay makes overnight stays necessary, accommodation and transport to a hotel must be borne by the carrier. There is no detailed information on respective national rules, but, in the absence of an extant European law and along the fact that these rules clearly follow the highly interventionist air passenger rights initiative, this set of provisions also figures as a net gain for the consumer side.

A fourth set of relevant rules concerns the rights of passengers with reduced mobility. Carriers are forbidden to charge higher prices for these passengers. They may generally not be refused service unless law-based safety requirements or the

---

31. The respective 2002 protocol of the 1974 Athens convention was already being transposed into European law at the time the proposals under analysis were formulated (cf. European Commission 2005a: 7–9).

size or structure of the vehicle make embarkation impossible. If such a refusal occurs, however, the passenger is entitled to reimbursement and to a reasonable alternative service. Furthermore, the respective passengers can request assistance as regards embarkation, luggage loading, as well as movement by bus, ship, or at terminal and port, free of charge. At the European level, such binding rules were new while the extant national regimes seem to have varied between voluntary standards and binding regulations. The strictest regime could be found in the UK, which had a duty of wheelchair accessibility for buses in place (European Commission 2006b: 15). Again, the Commission position places itself more towards the more interventionist regimes.

The fifth and final set of provisions prescribes the enforcement of the envisaged passenger rights regime. It allows member states to exempt transport services provided under public service contracts, but only 'if such contracts ensure a comparable level of passenger rights'. However, states must generally assign authorities that ensure the enforcement of the proposed regulation, prepare yearly reports, and monitor public service contracts in this regard. In legal terms, national governments shall enact effective, proportionate and dissuasive penalties for carrier infringements of the proposed regulation. Since no European regulation existed before, and apparently not all member states had regulated passenger rights, these provisions also entail a positive net effect for the consumer side.

This short legal analysis leads to a clear summary of the proposal in the light of the dependent variable: all five relevant sets of provisions establish a balance of rights among passengers and carriers that benefits the former at the expense of the latter. In relative terms, the Commission position thus moves the regulatory status quo in the direction of an interventionist model of consumer policy. But how did this position come about despite the apparently low public salience of maritime and bus passenger rights?

Both proposals were drafted in the DG TREN unit that was also responsible for the air passenger rights proposal. In fact, one official involved in this earlier initiative was now heading the drafting team, which operated mainly through group discussions to reduce individual workloads (COM33:376, 390). The major impulses and regulatory options came from the administrative level (COM33:164, 176, 500, 516), but the drafting officials knew very well that they would have to 'win all the levels of the hierarchy' (COM33:420). This was particularly important for the cases at hand, as they experienced a leadership change during the process. The accession of Bulgaria and Romania led to reshuffles among Commissioners, among which Jacques Barrot from the French conservative Union pour une Mouvement Populaire (UMP) left the post of Transport Policy Commissioner. He was succeeded by Antonio Tajani, from the right-wing conservative Forza Italia, who had previously been an MEP.

At least in terms of process, this change in leadership was relevant. By the 'end of 2007 [...] there was not the political will to go through [...] and the political will came six months later' (COM33:616). The plans to extend the passenger rights regime found the strong support of the new Commissioner Tajani who, as an ex-MEP, was said to have a general preference for 'devising policies that are in the interest of the European citizen' (COM33:482). Note, in addition, that the renewed political will for increased passenger rights also coincided with a resurfacing politicisation of European integration from the beginning of 2008.

The drafting officials also tested the waters among possibly affected stakeholders in the European market by engaging in several external studies in 2005, which covered individual aspects of the proposal. The studies highlighted a lack of uniform rules, an absence of any framework of predefined solutions for cancellations and delays, and a lack of passenger information in the case of critical events, thus providing the basic justification to cover also these modes of transportation under European law (see also Commission of the European Communities 2008f: 6; 2008h: 6–7). Not only these studies, but also the formal Communication to the Council in February 2005 (Commission of the European Communities 2005c) made industry and consumer stakeholders aware that the proposals were in the pipeline. In this document, 'the Commission already identified which rights should be strengthened by Community action irrespective of the means of transport' (Commission of the European Communities 2008f: 2), so that stakeholders were informed early about what the drafting officials had in mind. Specific policy papers for bus and maritime transport were issued in 2005 and 2006, respectively, and were followed by stakeholder meetings at the Commission (Commission of the European Communities 2008h: 6; 2008f: 5).

All official consultation documents took the extant law in air transport as the benchmark, and thus started from a comparatively high level of interventionism. While this did not trigger any opposition from the member states (COM33:362), the consultation uncovered a clear division between carriers and consumer associations, because 'the industry makes their analysis on the basis of trends and […] the majority of cases […] whereas the consumer organisations tend to focus on individual cases' (COM33:320).[32]

DG TREN took a clear stance in this regard. After 'market opening for international services' in both transport modes, 'passenger rights should be put in place to make the passengers benefit, not only the industry side or the operators' (COM33:140). Linking market liberalisation with increased passenger rights offered an interesting twist: the DG argued that a common passenger rights regime with a high level of protection could derive from the principle of the free movement of persons in the internal market (Commission of the European Communities 2005c: 3).

This provided the legitimation, and the air passenger rights initiative offered a suitable template (COM33:154). The starting point was 'the European policy of air passenger rights and [the drafting officials] tried to fulfil five, six, seven criteria that should be coherent between all the proposals' (COM33:160). With this blueprint in the drawer, the 2005 drafting process only amounted to adapting to the peculiarities of the respective transport modes (COM33:141). Also the

---

32. See also the minutes of the stakeholder meeting in this regard: http://ec.europa.eu/transport/ road/consultations/doc/2005_10_14_passengers_bus_coach_stakeholders_minutes.pdf (accessed 13 April 2010).

2005 Communication provides tangible evidence for the influence of the 2001 air passenger rights initiative (Commission of the European Communities 2005c): Both in structure and in substance, it almost perfectly mirrors the 2001 proposal, and this pattern was reproduced in the consultation documents (cf. European Commission 2005a, 2006a).

Moreover, this regime was to cover 'all kinds of services: national, international and within the national, local, regional and long distance networks' (COM33:456) – a position that was particularly favoured by consumer associations (European Commission 2006b: 7). Transport operators opposed and highlighted a range of voluntary commitments in both affected sectors, or tried to exclude their specific niches (UITP 2005, 2006; EPTO 2009; European Commission 2006c: 6). Yet DG TREN stuck with its position even though 'a large majority of member states […] accept the idea of regulating international services only' (European Commission 2006b: 7).

Similar arguments and stakeholder reactions abounded with regard to the liability rules for bus transport. DG TREN officials simply argued that the existence of such rules in other sectors made their application to bus transport necessary as well (Commission of the European Communities 2008h: 3; cf. also European Commission 2005a: 6–7). Consumer associations of course welcomed the proposed liability system, but asked for unlimited liability for any consequential damage. TREN initially shared this position but, in the railway passenger rights proposal, this request for unlimited liability had been rejected by Council and Parliament so that the drafting officials were more cautious about the proposal at hand.[33] Apart from that, however, member states favoured a liability system that was comparable to the air and rail transport sectors (European Commission 2006b: 8–9), and only the industry side fiercely opposed (EPTO 2009), arguing that the rules create 'ruinous insurance costs and financial exposure' (ECTAA 2009).

The industry similarly defied the proposed regime on delays and cancellations (European Commission 2006b: 11–14; 2006c: 15–16). However, particularly here, the air passenger rights proposal served as an archetype (COM33:434, European Commission 2005a: 9–10), and, as all consumer associations as well as all member states welcomed the idea of a passenger rights regime modelled around the air transport benchmark, DG TREN ignored industry opposition also in this regard.

The rules on disabled passengers are also derived from extant law. In February 2005, TREN had initiated a regulation 'on the rights of persons with reduced mobility travelling by air', which enhanced the old air passenger rights proposal and provided for mandatory assistance at airports, together with quality standards for assistance from airports and air carriers. Likewise, the proposed regulation on international rail passengers' rights contains rules that are directly similar to the ones in the proposal. (European Commission 2005a: 5). The resulting rules are particularly costly for the industry. For water transport, the accompanying material

---

33. This is evident in the minutes of stakeholder meeting; see particularly p. 4: http://ec.europa.eu/transport/road/consultations/doc/2005_10_14_passengers_bus_coach_stakeholders_minutes.pdf (accessed 13 April 2010).

estimates yearly costs of €3.9 million for the sector. The bus and coach sector was expected to lose 2.2 per cent of its annual revenues from these rules (Commission of the European Communities 2008a: 6–8). In this light, strong opposition from the operators is not surprising (e.g. EPTO 2009). However, DG TREN could also count on the support of national governments (European Commission 2006b: 14–17; 2006c: 7).

Finally, the enforcement rules were also derived from the existing TREN *acquis*. The national authorities the proposal requires are 'very similar in terms of the scope of [their] activity, tasks and structure' to the ones that were set up for the regulations on passenger rights in air and rail transport (Commission of the European Communities 2008b: 7). So, 'Member States welcome[d] also a complaint handling system based on national bodies' (European Commission 2006c: 29), and TREN could overcome returning industry opposition once again by sticking with its self-made role model regulation (Commission of the European Communities 2008f: 8).

Hence, despite lacking public salience of the covered issues during drafting, the clear interventionism in both proposals can be explained in DG TREN's will to expand its own competences along the air passenger rights regime, which itself was driven by politicisation and issue salience (cf. Chapter 4.3). Following this regulatory benchmark enabled DG TREN to build a much more encompassing regime after its original task of liberalising the covered transport sectors had been largely achieved (cf. Karsten 2007). A competence-seeking logic locked in and expanded earlier policy choices towards widespread regulatory benefits for consumers. And, while this aim was pursued against consistent industry opposition, the constellation of member state interests permitted DG TREN's regulatory ambitions.

4.8 A comparative perspective on regulating producer-to-consumer transactions

Distilling the preceding process-tracing efforts yields some more general insights into the development of the Commission's regime on consumer rights in the internal market. In fact, this subfield of consumer policy appears much driven by the need to emancipate it from a perspective driven only by the cross-border competition of producers. With the exception of DG MARKT's sales promotion proposal, the policy formulation processes analysed here indicate a changing perspective on the internal market in Europe. The aggregate picture moves the consumer, as a specific market participant with specific needs and interests, to the fore. This was particularly evident in the cases drafted in the sectorally specialised DGs. Both DG INFSO in the universal service case and DG TREN in the passenger rights cases had largely fulfilled their mandates of liberalising the respective sectors and needed new justifications for a further development of their regulatory competences. Tackling their respective sector from a consumer angle was very much welcomed in this regard. Further regulation was justified by the argument that earlier liberalisation now demands protective regulation at the supranational level.

Likewise, emancipation from mere negative integration as the traditional approach to market-making was mirrored in the intense turf conflicts between DG SANCO and DG MARKT. Upholding the consumer's interests was vital in SANCO's large-scale initiatives as it provided the only way to delineate and to justify its own competences against the traditional MARKT approach of subjecting national consumer policy regimes to mutual recognition. From a comparative perspective, these findings highlight that interventionist policy positions can be particularly expected where they meet the organisational self-interest of actors within the European Commission.

Yet the comparative perspective also shows that organisational self-interest alone does not necessarily lead to such outcomes. SANCO's unfair commercial practices proposal, for example, still showed a rather liberal stance compared to the regulatory status quo ante. In contrast, in those cases where the contemporaneous public salience of the regulated issues met a generally politicised climate of European decision making, the outcomes were much more interventionist policy proposals. As predicted by the theoretical model, politicisation and issue salience seem to direct the incentives of internal Commission actors towards regulations that mainly serve diffuse public interests. The proposals on air passenger rights and on consumer credit especially are cases in point. Here, the respective lead DG made its public commitment to more interventionist provisions at points in time when high levels of politicisation met high salience of the regulated issues.

What is more, the case histories also reveal within-case variation where the Commission's policy position aligns with the ups and downs of politicisation during the multi-annual drafting processes. And, most notably, such co-variation was also observed where politicisation declined during drafting as in the unfair commercial practices cases, for example, where individual SANCO positions turned more liberal at the later stages. In this case, such variation occurred despite increasing salience levels. In contrast, the strongly liberal sales promotion proposal came in a highly politicised climate, but under markedly low salience levels. While alternative explanations cannot be completely refuted for this latter case, the comparative perspective underlines that only politicisation *and* salience together provide the necessary incentives for interventionist policies.

In all cases discussed so far, the respective variations in the Commission's choice among liberal and more interventionist approaches were directly translated into responsiveness to interest groups on either the consumer or the producer side. On the one hand, there were no instances where the producer side demanded higher standards as the 'trading up' theories of consumer protection would predict. In contrast, more interventionism usually meant more opposition by industry representatives. On the other hand, higher politicisation and salience levels let the drafting units take the suggestions of consumer representatives. This highlights that organised representation of diffuse interests is vital to the more interventionist policies of the Commission as it provides the drafting officials with easy access to relevant policy options. However, existing and more protective regulatory templates from the national level may also serve as a useful source of information, as the consumer credit proposal vividly underlines.

In combination, the case histories imply that politicisation and salience have generated a permissive climate for interventionist ideas that already lingered at the administrative level of the Commission DGs. Where politicisation and issue salience met, the political leaders jumped on the bandwagon and often risked conflicts with other Commission departments. However, although the more interventionist provisions often stirred such policy conflicts, they were nevertheless most easily asserted when the final political negotiations followed periods where the legitimacy of European decision making was more strongly contested by the public. Again, consumer rights as well as consumer credit are cases in point.

Nonetheless, despite the fact that agreement of the political leadership of a DG was necessary to go forward – particularly with more interventionist policy proposals – there has been little evidence in favour of explanations centred on Commissioner partisanship or nationality. On the one hand, Commissioners have been relevant mainly as regards the timing of the drafting processes, and they often served as internal gatekeepers. But no internal sources revealed instances where they proactively tried to change particular policy options. On the other hand, we observe strong variation in the dependent variable even where the political leadership remains unchanged. This is most obvious if the largely liberal proposal on unfair commercial practices is compared to the highly interventionist consumer credit case. Both, however, came under the responsibility of Commissioner Byrne. In contrast, we observe stability in the policy position despite changes, for example in the Commissioner, across the three passenger rights proposals in the sample.

Yet national interest has played an important role along another route in almost all cases scrutinised so far. All lead departments of the Commission had invested intensively in collecting information on national preferences during drafting. Process tracing most often revealed a pattern where the Commission position on individual key provisions was consistent with the majority of member states' responses to early consultation efforts. Although to a lesser extent, similar contact with the EP occurred before proposal adoption; the comparative perspective generates clear support for those explanations of position formation that hinge on their anticipated political feasibility.

In summary, this first policy chapter shows that politicisation in combination with contemporaneous issue salience directs the competence-seeking behaviour of Commission DGs towards policy positions that are most responsive to diffuse public interest. This mechanism plays out within a leeway that is largely defined by the anticipated majorities in the Council. Can this basic finding be replicated in the two other subfields of consumer policy as well?

Chapter Five

Product Safety

The overall aim remains to create growth and jobs in the Internal Market,
without loosening our environmental and consumer protection standards.

Günter Verheugen, Commissioner for Enterprise and Industry,
Speech to the European Parliament, Brussels, 14 September 2006

This chapter analyses how the proposed model of Commission position formation performs in the four sampled product safety initiatives. Commission proposals in this domain aim to regulate the risk of physical harm that consumers have to bear when using products bought in the internal market. While the cases discussed in the previous chapter addressed only the risk of economically disadvantageous market transactions, possible accidents or injuries touch upon consumers' well-being much more fundamentally. Accordingly, the public's baseline awareness of product safety issues should be higher.

Our public salience indicator developed in Chapter 3.6 is on average consistent with this assumption (Figure 5.1). While around 0.12 per cent of newspaper articles contain keywords referring to economic consumer rights (cf. Chapter Four), the investigation period mean for articles with product safety related keywords is 0.17 per cent. Yet this media-based measure also shows that the salience of product safety issues is much more volatile in the short term, whereas its long-term course between 1999 and 2008 was rather stationary. We witness peaks of publicly visible reporting, however, which are confined to rather brief periods. Compared to the smoother timeline on the salience of economic and contractual consumer risks, this observation initially highlights that the salience of product safety appears to be driven more by specific issues rather than by sustained public attention.

Furthermore, this volatility in the aggregate salience indicator makes the cross-case comparisons more ambiguous. While the proposed directive on general product safety (case 1) in March 2000 was adopted during a comparatively low level of salience, its late drafting stages experienced a single, confined peak of more than one standard deviation over the mean during late summer 1999. Similarly, the drafting of the proposal on the marketing of pyrotechnic products (case 10) coincides with a strong peak of public attention one month before its adoption in October 2005. For the proposed framework on the marketing of products (case 12), we can make a similar observation, while the six-month trend indicates that this drafting process was also accompanied by above average levels of issue salience across a longer period. Yet with the exception of the huge leap in August and September 2007, the salience of product safety declined again afterwards so

Figure 5.1:Public salience of the issue area 'product safety'

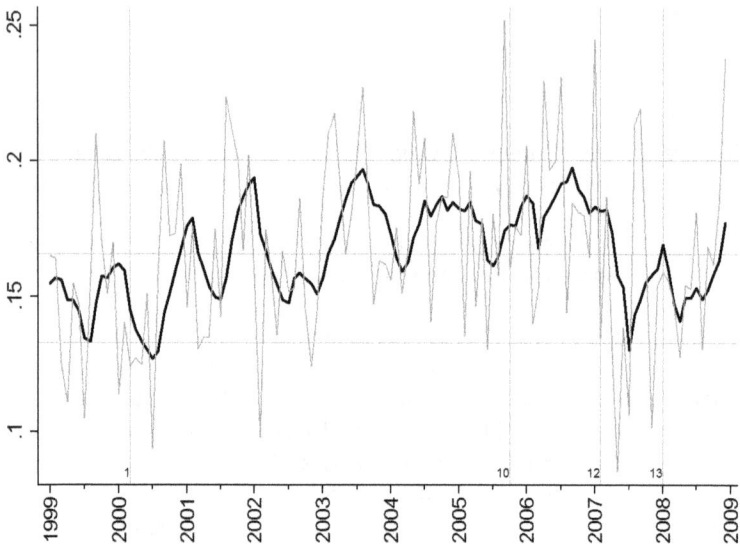

Note: Figures provide the average percentage share of newspaper articles with issue-area specific keyword combinations (see Chapter 3.6 and Appendix C in this volume for details). The grey curve presents monthly values while the bold curve indicates the six-month moving average. Horizontal lines indicate the investigation period mean +/–1 standard deviation. Vertical lines mark adoption months of sampled Commission proposals in the issue area.

that the proposal on toy safety (case 13) was adopted during a period of average salience.

Against the book's major theoretical model developed in Chapter Three, two expectations on the degree of Commission interventionism in product safety initiatives follow from these observations. First, the higher baseline salience of the issue area should make the Commission even more responsive to short-term variations in the politicisation of European integration. That product safety has a generally higher relevance for European citizens means that respective Commission proposals are more likely to impact their evaluations of European decision-making output more generally. During periods of high EU politicisation – when these overall citizen evaluations are immediately relevant for the Commission's future well-being – we would expect more interventionism for the benefit of consumers in product safety regulation. Second, the rather erratic salience indicator implies that the discussion of specific safety concerns – rather than the salience of the broader issue area – may moderate the effect of politicisation on the Commission's policy position. Thus a more detailed look at the substantial proposal contents and their actual prominence in public reporting is required if we want to know whether consumer interventionism is related to public attention.

However, before that, we need to outline which formal competences the Commission actually has to intervene in product markets for the sake of consumer safety. Chapter Four has shown that the regulation of economic consumer rights first had to be emancipated from competition policy. It developed mainly in the form of minimum harmonisation directives, and became more pressing only with increasingly direct contact between foreign traders and domestic consumers. In contrast, the dense and technically complex national product safety regimes have historically hampered market creation in Europe much more directly. Right at the onset of European integration, they presented the most important technical barriers for the free movement of goods in Europe – whether the foreign trader sold them directly to consumers or to local intermediaries only. The immense significance of trade for the political integration process made product regulation thus one of the first areas of regulatory market harmonisation.

In 1969, the Council had initiated a programme that foresaw the harmonisation of national rules on 'products of particular importance' in Article 100 of the Treaty of Rome (Falke and Joerges 2010: 248–53). This treaty base allowed Community action if national laws directly affected the establishment or functioning of a common market, but it required unanimity in the Council (Vos 1999: 24ff.). Under this 'traditional approach', a range of highly detailed European directives for specific products were drafted (ibid. 54ff.).

However, this approach to market creation was not viable for two reasons. First, the need to regulate each and every technical specification for particular products met scarce resources and a lack of expertise among the responsible Commission DGs. Second, the unanimity requirement led to cumbersome political negotiations in the Council which, in extreme cases, took more than ten years. In addition, the resulting directives contained many so-called optional harmonisation solutions, under which manufacturers had to comply with European rules only if they had planned to sell their product across borders. As a result, 'traditional approach' directives were often already outdated at the time of adoption, and only created highly fragmented product markets with a myriad of differing rules and specifications.

During the preparations for the Single European Act (SEA), the Commission and the Council therefore developed what became known as the 'new approach' to product regulation (cf. Vos 1999: 56–8: chapter 5; Pelkmans 1987). In an endeavour to arrive at technically sound and flexible norms for common European consumer product markets, the idea was to model supranational harmonisation on the distinction of general, legislatively established safety requirements on the one hand, and technical norms set by private standardisation bodies on the other. In most member states, outsourcing the technical implementation of legislative safety requirements to private bodies running on industry expertise was already common practice. Famous examples of privately driven standardisation bodies were the *Deutsches Institut for Normung* (DIN), the *Association française de normalisation* (AFNOR), or the *British Standards Institution* (BSI). And these national standardisation bodies in Europe were well prepared to extend their activities to the supranational level. Driven by the enormous market potential of comparable technical standards in Europe, they had set up the Committee for European Standardisation (known by its French abbreviation, CEN) by 1961 and the Committee for Electrotechnical standardisation (CENELEC) by 1973. These institutions were essentially made up of one representative from the national standardisation organisations and they developed voluntary technical standards (Vos 1999: 256–62).

The Commission – mainly driven by its DG for enterprise policy (DG XXIII and later ENTR) – made use of these structures. After the traditional approach had failed to create flourishing product markets, the Council was easily convinced that outsourcing technical product specifications to private bodies was a promising route. In 1984, it allowed the Commission to develop a regulatory technique that would rely more heavily on private standards. On this basis, the Commission immediately concluded a mutual agreement with CEN and CENELEC, whereby these bodies were entrusted with supranational standardisation if they guaranteed that their standards would satisfy product-specific and legislatively set safety requirements. Following these decisions, the White Paper on 'Completing the Internal Market' (also known as the 1992 programme) was published and transmitted to the Council in June 1985. It proposed to harmonise over 300 product categories using this new approach (Vos 1999: 268–71; Commission of the European Communities 1985: part two). Respective legislative acts were meant to fully replace any national rule on the covered product category, thus presenting a total harmonisation approach (Vos 1999: 44–5). The new approach, furthermore, was explicitly linked to Article 100a of the SEA, which meant that supranational product harmonisation no longer depended on Council unanimity but required only a qualified majority instead.

'New approach' directives followed a predefined regulatory technique, which determined the European regulation of product safety for years to come (cf. European Commission 2000). Each directive – drafted by the Commission and adopted by the Council – contains so-called 'essential safety requirements' for the product group in question. The directive then delegates the development of corresponding 'harmonised standards' to private bodies. The standards remain essentially voluntary for producers, but any product that complies is automatically presumed to conform to the European directive which, in turn, allows access to each and every national market in Europe. Member states then may only restrict trade through so-called 'safeguard clauses'; however they can no longer do so unilaterally but have to request a common decision of the Commission and a committee of all member state representatives. The 'new approach' thus presented a streamlined procedure, strongly limited national intervention policies and provided producers with clear standards that made their products immediately marketable all over Europe. Especially for the benefit of market surveillance authorities, but also for the consumer, the 'new approach' is visible in the famous CE marking (Conformité Européenne), which indicates compliance with the respective European directive.

In terms of decision-making efficiency, this regulatory innovation was a success (Vos 1999: 272–6). Average adoption times for respective directives dropped to eighteen months and a range of additional product markets were harmonised. However, its reliance on private, industry-driven bodies stirred concerns as to whether standardisation actually served consumer interests in product safety (Pelkmans 1987). The Commission, in response, actually lobbied and partially even financed the participation of consumer representatives in the standardisation committees from 1983 onwards, but they were only granted observer status (Vos 1999: 299).

Yet consumer interests in product regulation gained a more prominent role in the run-up to the 1992 Treaty of Maastricht. On the one hand, many products were not yet covered by the new approach and their trade was still hampered by national safety concerns. In fact, the European Court of Justice (ECJ) declared such national trade barriers legal where they served the aims of Article 36 in the Treaty which – among other matters – covered the protection of human health and safety. This exemption, however, was only seen as valid as long as no equivalent level of consumer protection was granted by a supranational regulation. On the other hand, the political discourse surrounding Maastricht also depreciated pure efficiency considerations and was oriented more towards the democratic deficit and the legitimacy of European decision making. Both this broader political climate and ECJ case law signalled that the supranational inroad to product safety regulation did not end with market creation using the 'new approach' (cf. Vos 1999: 58–81). And, as discussed in Chapter 3.2, the Maastricht Treaty indeed added 'a high level of health protection' and a 'contribution to the strengthening of consumer protection' to the official list of Community activities (Article 3).

In this context, the Commission initially aimed to strengthen consumer representation in product standardisation. While it was not able to force the standardisation bodies to grant voting rights to consumer associations – which would have endangered the efficiency gains of relying solely on industry expertise – the Commission empowered the consumer side by founding a single standing European Association for the Coordination of Consumer Representation in Standardisation (known by the French acronym, ANEC). Like BEUC, it is essentially made up of one representative from each national consumer organisation and is mainly financed by the EC budget (Vos 1999: 300–1).

Nevertheless, the increasing integration of product markets also enabled the Commission to push its legislative programme in the interest of consumers, initially by claiming the need for a truly European market surveillance system (Vos 1999: 280). Accordingly, the enterprise and industry DG of the Commission proposed the first version of the general product safety directive, which was adopted in 1992. Going beyond the product-specific safety requirements in individual 'new approach' directives, this horizontal instrument contained a general producer obligation to market only safe products, and included information exchange and coordination procedures if unsafe products were discovered in national markets (see also below).

In the subsequent years, the responsible Commission DG did not flesh this out further, but rather mainly pushed additional 'new approach' directives and revised existing ones. Yet as we have seen in Chapter 3.2, the Amsterdam Treaty of 1997 further enhanced the basic Community competences in the name of the consumer. Rather than only contributing to it, the Community was now committed to ensuring a high level of protection in all of its policies. Additionally, while all earlier product safety measures had been developed by the predecessors of DG ENTR, we have also seen above that the consumer policy service of the Commission consistently grew and turned into the fully fledged DG SANCO at the beginning of the investigation period in 1999.

In sum, European product safety regulation has been historically tied to the imperatives of market creation and efficiency rather than being motivated by enhancing the safety of European consumers. However, in this policy area attention to consumer concerns has been growing in parallel with the increasing politicisation of Community decision making throughout the 1990s. By the beginning of the investigation period in 1999, the Commission was thus equipped with both encompassing Treaty competences and an internal actor with the organisational incentives to push for more consumer protection. In this light, it is quite reasonable to ask whether the Commission's more recent product safety proposals indeed became more consumer-friendly and, if so, whether this can be traced to the short-term variation in general EU politicisation and the specific issue salience we have observed above.

5.1 Revision of the general product safety directive

The first product safety case in the sample, adopted on 29 March 2000, is highly revealing in this regard. It presents a revision of the 1992 general product safety directive (GPSD). Unlike its precursor, the proposal was not drawn up by the industry DG, but was written under the auspices of the only recently empowered DG SANCO, responsible for health and consumer protection. The DG had become responsible for managing the existing directive in 1998 and immediately started to discuss a potential review with low-level national experts (COM87:46).

During this period of policy formulation, the overall public politicisation of the EU exhibited quite some swings (cf. Chapter Two). One occurred in the first half of 1999 around the time of the resignation of the Santer Commission, the European parliamentary elections, a Berlin Council meeting on budgetary reforms and a trade dispute between France and the UK in the wake of the first BSE crisis. The politicisation indicator declines in the second half of 1999, but starts to rise again in the beginning of 2000. At this time, politicisation was driven mainly by the public visibility of political discussions on the envisaged Lisbon agenda, the Charter of Fundamental Rights and initial preparations for what was to become the Nice Treaty. Thus, the beginning and the finalisation of the legislative initiative under analysis here were, at least, accompanied by local peaks in the overall public politicisation of EU decision making.

What is more, this contestation addressed the performance and the future competences of the European Commission rather directly. First, the budgetary scandal leading to the sacking of the Santer Commission had only recently unveiled serious flaws in the Commission's decision making. Second, the recent BSE crisis had spurred widespread concerns as to whether particularly the Commission could ensure the safety of European citizens. And third, against a tight schedule for a further enlargement of the Union, it was clear that the next round of Treaty reforms was well under way. In the light of public criticism and upcoming institutional reforms, the Commission clearly had an incentive to serve widespread public interests and the revision of the GPSD was a promising vehicle in this regard.

While the public salience of product safety issues (Figure 5.1) remained below the long-term mean, the monthly values indicate two short but pronounced peaks in September and December 2000, that is, during the last half-year of policy formulation in the Commission. Digging deeper into the contents of the underlying newspaper data shows that these upsurges are directly related to the content of the Commission proposal under analysis here.[1] Besides some early hints of the Commissions plans at the beginning of 1999 (FAZ 1999b), a range of articles on counterfeit products and their safety risks was published during autumn and winter (e.g. Marsh 1999; Perez 1999; El País 1999b). And with an even stronger connection to the case at hand, newspapers reported intensively on a Commission prohibition of phthalates, a specific chemical softener in toys, shortly before Christmas in 1998 (e.g. Buckley 1999; El País 1999a). In fact, this particular issue made the Commission invoke a supranational decision on the basis of the existing GPSD (1992) for the very first time (FAZ 1999a).

The drafting officials themselves pointed out that the issue of softeners in baby toys created considerable public attention even before the revision of the directive started (COM87:63, 165). The carcinogenic effects of these softeners had become known during 1998, and the Commission was under public pressure for not banning these toys from the internal market. But despite a range of respective newspaper reports and Greenpeace protests in front of the Berlaymont building in Brussels, internal conflict between the industry and the consumer DG, as well as uncertainty about whether the existing directive allowed such a strong market intervention, forestalled a decision. The press accused the Commission of ducking down to industry demands, and linked this criticism to the Commission's mismanagement of consumer safety during the BSE crisis (e.g. Iskandar 1998a, 1998b; Tucker 1998). Against the high overall EU politicisation and the specific public pressure regarding product safety, the book's major theoretical model predicts a rather interventionist policy proposal in the case at hand. The systematic comparison of

---

1.   Given that this particular case covers product safety at the most general level, I refrained from designing a more specific issue salience search algorithm as in other cases. Rather, I relied solely on the search logic that has been constructed for the broader issue area along the lines given in Appendix C. The text of a relevant newspaper article had to contain 'product*' and 'safety' but not 'food*.' For the period 1 January 1999–29 March 2000, this resulted in 131 hits in Le Figaro, ninety-four in El País, eighty-three in the Frankfurter Allgemeine Zeitung and seventy-one in the Financial Times.

the Commission proposal with the predecessor directive (Directive 92/59/EEC) based on four sets of key provisions is indeed in line with this prediction.

First, the proposal widens the scope of the GPSD markedly. It now also includes products employed in consumer services (such as the scissors used by a coiffeur), which were explicitly excluded before. Like the existing directive, the revised GPSD is meant to apply only where no other specific Community safety regulation exists. However, under the old regime, this meant that no safety provisions beyond that of the product-specific legislation would govern the market (Centre de Droit de la Consommation 2000). The new proposal, in contrast, goes further. While the definition and the assessment of what constitutes a safe product is left to the more specific 'new approach' directives, the revised framework now explicitly covers all safety-related aspects that the more specific legislation leaves unregulated. In other words, the general rules in the GPSD also hold for all product groups regulated by the 'new approach' directives. In this way, the 2000 GPSD proposal also extends their level of protection and is explicitly designed as a 'safety net' for consumers (COM94:45).

Second, the proposal details a range of producer obligations that go beyond the regulatory status quo. Besides the general obligation to market only safe products, it makes explicit warnings or even product recalls mandatory in certain cases. Likewise, producers are required to cooperate with market surveillance authorities, which also entails new duties to store and pass on product-related information. The proposal furthermore declares that any information on product-related risks should be generally available to the public. It thus explicitly subordinates professional secrecy to the overarching aim of consumer protection. While the old directive urged member state authorities not to disclose any professional information, the new proposal turns this emphasis upside down by making public availability the general standard. And finally, while the proposal acknowledges private standardisation as a route to market access, it also explicitly allows member states to restrict trade in standardised products 'if it is dangerous to the health and safety of consumers' (Article 3.4). Compared to the 'new approach' technique, where such restrictions are tightly limited and come under a supranational and intergovernmental cross-check through the safeguard procedures (cf. above), this provision signals a much more consumer-oriented policy choice.

Third, the proposal widens the duties and responsibilities of member states in implementing the supranational product safety framework. Generally, member states are responsible for market surveillance and for counter-measures if unsafe products are discovered. National authorities are accountable to the Commission in this regard, and must now also notify their operational procedures. The proposal also deviates from the existing directive in that national authorities receive the powers necessary to enforce the newly established producer obligations. Also the requirement that procedures 'shall aim at guaranteeing a high level of consumer health and safety protection' (Commission of the European Communities 2000i: Article 9) is novel and results in the national duty to provide consumers with adequate information and access. Furthermore, the proposal reinforces and deepens the existing network of market surveillance authorities and their rapid information exchange system (RAPEX), which ensures that risks identified in one member state are immediately notified to the Commission and to contact points in other member states.

Finally, a fourth set of relevant provisions extends Community-level responses to the discovery of unsafe products. As in the extant directive, the Commission, together with a regulatory committee of member state representatives, may decide whether Community-level actions are necessary. However, extending the existing directive, product suspensions from the market have been increased from three months to one year and the proposal now additionally prohibits the export of products that have been recalled from European consumers. An even more important deviation from the regulatory status quo is the list of possible counter-measures, which has been particularly widened as regards the removal and destruction as well as the recall of dangerous products that are already marketed or even sold to consumers. Where producers and distributors enact 'insufficient' measures in this regard, the Community and individual member state authorities may now also intervene directly (Article 8).

Taken together, comparing the 2000 GPSD proposal to the existing 1992 directive indicates a clear move towards more consumer interventionism. This redistribution of rights from the producer to the consumer side comes about especially along a widened scope, making the instrument complementary to any existing product regulation in Europe, by more specific producer obligations and by increased duties and powers for market surveillance at national and European levels. But in how far can these individual policy choices be actually traced to the politicisation of the EU and public pressure on European product safety regulation?

Originally, DG SANCO started to analyse the product safety framework on the basis of a review clause in the existing directive (COM117:41). Drafting started as a 'bottom-up process' owing to the fact that the manifold overlaps with other European directives made the proposal 'very technical' (COM117:99). In fact, all involved SANCO officials were experts on the matter, not only because they managed the extant directive but also because they previously worked either on the national implementation of the old directive or in 'new approach' units of DG ENTR. Their manifold experience in product safety regulation guided the very first steps, and this freedom emerged not the least from the fact that SANCO's political hierarchy was absorbed by handling the BSE crisis at the time, which 'limited input from that side' (COM87:63).

The 1998 scandal on dangerous softeners in baby toys changed this. When the detrimental effect of phthalates became publicly known and the Commission failed to recall the affected products from the shop shelves, the extant directive's flaws and their political implications became obvious to the hierarchy of DG SANCO – an impulse that provided the administrative level with the political agreement to draft a stricter law (COM87:63, 165–79). Since neither the general public critique of the Commission nor the issue of chemically contaminated toys in the internal market declined throughout 1999, this basic political agreement was upheld even when the political responsibility was handed on from Commissioner Emma Bonino to David Byrne (COM87:97).

With this political backing, the drafting officials started to garner external opinion. This first happened in the implementing committee of the existing directive, where potential flaws were discussed with member state representatives (COM87:46). SANCO then financed a major academic study on the national transposition of the extant regime (Centre de Droit de la Consommation 2000). This study mainly delivers factual information, but it also comments on the application of national laws and on national preferences for a possible revision. Then, the DG SANCO officials published a discussion paper in summer 1999 after the toy scandal had led to the decision to actually re-regulate the area (DG XXIV of the European Commission 1999). This paper provided the structure for a meeting that followed shortly afterwards, for which the drafting officials proactively contacted consumer and trade union interests, retailers, employers and small and medium-sized enterprises, as well as networks of standardisation bodies and national market surveillance authorities (COM87:127 and 149, see also Commission of the European Communities 2000i: 18). Stakeholder contacts were limited to European umbrella organisations, while the input of individual companies was explicitly rejected during drafting (COM87:151). The officials saw the purpose of these consultation efforts as a way to gain a mix of factual expertise and strategic information on the political feasibility of particular positions. Stakeholder contacts provided a 'base for identifying the issues that needed to be looked after' while 'assuming that the positions that were given by the experts would then also be determining the political positions in the end' (COM87:51, 163).

In a similar vein, the drafting unit sought intense contact with the DG ENTR officials responsible for 'new approach' directives. This involved informal meetings right at the beginning of drafting, as well as almost daily contact by mail or phone, which was facilitated by the fact that one of the SANCO officials involved originally worked for DG ENTR (COM87:91; COM117:67, 75). However, in the light of clear overlap with the 'new approach', coordination was organisationally challenging from the start (COM24:414). Product safety has been traditionally a stronghold of DG ENTR, but the responsibility for certain product groups, including toys, switched back and forth between ENTR and SANCO during the 1990s (COM87:65, 79).

In this context, DG SANCO officials saw DG ENTR's legislation 'more oriented towards the free circulation and the harmonisation of technical rules and less towards really ensuring the safety of the products', while their proposal was intended to present 'the regulatory side more oriented towards protection' (COM117:49). This position served both to meet public criticism of Commission decision making in the light of unsafe toys and foods and the internal need to delineate their own competences against a historically grown product safety *acquis* controlled by DG ENTR. So while SANCO needed to find an alternative *raison d'être* beyond the mere removal of trade restrictions, the political context of publicly visible flaws in the safety framework provided the opportunity to establish such a new perspective in the Commission. In fact, SANCO's clear focus on consumer protection fed through to each individual key provision in the final proposal.

Regarding the scope, SANCO's ideal position was even more ambitious than the final legislative text. The officials originally also wanted to include services offered to consumers in line with one of the strongest demands of consumer associations (COM117:19, BEUC 2000d). However, early discussions in the implementing committee revealed that there was 'not much room for manoeuvre in the light of some bigger member states' interests' (COM87:147). Accordingly, the position was cut back to extending the directive's scope to products used in consumer services only. Still, this compromise position presents a large heap forward and was accordingly welcomed by consumer organisations, while leading to 'reservations' in the commercial sector (e.g. UNICE 2001). Being well aware of these outside preference patterns (Commission of the European Communities 2000i: 19), SANCO officials stuck to this position, which presented the most consumer-friendly solution within the leeway granted by the member states.

In contrast, the question of the proposal's relationship to other European laws was much more determined by internal discussions. For the drafting officials in DG SANCO, 'the most important aspect was not to which products but which type of provisions' the proposal should apply (COM117:53). From the start, they conceptualised the revision as a catch-all 'safety net', ensuring protection where extant and future legislation on product standardisation lacked this element (COM87:71). To the outside world, DG SANCO justified this with the commissioned legal study that emphasised the legal uncertainty in the relationship between specific legislation and the GPSD, thus recommending clarification (Centre de Droit de la Consommation 2000).

While this pleased member states, a much stronger debate unfolded within the Commission, particularly concerning DG ENTR (COM87:67). Interaction on this matter 'was not consensual' (COM87:103), but due to good informal working relations and the technicality of the issues involved, SANCO and ENTR officials were successful in 'trying not to go to cabinet level' (COM87:99). While the political leadership of DG ENTR preferred to leave the 'new approach' legislation completely untouched (COM72:118; COM87:123), experts at the service level tried to find 'workable solutions' that would legally reconcile the GPSD and the 'new approach' instruments 'without time delays and without major upheavals' (COM87:103). Apparently, the drafting officials and their ENTR counterparts avoided too much political conflict because its outcome was hard to predict in the political climate of 1999 and 2000, while political turf wars would have added to negative perceptions of the Commission's ability to ensure consumer safety. Against this background, DG SANCO was assertive in covering DG ENTR's legislation as well.

In return, the industry DG was appeased on the issue of standardisation. Originally SANCO was targeting at a uniform, Commission-driven standardisation procedure that was 'swift' and 'fair' but also 'firm' as regards the protection of consumer safety (COM87:59). As discussed above, however, ENTR's 'new approach' was driven essentially by privatised standardisation and came with a staged procedure of product testing that varied in strength as to the products and the risks involved.[2] Defending the presumably greater market efficiency of this system, DG ENTR argued strongly internally for sticking with this traditional role model of product standardisation. Given that ENTR's approach had previously been a defining feature of the internal market, their opposition was 'politically understandable' for the DG SANCO officials, who finally gave in on this issue in their endeavour not to raise the conflict potential of the proposal too much (COM87:99–103).

Yet on producer obligations in the cases where dangerous products were actually marketed, DG SANCO was much less flexible. Here, their ideal position mirrors the content of the final proposal and is informed by consumer information and recall duties that exist in other countries, most notably the US and Australia (cf. Commission of the European Communities 2000i: 9). Unsurprisingly, the producer side voiced serious doubts, considered the new duties as an administrative burden and wanted recalls to be explicitly considered as a measure of last resort (UEAPME 2000). SANCO officials discarded these industry arguments and found support from the consumer associations (BEUC 2000d) and in the legal study they had commissioned (Centre de Droit de la Consommation 2000). Both sources also explicitly recommend the information obligation and respective penalties in cases of non-compliance – a recommendation that is directly incorporated into the proposal. The officials acknowledge that this might be costly to the industry side, but have explicitly subordinated producer costs to the aim of consumer protection (Commission of the European Communities 2000i: 17).

On the enhanced producer obligations, the drafting officials also justified the tightened market-surveillance duties of member state authorities. Here, SANCO officials felt that the 'surprisingly low number of notifications [in the extant information system of the member states] did not really reflect the reality of dangerous products in the market' (COM87:59). In other words, just assuming that the regulatory status quo on this key provision was insufficient was enough to strive for 'more regulation' (COM87:127). Interest group responses can be easily predicted: Consumer representatives welcomed the approach (BEUC 2000d), while industry associations opposed it, even arguing that the GPSD 'is not needed', since sectoral legislation would provide sufficient control (COM87:127). Also DG ENTR opposed a tightened market-surveillance regime internally (COM87:71).

DG SANCO, however, held on to its original ideas and was even able to overcome industry opposition on this point. Contacting national federations, SANCO officials spread the view that strict but common market surveillance rules in Europe not only facilitated cross-border trade but also provided protection for the 'good guys on the markets' against 'free-riders'. Given that the toy softener scandal involved an industry under import competition, this perspective incrementally spilled over to European umbrella organisations, meaning that 'these federations are now united with the consumer associations in requesting

---

2. In the 'new approach', several modules of product certification are used, ranging from internal control by the manufacturer to individual unit verification by testing agencies (cf. Vos 1999: 277, as well as case 12 below).

member states in having a sufficient level of market surveillance' (COM87:127; COM117:19). This 'shift in stakeholder attitudes' is seen to have accounted for the surprisingly limited opposition on this provision during later negotiations in the Council (COM87:135).

Anticipated member state opposition also had to be overcome as regards the Community responses to unsafe products on the internal market. Again, the paralleling toy scandal helped. Both the failure to find a political agreement on banning the affected toys in 1998 and the inability to remove the already marketed products after an agreement was found in 1999 clearly lent support to SANCO's demand for stricter counter-measures with prolonged time periods vis-à-vis the Council (COM81:179).

With regard to banning exports of products that fail to meet the European safety standards, drafting officials mentioned cooperation on consumer issues especially with the US and China that was emerging at the time (COM87:63). Although information on this particular issue is scarce, it stands to reason that such an internal rule could be employed as a bargaining chip for external relations in consumer policy – it is politically easier to justify a high internal standard if it restricts not only importers but also domestic exporters. The member states provided the necessary leeway in this regard: The Louvain report suggests that '[m]ost countries are in favour of the idea of having the right to ban exports' (Centre de Droit de la Consommation 2000: part IV, p. 10). Again, SANCO faced a predictable pattern of stakeholder preferences on this last set of provisions: Generally, all parties favoured the simplification of the Community safety procedures, while industry demanded sticking with the shorter time frames and 'strongly opposed' the export ban on unsafe products (UNICE 2001; UEAPME 2000), which was welcomed by consumers (Commission of the European Communities 2000i: 19; AE 2000). Again, the final Commission position tended towards the consumer side also on this provision.

Taken together, both the outcome and the process of revising the GPSD in DG SANCO are consistent with the predictions of the major theoretical model analysed in this book. The overall level of EU politicisation particularly challenged the Commission's abilities in sound management and its ability to ensure public safety. Combined with the immediate public salience of a specific product safety issue, this resulted in a policy proposal that clearly demanded much more interventionism than the existing regime. The reconstruction of the policy formulation process highlights the influence of the 1998 toy scandal in particular. And also, the organisational self-interest of the only recently established DG SANCO and its need to delineate own competences from existing regulatory templates was an additionally necessary condition for this result.

The process perspective delivers a range of additional insights. As for most of the cases discussed in the previous chapter, DG SANCO tried to underline its approach by a broad consultation process, including academic studies, while its responsiveness on individual issues mainly favoured consumer demands. Also in line with the model, the drafting time of approximately two years is rather short, given the technical complexity that drafting officials repeatedly emphasised. Yet in evaluating the process hypotheses on the political level's involvement and on the degree of internal conflict, the case warrants a more fine-grained perspective.

Whereas SANCO's political leadership provided the agreement for more interventionist regulation when the issue area became salient in 1998, it was less involved in formulating regulatory details because political attention rested with food policy concerns in the wake of the BSE crisis (*see* also Chapter Six in this volume). This again highlights that Commissioners do not serve as internal agenda setters but rather as gatekeepers; yet it also highlights the possibility of issue competition. Parallel increases in the public salience of regulatory issues might distort the predictions of the model, which indicates an additional route for theoretical refinement.

This is also linked to the hypothesis on internal conflict. In the light of policy options that strongly differed on the continuum of market-making versus interventionist policies – ENTR's 'new approach' on the one hand and SANCO's protection focus on the other – the service level actively tried to keep the political level out of their search for a technically viable solution. Both sides had much to lose, in fact. DG ENTR saw challenges to the 'new approach' using privatised standardisation, while DG SANCO feared that the general product safety directive remained a weak policy instrument subordinated to ENTR's market-making policies. For both, however, it was clear that an open turf war would further undermine the contemporaneously challenged legitimacy of the Commission. A compromise was thus in the mutual interest of both DGs. This is essentially consistent with the expectation that a highly politicised context may mute internal conflicts (see Chapter 3.3 in this volume). But it also points out that underlying concerns do not play out only at the political level of the Commission DGs but also matter among the administrative echelons of Europe's central bureaucracy. In fact, Commissioner characteristics also did not add explanatory power in this particular case. The leadership of both DG ENTR and DG SANCO changed during the process without observable responses in the policy positions of these DGs.

In contrast, the case provides additional evidence for the constraining effects of the anticipated political feasibility of Commission positions in the Council. With regard to the scope provisions in particular, DG SANCO cut back its original ideas when early consultations revealed member state opposition to the inclusion of consumer services. But especially in this instance, the drafting officials chose the most interventionist solution – namely one that covered all products used in consumer services – that was possible in the light of the national preferences that the consultation efforts had revealed.

Unlike in most of the cases analysed earlier, the productionist view of position formation mattered in the GPSD revision. While we saw no specific producer demand for 'trading up' in the name of producers, SANCO was at least able to convince industry of the beneficial effects of a tighter market surveillance regime that would also provide protection for import-competing industries. And it must also be noted that increasing producer obligations on consumer information and recalls was justified with the higher standards that persisted among European trading partners such as the US.

So while internal conflict, the anticipation of member state interests and some trade considerations constrained SANCO's position formation process, the available evidence underlines that an explanation based on turf interests in combination with a politicised climate and a comparatively high issue salience matches the observed patterns of position formation quite well.

5.2 Pyrotechnic articles

The next product safety case in the sample – a proposal for a directive on marketing pyrotechnic articles adopted through written procedure on 11 October 2005 (Commission of the European Communities 2005d) – contrasts the drafting process for the GPSD in several dimensions. To start with, it was drafted by DG ENTR and firmly follows the 'new approach' of product harmonisation that focuses primarily on market efficiency.

In this regard, it is important to note that the product group of pyrotechnic articles covers not only fireworks, but also a range of products used in airbags, belt pre-tensioners, stage effects and distress flares, for example. While the market for fireworks was estimated at €1.4 billion annually, a much bigger turnover was achieved for such automotive components. Airbag igniters alone accounted for about €3.5 billion a year, while seat belt pre-tensioners generated another €2 billion (Commission of the European Communities 2005d: 6). Considering the size of these markets, much was to gain from harmonising the rules on this product group in Europe. In addition, a regulation also has implications for external trade. While the fireworks industry is based almost completely on Chinese imports, the EU-25 was a still net exporter for airbag igniters but imports from the Far East were clearly on the rise (Centre for European Policy Studies 2006: 9–10). So both overcoming internal trade restrictions and supporting European producers in import-competing sectors made a common European regulation attractive from a market point of view.

But most member states had restricted their trade on the basis of public safety exemptions granted by Article 28 TEU. For pyrotechnic articles, there was 'no mutual recognition of test results', so that cross-border trade required product approval in each and every member state (European Commission 2005c: 7). Clearly, producers could expect valuable efficiency gains from European harmonisation, and the European Committee for Standardisation (CEN) had already sought to develop 'a first series' of voluntarily harmonised standards (Commission of the European Communities 2005d: 2–3). Time was thus ripe for a supranationally driven market-making initiative, and officials in DG ENTR started to prepare the legislation under analysis in early 2002 (COM32:34).

In fact, a detailed comparison of the text of the proposal with the existing set of national provisions summarised in the impact assessment and the explanatory memorandum (European Commission 2005c; Commission of the European Communities 2005d) demonstrates primarily a market-making purpose, but also indicates some interventionist deviations from the 'new approach' pattern. Four sets of key provisions in the proposal illustrate this.

First, the proposal concerns the categorisation of pyrotechnic products according to the risks they entail. For fireworks, this ranges from category one, indicating products with low hazards that can be used indoors, to category four for products with high hazards that may be used only by professionals. For other pyrotechnic articles, a comparable three-step categorisation is prescribed. Such categorisation schemes existed in all member states, but differed in the way the exact lines were drawn. Most countries differentiated according the quantity of active substances while some did so depending on the location of use. The Commission proposal mixes these approaches which, however, simply mirrors the voluntary European standards that the industry-driven standardisation body had developed in the meantime (Commission of the European Communities 2005d: 2–3).

Second, the general obligations for pyrotechnic manufacturers in the proposal also simply follow a market harmonisation logic. As for any 'new approach' directive, these obligations are mainly codified in the essential safety requirements. Briefly summarised, the Commission's proposal requires pyrotechnic articles to be physically and chemically stable, to resist foreseeable handling and transportation as well as water and extreme temperatures, to come with safety features that prevent untimely or inadvertent ignition, and not to deteriorate over time (cf. Commission of the European Communities 2005a; 2005d: Article 4 and Annex I). In essence, these requirements are again broadly 'similar to those currently contained in the national legislation of most Member States' (European Commission 2005c: 9).

While the safety requirements thus hardly change the basic duties for manufacturers or importers, the actual distribution of risks among producers and consumers also hinges on the assessment of whether a specific product conforms to them. Here, the proposal requires producers to notify their products to a national authority, which then conducts a conformity assessment procedure detailed in Article 9 and Annex II of the proposal. In comparing this procedure to the regulatory status quo, the most important deviation is that the Commission proposal makes so-called type testing the rule. In short, the manufacturer must provide one product for assessment and guarantees that all other products conform to this type. If type assessment is positive, a CE mark can be affixed and all of the products conforming to the type can be marketed all over Europe. By contrast, some member states previously had a much more restrictive pre-market control in place. They required batch testing, meaning that one product from each production batch had to be assessed before it could be offered to consumers. In that sense, the Commission proposal takes a clearly liberalising position here.

This is different for a third set of provisions, which sets age limits for the use of pyrotechnic articles. For fireworks, the proposal prescribes twelve years for category one, sixteen years for category two and eighteen years for category three. Other pyrotechnic articles should not be made available to persons under eighteen, while all fireworks above category four and all pyrotechnic products above category two are limited to persons with specialist knowledge. Given that some member states had no age limits in place before (European Commission 2005c: 12), the net effect of these rules is a slightly increased level of consumer protection. What is more, the proposal explicitly allows member states to set higher age limits in the future if this can be justified in the interest of public health and safety. This contradicts the maximum harmonisation idea in the standard 'new approach' technique and also indicates more interventionism in the name of the consumer than a purely market-making consideration would lead us to expect.

Fourth and finally, the proposal regulates implementation obligations for member states, which by and large follow the 'new approach' template. Besides standard rules on the CE marking, market surveillance, rapid information exchange and safeguard procedures, any further restrictions on market access for pyrotechnic articles are forbidden. Given that the regulatory status quo consisted of twenty-five different approval and market-surveillance systems, these rules unburden the producer side in particular and ease market access significantly. But again, one important exemption is granted. National governments may still restrict the trade of category two and three fireworks to the general public on the grounds of public security or safety.

In summary, this overview of the proposal content reflects the 'new approach', in that the net effect of the proposed directive targets efficiency gains and liberalises market access. Producers have fewer duties both in quantitative and qualitative terms, particularly as regards pre-market control. Less control in terms of national checks and batch testing, however, also means that consumers bear more risk. The distribution of rights and risks among producers and consumers thus clearly tends to the *laissez-faire* end of the possible policy continuum. Yet we also observe some increased restrictions in terms of age and certain national exemptions. Relative to the standard 'new approach' models, these exemptions make the proposal somewhat more interventionist than one would expect. Can these individual choices be explained along the politicisation/salience logic scrutinised in this book?

During the drafting period of this particular proposal between 2002 and 2005, we do observe a rather high general politicisation of European integration. Around the initial failures of the draft constitution in 2003, the Eastern enlargement in May 2004, the EP elections in June and the conflictual replacement of the Commission in November 2004, the 2005 referenda and widespread protest against service liberalisation, all three component indicators developed in Chapter Two reach local modes. Together they account for the highest level of politicisation observed so far. Clearly, the legitimacy and the future of European decision making were widely contested in the final two years of the drafting period under analysis here. Thus, the Commission should have had the theorised incentives to serve widespread interests so as not to undermine public support for European unification.

However, there were small contemporaneous signals that the proposal under analysis would particularly matter in the public evaluation of supranational decision making. Our media-based measures for specific issue salience hardly indicate that risks of pyrotechnic articles were high on the public agenda at the time. While the broad indicator for the salience of product safety discussed above exhibits some local modes in 2003 and late 2004, the underlying newspaper reports deal with safety concerns on pharmaceutics, basketball shoes and car tyres, or they address safety aspects of the REACH regulation on chemical products.

Also a more precise search for the specific issues covered by the proposal at hand[3] does not produce a single report that directly deals with consumer health or safety risks associated with pyrotech. Against these results, the issue area hardly met any contemporaneous salience among the European public. From this perspective, the responsible Commission officials could be quite sure that the proposal at hand was flying way below the public radar. The theoretical model would thus lead us to expect it to be geared much more towards the Commission's traditional stakeholders, most notably the member states and producers interested in cross-border trade.

In fact, the drafting process almost looks like an ideal type of technocratic decision making at the supranational level. The basic idea of regulating pyrotechnic articles along the 'new approach' model dates back to the explosives directive from 1993 (Directive 93/15/EEC), which excluded pyrotech but mentioned a Commission plan to harmonise the area as well (Commission of the European Communities 2005d: 2). However, the enterprise and industry DG considered other products more important, and the resulting delay 'became increasingly embarrassing' (COM32:42). The reason that drafting finally set off in 2002 was repeated requests from individual member states as well DG ENTR's general drive to revive 'new approach' legislation (COM32:42; see also Chapter 5.3 below). The explosion at a fireworks company in Enschede in May 2000 also played a role, but only in that Dutch authorities started to lobby ENTR for a European solution (COM32:204).[4] In response, ENTR devoted one official from the chemicals unit to the proposal (COM32:34). The cabinet of Commissioner Liikanen was informed (COM32:264) but the major drive came from the day-to-day interactions of the DG ENTR officials with lower ranking representatives of national ministries in the implementing committee of the explosives directive (COM32:70, 124, 200).

Early preparations focused solely on fireworks and began with a questionnaire sent out to the national authorities (Commission of the European Communities 2005d: 2). Not all member states were happy about a supranational inroad into the area (ibid. 5). The UK in particular saw no need for supranational legislation as their non-participation in the Schengen accord allowed tight controls of fireworks influx at their national borders (COM32:148). Yet DG ENTR officials considered this to be a minority position in the Council because other member states were more vulnerable to faulty products that entered their markets on the basis of the

---

3. The search covered the period from 1 January 2002 to proposal adoption on 11 October 2005. A newspaper article had to fulfil the following condition in text or heading: 'safety AND (consumer* OR health*) AND (pyrotech* OR firework*)'. This was met by eight articles in the *Financial Times* and in *Le Figaro*, respectively, and five at a time in the *Frankfurter Allgemeine Zeitung* and in *El País*. Yet these hits did not address specific safety concerns, but use reference to fireworks in a metaphorical sense. The German *Frankfurter Allgemeine Zeitung* references an existing EU directive on definitions of pyrotechnic articles and ammunition, but this one reference makes no allusion to its safety dimension and uses it merely as an example for the types of regulation coming from Brussels (*FAZ* 2004b).

4. Note that the Netherlands at the time also held the chair of the CEN committee that drafted the voluntary standards on fireworks mentioned earlier.

general mutual recognition principle in the Treaties (COM32:148). Also, the UK did become 'more cooperative' after their representatives realised that they were largely alone with their general reluctance during working group meetings (COM32:144). Some concessions to member states were nevertheless necessary at this stage. For example, DG ENTR originally planned a regulation that would be less dependent on national transposition than the finally proposed directive. However, given that a range of governments wanted to stick to specific national deviations, these plans were given up early (COM32:124).

ENTR's planned regulation was also supported by DG SJ, and by ENTR's horizontal unit on the free movement of goods. Both argued for consistency with existing 'new approach' instruments, which had usually come as directives (COM32:96, 122). On the other hand, DG SANCO supported this view but from another perspective; they clearly favoured the maintenance of national deviations that provided more consumer protection (COM32:276). But apart from these issues, DG ENTR did not need additional – let alone political – negotiations with other Commission DGs (COM32:66, 68, 166).[5]

Three stakeholder meetings in September and December 2003 and March 2004 set the lines for other details in the proposal. The drafting officials clearly concentrated on 'representatives of the member states' who were asked 'to name their stakeholders' and to distribute the initial questionnaire to possibly relevant addressees. BEUC, the European consumer association, was informed but showed 'little interest' and did not participate in the meetings (COM32:64, cf. also European Commission 2005c: 11). But the industry became aware, and representatives from two associations – the European Pyrotechnics Association (EUFIAS) and the automotive components supplier industry (CLEPA) – answered the initial questionnaire and participated in the meetings (Commission of the European Communities 2005d: 5). Likewise, those technical experts from CEN who had been working earlier on voluntary industry standards took part (COM32:200).

These consultations widened DG ENTR's original ideas significantly, especially with regard to extending the scope beyond fireworks. This was demanded especially by automotive component manufacturers, and the Commission 'adapted its proposal accordingly' (Commission of the European Communities 2005d: 6). The decision to cover this much bigger market pushed the idea of reducing firework-related accidents to the background and rather emphasised market-making along the principle 'tested once, accepted everywhere' (COM32:44, European Commission 2005c: 6). The legal initiative was now mainly justified by a 'considerable reduction in costs as a single CE assessment of conformity will replace up to 25 parallel national approval procedures' (European Commission 2005c: 8). Consumer benefits of coordinated market surveillance came only second.

---

5. This is also confirmed by the internal CIS-documentation that was provided to the author under request GESTDEM 20104652. All consulted DGs agreed except DG ENV (environment) which request referencing a specific technical standard on chemicals which ENTR immediately wrote into the proposal.

This order of priorities affected other key provisions in the proposal. Regarding product categorisation and the definition of essential safety requirements, ENTR officials relied almost completely on the voluntary standards developed in the industry-driven CEN committee, which had been fixed at a 2003 meeting in Delft (Commission of the European Communities 2005d: 5; European Commission 2005c: 9). Given that most member states had already signalled their agreement on these industry standards (Commission of the European Communities 2005d: 2–3), officials could be quite sure that this particular choice would also fly in the Council.

Among member states and other stakeholders there were some arguments on the question whether importers of pyrotechnic articles could be held liable under the proposed directive. DG ENTR took the view that the import-competing nature of the fireworks market and increasing imports in the automotive sector placed importers 'on a key position in the value chain' (cf. Centre for European Policy Studies 2006: 10). So, if European consumers were to be protected against risks associated with imported products, a contact within the EU that could be held legally liable was seen as highly relevant. Beyond consumer protection, this position also favoured European producers as it balanced the duties of European and external producers.

The prescribed age limits were also contested among member state representatives and DG ENTR grudgingly allowed them to enact stricter limits in the future. Recognising differing levels of protection in Europe was ironically justified by the 'positive effect on the number of firework related accidents' (European Commission 2005c: 12), while it stood to reason that, on this issue too, gaining a Council majority was a primary consideration. Similarly, anticipating feasibility in the Council drove DG ENTR's position as regards national implementation duties. During stakeholder meetings, the maintenance of existing national restrictions on certain firework categories was a heatedly debated issue, and ENTR officials 'learned' about the national authorities' different approaches to fireworks (COM32:192, Commission of the European Communities 2005d: 6; also European Commission 2005c: 12). For ENTR's original idea to fully harmonise the respective rules, it was seen as 'highly unlikely that the Council could agree to such an approach because a number of Member States are very anxious to keep their national restrictions on certain types of fireworks' (European Commission 2005c: 10). Yet DG ENTR did not give in fully. Some member states even wanted to restrict trade in category one fireworks, which ENTR declined because otherwise the market-making effect of the common rule would have been fully undermined. Regarding all remaining national duties, the proposal content is simply transferred from the general 'new approach' model (cf. European Commission 2000).

So, how does this case fare in the light of the theoretical expectations developed in Chapter Three? Despite soaring politicisation levels during 2004 and 2005, the low levels of contemporaneous issue salience signalled that the regulatory initiative was not very likely to appear on the public radar. As expected against this combination of independent variables, the policy proposal is more oriented towards fostering market efficiency in the interests of the Commission's more traditional stakeholders. The process hypotheses also support this view. As expected for low-salience proposals, involvement of the Commission's political leaders was virtually absent and no significant intra-Commission conflict could be observed. In addition, the drafting DG was mainly responsive to producer demands, while consumer associations hardly participated at all. Also, the rather long drafting time of almost three years was ensured by frequent stakeholder consultations, as expected by the model. Yet the proposal contains some deviations in the direction of consumer interventionism which, however, can be explained without reference to public salience.

First, an explanation along the productionist view cannot be fully refuted in the pyrotechnic case. Direct evidence is hard to gather, but particularly the demands from producers of automotive components for an expanded scope and for the liability of importers are consistent with a perspective that explains DG ENTR's more interventionist choices on the basis of rising import competition in the relevant industry sector. Second, analysis of the legal text as well as insights on the early drafting process show that consumer protection concerns on fireworks were present, especially at the initial stages. Yet this was caused by the fact that existing national trade restrictions were justified along that line. In addition, the Dutch government, which had recently experienced a significant fireworks-related accident, lobbied for a more consistent regulatory framework at the European level. And third, some of the more interventionist choices in the proposal were driven by the anticipation of political feasibility in the Council. In summary, the bird's eye view on the drafting process allows theories anchored in member state interests appear to be the single most powerful factor in the case at hand.

5.3 Revised framework for the marketing of products

The next product safety case in the sample – a proposal for a decision on a common framework for the marketing of products adopted on 14 February 2007 (Commission of the European Communities 2007c) – was also drafted in DG ENTR. However, unlike the previous case, it does not regulate a specific product category, but presents a horizontal instrument that addresses European legislators themselves. The initiative is part of a broader overhaul of the 'new approach'.[6] It essentially provides a toolbox for future legislation that regulates market access for particular products only if such legislation enters into force. In that sense, however, the case is a sort of meta-regulation which, affects the distribution of rights and risks among producers and consumers in the long run.

The basic idea to reinforce the 'new approach' lingered in DG ENTR for quite some time. Clearly, DG SANCO's consumer-oriented emphasis in revising the GPSD had challenged the industry-focused approach to product regulation that DG ENTR was willing to defend. Only days after the Council and the Parliament

---

6. The proposed decision came together with one parallel directive that reinforced the mutual recognition principle and another one on accreditation and market surveillance (AE 2007a).

had accepted DG SANCO's general product safety regime in December 2001, the DG – in close cooperation with DG MARKT – published a consultation paper underlining that they considered the 'new approach' far from outdated (DG Enterprise 2001). The results of this consultation were summarised in a formal Communication to the Council, which then requested the Commission to review the 'new approach' (COM27:157, see also Commission of the European Communities 2007c). With this backing, the actual drafting process took off in early 2004 (COM27:49).

This endeavour nicely fitted the policy priorities of German Commissioner Verheugen, who took over political leadership of DG ENTR in November 2004. In line with President Barroso's focus on achieving the Lisbon goals, Verheugen seized ownership of the EU's 'better regulation' strategy. Starting off with a 2005 communication (Commission of the European Communities 2005b) as well as several newspaper interviews (e.g. Parker and Buck 2005; Parker 2005), the reduction of regulatory 'red tape' was stylised as a central instrument to achieve the growth and employment targets of the Lisbon agenda. In this vein, Verheugen published a 'strategic review' of the Commission's better regulation efforts, which emphasised simplification of legislation as a means of reducing 'administrative burdens' on business and industry in November 2006, only four months before the Commission tabled the decision under analysis here (Commission of the European Communities 2006a). These developments set the policy context for the drafting process and, also in more general terms, the drafting period between 2004 and 2007 presented stormy times.

The unusually high politicisation levels around the EU enlargement and the failed constitutional referenda in 2004 and 2005 were outlined earlier. Also the politicisation indicator in Chapter Two shows that the EU's legitimacy also remained contested for some time afterwards. Until spring 2006, the draft constitution kept moving the print media, and also public support for EU membership polarised more during this time. In summer 2006, the indicator fell below the long-term mean – a trend that was only paused by a minor plateau driven by the media visibility of intergovernmental preparations for the Lisbon Treaty. Our politicisation indicator thus suggests strong public challenges to the EU, especially during the first two years of policy formulation in the case at hand.

But was this matched with comparably high levels of issue salience? Except a minor slump during summer 2005, the moving average of the subfield's issue salience stayed above its mean levels between January 2004 and February 2007 (see above). In the preceding case study, we have already seen that the high levels during 2005 were driven mainly by concerns on specific products ranging from car tyres to sports shoes and chemical products. However, also in the first half of 2006, as well as one month before the decision under analysis was adopted, the indicator exhibits temporarily brief but pronounced deflections. Press reporting covered the safety of specific products – this time mainly pharmaceutical and skin care products – but unfortunately the indicator is distorted by a conflict on gas supplies between Russia and the EU. The newspaper search picked up quite a few reports on energy security, and is thus somewhat biased upwards here.

To arrive at a final judgement on issue salience, a more specific search is needed. Here I rely on basic terms circumscribing legislation of the 'new approach' type. Accordingly, an article is deemed relevant if it refers to safety concerns and deals with product certification, conformity assessment or the CE marking.[7] The results include some articles on the certification of technically innovative products (and the related economic performance of the companies selling them), and one article referring to the parliamentary adoption of the Commission proposal on pyrotechnic articles discussed earlier. However, rather than referring to the safety dimension of 'new approach', this report mainly covers the long drafting time contrasting with Verheugen's better regulation agenda (Stabenow 2006).

Given that the general product safety indicator hinged on specific products that were mostly not covered by 'new approach' law, and given that the essential features of the 'new approach' themselves did not make much news at the time, the issue salience related to the proposal under analysis must be considered intermediate at best. This bodes well with the perceptions of the Commission officials involved. They considered the proposal as far too complex for the public (COM27:243; COM94:37). While they clearly understood the public safety dimension in that the rules would have 'repercussions on the daily lives of us all', they were also well aware that it was based on concepts 'not everybody in the street has heard of' (COM72:282). Thus, the particular meta-regulation under analysis here was hardly relevant to contemporaneous public evaluation of overall EU decision making.

Given this combination of high politicisation on the one hand, but low contemporaneous issue salience on the other, the major theoretical model predicts that the Commission and particularly DG ENTR would stick with their classical, efficiency-based approach to product regulation in Europe. But did the legal text meet this expectation?

The meta-structure of the 'new approach' had not been legally codified before, but was mainly spelled out in the Commission's 1985 White Paper (Commission of the European Communities 1985: 17–23). One major implementing measure was Council Decision 93/465, which set the basic rules for CE marking and conformity assessments in technical harmonisation. This was complemented by several Council resolutions and by Directive 98/34 on supranational standardisation. There were more than twenty-five 'new approach' directives on specific products in place.[8] Besides, there was also SANCO's general product safety directive. Taken together, these diverse regulations present the regulatory status quo. Here I compare this scattered regulatory landscape with the proposed legal text

---

7. More specifically, the search covered the period from 1 January 2004 to 14 February 2007 and applied the following condition: (safety AND (product OR products) AND (certification OR 'conformity assessment' or 'CE mark') NOT (food* OR shares OR stocks). This resulted in twenty-nine hits in *El País*, twenty-four in *Le Figaro*, five in the *Financial Times* and only one in the *Frankfurter Allgemeine Zeitung*.

8. For a full list of 'new approach' directives including the links to the original legal texts, see: http://www.newapproach.org/Directives/DirectiveList.asp (accessed 23 September 2011).

of seventy-six pages, thirty-nine articles, and two annexes (Commission of the European Communities 2007c) along six distinct sets of provisions that matter to the distribution of rights and risks among producers and consumers.

The first of these sets circumscribes the scope of the instrument. Article 1 clarifies that the proposal is meant to determine all Community legislation harmonising the conditions for the marketing of products and serves as a blueprint in this regard. All product-related harmonisation 'shall have recourse to the general principles set out in this Decision', and future acts may deviate only 'if that is appropriate on account of the specificities of the sector concerned, especially if comprehensive legal systems are already in place' (Article 2). Hence, not only food and feed but also human blood and blood cells, human and veterinary medicinal products and tobacco products are explicitly excluded. Note, however, that no reference is made to SANCO's GPSD or consumer products more generally.

In comparison, the extant horizontal Council Decision 93/465 neither defines a scope nor excludes particular product groups, but only refers to all 'technical harmonisation directives'. The proposed rules thus present a clarification and simplification of future legislative work, which can be seen as a net extension of the 'new approach'. While the extant Council decision allowed some interpretation as to exactly what was covered by technical harmonisation, the new proposal basically targets all products apart from the now neatly defined exemptions.

The second set of relevant key provisions sets the general principles of the legal framework (Articles 2–5). Most importantly, Community intervention as regards the 'level of protection of public interests' should be limited to defining 'essential requirements' expressed 'in terms of the results to be achieved'. Where the Commission sets essential safety requirements, this should be done with reference to already harmonised standards. In any case, the so-called presumption of conformity applies: a product complying with a technical standard is deemed to comply with the directive's safety requirements. Beyond that, Article 3, in conjunction with a forty-page annex, defines a broad range of different 'modules' for assessing conformity. They basically vary in how tightly the manufacturer is supervised in design and production.[9] In deciding what module applies to a specific product, the proposed decision commits the Commission to the least burdensome method for producers.

These rules merely codify the 'new approach' principles that have guided the internal market since 1985 (cf. Commission of the European Communities 1985: especially p. 19; see also European Commission 2000). As such, it is not really a deviation from the status quo, but it promotes these principles to legal rank. If one additionally considers that this decision is thought to bind future legislators, this set of provisions presents a move towards a more market-oriented position on European product safety policy.

---

9. For example, one of the weakest procedures involves internal production control by the manufacturers with some random ex-post checks, then covers increasingly strict type approval procedures, and ends with certified QS systems under the surveillance of third-party bodies.

The third set of provisions (Articles 7–12) contains obligations on economic operators. This refers to their general responsibility for complying with essential safety requirements, corresponding technical documentation and labelling, affixing of the CE mark and keeping a complaints registry. Furthermore, manufacturers who believe that their product does not comply with the essential requirements must immediately enact corrective measures such as changing the product as well as withdrawing or even recalling it. Such measures must be reported to national authorities, who may also request information regarding the conformity of a product from the manufacturer. Especially this latter obligation can be transferred to an 'authorised representative' of the manufacturer, which is particularly relevant for imported products. In general, importers and distributors marketing a product under their name or trademark bear the full set of manufacturer obligations outlined above.

Compared to the regulatory status quo, Council Decision 93/465 does not regulate operator obligations in such great detail. However, some of the obligations were also already present in individual 'new approach' directives, for example on pyrotech (above) and toys (below). Also, the obligations proposed here closely resemble the respective provisions in the 2001 GPSD (cf. Chapter 5.1). In sum, this set of provisions essentially codifies the European regulatory status quo.

A fourth set of key provisions sets rules for the conformity assessment procedures, and especially those 'notified bodies' performing them. This abstract concept covers several types of actors; public authorities, public–private partnerships, private laboratories or institutes or even the manufacturer itself may take up this role. For each future directive, member states must notify the respective body to the Commission. Besides a range of operational and informational obligations, these notified bodies must be independent of the product assessed, must be free of possible conflicts of interest (among others this also prohibits consultancy on conformity assessment procedures), and must verify their product-specific competence by accreditation. They can require manufacturers to ensure compliance or otherwise withdraw the right to market the product. But as a general rule, the decision also prescribes that their assessment procedures have to be proportionate, avoiding 'undue burdens' on economic operators.

The relevant fall-back option for these rules is Annex I.A of Council Decision 93/465, which also demands the avoidance of undue burdens for operators but does not contain such detailed rules on the independence, impartiality and technical ability of notified bodies. These rules, however, were part of most 'new approach' directives and so does not present a significant step towards more or less consumer interventionism.

The rights and obligations of member states are regulated in a fifth set of key provisions. If a member state doubts that a harmonised standard satisfies the safety requirements of a specific directive, it may initiate a committee procedure under which the Commission and representatives from all member states decide on it together. In addition, a specific national authority inspects and monitors the compliance of the conformity assessment bodies and notifies them to the Commission. Generally, this body is also sworn to impartiality by detailed rules and has to share all of its product-related information with the Commission and the notifying bodies of other member states.

In comparative perspective, no possibility of making formal objections to harmonised standards could be found in the existing horizontal legislation, but comparable rules have been part of each and every vertical 'new approach' directive at least since 1998. As such, the choice made in the proposal at hand again closely resembles the status quo. The duty of notifying the relevant conformity assessment institutions was also part of the existing framework. Detailed rules on the impartiality of notifying bodies are new, in contrast, but impartiality was arguably already a standard for governmental agencies without this particular Commission proposal.

A sixth and final set of relevant provisions specifies the so-called safeguard clauses for future product safety directives. If national market surveillance suspects that a particular product does not comply with the applicable directive or presents other risks to health and safety,[10] it can initiate an evaluation in conjunction with the economic operator and, if necessary, might force the operator to bring the product into line or to withdraw, or even recall, the product. Such counter-measures must be enacted Community-wide, and the Commission as well as all other member states must be informed immediately. Article 36 specifies the corresponding Community response in more detail. Basically, it is the Commission that judges whether a national safeguard measure is unlawful. Affected producers or other member states may issue complaints in this regard. If the Commission deems the measure justified, all member states must enact it; if it does not, the initiating member state must withdraw the trade restriction. This clearly supranationalises safety surveillance in Europe, and also offers producers an additional route for challenging national market interventions.

For most of the preceding rules, the extant horizontal decision mentions safeguard clauses but does not prescribe details. Yet again, all existing 'new approach' directives contain safeguard clauses that more or less follow the rules outlined here. Also on this last set, the Commission's 2007 position does not present a politically meaningful deviation from the regulatory status quo – other than also prescribing these rules for all future product-specific legislation.

In summary, the baseline conclusion resulting from the analysis of this legally complex framework is rather clear. On the dependent variable capturing relative changes towards either the *laissez-faire* or the interventionist end of the policy spectrum, the 2007 proposal for a common framework basically reinforces the status quo. But by raising 'new approach' principles to legal status, the DG ENTR proposal aims to attach emphasis to the free circulation of goods, which has prevailed in the area since the 1985 White Paper, for future decision making. How did this decidedly liberal position come about?

The major impulse for the proposal came from the service level and emerged from the implementation of the extant 'new approach' directives and the

---

10. The respective procedures of market surveillance agencies are covered by a specific regulation that was proposed in parallel to the decision analysed here.

respective contact among ENTR officials, national civil servants and affected enterprises (COM27:175). The particular issues and problems, and thus the demand for a legal review, have slowly grown over time in this triangle of the major implementing parties (COM72:108). Based on a weekly meeting with all units managing the twenty-five extant 'new approach' directives (COM27:41), a team of five officials in DG ENTR's horizontal unit worked on the 'new approach' overhaul (COM27:233).

Only during the endgame did Commissioner Verheugen become increasingly involved, and push for a timely adoption of the proposal. This was ascribed to his better regulation agenda, and was also due to obligations emerging from the official Commission work programme (COM27:219). However, it must also be noted that the German government was 'very keen to make progress with this dossier', and held the Council presidency in early 2007 when the proposal was adopted (AE 2007b). As a strongly export-oriented country, it is thus possible that Germany pressured 'its' Commissioner on this particular proposal.

But what did ENTR pursue with the proposal? When asked directly, the involved officials identified 'simplification and congruence' as the most basic aims (COM72:78). The decision was designed to 'ensure as much coherence in future sectoral legislation as can be politically and technically possible' (Commission of the European Communities 2007c: 5). It aims to remove 'diverging interpretations, […] incompatibilities, legal uncertainty, unnecessary duplication and confusion', which all have a 'negative effect on industry' (Commission of the European Communities 2007a: 7). In their day-to-day interactions with ENTR officials, economic operators had criticised the existing rules as 'burdensome or for being uncertain or inconsistent' (Commission of the European Communities 2007a: 2). Having seen the legislative plans, the retail industry in particular unreservedly welcomed DG ENTR's overall approach as 'part of the more general commitment of the Commission in terms of better regulation' (EuroCommerce 2007: 2).

However, unlike DG SANCO's GPSD, ENTR's will to simplify technical harmonisation did not go as far to prescribe general product requirements. The sector-specific approach of product regulation was not questioned. While the decision is actually thought of as 'a toolbox which should ensure coherence, it should not force solutions that may be inappropriate' (Commission of the European Communities 2007a: 7). DG ENTR's position was geared to the original purpose of the 'new approach', namely to make trade in technically complex products more efficient. Rather than reforming the approach, it was more about 'deepening' existing provisions (COM27:69). This included functional adaptations necessary after the twenty-year history of the regulatory model, but it disregarded the parallel developments in consumer product safety that had been especially pushed by DG SANCO in the meantime (COM94:35).

Of course, ENTR officials were well aware that the whole idea of technical harmonisation related to the 'safety level' of consumers (COM27:271). However, this was not considered as a matter of legislative principle, but rather as a question of enforcement, or was framed as an issue of market surveillance (COM72:108). But since SANCO's GPSD had established the need for both a legislative consumer focus and a tight surveillance regime, this position was asking for internal trouble. From SANCO's perspective, the 'new approach' was seen actually seen as 'old legislation' which did not take into account 'the whole new structure of consumer policy' (COM94:37). SANCO, in response, demanded nothing less than that 'products falling under the GPSD should stay under the GPSD' (COM26:112). This pledge to fully exclude consumer products from the scope of the 'new approach' was not acceptable to DG ENTR (COM72:162).

The discussions on this fundamental point were 'a long, long story' and involved 'several rounds and layers of consultations' within the Commission (COM26:124). They began early at the service level (COM26:136) but SANCO officials felt that 'the proposal was already packaged at the level of DG Enterprise' (COM26:128). SANCO's demands for further exemptions fell on deaf ears. After SANCO had unsuccessfully made 'the same point all the time', this dissent finally resulted in a formal *avis negatif* during the ISC, which drew the political Cabinets of both DGs into policy formulation (COM26:162).[11] The Cabinets of Commissioners Verheugen (ENTR) and Kuneva (SANCO) met 'four or five times' (COM94:123). Indeed, the proposals kept cooking for about five months after the administrative ISC, and one Cabinet member of Commissioner Verheugen worked almost full-time on the package during this period (COM72:196). But also the administrative level took part in the 'bilateral meetings' with the Kuneva Cabinet. These meetings also involved officials from DG SJ who teased out legally viable solutions for aligning the GPSD framework with the 'new approach' (COM72:214).

Unlike the service level, the process for political echelons appears to have been much more oriented towards a solution. From the perspective of involved cabinet members, the administrative level had identified too strongly with their own legal instruments, because each side feared to become obsolete if the other side won. There was some regret that the political level had not been involved earlier because, from their perspective, policy making is not 'mathematics' but requires 'a political decision' (COM72:164, 394; COM94:85, 99). Nevertheless, the final outcome also does not indicate a clear-cut decision among the differing approaches, but suggests intense political haggling between the DGs involved.

Initially, the general obligations of economic operators are similar to the GPSD framework, making the future 'new approach' system at least more compatible with SANCO's framework directive. Beyond that, issue linkage with ENTR's parallel market-surveillance proposal has taken place (Commission of the European Communities 2007d: especially Articles 13 and 20). On the one hand, this proposal excludes all consumer goods from ENTR's market-surveillance measures and limits them to industrial products. On the other hand, the proposed regulation states that all information exchange measures under ENTR's new market-surveillance regime should use the RAPEX infrastructure, which is handled by DG SANCO under the GPSD. Therefore, while SANCO could not avoid some consumer products also being regulated under the 'new approach' in the future,

---

11. Note that this conflict on the principles of product regulation unfolded even more strongly on the parallel proposal on market surveillance that was also part of the package.

they ensured control of market surveillance and even gained implementing powers regarding the surveillance of industrial products (COM27:207). Beyond that, SANCO had been successful in ensuring that its own body of food and feed law was excluded from the 'new approach' for good (COM26:180).

These concessions were 'a matter of negotiation'. Internal observers mentioned that Commissioner Verheugen was particularly pushing for a solution as 'the pressure to bring something out was more important than finding the factually correct solution' (COM27:207). The technical complexity of the issues made concessions for DG ENTR somewhat easier, as the detailed compromise solution 'hardly play[ed] a role in the political display' (COM72:194).

Apart from these conflicts on principle, some of the more detailed policy positions can be traced directly to stakeholder demands. In fact, external consultation efforts on the overall overhaul project were immense. Altogether, DG ENTR prepared twenty working documents on individual issues in 2005, and circulated them widely among stakeholders, leading to about 250 individual responses. This was complemented by an online consultation resulting in another 280 answers.[12] In addition, ENTR drew up 'fact-finding questionnaires' for affected industries, national authorities, certification and assessment businesses and consumers. Beyond that, 800 face-to-face interviews with representatives from small and medium enterprises were carried out (COM27:273, Commission of the European Communities 2007c: 3–4).

In these consultation efforts, the national officials were seen as particularly 'pivotal' (COM27:273). But set against the aim to simplify the existing framework, officials primarily sought legal facts rather than strategic information from the member states. The 2003 Council resolution granted sufficient room for manoeuvre in strategic terms and, given that product standardisation was a 'highly technical area', further political interference from the Council was not feared (COM27:229).

Consumer associations, in contrast, did not exert much influence on the proposal. They criticised privatised standardisation because, in the respective committees, 'industry is normally in the majority [...] which does not ensure balanced decision making'. Their demand was a 'fundamental review of the New Approach' in which essential requirements would be translated into technical specifications via a member state committee complemented by a balanced stakeholder group. Only this approach would be technically flexible, and represent 'public interests' sufficiently (ANEC 2006: 1–2). Obviously, DG ENTR did not give in, as the removal of technical specifications from the political sphere was a 'basic principle' of the 'new approach' that was never intended to be changed (COM27:77; COM72:110) – a position that was strongly backed by business stakeholders of course (fn. 67).

12. A closer look at the response charts of this survey indicates that the overarching majority of responses came from Germany (seventy-three), followed by France (sixty) and the UK (twenty-five). Although removed from ENTR's official website, the consultation documentation is still available via the web archive: http://web.archive.org/web/20080206102518/http://ec.europa.eu/enterprise/newapproach/review_en.htm (accessed 9 August 2010).

Another issue discussed was the CE mark itself. ENTR considered the mark first and foremost as a symbol directed at market surveillance authorities and not consumers (COM27:106, COM26:112, Commission of the European Communities 2007a: 6). Since the requirements between the different product-specific directives differed, the CE mark had in fact a variable meaning. Depending on the conformity assessment module chosen, it meant that the product has been tested in one way or another in some product groups, but in other cases it amounted to nothing more than a manufacturers' declaration (Enterprise and Industry Directorate-General 2005c: 1–2). Thus, given that the 'new approach' left the exact, product-specific understanding of safety to the market, the CE marking was hardly seen as a good means of communicating product safety to the consumer.

Consumer representatives – as well as DG SANCO – nevertheless argued that 'consumers misread the CE marking' (COM27:106, ANEC 2006: 6). If it was really addressed only surveillance authorities, they argued, it would be sufficient to keep it in the technical files and not on the product itself. DG ENTR did not give in, but argued that the CE mark has to be visible as 'a real asset in international trade [that] strengthens the competitive position of European manufacturers' (Commission of the European Communities 2007a). This was an achievement of more than twenty years of ENTR policy, which has made the CE mark 'the image of the new approach' not only for operators but also for 'governments elsewhere looking at our legislative model'. It was the 'symbol of business-friendly legislation which at the same time ensures a high level of protection for consumers' (Enterprise and Industry Directorate-General 2005c: 2). As a minor concession, they announced a consumer education campaign on the CE mark in the future (Commission of the European Communities 2007a).

Consumer representatives also contested the rules on the independence of conformity assessment bodies. They would have preferred to prohibit in-house conformity assessment completely (ANEC 2006:5–6). Yet again, ENTR stuck to the product-specific point of view. Conformity assessors must be independent of the design and manufacturing process, but not necessarily from the manufacturer itself (Enterprise and Industry Directorate-General 2005a: 5–6). Likewise, ENTR decided against a deviation from the traditional 'new approach' as regards the control of conformity assessment bodies. At the beginning of drafting, 'one possibility was to centralise the whole notification system through the creation of an Agency at the EU level to centralise competence assessment, notification, and monitoring'. However, as this would be 'too costly' and 'too burdensome', ENTR stuck with the traditionally decentralised approach (Commission of the European Communities 2007a: 4). This, however, provided producers with forum-shopping options in conformity assessment.

Lastly, even the safeguarding procedures were slightly liberalised. National governments had complained that the safeguarding procedures were 'lengthy and difficult to apply in practice' (DG Enterprise 2001: 18). Most of the directives foresaw that any national measure constraining the free movement of goods under one of the directives would automatically result in a Community procedure. This, however, was obstructed by the 'lack of appropriate resources and technical expertise' on part of the Commission, and it was thus decided to trigger the procedure only if another member state, the Commission itself, or an economic operator objected to the national decision in question (ibid. 22). The other rules on immediate information disclosure under a safeguard procedure were partly transferred from the GPSD and its RAPEX system (cf. Enterprise and Industry Directorate-General 2005d: 3–5). This framework, however, also includes the requirement for other member states to react immediately. Although consumer associations would have liked to see this obligation in the proposal at hand (ANEC 2006: 7–8), ENTR did not go that far, underlining its pro-business position again.

In sum, the policy formulation process of DG ENTR was strongly influenced by the will not to change the fundamentals of the extant 'new approach', which was seen as a market-making success story and it also neatly fitted the better regulation agenda of Commissioner Verheugen. ENTR kept the basic principles fixed, updating only details. Considered against lacking public salience and the high level of technical complexity, the officials had little concern that their policy position would affect the evaluation of European integration among the wider public. Accordingly, the responsiveness to outside interests mirrors the traditional rank order of stakeholders under the 'new approach': first come the officials implementing it; then come the producers as the most directly affected stakeholders, and also as the most integral supporters of the system; and only lastly come consumer interests. DG ENTR left the basic principles of a liberal, efficiency-based approach to product safety untouched. While major deviations such as a centralisation of the notification system were contemplated during the high politicisation phases at the beginning of drafting, the final output, which was heralded by lower politicisation and absent salience, simply re-codified the 'new approach' that was developed in 1985.

Of course, some loopholes in the surveillance of the extant framework were closed. But as we have observed, these minor improvements were driven mainly by DG SANCO, which stepped up to defend its own framework under the GPSD. Ironically, SANCO was assertive in some dimensions because ENTR's political leadership was so keen on reinforcing the 'new approach' in time. Concessions were only made during the endgame when Commissioner Verheugen pushed for adoption after SANCO's cabinet had withstood five months of political negotiations. Interestingly, this turns the process hypothesis on internal conflict upside down (cf. Chapter Three). It was theorised that internal conflict initially rises with politicisation and salience, because this creates incentives for more interventionist policies of some DGs, which then meet the opposition of more traditionalist, market-making DGs (up to a certain politicisation threshold). We see a similar mechanism in the case at hand, but it works in the opposite direction. With SANCO's GPSD, the status quo was already rather interventionist. When ENTR now tried to get away with a more liberal proposal under low salience levels and declining politicisation during the final phases of drafting, SANCO waged conflict by defending the higher level of intervention that had already been achieved. In other words, the process hypothesis on internal conflict seems to depend on the location of the regulatory status quo. If a more interventionist status quo exists at the European level, intermediate politicisation and salience levels may trigger internal conflict if a DG proposes a comparatively more liberal position. If this is true, interventionism resulting from increasing politicisation and salience on one particular drafting process would account not only for more internal conflict on this particular case, but also for more conflictive interactions within the Commission in the long run.

As expected for low salience cases, furthermore, we have observed a rather lengthy fact-finding endeavour. More interesting is the involvement of DG ENTR's hierarchy. As expected, it hardly took part in the initial stages of policy formulation. However, after Commissioner Verheugen had publicly committed to 'better regulation', the proposal at hand moved up the political agenda. Essentially, it was the very idea of the 'new approach' to liberate industry from administrative burdens, so that its overhaul nicely suited the political priorities Commissioner Verheugen had set for his term in office. Verheugen's membership of the German Social Democratic Party does not account for the rather liberal approach to product safety his DG had reinforced. But influence of his nationality, in contrast, cannot be directly refuted. It was known that the German government had an interest in overhauling the 'new approach' – arguably so, because it is an exporting economy that relies strongly on Europe's internal market – and it wanted to bring the dossier forward during its Council presidency in the first half of 2007. While direct evidence is rare, Verheugen's pressure for timely adoption is clearly consistent with theories claiming that the Commissioner upheld national interests here. Yet given the strong pressure from his department to reinforce the liberal framework, it is questionable if the outcome would have significantly changed under a different Commissioner.

Beyond specific German interests, there was little evidence that the anticipation of other political preferences in Council or parliament mattered to the drafting process analysed here. The 2003 Council agreement was enough to ensure political feasibility, and detailed positions were not tested against majority preferences since their technical complexity shielded against political interference. In the same line, also MEPs did not consider it 'an interesting *sujet*' when the preliminary proposal was presented to the parliament during the drafting stages (COM72:302).

Finally, the protectionist view does not yield much insight to the case at hand. While ENTR emphasised the regulatory model's reputation in the world, producers appear not to have demanded protection from international competition. Rather, the final outcome simply reinforces an industry-focused regulatory approach to market access within Europe.

5.4 Toy safety

The subsequent product safety initiative in the sample – the proposal for a revised Toy Safety Directive adopted on 25 January 2008 (Commission of the European Communities 2008e) – actually presents a hard test case for DG ENTR's success in reinforcing a liberal model of product regulation in Europe. ENTR published the toy safety proposal just one year after the 'new approach' overhaul, which was negotiated in the Council and especially in the EP at the time. In addition, the proposal covers a market segment that had already provided a range of watersheds in the history of European product safety regulation. Toys were the first mass consumer product to be subsumed under the 'new approach' in 1988 (ibid. 2). Furthermore, formal responsibility for the extant toy safety directive switched back and forth between DG ENTR and DG SANCO during the 1990s (COM87:67). We have also seen above that the development of SANCO's GPSD was driven to some extent by specific toy scandals (Chapter 5.1). So, on the one hand, the sample's final product safety case was constrained by adhering to the liberal 'new approach'; on the other, it was subject to competence overlaps between the industry and the consumer protection DG, and it also risked facing high levels of public salience.

DG ENTR had also worked for quite some time on this particular proposal. Drafting set off with a first draft proposal that was informally distributed to member state representatives in the standing administrative cooperation group on toy safety in March 2002 (Enterprise Directorate-General 2002). The preceding cases have already shown that the overall politicisation of European integration exhibited marked variation during this rather lengthy drafting period. Particularly during 2004 and 2005 our indicator in Chapter Two indicates a stormy period in which European integration was strongly contested by the wider public. After a minor plateau around the initial discussions of the Lisbon Treaty in the second half of 2006 and early 2007, politicisation declined markedly only during the last six months of the toy safety proposal being drafted. So, during large parts of the drafting period, there should have been incentives to serve widespread public interest – but only if the issue of toy safety also remained publicly salient during these phases.

Undoubtedly, concerns on toys have repeatedly fed into the broader salience indicator on product safety. Also a more specific search underlines that either speculation, explicit safety warnings, or even recalls of toys kept the public aware during the early stages of the drafting period (e.g. *El País* 2002; Gadea 2004; Foster 2004; Lobe 2004; Gadhoum 2005).[13] Most interestingly, it was often DG SANCO that pushed the salience of toy safety in newspaper reports. During the drafting of DG ENTR's toy safety proposal, the Commission's consumer protection DG regularly published data from the rapid exchange system operating under the GPSD. These data often made the news, particularly because toys accounted for more than one-quarter of all safety notifications in the European market (Tait 2006; also: Fellsted 2005; Grande 2005; *FAZ* 2006). Virtually all these toys were Chinese imports, which resulted in a formal complaint of SANCO's Commissioner Kuneva during a visit in Beijing in early summer 2007 (Dickie 2007).

But all this was even dwarfed in August and September 2007. Within these two months, one of the largest toy producers in the world had to recall toys covered with lead-containing paint, then shortly afterwards dangerous magnetic toys, and, in a third recall, a huge tranche of the famous Barbie doll, which also contained toxic dye (Callan and Dyer 2007; *FAZ* 2007d, 2007f, 2007i; *Le Figaro* 2007b, 2007c;

---

13. The employed search phrase was 'toy* AND safety AND consumer* AND NOT toyota' which resulted in a total of 184 hits in the newspapers under analysis.

Kwong and Mitchell 2007; Pérez Gil 2007; Pérez Gil and Pozzi 2007; Visseyrias 2007). Since all these products were traded under the CE mark, the 'summer of recalls' (COM26:228) moved the 'new approach' into the public spotlight. On the one hand, the parliamentary discussion on the Commission proposal for the 'new approach' overhaul heated up markedly resulting in discussion about the meaning of the CE mark (COM27:285, 135). On the other hand, the envisaged toy safety proposal analysed here figured prominently in print media, which transmitted demands to rethink European toy safety regulation and challenged the 'new approach' as well (e.g. *FAZ* 2007e, 2007g; Pozzi 2007). In response, both Commissioner Kuneva (SANCO) and Commissioner Verheugen (ENTR) publicly promised swift reactions. The former announced a review of the toy market using GPSD surveillance data, and the latter promised a tightened regime on toy safety in the proposal at hand (e.g. *FAZ* 2007h; *Le Figaro* 2007a).

So, both the issue area and the proposal itself were clearly on the public radar. While some contemporaneous salience was also present during the early drafting stages, the issue of toy safety heated up during 2005 and 2006 in the RAPEX data, and peaked especially in summer 2007 when broad toy recalls abounded. Hence, while the high politicisation level can be expected to have created incentives to pander to public interest, the high salience levels indicated that toy safety was a particularly relevant issue area to tackle. Against this combination of independent variables especially in the second half of the drafting process, the theory predicts a rather interventionist policy position of the Commission. But did the cramped corset of the 'new approach' model allow such deviations from the regulatory status quo?

The status quo is given in the existing toy safety directive, 88/378/EEC. However, as we have seen, the general product safety regime had moved on in the meantime. Some provisions relevant to consumer goods were part of the GPSD. And, obviously, the general decision on the 'new approach' principles discussed in the preceding case study set basic lines for the proposed directive at hand. To assess consumer interventionism in the legal text (Commission of the European Communities 2008e), the following paragraphs will outline deviations from these existing regulations in seven sets of provisions.

The first relevant set circumscribes the proposal's scope. Article 1 specifies that the proposed directive sets rules for safety and free movement of toys, which are defined as 'products designed or intended, whether or not exclusively, for use in play by children under 14 years of age'. Compared to the existing toy safety law, the scope is widened now to products that are not exclusively intended for use by children. Beyond this, Article 51 of the proposal specifies the relation to other extant EU law and, among others, explicitly states that the GPSD (2001/95/EC) applies also to toys. The existing directive made no reference to other legislation. In comparison, thus, the scope provisions present a slight move towards more consumer protection by increasing the number of products covered and by reinforcing the protection granted under SANCO's framework directive.

A second set of key provisions contains the general obligations for economic operators, and follows the 'new approach' word by word (cf. Chapter 5.3). In some details, the particular rules go beyond what was in the extant toy safety directive, but these deviations merely mirror the general decision on the revised 'new approach' framework. As such, this set of rules does not deviate from the regulatory status quo in either a liberal or an interventionist direction.

Yet the product-specific, essential safety requirements do so. As for all 'new approach' products, these requirements are 'the only legal basis for taking dangerous toys out of the market in cases where a new risk is discovered' (Commission of the European Communities 2008e: 5–6). Basically, Article 9 prescribes that 'toys shall not jeopardise the safety or health of users or third parties when they are used as intended or in a foreseeable way, bearing in mind the behaviour of children'. Comparing these rules to the existing toy safety directive, one initially sees that the extant safety requirement was geared to the 'the *normal* behaviour of children' (emphasis added, Annex II of Directive 88/378/EEC). The new wording covers all possible behaviours of children instead; it thus widens the requirement, and makes manufacturers legally liable for a broader range of incidences. In other words, toy manufacturers are now obliged to foresee also unusual behaviours of children when designing their products.

Beyond this general requirement, Annex II specifies particular rules regarding physical, mechanical and electrical properties, as well as on flammability, hygiene, radioactivity and especially chemical characteristics. Particularly with regard to the latter, the annex is rather encompassing and derives requirements from a range of other Community legislation on chemicals. It explicitly bans the so-called CMRs – that is, substances that are carcinogenic, mutagenic or toxic for reproduction – and also prohibits a range of allergenic fragrances, or regulates their dosage and respective labelling. What is more, the Commission may adopt the rules on chemical requirements by a comitology procedure in the future (Article 45). With regard to these specific safety requirements, the extant directive differs in highly relevant details. The proposal now contains explicit rules for toys in food which must come in a separate packaging that is large enough to prevent swallowing or inhaling. In addition, toys that can only be accessed through eating are totally banned. Other rules on choking and suffocation risks have also been extended. However, most strikingly, the rules on chemical properties have more than doubled in length. A closer look indicates that neither the prohibition of CMRs nor the restricted uses of allergenic substances was part of the extant directive. In the spirit of the 'new approach', the existing directive had not foreseen future Commission involvement in specifying toy characteristics. Only with the proposed revision would such involvement become part of the European toy safety regime. With regard to both the general requirement and the specific safety rules, this set of key provisions thus presents a move towards a more restrictive regime for toy producers.

Another set of relevant provisions concerns those labelling requirements in the directive (KP13.4) that are not due to the general 'new approach' pattern.[14]

---

14. The only labelling requirements coming from the 'new approach' concern the CE mark in Articles 15 and 16. Again, these parts of the legal text provide a word-by-word transfer from the general decision discussed earlier.

Producers are obliged to affix warnings to the product, its packaging or the accompanying instructions. This holds, for example, for aquatic toys where the producer is forced to warn that they should only be used in shallow water and under adult supervision. Comparable rules are set for toys that are not intended for children under thirty-six months, slides, swings and rope rings, functional toys, sports equipment sold as toys, toys involving inherently dangerous preparation (e.g. photography development sets for children), as well as toys in food ('adult supervision recommended'). With the exception of toys in food, the extant directive prescribed rather similar warnings for these categories of toys. Some additional clarifications on age or weight limits as well as more emphasis on adult supervision are new in the proposal but, in sum, this set of rules does not really provide significantly more obligations for producers in protecting the consumer against particular risks.

Following the 'new approach' pattern, the subsequent set of rules covers conformity assessment and the respectively responsible bodies. Most of this is identical to the framework decision discussed above. But as noted earlier, the Commission has the power to decide how strict conformity assessment for a specific product category should be. For the toy safety proposal, it chose two sets of assessment modules from the menu offered in the framework decision. If a harmonised standard for a specific product has already been published in the Official Journal, and manufacturers have applied this standard in designing and producing the toy, they can rely on in-house production control. However, in cases where such a standard does not exist, has not been applied, has been published only with restrictions, or if the manufacturer thinks for other reasons that third-party verification is warranted, the so-called EC type examination procedure applies. Here a representative product is handed over to a third party who then evaluates conformity. In the extant directive, EC type examination was the rule for all toys, and internal production control was not allowed. Arguably, this was the case because no harmonised standards existed in 1988, but still, the present proposal liberalises the assessment procedure for toys when compared to the status quo. The liberalising effect of the chosen conformity assessment procedure is also underlined by the fact that the framework decision offered more restrictive modules – such as batch control – which, in principle, could have been chosen for toys as well. In this set of provisions, thus, the Commission position tends more towards the *laissez-faire* model of consumer policy.

Another set of key provisions following the 'new approach' structure contains national powers and duties under the proposed directive (KP13.6). Directly corresponding to the framework decision, member states may not, in principle, prohibit the free movement of toys (Article 11) and are responsible for monitoring the conformity assessment bodies. Likewise, mimicking the framework, national governments may challenge standards via a committee procedure. However, the toy safety proposal is more specific than the framework decision in terms of market surveillance. Interestingly, member states are obliged to 'organise and perform' market surveillance of toys along the lines defined by the GPSD. Yet while the explicit reference of the GPSD is notable, the preceding case study has shown that these decisions have already been made during the negotiations on the framework decision and the accompanying proposal on market surveillance and accreditation (Chapter 5.3). In this perspective, the toy safety proposal merely reinforces the existing regime, and thus marks no change on the dependent variable of interest in this regard.

The same conclusion applies to the rules on safeguard procedures enshrined in Articles 41–4, which again provide a literal transfer from the framework decision discussed above. In summary, the proposal under analysis here is neutral as regards general operator obligations, labelling requirements, national surveillance duties and safeguard procedures. As regards assessment procedures, furthermore, it has a liberalising effect. However, we have seen that the scope provisions and especially the enhanced safety requirements confine producers much more than the regulatory status quo did. In net terms, thus, we cannot really align the Commission position in the 2008 toy safety proposal with one of the ideal-type consumer policy models in Chapter 3.2. Rather, the proposal takes a middle ground between liberalised market access along the 'new approach' model and the stronger consumer orientation developed in the GPSD. So, how did this choice come about during drafting?

The drafting process started in a rather calm political context and followed a technocratic pattern during the years 2002 and 2003. The idea 'to revise the 88' emerged out of the implementation of the extant directive and the constant exchange with national civil servants. Many ideas on specific requirements had grown because 'the toy sector is a sector that changes every six months'. Both the Commission and the national authorities were constantly forced to rewrite implementation guidelines (COM25:60). At this stage, the ongoing exchange with the administrative stakeholders allowed the policy formulation to appear as merely a continuation of adaptation processes that were going on nevertheless (COM26:204).

The standing expert group on toy safety was the major forum for consulting stakeholders (Commission of the European Communities 2008e). It is made up of representatives from industry, standardisation and consumer organisations, but most of its members come from national authorities implementing the directive. This group of national administrators was deemed most important by the drafting officials (COM25:206). The expert group had accompanied the whole drafting process and discussed seven different draft proposals between March 2002 and July 2007. When the group identified the issues for revision, they were made subject to a public online consultation, which was answered mainly from the industry side (Commission of the European Communities 2008e: 3).

As noted above, similar revision processes also occurred for other 'new approach' directives. This, as well as SANCO's repeated attempts to conquer consumer product regulation, pushed DG ENTR into an overhaul of the general framework. In this context, the position formation on toy safety also involved intense coordination with other 'new approach' units in ENTR, the chemicals and cosmetics units, and at least weekly exchanges with ENTR's horizontal unit on the free movement of goods (COM25:160).

DG SANCO's product safety unit was also a logical contact, although interaction occurred mainly during the later stages of policy formulation (COM25:160; COM26:206). On the one hand, the product safety unit was a useful source of factual information. It employed a chemist and a toxicologist, and it controlled all RAPEX data containing detailed information on recalled toys and involved safety concerns. On the other hand, SANCO was strategically important. As the preceding case history has shown, they had blocked the general framework decision for quite some time and insisted on their regulatory competences concerning the safety of consumer goods. So, in the politicised context of 2005 to 2008, it was vital for ENTR to ensure SANCO's agreement so as to avoid internal conflict that – given the rising salience of toy safety – entailed the danger of alienating the European public further.

The resurfacing public salience of toy safety did indeed change the nature of the drafting process towards the end. The immense recalls during summer 2007 in particular spread through SANCO's rapid exchange system operating under the GPSD (COM26:216). Although the preparation of the toy safety proposal was well underway at the time, ENTR was 'put under much more pressure' by these events because 'people wanted to have immediate results' (COM25:234). For the drafting officials, this pressure came 'from the press' but also 'from above' (COM25:242). Particularly, the public commitments of ENTR's Commissioner Verheugen (e.g. *FAZ* 2007g) forced the unit to accelerate drafting, which would have taken another year otherwise (COM25:236).

Also the political leadership of DG SANCO increased the pressure. After repeated toy scares, Commissioner Kuneva started to negotiate voluntary agreements with the European toy industry. And she initiated the so-called Consumer Product Safety Review, a working group that was handled by SANCO's product safety unit and comprised national representatives, industry and consumer associations. Although it produced only reports (COM26:222; COM25:244) while the actual legislative regulation of toys remained under ENTR's auspices, the consumer policy Commissioner thereby underlined that the battle for consumer safety competences was not yet decided. Highlighting this, she made a speech to the EP, which was negotiating ENTR's 'new approach' framework package at the time, and used the toy issue as a reason to urge MEPs 'not to back proposals that would water down the existing regime of consumer product safety surveillance' (Commission of the European Communities 2007e).

But did these political pressures during proposal finalisation actually change ENTR's policy positions? The draft proposals submitted to the expert group give us additional leverage to answer that question. In fact, we can trace the development of ENTR's position across the rules drafted in March 2002 (Enterprise Directorate-General 2002), when both politicisation and issue salience were comparatively low; in July 2005 (Enterprise and Industry Directorate-General 2005b), when politicisation was extraordinarily high but salience levels remained intermediate; and in June 2007 (Enterprise and Industry Directorate-General 2007), when politicisation stayed at intermediate levels while the issue of dangerous toys from China became increasingly visible to the European public.

Comparing the scope provisions across these preliminary documents shows that the coverage of products that are not necessarily intended for children was discussed early on. The first draft in 2002 explicitly mentions 'double use' products, and both the 2005 and 2007 documents already contain the definition that one can also find in the final proposal. This particular widening of the scope cannot thus be traced to the political context. However, the explicit reference to the more protective GPSD was not part of the three preliminary drafts. Accordingly, this concession to DG SANCO occurred only in the last months of drafting between June 2007 and January 2008. In the final proposal, the issue was uniquely settled 'for the sake of clarity and legal certainty' by reinforcing the safety net function of SANCO's directive (Commission of the European Communities 2008e: 7).

The picture of essential safety requirements also highlights increasing consumer interventionism over the drafting period. We have seen that the 2008 proposal deviates from the status quo in that it extends safety needs also to incidences going beyond the 'normal' behaviour of children. In contrast, the 2002 proposal still focuses on 'normal behaviour of children' while also including the 'foreseeable abuse of the toy' and thus the 2008 proposal widens the requirement slightly. Similarly, the 2005 and 2007 documents cover 'misuse' of toys. However, the extension to any undefined instance beyond normal children's behaviour entered ENTR's position only in the last six months between the last draft and the final Commission proposal. Given that the general requirement is the only basis on which market access can be denied under the 'new approach', this widening is a clear move towards more protection in the very final stages of drafting – although consumer associations would have preferred an even more precautionary approach (BEUC and ANEC 2008: 3, 6).

Because of their complexity, safety requirements on the specific properties of toys are somewhat harder to trace. However, most obviously, the restrictive rules on toys in foods entered the proposals only after summer 2007. This can be considered as a gift to please the consumer associations as it was one of their major demands (e.g. BEUC and ANEC 2008: 13; Commission of the European Communities 2008e: 5).

Yet the really 'big issue' was the requirements on the chemical properties of toys. Since the phthalates issue in 2000 until the 2007 recalls, almost all toy scares were related to chemicals. In this light, the drafting officials invested utmost effort to provide a 'correct' provision, kept the details out of the expert group and instead commissioned two particular scientific studies on relevant chemicals (COM25:200). This covered explicitly CMR substances which had also caused big discussions during the preparation of Europe's major chemical regulation (REACH) in 2003. In this regulation, CMRs were distinguished into three risk categories with differently restricted usages – a solution also taken over to the toy safety proposal at hand (cf. Commission of the European Communities 2008e: 4).[15]

---

15. Note that the internal preparation of the REACH legislation had caused major rifts between DG ENTR and DG ENV (environment). DG ENV also intervened in the toy safety proposal at hand, but details cannot be provided because all relevant information was redacted in the documentation provided to the author under GESTDEM 2010/648.

Other technical details on specific substances were transferred from already harmonised standards (Commission of the European Communities 2008e: 5) while DG SANCO's product safety unit provided expertise on the thresholds of certain chemicals (COM26:60, 82). In addition, the exclusion of allergenic substances and fragrances was copied from the Cosmetics Directive that was drawn up in 1976 (Directive 76/768/EEC, see Commission of the European Communities 2008e: 4). Given that this directive already existed when the extant toy safety directive was adopted, including these more restrictive rules only now must be explained by the contemporaneously enhanced political relevance of consumer protection.

Nevertheless, consumers wanted much more restriction on chemical usage (BEUC and ANEC 2008: 4, 7–8), whereas member state governments were divided on the matter. Against this unclear pattern of external interests, the drafting officials in DG ENTR checked back with the cabinet of Commissioner Verheugen, which – because of the time pressure in the endgame – agreed with the approach taken in the final proposal (COM25:102). Note, however, that they kept an open back door. More protective rules in the future would be possible as the proposal enables the Commission to change the rules on chemicals through a comitology procedure. This provision is rather unusual under the regulatory model of the 'new approach' but it was specifically welcomed by consumer representatives as well (BEUC and ANEC 2008: 6). This finally allowed the Commission to exploit the improved regulations on chemical properties, and particularly the banning of CMRs as the major story angle in the public presentations of the proposal (e.g. Commission of the European Communities 2008j).

The labelling requirements were another slightly interventionist deviation from the 'new approach' model. The first draft of 2002 foresaw no specific warnings, but contained an empty category on the matter. The 2005 draft, in contrast, included warnings for all categories that were also covered later (except for toys in food) but did not specify rules on legibility. These rules became part of ENTR's position only in the last draft of summer 2007, which was also pushed by DG SANCO's product safety unit (COM26:60). Consumers welcomed these enhanced provisions (BEUC and ANEC 2008: 12).[16]

This leaves the rules on conformity assessment, the major instance where ENTR's 2008 proposal takes a clearly more liberal position than the status quo. The timeline of the draft proposal shows that this was intended from the start, but the consumer side strongly regretted that third party testing was not made obligatory for particularly dangerous toys (BEUC and ANEC 2008: 11–12). When toy safety became a publicly salient issue, however, the drafting officials required a 'political decision' in this regard and turned to Verheugen's cabinet. Here, the originally intended version was still seen as 'proportionate', so that it remained in the proposal and thus reinforced privatised standardisation as a central element of 'new approach' directives (COM25:82, 102).

---

16. Of course, the consumer side repeated its general criticism regarding the CE mark; but again, ENTR defended this central element of the 'new approach'.

As an analysis of the legal text already implied, the remaining provisions on general operator obligations, national duties and safeguard procedures are just transfers from ENTR's framework decision on the 'new approach'. But while ENTR's defence of this liberal regulatory model constrained the drafting process, the enhancements of consumer protection enabled the Commission to exploit the proposal politically. The press release announced that the 'European Commission has come forward today with measures to improve toy safety in Europe', quoting ENTR's Commissioner Verheugen saying that the 'health and safety of children is non-negotiable and cannot be subject to any compromises' (Commission of the European Communities 2008j).

To summarise, the drafting process on the revised toy safety directive initially appeared as another building block in DG ENTR's strategy to defend the 'new approach' against repeated political demands to enhance the protection of European product regulation. During the early phases of drafting – when neither the general contestation of European decision making nor the salience of toy safety figured prominently – the basic ideas were developed at lower Commission echelons and in close exchange with national bureaucrats, drafting was not rushed but could unfold across several episodes of expert group consultation, and little conflict abounded since nothing challenged the predominant regulatory model or the responsibility of the leading DG.

Against this start, the upsurge in politicisation after 2004 plus the exploding salience levels especially during 2007 almost appeared as a natural experiment. Suddenly, the drafting officials felt the need to consult their political leaders on specific decisions, and publicly committed to specific policy positions in the meantime. Proposal finalisation became rushed, involved some late gifts to the consumer side, and the emerging window of opportunity put internal rivalries back on the agenda. While similar demands from external stakeholders had been denied in the preceding case and SANCO's success came only after five months of negotiation, high salience levels in this parallel case allowed some late position changes on significant matters that had earlier been left untouched in more than five years of proposal preparation. Although it still follows the spirit of the 'new approach', the resulting policy output of the Commission – at least on some provisions – positions itself on the more interventionist side.

This outcome also highlights that the combination of politicisation and salience may override Commissioner characteristics. While Commissioner Verheugen defended the 'new approach' overhaul under his 'better regulation' agenda in the preceding case, in toy safety he allowed more interventionist solutions including a future comitology decision on chemical properties that are unpredictable for the industry. Likewise, the comparison of proposal drafts in 2002 and 2005 indicates no meaningful changes, even though the political leadership of DG ENTR shifted in 2004. Again, Commissioner characteristics do not appear as a strong explanatory factor for the policy choices of the Commission.

In contrast, neither the political feasibility in the Council nor the productionist view can be fully rejected for the case at hand. The policy choices on toy safety were repeatedly checked back with national representatives in the expert group.

And, given the huge importance of Chinese imports, which caused many of the actual toy scares, one could assume that European producers preferred higher safety standards as a means to protect them against external competition. However, in the only available evidence on the aggregate position of the European toy industry, stakeholders merely welcomed the directive without explicit reference to its more interventionist elements (cf. TIE 2008). Against this scarce evidence, however, DG ENTR's willingness to defend the 'new approach' together with the influence of issue salience provides the most compelling explanation for the policy choices that we observe in the case at hand.

5.5 The product safety cases in comparative perspective

Taken together, the four position formation process on product safety regulation offer considerable evidence on the theoretical expectations derived in Chapter Three. Working backwards and starting with the alternative explanations, the first striking fact is that the productionist view on position formation cannot be as easily refuted as for the cases in Chapter Four. This explanation contends that more interventionist policy choices of the Commission emerge especially where European producers demand protection against international competition. In fact, two of the sectors covered by the cases in this chapter – toys and pyrotechnic articles – operated under increasing import competition particularly from China. The case histories show that this at least facilitated the Commission's plans for tighter market surveillance regimes under the GPSD (Chapter 5.1) and for enhanced rules on chemicals in toys (Chapter 5.5). It also probably accounts for the inclusion of automotive suppliers under the 'new approach' to pyrotechnic regulation (Chapter 5.2). However, while protectionist arguments helped to convince the affected industries of the need for particular regulatory choices, we can hardly attest a causal effect, because direct producer demands in this direction could not be traced.

Another prominent account of Commission position formation hinges on the characteristics of the responsible Commissioners who are seen to represent either party-political or national interests. All four case histories in this chapter span changes in the political leadership of the participating Commission DGs. The drafting of SANCO's product safety directive involved the inauguration of the Prodi Commission in late 1999, while the other three cases were prepared as President Barroso entered office in 2004 and all political responsibilities were reshuffled. However, process tracing efforts did not yield corresponding changes in the positions of the DGs. On the product safety directive and on the pyrotechnic case, as well as on the 'new approach', the basic positions of policies on the liberal–interventionist continuum remained by and large stable throughout drafting, while the adaptations in the toy safety case occurred only in the last six months after the 'new' Commissioner had held responsibility for almost three years. The role of party politics is doubtful to say the least, if one considers that the most interventionist product safety case (SANCO's general directive) came under the independent Commissioner Byrne, while the most liberal one (ENTR's 'new approach' overhaul) came under the responsibility of a social democrat. With regard to Commissioner nationality, one interesting exception applies: the time pressure Commissioner Verheugen exerted during the finalisation of the 'new approach' at least coincided with the German government's interest in pushing this particular dossier through under its own Council presidency. But even if there were a causal link here, it must be noted that this does not affect our dependent variable, as this piece of legislation was prepared with a rather liberal approach even before Commissioner Verheugen became responsible for it.

Another prominent explanation argues that the Commission is first and foremost interested in drafting proposals that will survive negotiations in the Council. In fact, this view is particularly supported as regards the drafting processes in this chapter: all four cases show that the drafting DGs engaged in exchanges with national representatives in one way or another. However, the degree to which national preferences constrained position formation also varied across the product safety initiatives. In the general product safety case, SANCO had to cut back its ideal position on covering consumer services but nevertheless chose the most interventionist route – including products used in consumer services – that the set of national references allowed. In the pyrotechnic case, DG ENTR had to grant certain exemptions as regards age limits and specific firework categories because a more liberal solution would have been opposed in the Council. In the 'new approach' overhaul, in contrast, a green light from the Council at the initial stages of drafting was sufficient as technical complexity made further interference unlikely. In the toy safety case, seven draft proposals were presented to national representatives throughout drafting. In sum, this evidence underlines the expectation that the anticipated Council preferences constrain position formation in the Commission DGs, but do not determine a unique policy choice. Rather, the Council usually offers leeway in which the Commission can either take a more liberal or a more interventionist position.

This brings us to the combination of EU politicisation and issue salience which – according to the major theoretical model – should explain this Commission choice. Looking just at the combination of independent variables and the Commission's final policy output on the dependent side yields an interesting pattern across the four cases. Where DG ENTR and its political leadership could be reasonably sure that the public was currently not interested in the regulated issues – as was the case for pyrotechnic products and for the framework decision – they reinforced the existing regulatory model, which is geared to efficient trade, with as little political intervention as possible. But where specific incidences made the public aware that specific safety concerns were linked to the policy decision in question, the existing product safety regime could be stretched to allow more interventionist provisions. This was the case with regard to softeners in baby toys during the drafting of the GPSD, and with regard to the massive recalls of Chinese imports during summer 2007 when the toy safety proposal was finalised. Taken together, we clearly observe some co-variation of issue salience and the interventionism in the Commission's policy position.

Also a process-based perspective on the four drafting histories lends support to the model developed in Chapter Three. Most notably, the policy formulation process on toy safety exhibited co-variation of issue salience and interventionism in the Commission's position *within* the case. Similarly, the process hypotheses support the proposed model by and large. In terms of process duration, the two low salience cases on pyrotech and on the 'new approach' overhaul come with rather lengthy processes. Likewise, the toy safety proposal started calmly but became significantly more rushed when the public salience of toy safety kicked in. The general directive of SANCO, in contrast, could be finished within two years despite its general nature and its large scope. In a similar vein, responsiveness to consumer interest was allowed for the GPSD and the late stages of the toy safety process, while specific consumer demands were virtually absent in the other two cases.

Yet more complexity was involved with regard to the expectations on hierarchy involvement and the degree of conflict within the Commission. The exploding salience levels during the toy safety proposal immediately triggered the involvement of Commissioners Verheugen and Kuneva, who, in addition, publicly committed to more interventionist policies. In contrast, political involvement in SANCO's general product safety case was much less intense than the model would lead us to expect. As we have seen, this was due to issue competition on the public agenda. SANCO's political level was absorbed in the BSE crisis and it dealt with the corresponding food policies at the time. Also, while political involvement was virtually absent in the low-salience case on pyrotechnic products, ENTR's Commissioner engaged strongly in the 'new approach' overhaul, despite its lacking public salience. Since it nicely suited the political agenda he had set for his term of office, he jumped on the bandwagon that his DG had push-started. This implies that political involvement may be triggered or prevented by other mechanisms.

It is also undeniable that much of the observed Commissioner involvement was induced by the turf conflicts DG SANCO and DG ENTR led in the area of product safety. This was most notable when toy safety became publicly salient, but it also occurred at the final stages of the 'new approach' overhaul, which was not particularly salient but profoundly contradicted SANCO's rather young regime on consumer goods. As the public was not watching, SANCO's political level waged internal conflict, blocked ENTR's proposal for more than five months and finally achieved a range of concessions. Interestingly, this is consistent with the basic theoretical expectations on internal conflict. Yet the roles of the interventionist and liberal players are exchanged because the liberal position was no longer the status quo after SANCO's general product safety regime became European law in 2001. The drafting process on the general product safety regime also provided interesting insights on conflict within the Commission. This case highlights that the administrative level anticipated possibly detrimental turf conflicts. Given that their outcome could not be predicted at the time, the drafting officials tried to settle the issues at their own level, hammering out a neat border line that delineated their turfs.

In sum, evidence on the major theoretical model implies some refinement, but in the aggregate, it is consistent with the basic assumptions and the proposed hypotheses. Yet the alert reader might notice that this conclusion comes with a few caveats regarding the area of product safety. While the influence of contemporaneous public salience could be outlined nicely in the four cases, we cannot fully determine the theoretical model as regards EU politicisation because we lack a product safety case with high salience in combination with low politicisation values. Only such a case would allow us to say whether the influence of salience is dependent on politicisation. In this regard, the insights presented here must be complemented with the broader sample including the market transaction and food safety cases.

On a less abstract level, the case histories on product safety show that specific policy characteristics might constrain the proposed theoretical mechanism. On the one hand, contemporaneous public salience of the issue area was much more erratic, and the Commission's interventionism seems to hinge on a direct link between incidences making the public aware of the regulation in question. The failure to remove toys with chemical softeners in 1998 directly pointed to flaws in the particular regime the Commission was working on, as did the massive recalls of chemically contaminated toys in 2007. In contrast, other safety concerns that were visible to the public during the renewed 'new approach' decision were not directly attributed to European competences – arguably because of the technical complexity of this meta-regulation.

On the other hand, the history of the policy area hindered more interventionism in the Commission's policy proposals. The introduction to this chapter has made clear that product regulation was profoundly linked to the creation of the internal market since the 1960s, and that a specific regulatory model has developed and flourished over time. This tradition led to an encompassing body of law and vested interests on the part of DG ENTR and producers operating on the European market. Against this background, the consumer protection DG appeared much more constrained as compared to its battles with DG MARKT discussed in the cases in Chapter Four. In these earlier cases on contractual consumer rights, the principle of mutual recognition and mainly national rules formed the regulatory status quo; but in the product safety domain, SANCO had to fight an existing body of European law that was directly linked to extant competences of another Commission DG. In this view, the politicisation–salience–policy nexus may hinge even more strongly on the regulatory status quo. The following chapter on food safety regulation will shed more light on this.

Chapter Six

Food Safety

In the quest to win over the hearts of its citizens, the European Union is increasingly targeting their stomachs.

Headline of *Financial Times* article, 1 February 2003

This final policy chapter studies five drafting processes in the Commission that led to legislative proposals in the area of food safety. This area presents a particularly relevant testing ground for the expectation that high levels of EU politicisation in conjunction with high levels of public issue salience lead to policy choices that explicitly favour consumers over producers. Four features render this policy area particularly sensitive in this regard (cf. Ansell and Vogel 2006: chapter 1).

First, policy choices on food safety in Europe can unfold immense economic implications. Outperforming the automobile, metal and chemical businesses, the food and drink industry is the largest manufacturing sector in the EU as measured by a turnover of €954 billion and employing 4.2 million people in 2009 (CIAA 2011: 3). The sheer size of the European food industry implies that the regulatory distribution of rights among producers and consumers could also lead to a significant redistribution of actual resources in the European market.

Second, food policy has a strong international dimension. Diverging food standards have historically presented significant barriers to international trade (cf. Vogel 1995: chapter 5), and at the same time as being the world's largest food producer, the EU is also one of the largest food importers (in 2009 food imports amounted to €50.8 billion, which resulted in a small trade surplus of only €3 billion: CIAA 2011: 3; see also MacMaoláin 2007: 5–6). European food safety regulation has thus always given rise to serious trade, as fervently illustrated in the cases of genetically modified foods or hormone-treated beef (e.g. Young and Holmes 2006; or Noiville 2006). By 1961, the World Health Organisation (WHO) and the Food and Agricultural Organization (FAO) had established the Codex Alimentarius Commission, a body that developed voluntary standards to promote trade and consumer protection. With the establishment of World Trade Organization (WTO) in 1995, the Codex standards acquired law-like status (Ansell and Vogel 2006: 6–7; Taylor and Millar 2002).

Third, food regulation also has a strong cultural dimension: 'Both national and ethnic cultures are associated with distinctive attitudes toward food' (Ansell and Vogel 2006: 5). This is important for our purposes, as differing food cultures are mirrored in diverging regulatory approaches within the European member states (Waarden 2006). Whereas the French and Italian regulatory traditions, for example, are more concerned with quality grading, the German approach has traditionally regulated the chemical composition of foods directly. For any given food safety issue, the Commission thus must choose among a variety of regulatory models that impinge on individual member states differently.

Fourth, and most important for the major theoretical claim of this book, 'few other areas of public policy so directly, personally, and continually affect the well-being of every citizen' (Ansell and Vogel 2006: 4). The regulation of food invariably touches upon the most basic needs of individuals and we can assume that it attracts an even higher degree of public attention. The Commission may thus have a strong incentive to serve widespread interests in this policy area – and these may even be stronger than the other areas of consumer policy discussed so far.

In fact, the media-based salience measure developed in Chapter 3.6 is in line with this expectation. On average, 0.36 per cent of newspaper articles contain key word combinations that point to food safety issues, while this indicator reaches only 0.12 per cent and 0.17 per cent for contractual consumer rights and product safety respectively. Along this line, public visibility on average is indeed higher for food safety than for the consumer policy issues discussed in the two preceding chapters. Nevertheless, Figure 6.1 shows that the contemporaneous public issue salience of food safety also varies during the investigation period.

In particular, the newspaper data identify two modes of issue salience in early 2001 and mid-2008. The first peak reflects renewed outbreaks of both mad cow and foot-and-mouth diseases, and subsequent restrictions in meat trade throughout the EU. Afterwards, the salience indicator stays below its mean, which changed dramatically from mid-2007 onwards. During this time, the heightened media attention was driven by world-wide soaring food prices, WTO disputes on agricultural products and genetically modified foods, and various discussions on food labelling in different European countries. The five drafting processes discussed in this chapter thus come under varying levels of public attention to the issue area, providing empirical leverage for the comparative evaluation of the book's major argument.

Taken together, the food safety issue area constrains the Commission's choices on how to distribute rights and risks among consumers and producers by huge internal and external trade considerations, varying national regulatory approaches and an attentive public. One the one hand, the high baseline salience provides the hypothesised incentives for serving diffuse consumer interest in a context of politicised European decision making. On the other hand, the size of the food and drink sector leads us to expect powerful producer pressures not to openly favour the consumer side. In addition, food policy allows insights into the major complementary explanations: varying national regulatory approaches, as well as the international repercussions of food safety decisions, make the alternative theories of Council anticipation, nationally motivated Commissioner influence, or protectionist logic following producer interests equally likely candidates for explaining Commission choices in individual food policy measures. But what is the actual regulatory leeway that the Commission has in regulating food safety?

Figure 6.1: Public salience of the issue area 'food safety'

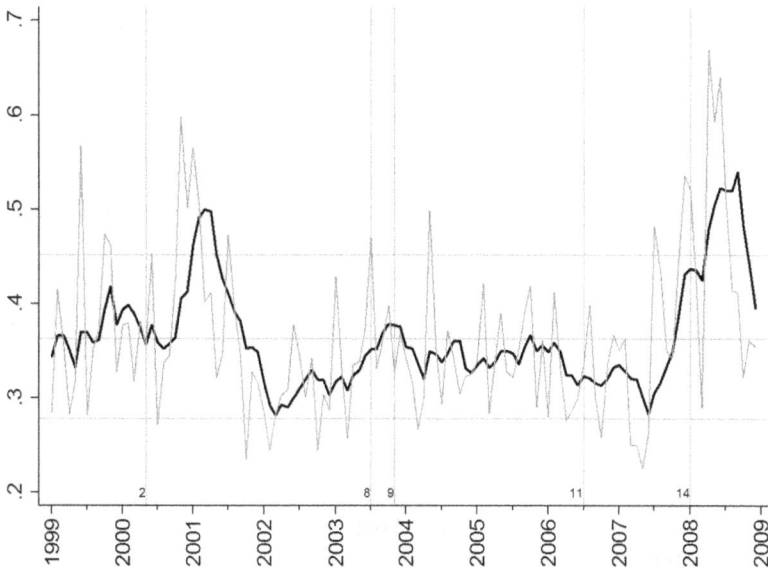

Note: Figures provide the average percentage share of newspaper articles with issue area-specific keyword combinations (see Chapter 3.6 and Appendix C in this volume for details). The grey curve presents monthly values while the bold curve indicates the six-month moving average. Horizontal lines indicate the investigation period mean +/−1 standard deviation. Vertical lines mark adoption months of sampled Commission proposals in the issue area.

During the 'genesis' of European food policy, trade considerations have clearly surmounted public safety and health concerns. From the 1960s to the mid-1980s, supranational activity mostly pursued the goal of a harmonised marketplace for foodstuffs (Alemanno 2006: especially 239ff.). Much like the patterns observed for product regulation in Chapter Five, the Commission tackled diverging national rules by drawing up almost fifty 'recipe laws' that should ensure the free trade of individual foodstuffs by harmonising their composition across Europe (ibid. 240). Major examples are the directives on the composition of chocolate (1973), honey (1974), and jams and marmalades (1979, MacMaoláin 2007: 4). These directives prescribed food composition in a highly detailed fashion, but health and consumer protection implications were left to member states and were only tackled 'to the extent that it was necessary to ensure regular intra community trade' (Alemanno 2006: 240).

The preponderance of economic considerations in supranational food policy was underlined by case law in the ECJ. Two of the ECJ judgements most important for European integration actually revolved around trade in foodstuffs (cf. Scharpf 2009: 10–13). In the 1974 *Dassonville* case on Belgian import rules for whisky, the ECJ established the principle that 'all trading rules enacted by Member States that are capable of hindering, directly and indirectly, actually or potentially, intra-Community trade are to be considered as measures having an effect equivalent to quantitative restrictions', which were illegal under the EC treaty (Case 8/1974 as cited in MacMaoláin 2007: 20–1). Furthermore, in *Cassis de Dijon*, revolving around French liquor imports to Germany, the ECJ initiated the principle of mutual recognition. According to this 1978 judgement, any product lawfully marketed in one member state must be lawfully marketable in all member states (Case 120/1978, discussed in MacMaoláin 2007: 22). This judgement basically put existing national food safety rules into question. But subsequent case law also diluted the mutual recognition principle slightly by granting exceptions if national rules on public health are necessary and proportionate (ibid. 23, Clergeau 2005: 115). This left a range of diverging national rules, an obstacle that could not be overcome by further 'recipe laws'. These directives were subject to unanimity in the Council, where 'sensitive questions of culinary cultures and traditions contributed to render the decision-making procedure extremely cumbersome and time-consuming' (Alemanno 2006: 240–1).

As for product regulation, the Commission thus also made food subject to its 'new approach' in the 1985 internal market programme (ibid. 240–1; cf. Chapter Five). European food law should accordingly harmonise only those 'essential safety requirements' that were necessary to ensure the free circulation of foodstuffs in the EU, while all national legislation exceeding these requirements was explicitly made subject to the mutual recognition principle. The minimum requirements for particular food risks were set in a rather obscure committee system, in which member state representatives, interest groups and scientists deliberated on individual standards (Vos 2000). This committee system rested on the 'fiction of objective science' (Joerges and Neyer 1997), but 'EC food law was still mainly focused on issues of trade and the free movement of goods rather than on safety issues' (Alemanno 2006: 243).

However, this regulatory model was strongly shattered when it became clear in 1996 that the BSE disease in cattle was transferable to humans. As the BSE crisis had already smouldered in Europe since 1985, this resulted in public outrage that triggered immense and lasting distrust in the means and regulation of meat production in Europe (Vos 2000: especially 231–3). Under President Jacques Santer, the Commission reacted to this crisis both in institutional and in policy terms. With the declared aim of avoiding producer capture of standard setting committees, risk assessment (meaning the generation of scientific expertise on food) was to be separated from risk management (meaning the actual setting of legislative food standards). Internally, this particularly favoured DG SANCO, which gained all risk assessment responsibilities at the expense of DG ENTR and DG AGRI (agriculture, Vos 2000: 233–4). Yet this institutional separation left open 'how the balance was to be found between the scientific elements guiding the expertise applied at DG [SANCO] and the economic considerations of the agriculture and industry DGs, which were still in charge of drafting laws' (Clergeau 2005: 123–4).

In policy terms, the Commission reacted to the crisis with a 1997 Green Paper that 'first stated that that the main objective of the Community's approach to food safety is to reinforce consumer health protection' (Vos 2000: 234). Besides this single signal from the Commission, the BSE crisis affected the intergovernmental conference in Amsterdam 1996/7 much more, leading to a range of consumer-related treaty changes including the goal of a high level of human health protection in Article 152 of the Amsterdam Treaty.

However, many critics still considered these responses as insufficient, and this gave rise to another phase of European food regulation (Clergeau 2005: especially 125–30; likewise: Alemanno 2006: 245–7). Leaving legislative powers in the hands of DG AGRI and DG ENTR spurred fears that food regulation would remain a producer-driven policy, which made commitments to consumer health concerns much less credible. Many experts doubted the separation of risk assessment and management, and called for a more direct role of science in drawing up legislation. Public attention on these issues remained high as the BSE crisis kept cooking and this was compounded by further food scandals on dioxin in Belgian eggs and swine fever in the Netherlands (cf. Paul 2008). The high issue salience of food safety combined with a broader political crisis in the EU's political system. During late 1998 and early 1999, the European Commission saw itself publicly accused of seriously flawed management procedures after the misappropriation of funds by Commissioner Cresson ultimately led to the resignation of the whole Santer Commission in spring 1999.

In this climate of politicisation and high issue salience, the new Commission President Romano Prodi and his fresh Commissioner for health and consumer protection, David Byrne, moved quickly. Only a few days after entering office, they held a combined declaration on food safety in the EP, and made several commitments. Among others, they promised a White Paper including concrete legislative proposals, the creation of an autonomous food safety agency providing risk assessment services and the creation of a single Commission DG responsible for food policy. The actual 'White Paper on Food Safety' was published in January 2000 (Commission of the European Communities 2000j) and, during spring, all food-related units were moved from DGs AGRI and ENTR to DG SANCO. In fact, the Commission had changed the playing field in which 'a balance needs to be found between consumers' protection and their health, the rules of the single market, technological innovation, and international trade' (Clergeau 2005: 129–33).

So, at the beginning of our investigation period, the stage was set for politics theorised in Chapter Three. As a formerly market-driven policy area, European food policy was now equipped with Treaty rules that enabled the Commission also to push consumer concerns. With DG SANCO, an internal player was established with both the competences and the organisational incentives to do all this. Yet in DG ENTR and DG AGRI, the alleged 'consumer' DG had internal counterparts with overlapping and countervailing competences in food safety matters. Additionally, all internal Commission players had recently experienced the salience of food safety easily spilling over into the politicisation of European integration as a whole. Taken together, the context of European food safety regulation fulfils the basic scope conditions of the theory proposed in Chapter Three.

6.1 Food supplements

The first food safety case that the sample yields is a proposed directive on food supplements, which was formally adopted by the Commission's College on 8 May 2000 (Commission of the European Communities 2000g). Food supplements are concentrated sources of vitamins and minerals that are sold to the consumer in dose form such as pills, drop-dispensing bottles or tablets in order to complement the normal diet. Among the most commonly known consumer products in this category are soluble tablets of vitamin C and magnesium.

At the time of drafting, food supplements presented a growing market (BEUC 2000a). In the early 1990s, they emerged in Europe through US imports to the UK as an access point to the European market via mutual recognition (COM88:106 and 154, DG III of the European Commission 1997: 1). But this product group met a range of scientific concerns, which was also mirrored in strongly varying regulatory approaches in the other member states. Evidence about the positive health effects of these products was 'shaky' (Eberhardie 2007) and some initial studies on overdoses began to emerge (cf. BEUC 2000a: 3). In this context, the regulation of food supplements clearly involved the challenge of balancing market freedom and consumer safety (Lewis and Strom 2002). While no supranational legislation existed, producers faced very liberal regimes in the UK and the Netherlands, followed by Ireland and Belgium, where food supplements were treated as foodstuffs. The southern and Scandinavian countries in particular, however, were much more restrictive in terms of market access. In France, Spain, and Italy especially but also in Germany, food supplements were treated as medicines, allowing for trade restrictions based on public health concerns (COM88:26, Europe Information Service 1997a; Europe Information Service 1999, 2000; see also Commission of the European Communities 2000g: 2). This set-up justified Commission action in line with its original market-making mandate and the very idea of regulating the sector was induced by 'complaints from manufacturers' filed with the drafting unit (COM88:30). But did the political context during 1999 and 2000 actually allow a *laissez-faire* approach to food supplements?

We have seen in Chapter Two that the overall politicisation of European integration was slightly on the rise during the last stages of the drafting process analysed here. Visibility, polarisation, and mobilisation exhibited local peaks in early 1999, and were on the rise during spring 2000 when the food supplements proposal was finished. Apart from the cumulative effects of the sacking of the Santer Commission, the EP elections in June 1999, and the arrival in office of Romano Prodi, however, it has to be noted that our politicisation indicator does not exceed its long-term average. Public criticism of EU politics during 1999 and 2000 especially concerned the European Commission and may thus have created incentives for pandering to diffuse interests; but, in comparative terms, the drafting period was calmer than at other points in time.

The salience indicator discussed above indicates no extreme swings, but its levels were slightly above the investigation period mean during the final stages of drafting. From summer 1999 onwards, the underlying media data cover three related public debates. First, genetically modified foodstuffs, their traceability, and further WTO negotiations on the matter were discussed. Second, the EU/US debate on hormone-treated beef cooked up since the US announced severe sanctions in late 1999. The third and most important factor driving public food safety salience was a scare on dioxin in Belgian poultry, cattle and pig feed, which resulted in a public outcry and trading bans within and across Europe.

Yet while these developments focused public attention on nutritional safety, the debates did not revolve around the niche product of food supplements covered by the proposal. Searching the available quality newspapers for particular articles on food or dietary supplements during the period from January 1999 to the proposal adoption on 8 May 2000 revealed only one *Frankfurter Allgemeine Zeitung* article discussing the economic potential of these products for the Nestlé company.[1] So while consumer demand for food supplements was present, particular risks or regulatory issues were not high on the public agenda when the Commission finished the proposal. Taking an intermediate level of EU politicisation together with the apparently meagre public interest in safety issues related to dietary supplements, our major outcome hypothesis predicts a market-making proposal with little consumer policy interventionism for the case at hand.

The Commission's choice on the consumer policy continuum developed earlier can be tracked through four sets of provisions in the final legal text (Commission of the European Communities 2000g), which directly affect the distribution of rights and risks among producers and consumers. The first concerns the proposal's legal scope, which defines food supplements explicitly as foodstuffs. But in those countries where food supplements were treated as medicines – Germany and Austria, for example – authoritative pre-market control under medicinal licensing law applied, and the burden of proving the product's safety lay with the producers. The more liberal regimes in the UK and the Netherlands generally treated them as foodstuffs, and required much less pre-market control, shifting risk assessment duties more towards the individual consumer (COM88:26, Europe Information Service 1999, 2000).[2] The Commission's choice clearly reflects this more liberal approach.

This is underlined by the second provision in which the Commission prohibits member states to restrict trade in food supplements, complying with the proposed directive. Under this full harmonisation approach, any national consumer protection measure referring to the composition, manufacturing or labelling and presentation of food supplements would become invalid. Given varying levels of

---

1. Newspapers were searched for either 'food supplements', 'nutritional supplements', or 'dietary supplements', and the corresponding translations.

2. Following a study of the pro-harmonisation industry group EHPM, in the UK, 50 per cent of food supplements were only allowed to be sold through chemists', while this figure amounted to 90 per cent in other European countries (Europe Information Service 1997b).

protection in national approaches and given that national governments had actually restricted trade on public health grounds before (Commission of the European Communities 2000g: 2), this presents another move towards a more *laissez faire*-motivated re-regulation.

Yet an overall judgement has to be made in conjunction with the actual product specification the Commission proposal prescribes. In the third set of provisions distributing rights among consumers and producers, the rules in the proposal and its annexes prescribe a conclusive list of permitted vitamins and minerals while establishing the criteria by which their purity as well as their upper and lower levels are to be set in the future. Comparing these rules to the regulatory status quo indicates an at least slightly more interventionist Commission position. On the one hand, the list excluded some nutrients that were allowed under the hitherto most liberal regime in the UK (Eberhardie 2007); on the other, legislatively establishing a positive list of allowed nutrients presents a much stricter constraint for producer freedom than a negative list of prohibited ingredients or dosages would have provided. Compared to this conceivable alternative, a positive list raises producer costs of product innovation, particularly because the proposal makes any future changes to this list subject to a committee procedure and a corresponding Commission decision.

Also the fourth set of relevant key provisions on labelling requirements for food supplements deviates slightly from the regulatory template of the most liberal national regimes. It demands that any product must bear the term 'supplement' in its name while prohibiting allusions to the product's effectiveness in preventing or treating human diseases. In addition, producers are obliged to indicate the recommended daily amount of consumption and the health risks of exceeding it. Further, the product label needs to state that food supplements 'should not be used as substitute for a diversified diet' (Commission of the European Communities 2000g: Article 6.3), while labelling must not imply that an adequate diet is insufficient without supplements. Clearly, these rules raise the responsibilities of producers and, on the flipside, provide consumers with information rights. However, given that dietary supplements were previously treated as medicines in some European countries – which usually involves much stricter packaging, labelling and information requirements – the Commission position can also not be deemed too interventionist here. This is also underlined by the fact that the proposal enables member states to suspend pre-market control of new products' labels.

Across these rules, the overall proposal tends more towards the lower end of the *laissez-faire*–interventionist continuum. It is geared towards removing trade obstacles, strips national governments of further opportunities to regulate food supplements, and proposes a supranational approach that resembles the most liberal rather than the most restrictive national regimes. The distribution of rights and risks the Commission proposes clearly favours food supplement producers operating cross-border. So, how has the Commission taken this choice?

The food supplements proposal did have an unusual history, as the formally responsible DG changed during drafting while the drafting officials remained the same. The drafting process was affected by the organisational reshuffles in the wake of the BSE crises that have been discussed above. The 'main work' of drafting was actually done at DG III, a predecessor of DG ENTR responsible for enterprise and industry (COM88:22), and the responsible unit and the pen-holding desk official did not become part of DG SANCO until October 1999 when President Prodi started to move all food safety units to this DG (COM88:42; COM115:31).

In addition, staff in this particular Commission had a long history of trying to create a European market for supplements. When the first US imports hit the UK during the early 1990s, the unit in the enterprise DG was already starting to draft a European law (COM88:106, 154), but had to shelve this proposal in 1993, because 'some interests felt their marketing area threatened' and 'lobbied against the proposal' as one of the drafting officials mentions, alluding to producers holding medicinal licenses in the stricter member states (COM88:112). This national opposition, driven by 'pharmaceutical companies', was transmitted via the Commissioner level into DG III (COM88:194) and – while no direct allusion was made during the interviews – one should note that the then Commissioner Bangemann came from Germany, one of the more restrictive states with regard to food supplements.

Yet the officials kept the issue cooking. A staff working paper accompanying the broader 1996 single market review mentions food supplements as an area in which regulatory action against technical trade barriers was needed (Commission of the European Communities 1996: 27). Emphasising this commitment, the unit issued a discussion paper,[3] which can be considered as the prelude to the drafting of the 2000 proposal (COM88:116). In parallel, it initiated infringement procedures against Germany and Austria, both of which imposed trade restrictions based on treating supplements as medicinal products (Europe Information Service 1999, 2000).

This persistence is remarkable and it points out that the major groundwork for the 2000 proposal was done before the big food scares occurred in the late 1990s. During a period when European food policy served mainly market creation purposes, the main regulatory ideas 'came from the service level' (COM88:86), with the primary aim 'to facilitate trade in these products' (COM88:26). This was in line with the overall tasks of DG III and particularly those of the foodstuffs unit, but also nicely suited the prevalent context of the single market review (Commission of the European Communities 1996). Even though formal responsibilities had been shifted to DG SANCO during the endgame, the proposal contents were 'more or less a continuation' of what has been developed earlier in DG III (COM88:22).

However, a changing context brought not only new opportunities but also adaptations of the drafting unit's position on food supplements. On the one hand, a

---

3. DGIII/5934/97; *Addition of vitamins and minerals to foods and food supplements: a discussion paper*; also cited in (BEUC 2000a). Access has been granted by the Secretariat General of the Commission under formal request GESTDEM 2010/623.

rising and more 'pushy' market for dietary supplements and ongoing infringement procedures led the member states increasingly to prefer 'a Community solution rather than having to face it case by case' (COM88:98, 30). On the other hand, the higher political importance of food safety in the wake of the BSE crisis raised demands for consumer protection, which now also informed DG III's position on the proposal (COM88:134). Adding to the market-making goal, another justification was now 'to ensure that people have safe products that will not put them in danger of excess' (COM88:90).

This ranking of market-making and consumer safety informed the policy choices formation on all four individual proposal provisions that distributed rights among producers and consumers. Regarding the scope, the officials were well aware that they had to decide whether to have supplements 'regulated under food law […] under medicinal law […] or as a category apart' (COM88:34). The major reason to treat them as foodstuffs, it was claimed, was the existing horizontal framework on food. This made legislative drafting less resource-intensive, because one already 'had all this general food law and […] only needed a specific piece of legislation that dealt with the particularities of the products' (COM88:38). Yet this does not explain fully why supplements were not treated as pharmaceuticals, an area that was also subject to a legislative Community framework (e.g. Directive 65/65/EEC). This decision was actually justified by the fact that supplements 'did not cure, they did not claim to cure or to treat diseases' (COM88:34), which appears quite unconvincing given that these products were actually marketed on the basis of their health effects (Eberhardie 2007). Rather, the decision to consider supplements as foodstuffs seems to have been at least partly predetermined by the fact that the original producer complaints were filed under this heading, and that treating them as pharmaceuticals would have shifted responsibility away from the unit that held the original 1992 proposal in the drawer. In addition, treating supplements as foodstuffs was likely to render less member state opposition as it did not need to interfere with national licenses to sell medicinal products (COM88:30). In this view, further producer duties to protect and to inform consumers were subordinated to the envisaged trade-promoting effects.

The same can be said about the unit's choice of a full harmonisation approach, which prohibits any trade restrictions by member states. Even in the 1990s drafting officials considered mutual recognition the *de jure* status quo, which is evident in the infringement procedures against Germany and Austria. As incoming producer complaints provided evidence that this was not working, simply re-codifying mutual recognition in the proposal would not have furthered market-making, and thus the full harmonisation approach was chosen (COM88:26).

As noted above we can only judge what this full harmonisation means for consumer protection by assessing the rules on the specification of food supplements where the proposed degree of interventionism exceeds a purely *laissez-faire* solution. Before the food scares in Europe, a discussion paper from the drafting unit left open whether it preferred only a negative list of prohibited substances or the finally chosen and much more strict regulatory instrument of a positive list (Europe Information Service 1992). Given the attention to food safety when the initiative was renewed in 1997 and the scientific uncertainty regarding the effects of an artificially enriched diet (Eberhardie 2007; Lewis and Strom 2002), this can be explained by the Commission's willingness to avoid any risk associated with potentially unknown and thus unregulated nutrients. The actual list of allowed nutrients as well as the purity criteria and levels result directly from the input and expertise provided by the Scientific Committee on Food, in which one of the drafting officials was actively involved (COM88:186, 190, Commission of the European Communities 2000g: 2). It further has to be noted that the required minimum levels of nutrients contained in each dosage of food supplements represent a clear accommodation of consumer interest. The very idea that a product must contain enough active ingredients before it can be expected to work properly goes back to early demands from consumer associations (e.g. EURO COOP 1997), which welcomed this particular Commission position (BEUC 2000a: 7).

Congruence between consumer demands and the Commission position can also be found on the labelling provisions. However, this responsiveness to diffuse interests did not emerge from a politicised or salient context but rather out of extant and emerging parallel legislation. This was the general framework on nutrition labelling (Directive 90/496/EEC), as well as the regulation on health claims that was also prepared at the time (see below), drafted in the same unit, and principles established in the regulation on misleading advertising (COM88:38, COM30:51, BEUC 2000a: 9). Despite the consumer-friendly position on this key provision, it should be noted that DG III did not take every packaging requirement of consumer organisations on board. Among other things, they demanded child-resistant closures (cf. EURO COOP 1997; BEUC 2000a), which were not considered in the proposal.

Taken together, the choices taken by DG SANCO and ex DG ENTR Commission officials can be explained by three elements: the market-making motivation was instilled by industry demands, strategic limits were set by member state interests, and an accompanying focus on consumer-oriented food safety concerns was informed largely by a changed policy context in the wake of the BSE crisis. This is initially consistent with our major outcome hypothesis. We find a medium level of politicisation combined with lack of public interests in the particular issues addressed in the proposal, resulting in a proposal that tips towards market-making on a regulatory level that is closer to the *laissez-faire* model of consumer policy. Both the observable outcome implications and the process hypotheses support this view. The proposal entails templates from the least interventionist member states, mirrors producer demands and prohibits further national intervention, thereby harmonising at a comparatively low level of consumer protection. The drafting process, in addition, is dominated by the administrative sphere, has a long time horizon, and involved little intra-Commission conflict (COM88:54, 88).

Yet the Commission position on the product specification rules runs counter to such a clear conclusion. While these provisions undercut the most protective national regimes, some consumer protection at the expense of producers has been included in response to the combination of issue salience and politicisation that emerged from the BSE crisis and the management scandals of the Santer

Commission, as discussed earlier. Here, consumers profited in the wake of these developments, while the influence of politicisation and salience was only indirect.

In addition, we see some of the complementary and alternative explanations at play. First, anticipated member state opposition initially accounted for the shelving of the proposal in the early 1990s. Interestingly, the case history suggests that this anticipation was transmitted via the nationality of the then responsible Commissioner, who came from a country with high regulatory standards. Yet there is no evidence for this 'Commissioner characteristics' explanation during the actual conclusion of the process where David Byrne from Ireland – another country with high regulatory standards for food supplements – was the responsible Commissioner. Likewise, there was no evidence that the Commissioner's party affiliation played any role – in fact, given the limited involvement of the Commission's political leadership there was hardly any scope for this explanation. Furthermore, the 'productionist' view of position formation in consumer policies cannot account for the outcome. Rather, the contrary was the case. Triggered by US imports, the decisive producer arguments were those for lower standards across Europe rather than demands for protection against international imports.

6.2 Health and nutrition claims

The next proposal in the sample aims at regulating labelling, presentation and advertising of foodstuffs with regard to marketing claims that refer either to the nutritional content of foods (e.g. 'low fat') or the health effects of certain nutrients (e.g. 'calcium aids in the development of strong teeth'). The College of Commissioners adopted the initiative (Commission of the European Communities 2003c) by an oral procedure on 16 July 2003.

Since the food supplements proposal was adopted, the Council and the Parliament have also largely accepted the Commission propositions made in the 2000 White Paper. Regulation 178/2002 established the general principles of European food safety legislation, which also included the foundation of the European Food Safety Authority (EFSA) in Parma. The 2000 White Paper had also already announced legislation on marketing claims (Commission of the European Communities 2000j: 32), which were hitherto only partially regulated. For example, Directive 96/8/EC on energy-restricted diets prohibited any claims as to expected weight loss. More broadly, Directive 90/496/EEC generally prohibited misleading the consumer on nutritional labelling while the even broader Directive 2000/13/EC prohibited the attribution of preventing, treating or curing properties to foods. Beyond these general rules, some member states have also enacted specific laws, either restricting and regulating claims – as, for example, in Sweden – or even banning all health related claims – as in Denmark or Belgium (BEUC 2000e).

Food-related marketing claims were also on the agenda of the international regulatory community. The Codex Alimentarius has provided specific guidelines on nutritional claims since 1997. With regard to health claims, discussions 'proved to be much more difficult and controversial', and a preliminary settlement under

WTO rules was only reached in May 2003, two months before the Commission proposal under analysis was tabled (Commission of the European Communities 2003c: 4). All these regulatory efforts also reflect the fact that both the supply of and the demand for functional foods has been consistently rising since the early 1990s (COM30:51).

In this context, the drafting unit in DG SANCO prepared an internal 'scoping paper' on claims shortly after the 2000 White Paper appeared. In early 2001, the officials summarised their original ideas and gathered their line hierarchy's permission to push forward (COM30:127, 271). This timing of proposal initiation is important since our measures for both politicisation and public food safety salience show deflections during this period. In early 2001, we observe above-standard politicisation levels around the heavy media reporting on the Nice Treaty and the subsequently failed Irish referendum (cf. Chapter Two). Then, in June 2001, we see a brief but pronounced peak driven by an unusually high number of Europrotests culminating in violent anti-globalisation riots at the Gothenburg Council meeting. In addition, summer 2001 saw various strikes against the EU's fishery and transport policies as well as manifestations against the EU's handling of the BSE and foot-and-mouth diseases. These data suggest that the legitimacy of European governance was publicly contested in the early stages of drafting the health claims proposal. Yet the politicisation index drops during 2002 and only sets to sharply rise again around the debates on the Constitution shortly before the proposal was finally adopted in the first half of 2003.

The indicator for the public salience of food safety shows an enormous peak in early and mid-2001, which exceeds the investigation period mean by more than one standard deviation (cf. Figure 6.1). The media analyses indicate that this salience level was driven mainly by renewed outbreaks of BSE and food-and-mouth disease, which resulted in lasting and publicly contested trade bans of British and Dutch meat in the European market. But also salmonella occurrences and renewed transatlantic trade talks, as well as discussions surrounding the creation of the EFSA, account for the media prominence of food safety topics during this period. Yet aggregate food safety salience levels fall below their mean in autumn 2001 and drop further until February 2002. But shortly before the proposal at hand is adopted, the salience curve starts to rise again. This mirrors radical reform plans for EU agricultural policy, an EU ban of genetically modified crops from the US and newly published UN standards on genetically modified organisms (GMOs). Most importantly, however, this increase during the first half of 2003 also entails a range of prominent reports on nutrition and health claims, which even made direct reference to the regulatory plans of the Commission (e.g. Buck 2003b, 2003a; FAZ 2003a, 2003c, 2003d; Katan and Roos 2003; Sigaud 2003).[4]

4. A detailed search for the issues covered by the proposal ('health claims' OR 'functional food' OR 'food marketing' OR 'food labelling') results in the unusually high number of 122 hits in the newspaper sample. Note that all scrutinised newspapers also reported intensively on the later inter-institutional reception of the proposal, which contributes to the minor peak in food safety salience after proposal adoption (cf. Figure 6.1).

Against the comparatively high levels of EU politicisation and issue salience particularly during the early drafting stages, and the pronounced media visibility of the proposal itself shortly before its adoption, the theoretical model leads us to expect a Commission position that explicitly prefers diffuse consumer interest over the economic advantages of food producers.

Along three sets of key provisions that distribute rights and risks among consumers and producers in the legal text of the proposal (Commission of the European Communities 2003c), we can see that this expectation is met. Initially, this concerns the general principles regarding producers' usage of claims. The proposal understands claims widely, including not only verbal statements but also 'pictorial, graphic or symbolic representations' (ibid. Article 2.1). Any food product marketed with a health or nutrition claim must provide a full nutrition label. Claims must not be false or misleading, raise doubts about the safety or adequacy of other foods or imply that a balanced diet cannot supply appropriate quantities of nutrients in general. In addition, the proposal sets a comparatively high threshold with regard to the truthfulness of claims. Substances giving rise to a marketing claim must be included in sufficient quantity and in a form that the human body can use (bio-availability). What is more, the use of claims is only permitted if the 'average consumer' can be expected to understand the beneficial effects (Article 5). Most importantly, the Commission proposal requires the substantiation of a claim by 'generally accepted scientific data'. The burden of proof lies with producers or distributors, who must at all times be able to provide respective evidence.

This initial set of rules frees consumers from the duty to evaluate marketing practices in detail. In turn, it burdens producers by constraining their strategies in an expanding market of functional foods. This judgement also holds when we consider the net effect by comparing this Commission position to the regulatory status quo. Of course, misleading advertising was illegal under European and almost all national regimes. Yet except in Sweden and Denmark, more specific restrictions on health and nutritional claims did not apply in the European market. In particular substantiation by scientific data, a clear burden of proof on producers, and intelligibility by the average consumer were regulatory innovations tending clearly towards an interventionist model of consumer policy.

This picture is reproduced in the second set of key provisions, which adds general restrictions on the usage of claims. Article 4 of the proposal announces that the Commission will establish specific nutritional profiles – that is, combinations of fat, fatty acids, sugars and salt – which are deemed to be non-detrimental to human health. Any product failing to respect these profiles will not be allowed to bear any nutrition or health claim in the future. Beyond that, beverages with more than 1.2 per cent by volume of alcohol are excluded while the Commission proposal generally allows the future exclusion of further foods by a European committee procedure.

Compared to the regulatory status quo, these rules mostly present regulatory innovations. While marketing on alcoholic beverages was limited in many member states, making health-based advertising subject to the overall nutritional profile of a food was a wide-reaching intervention. It aimed to render some of the then most common advertising strategies for sweets, snacks, or sodas illegal. What is more, the possibility of further restrictions in the future presents an economic risk for producers in the development and marketing of new products. On the flipside, the rules strongly protect the consumer against the detrimental side-effects of foods that contain only single health-promoting ingredients. This set of rules thus pushes the Commission position more towards an interventionist model of consumer policy.

A third set of relevant proposal provisions contains rules on health claims in particular. Once a producer uses a health claim, the food's presentation must state the importance of a balanced diet and a healthy lifestyle, it must provide the quantity of the food and the pattern of consumption needed to achieve the claimed effect, and it must warn potential risk groups. Furthermore, the Commission aims to prohibit so-called 'implied health claims' meaning assertions that refer to either the overall well-being ('preserves youth'), the psychological or behavioural functions of food ('helps your body to resist stress'), to slimming or weight control, or to claims that make reference to health professionals.

All other health claims are made subject to a pre-market authorisation procedure. The producer must apply to the EFSA by submitting the proposed claim and data on the food's characteristics, as well as peer-reviewed scientific evidence. Having assessed these data, the EFSA then informs the Commission, which in turn holds a public consultation before a committee decision finally decides on the claim's authorisation. The same seven-month procedure applies if a claim is to be modified, suspended or revoked. It has to be noted that the proposal also foresees the establishment of a positive list of 'generally accepted' claims in the future. Yet such claims must be based on unequivocally agreed scientific results, such as the often-mentioned example of the relationship of calcium and the growth of human bones. Comparing these rules to the regulatory status quo again indicates a policy choice that tends towards consumer interventionism. As long as they were consistent with more general provisions on misleading advertising, health claims had been legal in the European market before (again with the exception of Denmark). In fact, only Sweden had a pre-market approval system for health claims in place when the Commission proposal was drafted. Thus, from a net perspective, also this third set of rules also burdens the producer side in an effort to improve consumer information.

Taken together, the Commission position on nutrition and health claims proposes to alter the distribution of rights among producers and consumers to the advantage of the latter. Food manufacturers and retailers complained that 'proposal no longer places priority on improvements in the functioning of the internal market' (CIAA 2003; likewise: EuroCommerce 2003b). So, which internal processes produced this proposed policy choice?

As highlighted in the preceding case study, the discussion on functional foods had a longstanding history in the Commission, which was accompanied by high personnel persistence in DG SANCO. The officials working on the claims proposal had drafted, negotiated and implemented most of the preceding food legislation for over twenty years, which provided them with a strong strategic capacity. From the beginning of the drafting process, the SANCO (and formerly ENTR/DG III) officials used their contacts with all relevant stakeholders and were able to oversee their preferences. In fact, the basic idea to regulate marketing claims materialised when the drafting officials discussed the issue in 'frequent meetings with member states' as well as with 'multinationals [...] that would like to produce in markets with the same label and the same claims and the same composition in the whole of Europe' (COM30:55, COM88:25). These early contacts explain why the idea to regulate claims supranationally found entry to the White Paper on Food Safety, and, at least since January 2000, all major stakeholders had known that the proposal for a regulation was coming up.

In response, the main European consumer group had published a policy paper by August 2000. This paper actually foreclosed the later Commission position to a large extent, for example, by proposing comparable general principles, restricted usage in the case of unhealthy nutritional profiles, and the pre-market approval of health claims (BEUC 2000e). The producer side, in contrast, tried to evade formal regulation and concluded a voluntary code of practice on health claims in January 2001 (CIAA 2003).

Yet during a period that also saw high EU politicisation and high public issue salience, DG SANCO sided more with the consumers and initiated the preparation of binding European law. After the initial scoping paper in early 2001 and the agreement of the internal hierarchy (COM30:127, 271), the drafting efforts were immediately made public with a widely distributed discussion paper in summer 2001 (Directorate-General Health and Consumer Protection 2001). Further milestones were another discussion paper in early 2002, which already came in the form of a legal text and was followed by an open stakeholder meeting (Directorate-General Health and Consumer Protection 2002) (BEUC 2003a). In addition, a revised draft was circulated informally in June 2003 shortly before the proposal was officially adopted.

These documents allow us systematically to track the development of the Commission's policy choice over time. During the high politicisation and high salience phase in 2001, the initial discussion paper tested the most interventionist and most contested regulatory ideas such as the burden of scientific proof, the pre-market authorisation and limiting claims to particular nutritional profiles (Directorate-General Health and Consumer Protection 2001: 4, 9–10). Yet particularly this latter idea was dropped from the 2002 draft proposal (Directorate-General Health and Consumer Protection 2002), which was published during a period in which both EU politicisation and food safety salience had fallen to local lows. But following consumer protest, the nutritional profiles issue re-emerged in the final proposal in 2003 when issue salience had reached its mean level again and politicisation had also started to rise.

This 'late introduction' of the provision into the proposal led to 'strong concerns with the food and drink industry', which expected it to stifle innovation and present new barriers to trade with third countries (CIAA 2003; EuroCommerce 2003b). Industry critics argued that this provision went beyond the market-making justification of the proposal indicated by its legal basis, Article 95 of the EC treaty. In their view, the Commission had unlawfully entered the field of public health, which would stall major marketing opportunities for companies operating in Europe (AE 2004a; Hauer 2006). Consumer representatives, in contrast, welcomed the requirement of healthy nutritional profiles 'unreservedly' (BEUC 2003a).[5] For our purposes, it is most important to note that the Commission's positioning on this particular conflict developed exactly in parallel with the swings in EU politicisation and public food safety salience.

The view that the political context drove SANCO to an interventionist position early in 2001 was also supported when a middle-ranking official was asked to rank the policy goals. In his words:

> [t]he first is the protection of consumers, whether it is interests, whether it is health, public health because of safety issues. But in the claims and the labelling, of course, we didn't have direct safety concerns. It was more protection of the consumer interest. Second, of course – and maybe one would say this is the first reason for harmonisation because it is our true basis – is to facilitate the functioning of the internal market. Last but not least, is that we also aim to provide the economic operators with a legal framework that is the same across Europe. (COM30:47)

Compared to the food supplements case, which was drafted by the same unit, the ranking of consumer protection and market creation was reverted for the health claims proposal – consumer interests suddenly came first.

Consistent with this rank order, the likewise strongly contested provision on pre-market approval of health claims was consciously modelled on the most interventionist pattern that could be found in Europe. In fact, the Swedish regime was the only one including a respective requirement, and DG SANCO officials thus intentionally chose it as a regulatory template (Directorate-General Health and Consumer Protection 2002: 10) – another move particularly pleasing to consumer demands (cf. EURO COOP 2003c).

However, consistency with our main hypothesis does not mean that the political context alone can explain all individual choices in the proposal. Many of the general principles on claims were taken over from the Codex Alimentarius (Commission of the European Communities 2003c: 3). SANCO's basic argument for this transfer was 'to avoid confusion and limit potential trade disputes' (Directorate-General Health and Consumer Protection 2001: 9). Clearly, the parallel international negotiations led by the DG affected position formation in the case at hand. But by also covering 'pictorial, graphic, or symbolic representations' and by shifting the responsibility to provide scientific data onto producers, SANCO exceeded the internationally agreed Codex rules in the name of the consumer, which again earned the applause of consumer representatives (BEUC 2003a).

---

5. Note that this was also the most contested issue in the inter-institutional negotiations (http://www.euractiv.com/en/health/nutrition-health-claims-foods/article-133154, accessed 5 July 2010).

Likewise, the prohibition of so-called implied health claims went beyond national and international rules, which again was fancied by consumers (ibid. 4), but presented another red rag for the European industry (AE 2004a; EuroCommerce 2003b).

Besides responsiveness to consumer interests and transfer from international rules, other strategic considerations played a minor role as well. The officials used their regular interactions with member state representatives to find out 'how any changes, any proposals would be received in Council', because 'at the end of the day the name of the game is to have a proposal that will go through by qualified majority' (COM30:163–5). Likewise, an EP resolution in June 2001 had signalled support for making 'enhanced function claims and disease reduction claims [...] a priority for legislation' (Commission of the European Communities 2003c: 7–8). Yet this anticipation of support from external political actors was incorrect as later debates on the proposal in Council and Parliament glaringly revealed (e.g. AE 2004a).

The political sensitivity of SANCO's interventionist thrust was already visible during drafting, most notably as other internal actors raised serious concerns and formal interventions. The internal documentation[6] indicates that two rounds of formal ISC were necessary. Even the second round, held roughly two weeks before official proposal adoption, did not bring about an agreement. In fact, 'the questions often came from DG Enterprise where, of course, the interests of the producers and the interests of manufacturers have been sort of represented' (COM30:73). Unfortunately, the official ISC document of DG ENTR was largely redacted, hence we cannot uncover the details of their substantial comments on DG SANCO's drafts.

Besides ENTR, the DG for agriculture also withheld its formal agreement. Like DG ENTR, DG AGRI voiced producer concerns, fearing that the proposal would 'discriminate between food business operators that can afford the costs of an authorisation procedure, and those that cannot'. Further, DG AGRI pointed to inconsistencies with fruits and wines regulations that it had recently concluded with the agreement of DG SANCO. Lastly, AGRI opposed the prohibition of claims for alcoholic beverages; a position that ranked also highly on the wish list of the food industry (CIAA 2003).

This lasting disagreement among the administrative levels ensured that the final decision on the proposal had to be negotiated among the political leaders of the involved DGs. It appears to have been taken only at the Commissioner's meeting of 16 July (European Commission 2003). But as we know from the analysis above, almost all of the interventionist choices of DG SANCO have survived in the final common Commission position. Direct evidence on College-level negotiations is lacking, but arguably the political context made a markedly consumer-friendly proposal very welcome, which may explain SANCO's internal success. In fact, the Secretariat-General of the Commission, which is often seen as the administrative

---

6. Internal documentation has been provided by the Secretariat-General in response to a formal request. The internal reference number is ISC 440018.

arm of the Commission President (Hartlapp *et al.* 2010), had supported SANCO during the ISC, adding that 'the revised proposal constitutes a strong signal about the intention of the Commission to respond to the challenge of promoting public health through different actions such as labelling of foods'.[7]

In summary, the case of health and nutrition claims exhibits a striking consistency with the theoretical model proposed in Chapter Three. The predictions of the outcome hypotheses apply: the combination of a politicised context and a salient issue area coincides with a Commission position that contained regulatory innovations supporting the consumer and built on templates from the most interventionist EU member states. A particularly striking piece of evidence is that the proposed levels of consumer interventionism co-varied with the key political context variables during the drafting process.

Also on the derived process implications, the case supports the model developed in Chapter Three. As predicted, the hierarchies were drawn early in the process, and the political level took the final decision. At two-and-a-half years, the time horizon of drafting was comparatively short and, from the start, drafting officials had been much more responsive to the demands of consumer interests despite apparent industry opposition. As predicted by the final process hypothesis, the more interventionist position of DG SANCO stirred internal conflict which, however, could be overcome without real concessions to internal opponents during a phase when high levels of EU politicisation combined with high issue salience.

Moreover, alternative explanations have little explanatory power in this particular case. Some anticipation of Council and EP positions has taken place, but given that the proposal caused intense debate after its adoption, Council and EP anticipation do not seem to have constrained SANCO very much. Likewise, little evidence on the national or partisan identity of the involved Commissioners could be found – particularly so since the issue of health claims does not affect particular national industries but rather affects all European food producers to the same extent. In addition, although Commissioners were informed from the beginning about the proposal, policy formulation took place mainly at the administrative levels. Lastly, the productionist view cannot account for position formation on health and nutrition claims. We have seen that parallel trade negotiations on the Codex Alimentarius have indeed influenced SANCO's position, but this did not take place in response to producer demands for more protection, and indeed even exceeded the internationally negotiated level of consumer protection.

6.3 The addition of vitamins and minerals to food

Less than five months after the health claims proposal, the following food safety case in the sample was adopted on 10 November 2003 and a regulation was proposed on the intentional addition of vitamins, minerals and certain other substances to foodstuffs (Commission of the European Communities 2003d).

---

7.   Reply of the Secretariat-General to ISC 440018.

For food producers, this so-called food fortification initially presents a valuable marketing strategy, for example, by advertising the health effects of 'enriching' food products with vitamin C. However, food fortification also was a tool in various national health policies, which made enrichment obligatory in certain staple foods so as to cure population intake deficiencies.

Extant national rules and justifications accordingly varied as to the purposes for which nutrients could be added, the types of foods in which enrichment was allowed, and the extent to which such foods could be actually artificially augmented. This ranged from the most liberal regimes, in which addition was allowed with hardly any restrictions, over a widely spread middle ground in which different sets of nutrients were allowed to different maximum levels, to the most restrictive systems in which nutrient addition was only possible if population deficiencies could be scientifically proven (Commission of the European Communities 2003d: 3, see also DG III of the European Commission 1997: 7–8). On this dimension, the UK tended to be the most liberal, while Denmark had one of the most restrictive regimes on food fortification in place (cf. European Court of Justice 2002).

The initiative to harmonise these regimes was once again drafted by the DG SANCO unit that had drawn up the earlier proposals on food supplements and marketing claims (COM88:154). While the idea of regulating the area dates back to the 1990s (see below), a major milestone was a draft proposal circulated among stakeholders in Brussels in June 2000 (Commission of the European Communities 2000f). The actual drafting period thus overlaps largely with the preceding case and was subject to the main peaks of EU politicisation in 2001 and 2003. With regard to the issue salience of food safety, the renewed outbreaks of various animal diseases as well as the discussion on health claims was high on the public agenda. But more specific keyword searches in the quality newspapers speak for little contemporaneous public attention to the specific content of the proposal at hand. Between January 1999 and the proposal adoption in November 2003, no particular articles on food enrichment could be retrieved, except some references to the economic performance of companies such as Unilever.[8]

Note, in addition, that the proposed regulation on nutrition and health claims was negotiated by Council and Parliament while the proposal on food fortification was finalised in the Commission. Not the least due to its interventionist thrust, this earlier proposal had become a high-profile and politically sensitive issue that stirred lively debates among interest groups and European politicians (AE 2003c, 2004a; Bream 2004).[9] Given that the claims proposals had much broader

---

8. All for newspapers were searched for ((food*) AND (enrichment OR fortification OR restoration) AND (vitamin* OR mineral* OR nutrient*)) and the respective translations as used in the differing language versions of the Commission proposal. The covered period was 1 January 1999–10 November 2003.

9. Besides, another relatively far-reaching consumer policy proposal of the Commission had been published in parallel. The Council and EP discussions on the unfair commercial practices proposal (cf. Chapter 4.6) also attracted significant attention from producer and consumer groups during the second half of 2003.

scope and that the drafting unit was also responsible for defending this proposal in Council and Parliament, the drafting officials were quite sure that 'all the attention was on the claims' when they issued the food fortification proposal under analysis here (COM88:130).

With a view to the theoretical expectations, this political context is rather inconclusive. Rising EU politicisation and at least mean levels of public salience of related issues during parts of the drafting period could have provided the Commission officials with incentives to draw up a more interventionist proposal on food fortification. Yet the longstanding history of this particular proposal, as well as the low public interest in the specific issues it covers, leave some question marks on this expectation. So, which policy choices did the Commission actually make in the legislative initiative at hand?

Four sets of rules in the final legal text (Commission of the European Communities 2003d) directly address the distribution of burdens among consumers and producers. Initially, these are the purposes and categories of foods for which artificial fortification is allowed. According to the proposal, adding vitamins and minerals would only be forbidden for non-processed products and alcoholic beverages. For all other foodstuffs, artificial enrichment is allowed if it serves one of three purposes. First, is 'restoration', meaning the addition of nutrients that were originally present in a product but were lost during processing or storage. The second purpose is the 'nutritional equivalence of substitute foods'. This refers to cases such as margarine, which serves as a substitute for butter but naturally contains considerably less vitamin D, and was thus mandatorily enriched, for example, in Germany. Another allowed purpose is the narrower 'enrichment' of foodstuffs, which refers to the addition of vitamins or minerals that are not usually part of the respective product. The Commission maintains that such a producer action must either be based on deficiencies in the population, on the potential to improve the nutritional status of the population, or on 'evolving generally accepted scientific knowledge' regarding the role of vitamins and minerals and their health effects.

The broadness of these rules obviously ensures that all foods and purposes of fortification that were granted in any of the extant national regulations were also covered by the supranational law that the Commission proposed. For the most liberal regimes, this key provision enshrines the status quo while it clearly deviates from the more restrictive regimes that had previously allowed addition for usually one of these purposes before. The net effect of this key provision throughout Europe is thus a liberalising one, which sits well with a *laissez-faire* model of European consumer policy.

A second set of provisions affecting the distribution of risks among consumers and producers specifies the substances that can be added to foods. The proposal establishes a conclusive list of allowed vitamins and minerals and establishes purity criteria as well as minimum and maximum levels. This list, as well as potential future changes to it, is based on scientific risk assessments. In addition, the proposal establishes minimum amounts of nutrients to be added, and refers all more specific decisions in future to a committee procedure.

Beyond vitamins and minerals, the proposal also provides some rules on other substances added to foods. While not directly listing such substances, the Commission proposes a categorisation that structures future regulation. If the EFSA sees sufficient scientific evidence that the respective substance is harmful to health, its addition to foods may be prohibited or restricted. This happens through either Community initiatives or a member state provision, which, however, has to be notified and requires the Commission's agreement. Further, a category of substances for which 'scientific uncertainty persists' is established. For this category, food producers, distributors, or any other party may submit scientific data supporting the substance's safety. The Commission and a committee then make a final decision on prohibition, restriction or clearance of that substance in foods within four years.

Assessing the degree of interventionism in this set of provisions is tricky without biological or chemical knowledge. But from a layman's perspective, a list of thirteen allowed vitamins and fifteen allowed minerals does not appear to be too restrictive for producers.[10] Article 4 provides for a seven-year transitional period during which member states may allow trade in foods enriched with additional vitamins and minerals, but exploiting this derogation requires notification with the EFSA and a positive risk assessment of the respective substances. This shows that the proposed list of allowed substances is more interventionist than provisions in the most liberal member state regimes. But an overall assessment of consumer interventionism in these provisions is difficult, as it presents a moving target. The Commission does not fix its position regarding future extensions of permitted vitamins, minerals or other substances, but refers them to tertiary committee decisions in the future. In this light, the second set of key provisions takes a flexible middle ground between an interventionist and a *laissez-faire* approach to consumer protection.

The picture is similar for provisions on the labelling, presentation and advertising of enriched foodstuffs. According to the proposal, the addition of nutrients must be declared on the label, and full nutrition labelling is mandatory for enriched foodstuffs. Labelling must not be misleading or deceptive, and should not imply that a normal diet is an insufficient source of particular nutrients. Insofar, the labelling rules are consistent with the basic principles DG SANCO had proposed with the health claims proposal a few months earlier. In this view, they also deviate from a pure *laissez-faire* model by constraining the producer side more than the most liberal regimes – for example, the UK – had done before. Yet labelling is not made subject to obligatory pre-market control as had been the case in the claims proposal. In sum, thus, the Commission's position on this third set of provisions is also placed somewhere in between the most restrictive and the most permissive member state regimes.

---

10. In terms of vitamins, the proposal allows vitamins A, D, E, K, B1, B2, niacin, pantothenic acid, B6, folic acid, B12, biotin and vitamin C. Regarding minerals, the following substances can be added by food producers: calcium, magnesium, iron, copper, iodine, zinc, manganese, sodium, potassium, selenium, chromium, molybdenum, fluoride, chloride and phosphorus.

The fourth and final set of provisions regulates the remaining national powers. In principle, the proposal prohibits any further trade restrictions with regard to the addition of nutrients to foods. But it also foresees a safeguard measure similar to the 'new approach' model if a member state suspects immediate danger to human health. National authorities may then restrict trade, which, however, requires notification with the Commission. Following an EFSA opinion, then, the Commission decides together with a committee of representatives from all member states on the suspension of the unilateral trade restriction. A similar picture holds for the mandatory addition of vitamins and food. While several member states prescribed the addition of vitamins A and D to margarine, of iron and calcium to flour, or of iodine to salt at the time the proposal was drafted (Commission of the European Communities 2003d: 3), the proposal requires notification and a positive opinion of the Commission for such measures in the future. Essentially, these rules remove extant limitations on freedoms of food producers in individual member states and transfer them to supranational decision making.

In conjunction with the wide leeway on allowed fortification purposes and categories and against the intermediate position on allowed substances and labelling requirements, the overall effect of the Commission proposal thus tends to be a liberalising one. The Commission did not choose to remove any producer restrictions in the issue area completely, but its relative positioning in the space of extant regulatory templates in Europe is closer to a *laissez-faire* than to an interventionist conception of consumer policy. So, how did this rather liberal position come about?

Interviews with the involved Commission officials revealed that policy formulation on food fortification was strongly intertwined with the (likewise rather liberal) food supplements proposal (cf. Chapter 6.1).[11] As early as 1991, the drafting unit – then still part of DG III, responsible for industry policy – had planned to regulate both food supplements and food fortification in a single piece of European law. However, we have seen that this early endeavour failed due to anticipated Council opposition, which the officials explained as 'particular commercial interests' from member states with more restrictive regimes (COM88:194). Yet a growing market for enriched foods and supplements increased political pressure for liberalisation over time (COM88:98). This led to a high-level meeting of national authorities and European Commission services in 1995, which the officials took as a request to restart work on the matter (DG III of the European Commission 1997: 1). In 1997 they drew up a renewed version of the 1991 discussion paper (ibid. 3), but the national responses were not as encouraging as assumed. In this context, the drafting officials decided that tackling food supplements and food fortification at the same time was 'too much' for the member states (COM88:90). They split both issues into separate proposals – nevertheless, DG SANCO's 2003 position on food fortification is also 'more or less a continuation' of what had been developed by DG III during the early 1990s (COM88:22). The major aim of

---

11. Note that the food supplements proposal became binding European law in the meantime; on 10 June 2002, it was officially signed by the Council and the EP.

this regulatory endeavour, was thus first and foremost the creation of a European market for fortified foods.

In this vein, the drafting unit tried to break opposition from the more restrictive member states using a judicial approach. Formal infringement procedures against national trade restrictions on fortified foods were initiated against France, Denmark and the Netherlands. Based on individual producer complaints, the Commission sent reasoned opinions to which the three governments replied negatively, which ultimately led to the invocation of the ECJ.[12] Mirroring the strategy the unit had used with regard to food supplements, this judicial approach was meant to convince reluctant member states of a 'Community solution rather than having to face it case by case' (COM88:98) – a prime example of what Susanne Schmidt (2000) has termed the 'lesser evil' strategy of the Commission. But did the original market-making aim stemming from the 1990s insulate this particular drafting process from the pressures of EU politicisation and public food safety salience that we observed at the turn of the century?

For the first set of key provisions, this appears to be the case initially. The three purposes of adding nutrients – restoration, nutritional equivalence and fortification – are transferred from the international regime of the Codex Alimentarius (COM88:70, Commission of the European Communities 2003d: 5). Yet with regard to fortification the position of the drafting officials was 'less strict, much less strict' (COM88:74). The Codex requires that actual population deficiencies in the respective nutrients must be scientifically proven, while the drafting unit considered 'future changes in dietary habits' sufficient to allow fortification – a very liberal position that was already fixed in 1997 (DG III of the European Commission 1997: 4–5). Consumer associations strongly disagreed, arguing that 'changes in dietary habits' is too flexible a concept that shifts the risk of unbalanced diets and nutrient overdoses onto consumers (BEUC 2003b: 4).

Yet process tracing shows that the market-making aim of the 1990s was not carried forward blindly. In fact, the drafting officials – now part of the Commission's health and consumer DG – tried to install a much more interventionist rule into this first set of key provisions. According to documentation from the ISC,[13] SANCO's latest internal draft proposal dating from August 2003 foresaw 'establish[ing] specific nutrient profiles that food or certain categories of foods must respect in order that vitamins and minerals [can] be added to them'. During the late stages of drafting, SANCO actually tried to limit enrichment only to foods that are generally healthy, thereby responding to the main demand of European consumer

---

12. To illustrate the markets we are speaking about here, the relevant complaint in the case of the Netherlands was lodged by Kellogg's, a company selling a range of fortified cereals (European Court of Justice 2004). In the case of Denmark, the stumbling block was 'Ocean Spray Cranberry', a fruit drink enriched with vitamin C (European Court of Justice 2002). The reasoned opinions were sent to the Netherlands in December 1997 (European Court of Justice 2004), to France in October 1998 (European Court of Justice 2001) and to Denmark in September 2000 (European Court of Justice 2002).

13. These documents have been provided by the Secretariat-General in response to a formal request. The internal reference number of the respective ISC is 440452.

associations (BEUC 2003b, 2004a). Given that enrichment was a practice mainly reserved for sweets and sodas, this regulatory approach would have seriously constrained producer freedom, making the flexibility mentioned above much less significant in terms of the distribution of rights and risks. This nutritional profile idea was not yet contained in the 1997 paper, nor was it part of the 2000 draft proposal on food fortification. It emerged only in the partially parallel claims proposal in early 2001, during a period when both politicisation and issue salience peaked (cf. Chapter 6.2).

Yet while the unit had been successful with this in the claims proposal half a year earlier, the idea of nutritional profiles now stirred much stronger internal opposition. DG ENTR in particular asked for the deletion of the whole paragraph in SANCO's draft proposal. At the internal consultation they argued that the proposal at hand was different from the claims initiative. While the latter targeted 'only' marketing, the fortification proposal intervened much more as it regulated the actual production of food. Allowing the addition of vitamins and minerals only to foods that have a favourable health profile would 'eliminate any opportunity to improve some foods', 'block any innovation in certain sectors' and thus 'unnecessarily reduce the competitiveness of European industry'.[14] Since nutritional profiles are not part of the final Commission position, ENTR was clearly successful in this internal bid – also owing to the fact that the idea of nutritional profiles in the claims proposal was already strongly contested in the Council at the time the food fortification initiative was finalised.

In contrast, DG SANCO asserted a more interventionist position with regard to the conclusive list of allowed vitamins and minerals. Both the 1992 and the 1997 draft proposals had presented a negative list of forbidden substances only, a much more liberal alternative leaving more freedom to producers (cf. Europe Information Service 1992; DG III of the European Commission 1997). Yet in June 2000, the leaked draft proposal fixed SANCO's position to a positive list (Commission of the European Communities 2000f: Article 4). The decision for this much more precautionary policy option was thus made only after the BSE crisis and after the resignation of the Santer Commission; that is after the Commission had experienced high levels of food safety salience and a high level of general EU politicisation.

But national interests mattered as well. The blueprint for the future regulation of adding other substances to foods entered the proposal at a very late stage. Neither the 1997 discussion paper nor the 2000 draft proposal mentions any substances apart from vitamins and minerals. However, during 2001–2 Council negotiations on the sister proposal on food supplements extended this initiative to other substances (see Directive 2002/46/EC: especially Article 2). Since they personally took part in these negotiations, the drafting officials anticipated that similar national demands would be made for the fortification proposal and tried at least to sketch how enrichment with such substances could be regulated supranationally.

---

14. Author's translation of the internal ENTR response to ISC 44045.

198 | A Responsive Technocracy?

Interestingly, DG ENTR used this as an additional access point for their internal critique. The officials from the industry DG argued that if nutritional profiles were a necessary condition for the enrichment of vitamins and minerals, this needed to hold for other substances as well. But this would have made SANCO's proposal technically and politically too demanding. Technically, it would have required a complete framework on a specified list of all other substances that might be added to foods. Politically, it would have increased interventionism further by extending the proposal to an even broader range of foodstuffs. Faced with these alternatives, SANCO stayed away from nutritional profiles and kept future regulation of substances other than vitamins and minerals sketchy. Consumers were hardly satisfied with this cautious approach, pointed out that 'certain other substances' were 'too vague a concept' and demanded positive lists 'prior to any market integration' (BEUC 2004a: 9).

Similarly, the consumer representatives considered the labelling provisions as insufficient. They wanted a label with nutrient values per portion, specific advice for vulnerable groups, an explicit remark that enriched foods cannot substitute a balanced diet and obligatory pre-market control of all labels (BEUC 2004a: 11–3). However, during early drafting, the then DG III officials had considered these demands as 'too burdensome' for food producers in the light of their aim to create a competitive market for enriched foods in Europe (DG III of the European Commission 1997: 21) While DG ENTR would have liked even fewer restrictions on labelling, the SANCO officials kept their intermediate position until the final proposal was adopted in 2003.

With a few minor exceptions, thus, the final proposal carried over the original ideas that were developed in the early 1990s and that 'came up from the service level' (COM88:86). In fact, the internal hierarchy was hardly mentioned and also all issues that emerged during the formal ISC appear to have been hammered out at the administrative echelons so that the proposal could be adopted by a written procedure in the College of Commissioners.

All things considered, the food fortification case is not fully consistent with the major outcome hypothesis scrutinised in this book. While politicisation and issue salience exhibited strong and overlapping local peaks especially during 2001, this did not instil a significantly higher degree of interventionism in the policy position that the Commission finally proposed. Yet a closer look at the drafting process indicates that the case history does not fully refute the theoretical model. With regard to nutritional profiles and the allowed substances, DG SANCO's position indeed changed towards more interventionism during the period 2000–3. This resulted in enhanced responsiveness to consumer interests, and led to some rushed proposal adaptations. Yet due to two constraints, the expected interventionism did not carry over to the final Commission proposal.

First, SANCO's late pandering to consumer interests met clear internal opposition, particularly from DG ENTR. Given the intermediate level of specific issue salience during proposal finalisation in late 2003, this is exactly what the process hypothesis on internal conflict would lead us to expect (cf. Chapter Three). The political context was not sufficiently heated to provide for a common interest that could trump the typical differences between departments of consumer protection and industry. Second, member state preferences constrained further interventionism. The case history shows that policy formulation on food fortification, as well as on supplements, has struggled with national opposition since the early 1990s. Given this experience of the drafting officials, the signals from parallel Council negotiations on food supplements and marketing claims clearly warranted caution with regard to nutritional profiles or other substances added to foods. Also in this case, political feasibility in the Council appears as a significant complementary explanation for policy choices taken within the European Commission machinery.

The other three alternative explanations have little to add for the case at hand. The political hierarchy was hardly involved. Both responsible Commissioners, Bangemann (Germany, Freie Demokratische Partei) and Byrne (Ireland, Fianna Fáil), came from member states with high standards on food fortification, and from relatively liberal party backgrounds. In the light of partisan and nationality hypotheses, we should thus not have observed the variation in DG SANCO's positions that occurred in parallel to rising politicisation and issue salience. Likewise, the case hardly involves a 'trading up' following producer demands for external protection – it was actually rather triggered by trade interests emerging from US imports in the early 1990s.

6.4 Food additives

Much further down the timeline, the next food safety case in the sample was adopted by the Commission on 28 July 2006. It was a proposal for a regulating the use of additives in foods traded in the European market (Commission of the European Communities 2006b). Food additives are substances added during manufacturing, processing or packaging that are usually not consumed or used as characteristic food ingredients. This explicitly excludes nutrients covered by the preceding case, but encompasses sweeteners, colours, thickeners, anti-foaming and glazing agents and packaging gases, to name a few. If at all, these additives are known by their E-numbers in the ingredient lists on foodstuff packages.

In this area, the regulatory status quo was defined mainly in already existing European law (MacMaoláin 2007: 210–9). Food additives were covered by four directives which, among others, contain general principles (Directive 89/107/EEC), as well as specific rules for sweeteners (Directive 94/35/EC), colours (Directive 94/36/EC) and all remaining additives (Directive 95/2/EC). This was complemented by Decision 292/97/EC on national exemptions and six further implementing acts. These laws were all drawn up and managed in DG III – the predecessor of DG ENTR. Formally, all of them were to be repealed by the proposal at hand (Commission of the European Communities 2006b: 7).

The proposal studied here was published in parallel with three acts on enzymes and flavourings, and a common authorisation procedure for these substances. In the regulatory community, this set of proposals became known as the 'food improvement package' (COM80:39), and it was drafted in a SANCO unit responsible for chemicals, contaminants and pesticides (COM29:50). This unit had also been transferred from DG III during the restructuring at the onset of the Prodi Commission in 1999 (COM115:121). Like the other proposals discussed so far, the food improvement package was announced in the 2000 White Paper on Food Safety. Initial drafts were put forward as early as August and November 2003, and then continuously revised until another set of working papers was made public in February 2005, one-and-a-half years prior to its final adoption (Hagenmeyer 2006: 296; Directorate-General Health and Consumer Protection 2005).

In Chapter Two, we have seen that this three-year drafting period marked particularly stormy times with regard to the overall public politicisation of European integration. The unseen heights in the politicisation index observed from late 2003 onwards are related to the upcoming Eastern enlargement in May 2004, as well as the EP elections and the inauguration of the Barroso Commission in the same year. A further upward trend in 2005 was driven by debates on the Growth and Stability Pact following suspension of the deficit procedures against France and Germany, but were also mainly spurred by the draft Constitution and most importantly, of course, by the failed referenda in France and the Netherlands in summer 2005. Debates on the services directive in early 2006 sustained these high levels of public politicisation. Thus, the need of public support for further integration should have provided the Commission with clear incentives to demonstrate the usefulness of its legislative output to the broader public. But actually, the drafting officials received few contemporaneous signals that the food additives proposal was a useful vehicle in this regard.

Our measure for the public salience of food safety issues plotted above drops markedly after 2003. The share of food safety-related media reporting falls below the investigation period mean and stagnates there for the complete drafting process analysed here. This picture of comparatively low contemporaneous salience also holds for the narrower perspective on the specific issues covered by the proposal. During the three years of drafting, the sample of analysed European quality newspapers contains few discussions on the consumer risks involved in food additives.[15] The few hits that can be found are reports on the economic performance of chemical or food producers, some editorials that merely mention food additives as one of the realities of the modern world – especially with reference to the 2006 Nobel prize in chemistry and the REACH regulation – and single articles on individual additives. Only one article mentions the regulatory competences of the EU, arguing solely that it creates 'red tape' for UK food producers (Eaglesham 2005). Given the comparatively low numbers of press reports (which, in addition, come with a strong industry rather than a risk focus) the issue area was not

15. This result comes about by a relatively open search procedure. Using the databases described in Appendix C and covering the period 1 January 2003–28 July 2006, I evaluated all articles that contained the phrase 'food additives' or the Commission based translations of it ('Lebensmittelzusatzstoffe', 'additifs alimentaires', 'aditivos alimentarios') in text or title. This resulted in only twenty-five hits for the *Financial Times*, ten in *Le Figaro*, five in *El País* and none in the *Frankfurter Allgemeine Zeitung*.

particularly visible or important to the diffuse public at the time. In this vein, the involved Commission officials themselves considered the proposal as 'essentially low key' and a 'low level piece of legislation' (COM80:67, 133). Thus, the model developed in Chapter Three does not lead us to expect that the Commission to propose strong market interventions in the interest of the consumer.

This can be illustrated with four sets of provisions in the Commission proposal (Commission of the European Communities 2006b). The first one defines the approved substances and the purposes for which they can be added to foods. The legal text establishes a positive list of additives and specifies the general conditions that any future additive on this list must fulfil. Additives must not impair the health of consumers, there has to be a 'reasonable technological need', and the food additive usage must not mislead the consumer.

Additives are allowed if they either preserve the nutritional quality of the food, support special dietary needs of certain consumers, or aid manufacturing, processing, preparation, treatment, packaging, transport or storage of food. Usage of sweeteners is only allowed if no sugars are added, if sweeteners replace sugars in energy-reduced foods, if they extend shelf life by the replacement of sugar or if they serve particular nutritional uses for conditions such as diabetes. Colourings are allowed if they give colour to otherwise colourless foods, if they restore the food's 'original appearance' or if they make the food 'visually more appealing'. Producers are advised to use substances 'at the lowest level necessary to achieve the desired effects'.

Explicitly, none of these limitations applies to so-called processing aids (ibid. Article 2). The legal definition of processing aids differs from food additives only insofar as the former 'may result in the unintentional but technically unavoidable presence in the final product [...] provided they do not present any health risk and do not have any technological effect on the final product' (ibid. Article 3). While processing aids may be present in the food sold to the consumer, the fact that they have already fulfilled their technological purpose earlier in the production chain frees them from the restrictions that 'active' food additives encounter.

Given the extremely wide definition of purposes and the loophole of processing aids, the Commission's choice on this set of provisions hardly signals interventionism. In fact, a closer comparison with the extant regime shows that the proposal hardly changes anything (cf. MacMaoláin 2007: 215–6). The extant directives foresaw the positive list of food additives and specified the same general conditions, and allowed the purposes of additive usage and the requirement to operate at the lowest level necessary. Likewise, limitations on sweeteners and colourings had already been set in the recitals of Directives 94/36/EC and 94/35/EC. Also processing aids had previously been excluded; these rules thus present a mere re-codification of the formerly scattered European law.

The second set of key provisions specifies some general rules on the usage of food additives. Food additives are forbidden in unprocessed foods. The proposal also establishes a carry-over principle, meaning that if a food additive is allowed in one ingredient of a compound food, it is also allowed in the final product. Previously this rather self-evident rule, and the rule excluding unprocessed foods, was explicitly mentioned only in the colourings directive. According to the proposal, governments may prohibit food additives only in specific traditional foods that are exclusively specified in Annex IV. Among others, this covers German beer under the *Reinheitsgebot*, Austrian *Hüttenkäse*, French preserved truffles, Danish *Kodboller*, or Italian *Mortadella*. A rather similar list was previously excluded from food additive usage by Directive 94/34/EC. Therefore, this second set of provisions provides legal clarification at best, but hardly indicates meaningful shifts in either a producer- or a consumer-friendly direction.

This also holds with regard to the labelling requirements in the proposal. They specify that food additives have to be traceable throughout the production chain and, more importantly, they prescribe that food additives must be listed on the packaging of the final product. Here the producer may choose to either use the name of the additive or its E-number as specified in the annex of the proposal. These labelling rules do not deviate from what had already become European law in 1989 (cf. Directive 89/107/EEC: especially Articles 7–9), and also this set of provisions does not place the Commission position on a relative continuum between the *laissez-faire* and interventionist models of consumer policy.

This only leaves the rules on the future regulatory management of food additives at the supranational level. They entail an obligation for producers to immediately inform the Commission if there is any new information that 'might affect the assessment of the safety of the food additive'. Member states are expected to monitor consumption and use of food additives and to report their findings to the Commission and the EFSA. But the most important element of the proposal refers to future changes in the list of allowed food additives. While adding or removing food additives from the list of allowed substances had previously required a full legislative procedure involving the Council and the EP, Article 9 of the 2006 proposal makes this subject to a new authorisation procedure that the Commission proposed in parallel with the case at hand. Future evaluations of food additives will undergo a risk assessment by the EFSA, but the actual decision will then be taken only by the Commission in conjunction with a committee of member state representatives.

How can one judge these rules with regard to our dependent variable? Clearly, the information obligations for producers, as well as the monitoring duties for the member states, were not part of the extant regime; thereby the Commission position raises the level of consumer protection slightly. Yet shifting future decisions on additives to the administrative sphere is clearly a net gain for producers. Removing the EP can be expected to significantly lower the transaction costs involved in approving new substances that could be added in the production of food. From the perspective of the food consumer, however, moving the decision from the Parliament to an administrative committee is a net loss with regard to public scrutiny of the biological and chemical technologies used in the production of food. Without claiming that this is a fully liberalising move, this Commission position tends towards the *laissez-faire* model in that it decreases producer costs at the expense of the information rights of the consumer.

In summary, the Commission's position in this sample case hardly alters the regulatory status quo. Given the few substantial changes, commentators claim that 'whether such a revival was worth a year-long legislation process remains debatable', seeing it as 'legislation for legislation's sake' (Hagenmeyer 2006). The distribution of rights among producers and consumer has not changed much, and where it has, it tends to benefit the producer's side. What processes drove the Commission to this conservative approach?

Food additives were also listed in the 2000 White Book on Food Safety, and so the drafting officials considered a corresponding regulation as 'one of the tasks the Commission had to carry out (COM29:74). But in contrast to the huge political upheavals that had stimulated the White Book, the basic impulses for the particular food additives regulation in early 2003 came mainly from the 'regulatory community', meaning 'colleagues up to Head of Unit, their opposite numbers of the member states officials and the middle-ranking regulatory affairs coordinators for the food associations involved' (COM80:55). In other words, neither consumer associations nor the leadership of the Commission were involved in setting the basic lines of the proposal. Naturally, the drafting officials reported to the cabinets of the responsible SANCO Commissioners – David Byrne from Ireland followed in 2004 by Márkos Kyprianoú from Cyprus – but received no guidance as regards the specific proposal content (COM29:161).

From the start, the drafting officials themselves had no plan to transcend mere 'simplification'. It was foreseen to include 'very little changes' in the proposal, with the major exceptions of streamlining authorisation procedures and including the EFSA, as warranted under the new general principles of European food legislation. The exercise was largely meant to 'adopt a coherent approach' on additives, flavourings and enzymes (COM29:58; COM80:51). Also the duration of the drafting process was driven mainly by the parallel proposals in the food improvement package. Since enzymes and flavourings were much less densely regulated at the European level, preparing the respective proposals took some time, while 'for food additives it could have been much faster' (COM29:126).

The drafting officials used the three-year period for testing responses from their major stakeholders. Regarding consumer associations, however, the drafting officials noted the experience that they 'have to explain a little bit the issues before we get their opinion' because 'consumer organisations unfortunately [...] have very little resources and they have to follow a lot of topics' (COM29:50). This hardly indicates proactive consumer lobbying on this particular proposal. But the industry side was very active. Consultations involved the International Sweeteners Association, the Confederation of the European Food and Drink Industry (CIAA), the European Chemical Industry Council (CEFIC), the Federation of European Food Additives and Food Enzymes Industries (ELC) and the Association of the Chocolate, Biscuit and Confectionary Industries of the EU (CAOBISCO, Commission of the European Communities 2006b: 3, COM29:54). The sheer number and specialisations of these pressure groups highlight the economic value involved in the production and application of food additives.

However, while the position of the affected market participants was known to officials during drafting, anticipating member state interests did not work well. Contact with member state representatives occurred at 'working group level', but did not help the drafting unit to see 'where the obstacles are', because 'between [the] last discussion with the member states and the real discussion in the Council quite some time has gone by'. Given the long time frame, member state representatives in the working group did not take things 'serious[ly] enough' (COM29:180). But how far did these various contacts with external stakeholders (or the lack thereof) influence DG SANCO's policy choices?

Initially, the particular definition of processing aids and their exclusion, was a point of contestation. Consumer associations would have liked to see all artificial substances in foods regulated under the same tight regime (BEUC 2006: 4), but the industry opposed avidly (Commission of the European Communities 2006b: 4). Originally, SANCO tried to take a middle ground in the 2005 draft proposal where the definition of processing aids included an additional provision that the substance must be intentionally removed after treatment or processing (Directorate-General Health and Consumer Protection 2005: 15). Effectively, this would have satisfied consumer concern, as any substance remaining in the foodstuff sold to the consumer would be treated under the additives regime. However, this rule would have made particular enzymes nowadays commonly employed in food production subject to the proposal: They cannot be removed for technical reasons and are usually inactivated only in the final product (Hagenmeyer 2006: 297). Producers protested, and sometime during the last year of drafting, SANCO officials apparently gave in. Given 'considerable impact, it was [...] decided not to progress such a change at this stage' (Commission of the European Communities 2006b: 4).

Most other provisions were basically just transferred from extant directives. The general rules on food additive usage saw little contestation or policy adaptations. The carry-over principle 'has been generally welcomed by all stakeholders' (Commission of the European Communities 2006b: 4). SANCO dropped Greek *feta* and Italian *salame cacciatore* from the list of excluded traditional foods (Directorate-General Health and Consumer Protection 2005: 44, 56), but this was simply a technical issue as DG AGRI pointed out that both products were already covered by European law on protected denominations, which made an additional additives regulation unnecessary.

In the same manner, labelling requirements were left untouched during the process of position formation (Directorate-General Health and Consumer Protection 2005: 36–40). The drafting officials consulted internally with the unit responsible for general food labelling as a broader framework on these questions was prepared at the time (see Chapter 6.5 in this volume). But since the extant rules appeared to be consistent with this framework (COM29:174), officials saw no need to follow consumer demands to remove from additive labelling any confusion emerging from the fact that some additives are identified only by their E-numbers, others by their name, and still others by both (BEUC 2006: 3).

Only provisions on the future management of food additives presented deviations from the regulatory status quo and were also much more contested. First of all, there is the producer obligation to make new information on additives available. Here, DG SANCO had planned to be much more interventionist, proposing that producers would have to reapply for authorisation after ten years (see also Directorate-General Health and Consumer Protection 2005). This approach is consistent with the lessons drawn from the BSE crisis, and can be traced to the 2000 White Book and the 2002 food safety framework, which are based on the principle of binding food regulation to the most recent scientific data (Hagenmeyer 2006: 301). While national governments and consumer associations strongly argued for 'some form of review to ensure that the [proposed] Regulation remains current', the food industry feared additional controls and saw this approach as a 'barrier to innovation' that 'would introduce uncertainty in the food additives market'. Unlike at the turn of the century, when food scares had driven the general food safety framework, the competitiveness argument was now suddenly successful again in the context of the comparatively low public salience of food safety. Responding positively to industry demands, DG SANCO sold the requirement of information disclosure as a 'compromise solution', balancing consumer and producer demands (Commission of the European Communities 2006b: 4; see also Hagenmeyer 2006: 296–7).

Following a producer-friendly line further, DG SANCO was much more uncompromising when it came to the most 'fundamental change' concerning the question on how future 'changes to the list' of authorised food additives should take place. Indeed, moving these decisions to a comitology procedure with EFSA participation was seen as the essential aim of the overall drafting exercise. It was a way to 'make the very technical issues' subject to 'a more efficient way of working' (COM29:58, 66). Efficiency in this case meant that 'through the proposals a lot of responsibility is given to the Commission', which becomes 'completely responsible for the management of additive authorisation, so the Council and the Parliament no longer have to do anything with it' (COM29:31).

Surely, the drafting officials were fully aware that this was a contested position. They recognised that the old regime of making every detail of food additive authorisation subject to a co-decision procedure was in place because national governments wanted to limit the use of additives only to instances in which it was absolutely necessary to use them (COM29:339). In addition, the Commission's grasp on regulatory powers met the fierce resistance of the EP, which naturally lost influence under the proposed comitology rules, and argued for stakeholder consultations even in these tertiary decisions (AE 2007c; Hagenmeyer 2006: 297). Consumer associations were equally strong opponents of this position because they feared that they would 'not be able to provide input or the basis for these important decisions' (BEUC 2006: 2).

However, in such a low salience context, these demands for more stakeholder control over additive usage were apparently not very relevant to DG SANCO. Their political justification ranked efficiency higher than public interest as they argued that without this competence gain 'the process of amending additive authorisations would still require the lengthy co-decision procedure [...]. This would continue to act as a barrier to innovation by industry and as a consequence technological developments would not be encouraged' (Commission of the European Communities 2006b: 5). Producers cheered and the biggest associations of affected industries – the ELC, the Association of Manufacturers and Formulators of Enzyme Products and the CIAA – teamed up to support the envisaged procedure in the Commission negotiations with the Council.[16]

Within the Commission, SANCO's plans to gain full control over the future regulation of food additives were also supported by the DG ENTR – a rather unusual internal ally. Against the lowered transaction costs for producers, ENTR supported the move not the least since it conformed to similar procedures ENTR had handled itself with regard to other chemicals (COM115:137).[17] Along these lines, the DG SANCO officials could stick to their original plans. The position fixed in the final Commission proposal on food additives removed all political constraints on additive authorisation and ensured a consistent future workload for the DG.

Summing up, the food additives proposal was drafted during a period of extraordinarily high politicisation of supranational decision making in the EU, but, as judged by our general salience measure, a specific newspaper content analysis and the assessment of involved officials, it did not touch upon contemporaneously salient issues. In line with the theoretical claim that politicisation will affect the policy position of the Commission only in conjunction with contemporaneous issue salience, this allowed a policy proposal that is essentially guided by market-making considerations. The proposed regulation entails only few deviations from the regulatory status quo, but where it does, it rather disproportionately benefits the producer side, which profits mainly from an accelerated authorisation procedure circumventing parliamentary scrutiny.

With regard to processing aids and the time-limited authorisation of additives, DG SANCO had contemplated fairly more interventionist positions, at least until the February 2005 draft when politicisation had just passed its local mode while issue salience stayed shortly below the mean. Nonetheless, in parallel with the decreasing levels on the major independent variables of the model, these ideas were dropped in the final year of drafting. In the low salience context, there was little intervention from the internal hierarchy, the proposal preparation took rather

---

16. See: http://www.amfep.org/docs/ELC-Amfep-CIAAjointpositiononcomitology.pdf (accessed 27 July 2010).

17. In granting their internal support, ENTR also successfully lobbied for even shorter deadlines in the authorisation procedure (COM115:157). Internal support seems to have been necessary as not all actors within the Commission were happy with SANCO's increase in competences. Reviewing the ISC documents (internal reference: ISC 431037) indicates that DG AGRI opposed it strongly. Yet this opposition did not emerge from political objections, but was grounded in the fact that SANCO's future resources for managing food additives should be funded by the European Agricultural Guarantee Fund.

a long time, and we saw little internal opposition to the policy content proposed by the lead department. In essence, the food additives case presents a fairly standard process in traditional, technocratic position formation in the European Commission.

Surprisingly, however, the political feasibility of SANCO's ideal positions in the inter-institutional process mattered little during drafting. Opposition to the streamlined authorisation procedure in the Council and particularly in the EP was expected, but did not result in policy adaptations. Instead, the drafting officials appeared confident that the argument for more innovation resulting from more efficient procedures, the corresponding support from the producer side and consistency with the general 2002 approach to food regulation would be sufficient to assert their position in inter-institutional negotiations. With the benefit of hindsight, this strategic consideration was correct (cf. Regulations EC 1333/2008 and 1331/2008).

Explanations based on the Commissioners' characteristics also fail to reach far in this drafting process. While Commissioners were hardly involved, timing provides a natural additional experiment. The responsible Commissioners changed in autumn 2004, and we also observed decreasing interventionism in DG SANCO's policy choices around the same time. Yet this co-variation is hardly consistent with arguments that explain policy choices by Commissioner partisanship. The outgoing Commissioner Byrne was member of a liberal party (Fianna Fáil) and the incoming Commissioner Kyprianoú came from a centre-left party (the Cypriot Dimokratiko Komma). While this might have accounted for an increase, it does not account for the observed decline in SANCO's interventionism. On the other hand, nationality cannot explain this decline given the similarity in Irish and Cypriot dependence on food production. Clearly, position formation was not influenced by party membership or the nationality of the responsible Commissioners.

Finally, the productionist view cannot account for the Commission position on food additives. The easier authorisation procedure benefits European and foreign food producers alike. From the explanations systematically considered in this book, the politicisation–salience–policy nexus thus presents the most fitting approach in the food additives case.

6.5 Food information

The final sampled case in the realm of food policy came two years after the additives proposal. The proposed regulation, adopted by an oral procedure in the Commission's College on 30 January 2008, targets 'the provision of food information to consumers' on a much broader scale and specifies the general labelling and nutrition declarations accompanying any food sold to European consumers (Commission of the European Communities 2008g). Two supranational laws, both of which were to be repealed by the proposed regulation, formed the general status quo on these issues. Directive 2000/13/EC covered labelling, presentation and advertising of foodstuffs while Council Directive 90/496/EEC regulated nutrition labelling in particular. Especially with regard to the latter, the national regimes varied considerably (Commission of the European Communities 2008g: 3).

Again, DG SANCO was responsible for this proposal. Since the claims initiative (Chapter 6.2) was adopted, the DG had pursued a range of soft-law initiatives on healthy foods. Not the least due to the personal mission of its Director-General, Robert Madelin, the health and consumer protection DG pushed a strategy on fighting obesity in Europe. Among other things, Madelin had initiated the EU Platform for Action on Diet, Physical Activity and Health in 2005, a voluntary stakeholder network including producers and consumer associations, sport federations and WHO observers. This network was to develop voluntary approaches under the leadership of the European Commission. In May 2007, DG SANCO also published a White Paper entitled 'A strategy for Europe on nutrition, overweight and obesity related health issues'. This document explicitly stressed the need for consumer access to obesity-relevant information (Commission of the European Communities 2008g: 2). In the end, obesity reduction was actually one of the most important frames in defending the proposal publicly (see e.g. Bounds et al. 2008).

Paralleling these efforts, the actual legislative work for the proposal set off sometime in early 2005 (COM30:131). It was revealed to external stakeholders, at the latest by a broadly distributed discussion paper in February 2006 (Directorate-General for Health and Consumer Protection 2006). We have already seen above that the general public politicisation of the EU reached rather high levels at the initial stages of drafting. But after the marked politicisation peak in 2005 following the failure of the Constitution, the EU's public visibility and the public mobilisation on European issues in particular declined rather quickly. A minor plateau of politicisation was sustained with the discussions on a renewed Lisbon agenda in early 2007, but afterwards, the politicisation index developed in Chapter Two continuously declined and only started to recover at the beginning of 2008 when the proposal under analysis was finally adopted. So, while the onset of drafting was paralleled by extraordinarily high levels of politicisation, the final decisions were taken in a comparatively quiet period with regard to the public contestation of European governance.

Quite the opposite seems to be true for the contemporaneous public salience of food-related issues. Our indicator for the broad issue area above fluctuates at sub-standard levels during 2005, and declines even more throughout 2006. However, it forcefully turns around in July 2007, entering a phase of steep, continuous increases. When the proposal at hand was adopted half a year later, the salience measure had almost reached one standard deviation above the investigation period mean. A closer look at the media data feeding into this measure indicates that world-wide soaring food prices, WTO disputes on agriculture leading to another failure of the Doha round and renewed discussions on genetically modified foods in Europe spurred the public visibility of the issue area. But most important for our purposes, the more specific issue of food labelling was also part of the public debate at the time.[18]

While food labelling was a topic in the broader GMO debate, the strongest media presence could be detected in the UK where an initiative of the Food Safety Agency (FSA) to tighten laws on nutrition labelling resulted in a major public debate involving publicised opposition from large producers and retailers such as Kellogg's, Cadbury, Schweppes and Tesco (e.g. Wiggins 2007). The debate – which paralleled the whole drafting process – revolved mainly around the so-called 'traffic light system', according to which foodstuffs would be labelled on an overall rating of their nutritional value, with 'red' recommending sparing consumption, 'amber' advising moderate intake and 'green'-marked foodstuffs, which consumers should eat frequently (Wiggins 2005). British consumer associations strongly welcomed this approach, while the industry forcefully fought the FSA initiative, which had not become a binding UK law when the Commission proposal under analysis was adopted in January 2008.

But the labelling of foods and its implications for nutrition were also publicly debated in other member states. A scandal on rotten meat in Germany led to a publicly discussed revision of labelling law in Germany, and also a range of more general reports on increasing population obesity, the need to make respective food information available, and corresponding obligations on producers were present in all scrutinised outlets (e.g. FAZ 2007a). Furthermore, newspapers focused on the highly controversial claims proposal, which was discussed in the Council and the Parliament at the time that the food information proposal was drafted within the Commission (e.g. Perez 2005).

Beyond that, the newspaper content analysis indicates the care that the Commission took to ensure that its competences on food labelling were publicly visible. On the one hand, its various soft-law initiatives on obesity found their way to a range of news reports (e.g. Petitnicolas 2007; Carbajosa 2005); on the other, DG SANCO itself actively paved the way for the proposal by loudly justifying a tighter labelling regime in Europe. This started with an interview with SANCO's Commissioner Márkos Kyprianoú, who announced the fight against obesity on 20 January 2005. Discussing envisaged voluntary producer agreements on labelling practices, he threatened on the front page of the *Financial Times* that 'if this doesn't produce satisfactory results, we will proceed to legislation' (Mason and Parker 2005). Only one year later, DG SANCO's spokesman wrote a letter to the *Financial Times* announcing that they 'also plan to look at how to make nutritional information easier to understand as part of a review of EU

---

18. The following paragraphs summarise articles retrieved by a more specific keyword search in the newspaper described in Appendix C. The search was limited to the period 1 January 2005–30 January 2008, and required an article to contain the three major keywords and their deflections from the Commission's proposal description: 'labelling', 'food', and 'consumer'. This resulted in ten hits for the *Frankfurter Allgemeine Zeitung*, sixteen in *Le Figaro*, forty-four in *El País*, and as many as seventy-eight in the *Financial Times*.

food-labelling legislation' (Tod 2006). Various newspapers then also reported on the proposal itself shortly before it was officially adopted (e.g. FAZ 2007c). In this context, drafting officials in DG SANCO expected their proposal to be highly visible to the public once adopted (COM80:59, 138).

Given this combination of context variables, the food information case is fairly challenging for the theoretical argument developed in Chapter Three. In a strict sense, the drafting process at hand was never subject to high politicisation and high issue salience at the same time.

Looking only at the co-variation of the broader measures, one would accordingly expect limited interventionism and a concentration on market-making in the Commission proposal. Yet during early drafting in 2005 and 2006, Commission officials arguably learned how strongly future European integration might actually be contested by the European public. This would also be relevant in anticipating reaction to the Lisbon Treaty, the text of which was already prepared when the proposal under analysis was finalised. An increasing and actively pushed public salience in food labelling and obesity throughout the drafting process and the fact that labelling was particularly visible in the national debates in the UK and Germany could thus have created the theorised incentives for the Commission to push for an interventionist and easily sellable policy proposal. Besides this expectation, we would anticipate a slight decline of interventionism towards the end of drafting, when politicisation declined. So, which policy choices does the proposal actually reflect?

Comparing the final legal text (Commission of the European Communities 2008g) with the regulatory status quo is done using five sets of provisions that distribute rights and risks among producers and consumers. As a starter, the proposal defines general principles for food information. The Commission proposes that 'food information shall pursue a high level of protection of consumers' health and interests' by enabling them to make informed choices with regard to 'health, economic, environmental, societal and ethical considerations'. This principle does not refer only to population health in the context of debates on rising obesity, but it also explicitly allows regulation in consumers' economic interests and enables future decision makers to intervene in producers' freedom on a range of societal goals apart from market creation.

Refining this principle creates such regulatory leeway. Any mandatory food information must fall into one of three categories: information on nutritional characteristics, information on consumers' health and safe use of the food (covering durability and storage but also 'the health impact'), as well as information on composition and 'other characteristics of the food'. These regulatory categories leave room for interpretation, but the proposal also states that future food information law shall always support the free movement of goods and contain a transitory period for producers to adapt. Such general principles have not been part of the extant legal framework. Particularly by committing regulation to consumer health and interests, the proposal opens the door for a more interventionist approach to European consumer policy without, however, allowing unlimited interference with producer freedom.

On a less abstract level, the second set of relevant provisions translates these general principles into more detailed information characteristics and the corresponding responsibilities of 'economic operators'. Following Article 7, information must not mislead the consumer and any indication on the prevention, treatment or curing of human diseases is prohibited. These rules are commensurate with the regulatory status quo present in Article 2 of Directive 2000/13/EC. In contrast, the subsequent, more specific producer responsibilities were not part of extant EU directives and present a tightened regime for food producers and retailers. Article 8 in the proposal regulates the burden of proof, and extends food information responsibilities to the whole production chain. No food operator is allowed to modify information received from an earlier link, and all operators are obliged to pass on information at all steps. The final retailer bears responsibility for the presence and accuracy of the information provided to the consumer. Clearly, producers and retailers can no longer pass the buck if the final consumer is disadvantaged by faulty information.

Pushing this further, a third set of key provisions prescribes what information is mandatory and how it should be presented to the consumer. Among others, producers must provide an ingredient list, the net quantity, minimum durability dates, and allergenic contents. Calculation and composition of these mandatory particulars is regulated in a highly detailed manner. Furthermore, the proposal stipulates that information on the country of origin must not mislead the consumer as regards the true origin of all ingredients.

Besides these general obligations, specific rules for individual product groups apply. For example, beverages with more than 1.2 per cent alcohol must be provided with the actual alcoholic strength, and a range of further products – such as foods with sweeteners or high caffeine beverages – are regulated separately. The proposal furthermore exempts certain food categories from the need to provide an ingredient list. This includes fruit, vegetables and milk products, but also wine, beer and spirits. For these alcoholic beverages, the proposal explicitly foresees a five-year review clause.

This set of rules equals the lists in Directive 2000/13/EC, but the rule on allergenic substances and the required nutrition declaration are new. In this view, it increases producer obligations, which is further underlined by the new and rather restrictive rules on how this information must be provided. Producers have to present food information in a conspicuous position and in an easily visible, clearly legible and indelible way. This prescription goes so far as to require a font size of at least 3 mm plotted in so as to 'ensure a significant contrast between the print and the background'. Finally, information must be provided in a language that is easily understood in the country where the product is marketed. For our dependent variable, these presentation rules are important because they affect how easily the consumer can access food information, and because they strongly limit producers in package design and marketing possibilities. Given that the extant legal regime contained no comparably detailed presentation rules, these provisions move the Commission position clearly towards stricter producer obligations to the advantage of widespread consumer interests.

A rather interventionist Commission position is also visible in provisions on nutrition declarations. The proposal demands that producers provide the energy value as well as the amounts of fat, saturates and carbohydrates – the latter with specific reference to sugar and salt.[19] Making such declarations mandatory on food labels confers an additional constraint upon producers, which is highly relevant given the important role of nutrition, health and body weight in the marketing of foodstuffs. Only food supplements and mineral water, as well as beer, wine and spirits are excluded from this obligation. These provisions present a clear deviation from the status quo as nutrition labelling was optional under the applicable directive 90/496/EEC (except if vitamins and minerals were artificially added; cf. Chapter 6.3).

What is more, the proposal details how nutrition information has to be presented. The declaration has to appear in 'the principle field of vision', that is, on the front-of-package. The respective articles in the proposal specify the relevant measurement units, and allow energy and nutrient values to be presented on a 'per portion' basis only if the portion is quantified on the label and the number of portions contained in the package is stated. In addition, nutrition values must also be provided as a percentage value of particular reference intakes (Reference Daily Amounts, or RDA). Reference values were previously compulsory only for vitamins and minerals and, combined with the fact that the old directive did not make nutrition declarations mandatory, the 2008 Commission proposal presents another clear move towards a more interventionist model of food labelling regulation.

The proposal furthermore explicitly allows the development of non-binding national schemes for nutrition declarations – which may also involve graphical representations. In essence, such schemes must comply with the general principles of the proposal, must be based on 'sound consumer research', and must involve a broad consultation of stakeholders and best practice efforts. National schemes must be notified to the Commission, which can request a member state to repeal the scheme if it gives rise to trade obstacles. So, while producers may no longer fall behind on obligatory nutrition declarations, this latter set of rules explicitly allows more consumer-friendly deviations if they do not hamper trade in the internal market. In other words, the Commission allows a 'trading up' effect without prescribing such highly interventionist rules as the traffic light system for example.

Finally, the proposal specifies the remaining national powers and the future implementation of food labelling rules. National laws on food information will be subject to notification and inspection by different comitology procedures. The Commission may propose qualified majority decisions on matters including the labelling of allergenic substances, the precision of nutrition declarations, and implementing the rules on further national schemes. Unanimous committee decisions apply, among others, to future decisions on additional mandatory food

---

19. Besides these, producers are free to include the amounts of certain other substances such as fibre, protein, or certain vitamins and minerals.

information, possible exclusions of particular food categories or changes to the content of nutrition declarations. This transfers a number of significant powers to the Commission and respective committees. In principle, these issues could have also been resolved by the proposal at hand or could have been made subject to standard legislative procedures involving the Council and the Parliament. Committee procedures were an element in the extant directives, but the transfer of competences in the proposal at hand is much more pronounced, and dilutes the transparency of future consumer policy decisions.

However, this cannot disguise the overall interventionist character of the 2008 Commission approach towards food labelling. Particularly with respect to the general principles and the mandatory nutrition declarations, the proposal far exceeds the extant European regime. The Commission's policy is much more restrictive for producers, and emphasises consumer health and interests much more strongly. Which factors drove the processes towards such an interventionist position?

Initially one has to acknowledge that DG SANCO had a longstanding intention of overhauling the labelling regime. Like other food policy proposals discussed so far, labelling was mentioned as one area of future regulation in the 2000 White Book on Food Safety (AE 2003a). At that time, however, food labelling was still seen by other parts of the Commission mainly as an industry policy, as is evident in a 1999 legal revision initiated by the legal service and DG ENTR, just shortly before all food-related units were finally transferred to DG SANCO. After this transfer of competences within the Commission, the issue popped up as a consumer-oriented policy when the then SANCO Commissioner David Byrne announced his intention to overhaul labelling in 2003. Yet he still treated food labelling separately from nutrition labelling: both areas were covered by different directives that were not all equally restrictive (AE 2003a; European Evaluation Consortium 2003). But his officials had also cautiously consulted member states on the question whether nutrition labelling could be made mandatory.[20]

In fact, the decision to also make nutrition labelling obligatory was taken early in 2005 at a time when both the overall politicisation of European integration was high and the salience of food labelling started to increase following debates in the UK and Commission efforts in tackling obesity. From there 'it seem[ed] logical to have put it into one proposal rather than into two separate ones', and two SANCO officers started to work on a common framework. Drafting in these initial stages went 'fairly smoothly' and was supported by the respective head of unit, the responsible Director-General and the legal and horizontal units of DG SANCO (COM30:131; COM80:109). Once again, the alert reader should keep in mind the high personnel persistence and the functional concentration of almost all food legislation in the drafting unit. The same people who had drafted and negotiated the initiatives on supplements, nutrient addition and, most importantly, on health

---

20. See: http://ec.europa.eu/food/food/labellingnutrition/nutritionlabel/index_en.htm (accessed 12 July 2010).

claims were responsible for the case at hand. In other words, an extraordinarily high degree of factual and also strategic knowledge can be taken for granted.

So the administrative level of DG SANCO had a strong take on this proposal, which fits the overall development of the Commission's food policy rather neatly. However, unlike most other cases discussed in this chapter, the administrators were aware that the proposal at hand 'relate[d] directly to debates around managing obesity and poor food and what the supermarkets [we]re doing', and considered it as 'much more politicised' than other food initiatives (COM80:59). So, the fact that 'the food information proposal was an important proposal in the pipeline' increased their interaction with the political hierarchy (COM30:269). This involved the Director-General and the management board of SANCO, which included all directors as well as the Commissioner's cabinet. These higher echelons provided political guidance, mapped possible constituency reactions to different routes the proposal could take and explicitly asked the Commissioner for decisions in this regard (COM80:152).[21] And, as noted above, Commissioner Kyprianoú committed himself publicly to a restrictive route on obesity when he threatened the industry with legislation in January 2005.

Already during early drafting, the process was headed more towards an interventionist model of consumer policy and officials knew that there was a 'sharp end of the debate' (COM80:150). Yet with political backing, SANCO officials conducted a public consultation which resulted in 175 individual responses from companies and business associations, as well as consumer and other non-governmental organisations (NGOs, Commission of the European Communities 2008g: 5; cf. Directorate-General Health and Consumer Protection 2006). The document was also sent proactively to member state governments and was further discussed in several stakeholder groups. This was further flanked by direct contact with 'sectoral umbrella organizations' and 'individual companies'. These contacts were deemed as 'very important', for obtaining both factual and strategic information (COM30:149).

The initial interventionist stance, however, survived all these consultation efforts. While the basic aims of the drafting process were sold as a mere 'consolidation' or 'simplification' (COM80:59), discussion of key provisions and fierce reactions, particularly from the industry side, indicate that the final proposal remained costly for producers. Clearly, SANCO made no secret of the fact that the focus was more on protecting consumers than on facilitating trade in the internal market. The proposal's memorandum states:

[t]he main political will that motivated the first 'horizontal' legislative instrument on food labelling [...] was to provide rules for the labelling of foods

---

21. One of the interviewees summarised this process in the following way: 'We tended to say to the Commissioner: Well, here, you have three options and – broadly it is a matrix presentation – you have three constituencies. You have the suppliers, of which the big and the small. You have the consumer groups, you have media, you have MEPs. And here it is: smileys and frownies. This is how they will react. It is a necessary simplification!' (COM80:150)

as a tool for the free circulation of foods in the Community. Over time the protection of consumers' rights emerged as a specific objective of the European Community. (Commission of the European Communities 2008g: 1)

This shift in emphasis was not so welcome to other actors in the Commission. Again, the adverse position was presented mainly by DG ENTR, for which the 'accomplishment of the internal market' was the 'most important concern' because otherwise one would 'change the [legal] basis for the necessity of such legislation' (COM115:63). In fact, ENTR officials proactively encouraged industry representatives to also lobby their own directorate, as well as DG SANCO, so as to stay in the game on food legislation (COM115:95).

Internal coordination was experienced as 'quite controversial' in response (COM80:71), and SANCO tried to evade conflict as long as possible. In the formal ISC, three months before the adoption of the proposal, ENTR complained that there 'hasn't been any preliminary information' on the substance of the proposal and they 'blocked it with a four/five pages answer' (COM115:55).[22] ENTR officials voiced the suspicion that drafting officials in SANCO had 'instructions not to consult us' so that the final inter-service proposal was actually the first legislative document they had seen. This resulted in a '"*njet*" on a number of issues' (COM115:59; COM30:255). The proposal was then quickly handed up to the political level where the cabinet of Commissioner Verheugen (DG ENTR) negotiated directly with Kyprianoú's political officers (COM115:66). Unfortunately, little is known about these final negotiations but there are hints that issue linkage took place as the ENTR cabinet allegedly backed off because 'today you may refuse that but tomorrow you will ask something else' (COM115:72).

These internal and external rifts are mirrored in all individual policy choices contained in the proposal. With regard to the general principles on food information, consumer associations applauded the inclusion of 'environmental, social and ethical considerations', as they indicate that food labelling is more than only 'dealing with the smooth functioning of the internal market' (BEUC 2008: 2). Retailers, in contrast, feared that this would give rise to 'several additional mandatory requirements' in the future, thus contradicting the 'Better Regulation objective pursued by the Commission' (EuroCommerce 2008; likewise UEAPME 2008). Internally, ENTR opposed this point particularly (COM115:63) but was not successful, as the final Commission proposal shows.

Regarding the general obligations of economic operators, the retail sector complained that its own responsibilities were not clear, and wanted to clarify that they could only be responsible for labelling rules if food was produced in their name (EuroCommerce 2008). Likewise, food lawyers considered the burden of proof too wide (O'Rourke 2008: 304–5). Yet SANCO's choice to extend it to the whole production chain was consistent with the general food safety regulation 178/2002 that had been drafted by the very same unit in response to the BSE

---

22. Direct access to these documents was denied by the Commission – most likely because the proposal was still being negotiated in the Council and the Parliament at the time of the request.

crisis. This framework law had established a 'farm to fork' approach, so that the responsibilities in the proposal at hand could be seen as a mere transfer of these principles to the more specific issue area of food labelling (cf. Hagenmeyer 2008: 167).[23]

The question of what food information would to be made mandatory was even more conflictual. Initially, this concerns the exclusion of alcoholic beverages from the need to provide an ingredient list. The very first food labelling directive had asked the Council to regulate the ingredient labelling of alcoholic products in 1982 – a request that the Council has never met, despite three corresponding proposals of the Commission (COM30:77). SANCO's 2006 consultation showed that member states were still evenly split on this question, making regulatory progress on this matter appear politically infeasible (Directorate-General Health and Consumer Protection 2006: 11). However, anticipated member state opposition was not the only constraint. DG AGRI also opposed internally. The DG controlled legislation of alcoholic production and was proposing its own initiative on wine labelling in parallel (COM30:113, Vaqué and Melchor Romero 2008). While there are factual arguments on the changes in ingredients during fermentation, AGRI's opposition was also a way of defending its own competences in the area (COM30:207–13). The drinks industry and a number of governments supported this, and 'lobbied hard against revealing either the calorie content of their products or the full ingredient list for fear of putting off drinkers' (Bounds *et al.* 2008). The drafting officials were convinced in hindsight that they had 'let that go a little easily', having 'undersold the concession' because 'of it not being central to this piece of legislation' (COM80:170).

In publicly promoting the proposal, DG SANCO put much effort into ensuring that this concession did not appear as a weakness in defending consumers' interests. Most notably, it was emphasised that the exemption did not affect mixed alcoholic beverages – so-called alcopops – which were prominent in public debate at the time (and usually have a rather unhealthy nutritional profile, cf. Commission of the European Communities 2008i: 7). Commissioner Kyprianoú euphemised the revision clause by claiming that '[w]e will need to examine this in greater depth in order to define the notion of obligatory information and determine whether they should be provided under specific legislation applicable to wine or via this new horizontal regulation' (AE 2008b), while claiming in the *Financial Times* that 'alcohol is not a 'privileged product'' (Bounds *et al.* 2008).

Another contested issue was origin labelling. Consumer associations wanted mandatory origin labelling for all significant product ingredients (BEUC 2008). The industry, in contrast, clearly preferred the status quo; adding the origin of

---

23. Note that SANCO's position was also consistent with a 2005 ECJ judgement against Lidl Italia. Here the retailer had argued that it was not responsible for the faulty provision of alcoholic strengths on products it sold, while Italian law claimed the opposite. The ECJ argued that the extant labelling directive did not provide for distributor liability but that the Italian law was nevertheless in conformity since it contributed to the directive's original aim of protecting consumers. In that sense, SANCO's position might be seen as a legal clarification as well.

individual ingredients was simply seen as 'unmanageable' (CIAA 2008). Again, DG ENTR defended the industry position internally. During ISC, they argued that the costs are unsustainable for large companies that buy their ingredients from varying locations. Country-of-origin labelling would furthermore create 'sections in an internal market' that endanger 'all the achievements of the Commission until now' (COM115:31). The final SANCO proposal makes origin labelling of individual ingredients mandatory only if the consumer could be otherwise misled.

Nevertheless, this accommodation was only a limited success for DG ENTR. The rules on the presentation of mandatory food information were much more relevant to the food industry. SANCO defended particularly the minimum font size as a 'clarification' of the general principles governing labelling (AE 2008b). European retailers were outraged, and claimed that it will 'engender considerable cost for food businesses'. They pointed out that the prescription even exceeded usual newspaper font sizes, even those of the Official Journal of the EU (AE 2008a; UEAPME 2008; EuroCommerce 2008: 3–4). Despite these arguments, SANCO stuck with its consumer-oriented position. The DG could be sure about public support on this matter, as the 2006 consultation revealed that consumer associations and member states identified readability as a major demand (Directorate-General Health and Consumer Protection 2006: 11–2; cf. also BEUC 2008).

Even more consumer applause could be gained by making nutrition declarations mandatory. As noted, this decision was taken rather early in the process. Despite knowing that it would be a 'burden' for the industry, DG SANCO sided with consumer doubts about existing voluntary industry agreements: '[T]here were really worries, you know, that the relevant information was being provided' (COM30:65). In addition, the 2006 consultation showed that 'Member States on the whole tend to favour a mandatory system, with some reservations expressed that derogations for certain products or types of business should be considered' (Directorate-General Health and Consumer Protection 2006: 15). As this was equal to the position taken in the final proposal, anticipation of political preferences in the Council seems to have taken place here as well. But DG SANCO did not follow completely the demands of consumer associations. Consumers would have preferred a mandatory declaration of the 'Big-8', which additionally includes fibre and protein (AE 2008a). A study outsourced by DG SANCO, however, found that the inclusion of additional nutrients beyond the big four included in the proposal would have more than quadrupled producer costs, spurring even more industry opposition (Rabinovich et al. 2008: xv).

All these conflicts were trumped by stakeholder debates on the actual presentation of the nutrition declaration. This provision has the most direct repercussions for marketing food products and especially snacks. DG SANCO defended its decision to make nutrition declarations mandatory on the front-of-package by referring to the impact assessment, according to which it would have 'the greatest potential impact on consumer decisions' (Commission of the European Communities 2008i: 3; Rabinovich et al. 2008: xvi–xvii). The early threats of Commissioner Kyprianoú had startled the industry, which quickly concluded a voluntary commitment on nutrition declarations in 2006 under the auspices of the

CIAA. This 'guideline daily amount' (GDA) system was clearly expected to keep the Commission from enacting a mandatory scheme: 'Businesses have invested a lot of time, efforts and money, and yet, are faced with a prescriptive legislation on nutrition information' (EuroCommerce 2008). DG SANCO, however, sided again with the 'inherent distrust of self-regulatory initiatives' that consumer NGOs had voiced in the public consultation (Directorate-General Health and Consumer Protection 2006: 3).

Nevertheless, the voluntary industry agreement left some imprints on the proposal. The reference values on which nutrients are to be standardised were largely transferred from this scheme. But compared to the SANCO proposal for binding law, the voluntary scheme was much more liberal with regard to expressing nutrient values per portion or serving (CIAA 2008, 2006; cf. also BEUC 2008: 3). Likewise, the industry scheme only required the energy value shown on the front-of-package, while all other nutrients were indicated only on the back. Also on this provision the Commission ultimately went for the more interventionist position in the interest of consumer information.

Closely related to this discussion was the question of further national nutrition declaration schemes, in particular those with 'interpretative elements'. Here, the most-consumer friendly end of the debate was the so-called traffic light system discussed in the UK (Bounds *et al.* 2008). The major consumer association wanted to make this binding European law as it allowed consumers 'to calculate the nutritional value of a foodstuff at a glance' (AE 2008a; also BEUC 2008). But in an obvious attempt to avoid the resulting competition between healthy and less healthy foods, the existing industry agreement explicitly ruled out a colour scheme (CIAA 2006). In this vein, producers regretted that the Commission proposal still allowed for different presentation schemes, particularly since the GDA system was spreading quickly (CIAA 2008). The position in SANCO's proposal that was finally chosen thus presents a muddy middle road between consumer and industry demands.

Here, DG SANCO did not have the heart to raise the level of protection beyond everything that existed in member states, particularly since the consultation of the national governments did not convey clear political signals on this matter (Directorate-General Health and Consumer Protection 2006: 17). Defending this compromise position publicly, Commissioner Kyprianoú claimed that 'the substance of the information will be the same throughout the EU but we defer to the producers or to national schemes based on a colour code (as in the UK, for example) or anything else, as long as it does not hinder the smooth functioning of the internal market' (AE 2008b). Yet the food industry feared that this compromise in particular 'threaten[ed] the single market' because voluntary schemes would become the de facto rule for national markets (EuroCommerce 2008: 5).

Internally, this industry criticism was again well received by the administrative level of DG ENTR, which argued that 'there would be no internal market at all' with different national schemes (COM115:39). Interestingly, however, Commissioner Verheugen, heading DG ENTR, pushed much less strongly than his department on the issue (COM71:53). This fact – together with the insight that SANCO's position pushed neither consumer nor producer interests – underscore the impression that position formation on this particular issue was constrained by both a low signal for political feasibility in the Council on the one hand and the attempt not to alienate consumers on the other.

Similarly, caution appears to be the driving factor behind provisions on future implementation: the wide usage of committee procedures appears to be a sort of dump for possibly highly contested issues. The consumer association BEUC (2008: 3) is 'particularly worried that the proposal makes wide-ranging use of the application of the Comitology procedure to amend key elements of the Regulation', and finds 'that this procedure would severely limit the transparency of the legislative process'. Like the additives and the claims proposals discussed above, however, DG SANCO seems to have moved potentially conflictive issues into the realm of administrative decision making so as to let the proposal pass more easily without losing its own grip on future decisions.

To sum up, the food information case conforms to the theoretical expectations developed in Chapter Three. The highly politicised climate of EU decision making in 2005–6 and a rising public salience of the issues covered by the proposal come together with a policy position on food labelling that tends to a more interventionist model of consumer policy. Yet one major caveat applies. It is not the high public salience of the broader issue area that fell together high levels of general EU politicisation, but rather an emerging discussion on the narrower topic of food labelling that signalled the proposal's chance of scoring positively among the diffuse European public. Rather than the actual level of salience, it appears to have been more the anticipation of public visibility that drove the lead DG towards more interventionism. This is underlined by early and active efforts to raise the public visibility of corresponding issue by related soft-law initiatives on obesity and an early political commitment from the responsible Commissioner.

The within-case variation in DG SANCO's position during the process, in addition, mirrors declining levels of EU politicisation during 2007. While the salience levels of food safety and labelling were on the rise, the later phases of drafting involved some concessions. Particularly on the exclusion of alcoholic beverages and on origin labelling, SANCO sacrificed its original plans in the light of internal resistance from DG AGRI and DG ENTR. This highlights that public issue salience without general EU politicisation hardly accounts for moves towards interventionism. It is furthermore consistent with the process hypothesis on internal conflict. The argument proposed in Chapter Three claims that internal conflict will be trumped only under high salience but not under intermediate levels of EU politicisation, which fits the observations made in the food information case.

Other process implications are also in line with the theoretical model. Both the political and the administrative hierarchy of the lead department were involved to a great extent, accompanied the whole drafting process, and negotiated the final decisions following ISC in November 2007. On the whole, positions on individual key provisions have been responsive to consumer demands, as predicted for salient initiatives in a highly politicised context. Lastly, compared with the less salient initiatives on food supplements and nutrient addition, a duration of two years appears to be rather short, particularly given the comparatively broad scope of the food information proposal.

However, DG SANCO's interventionism was clearly constrained by anticipated member state preferences regarding the basic decision to make nutrition declarations mandatory, or by low signals on whether strongly interventionist positions such as traffic light system would survive intergovernmental negotiations. In this view, the 'political feasibility' explanation of position formation clearly exhibits explanatory power for the case at hand.

In contrast, this process reveals little about explanations resting on Commissioner characteristics since no within-case variation occurred. In a comparative perspective, however, one has to note that the less salient and less interventionist proposal on food additives discussed above was adopted under the same leadership as the salient and much more interventionist case at hand.

Lastly, the productionist view on position formation consumer policy can add little to the understanding of the food information case. While we have a proposal involving high regulatory standards, as predicted by this explanation, the case history shows that these standards were not demanded by European producers. Rather, the opposite is true. Producers had concluded a voluntary agreement at a level of consumer protection that was acceptable to them, but the Commission proposal clearly exceeded this industry preference.

6.6 Comparative lessons from the food safety cases

From a comparative perspective, the five cases unpacked in this chapter initially exhibit a great deal of stability. All of them were drafted under the responsibility of DG SANCO and, except one, all of them were drafted in same unit. Some of the involved officials worked in European food regulation for more than twenty years. In addition, the latter four cases have a common regulatory root, as they were all announced as legislative priorities in the 2000 White Paper on Food Safety. This framework document itself emerged out of the interplay of a political crisis in the Commission and a high salience of food safety due to the BSE crisis at the change of the century. It strongly refocused European food policy on consumer concerns and led to a bundling of respective competences in DG SANCO. For our theoretical endeavour, this stability across the investigation period has the advantage of holding a range of alternative explanations for the Commission's policy choices constant.

Nevertheless, the detailed analyses of the proposals' legislative content and their comparison to the respective status quo show that there still is considerable variation in the degree of interventionism the Commission proposed. Whereas the cases on food supplements, food fortification and food additives tend towards liberalisation by undermining protection levels that existed in some member states or in relevant European regulation, the proposals on claims and on food information went in the opposite direction and entailed far-reaching regulatory innovations in the name of consumer protection. What accounts for this variation?

Explanations based on Commissioner characteristics exhibit a weak performance in comparative perspective. While the investigation period covered two SANCO Commissioners – David Byrne from 1999 to 2004 and Márkos Kyprianoú until 2008 – both office terms contained a highly interventionist proposal, as well as one or two proposals that tended towards mere market creation. From a purely co-variational perspective, the change of Commissioner cannot account for a change in the Commission's position. The food additives case, in addition, particularly underlines this conclusion. Since its drafting process lasted throughout the change in SANCO's political leadership, it provides a sort of natural experiment. However, since the degree of policy interventionism did not meaningfully align with the party memberships or nationality of the outgoing or incoming Commissioners, the characteristics of the political leadership have no explanatory power.

Likewise – and despite the economic importance of external trade in foodstuffs – the productionist view on position formation cannot account for the level of consumer protection chosen by the Commission. In the two more interventionist proposals, the relevant key provisions came about despite clear producer opposition. Also, even where EU imports or the international Codex Alimentarius informed DG SANCO's position, the resulting proposal provisions benefitted importers rather than European producers, as in the examples of food supplements or the authorisation of health claims. The claim that the Commission's fight for consumer rights is in fact masked protectionism benefiting European industry cannot be upheld against the evidence on food safety regulation discussed in this chapter.

In contrast, varying national approaches to food regulation and correspondingly varying governmental preferences have impinged on position formation in each of the five food safety cases studied here. Where member states opposed liberalisation, as in the supplements and fortification cases, the Commission exhibited great persistence, worked on the issue for several years and employed those judicial strategies to overcome national opposition that Susanne Schmidt (2000) has famously analysed. In contrast, where possible national opposition to more interventionist positions was anticipated – as in the health claims and the food information proposal – DG SANCO formulated a maximum position and then tested throughout the drafting process how far it could actually go in the Council, adapting its position in response. These observations support the view that member state preferences are a constraint on position formation without, however, determining the Commission position conclusively.

The varying time horizons of the liberalising and the more interventionist proposals then bring us to the major theoretical interest analysed here, that is, the politicisation–salience–policy nexus. In fact, thinking of the import-driven position on supplements and fortification, of the decision to simplify authorisation of food additives and of the consumer responsiveness on claims and the early political commitment on food information, varying contexts of politicisation and issue salience *at the onset* of each drafting process show clear consistency with the major outcome hypothesis. In the cases in which drafting began, during periods where both context conditions exhibited low levels or where only one of them exceeded its mean, the Commission position remained fairly liberal and oriented towards market creation. In contrast, if the initiation of drafting happened when EU politicisation coincided with high public issue salience, the process followed a much more interventionist thrust.

While this clearly distinguishes claims and food information from additives, fortification and supplements, the exercise of tracing the position formation process reveals highly interesting within-case variation as well. Interventionism in individual key provisions often followed the pattern of the political context and decreased or increased along variations in politicisation and issue salience. Examples are the rules on product specification and labelling in the food supplements case, the issue of making health claims subject to nutritional profiles or the question of processing aids in the additives case.

What is more, the pattern of co-variation in the cross- and the longitudinal section reinforces the claim that politicisation can only be a sufficient condition for Commission interventionism in conjunction with a high issue salience. The food additives case was drafted at a time when EU integration was highly contested, but the contemporaneous public did not care about the specific issues in the proposal, so the Commission could get away with altering the status quo to the benefit of producers. In contrast, the food information drafting process was paralleled by decreasing politicisation but rising salience. But in internal arguments, DG SANCO conceded some of its more interventionist positions only at the end of the process, which makes it clear that salience alone is insufficient for the assertiveness of consumer protection in the Commission.

This also points to the process implications of the main theoretical argument. Besides a politicisation-dependent pattern of internal conflict, the predicted variation in the time horizon of drafting and the responsiveness to consumer demands has already been mentioned. Similarly, involvement of the political level occurred as assumed by the theoretical model in Chapter Three. However, the early commitment of Commissioner Kyprianoú in the food information case particularly raises the question whether involvement of the Commission's political leadership is an effect of politicisation and salience, or whether it is an additionally necessary condition for an interventionist position. This question points us back to the endogeneity in the theoretical argument, and it can only be answered by comparing the food safety results with other issue areas discussed in this book.

Chapter Seven

Conclusions: The Commission's Agenda-Setting Activity in a Politicised Context

This book set out by observing an increasing 'polarization of opinions, interests or values and the extent to which they are publicly advanced towards the process of policy formulation within the European Union' (De Wilde 2011: 560). Debates on the magnitude of these developments are far from being settled, but the aggregate picture in Chapter Two of this book underlines once more that supranational decision making in the EU is moving increasingly away from a permissive consensus and towards the logics of mass politics.

This public politicisation stands in stark contrast to the often rather technocratic and elite-driven approach that has characterised EU politics for large parts of its history. Whereas supranational policy has traditionally focused on market-making and trade interests, widespread awareness and contestation of supranational matters raise the question whether public interests now resound more strongly in Brussels' complex and often arcane decision-making machinery. Such responsiveness to political pressures, different camps argue, may directly affect both the efficiency and the legitimacy of supranational decision making. Normative expectations of EU politicisation are flying high and range from a declining problem-solving capacity to an enhanced democratic quality in politics beyond the nation state. But in spite of these far-reaching expectations, there is surprisingly little empirical research on the actual effects that the high politicisation periods already experienced in the EU exert on the procedures and content of day-to-day supranational policy.

Accepting this challenge, this book concentrates on the European Commission. This key actor was designed – and is still often perceived – as a rather detached supranational bureaucracy. At the same time, the institution also controls significant political powers to set the European legislative agenda. Starting from the assumption that the Commission, and its DGs, are fundamentally interested in retaining or even expanding these competences, Chapter Three argues that politicisation renders the diffuse European public a more relevant stakeholder in achieving that goal. The more supranational decision making is politicised in general, the more the Commission has incentives to appeal to immediate widespread public interests in its policy choices. Otherwise, it risks stalemate in future European integration, and further pooling and delegation of regulatory competences to the supranational level coming to a halt. As one of the Commission officials interviewed for this book put it: 'Certainly, if we want to continue, probably best would be to improve people's acceptance of the EU integration process – we should legislate in such a way that people can identify with the level at which the decision is taken and with the substance of what we are doing' (COM81:40).

Yet public attention is selective and varies across time but also across regulatory issues. In order to be relevant to the Commission's policy position, periods of high EU politicisation must fall together with the contemporaneous public salience of the issues covered by the specific policy on the drafting table. Without such public attention to the matters that Brussels is about to regulate, the initiative in question hardly affects the public evaluation of supranational decision making, and the Commission thus lacks incentives to deviate from its traditional regulatory patterns.

This general argument is then translated to European consumer policy. In this area, legislative initiatives from the Commission essentially propose how to distribute rights and risks among European producers and consumers. While respective supranational law has often focused on the creation of the internal market, benefiting mainly producers operating across national borders, politicisation should turn the distribution of political benefits to the diffuse mass of European consumers into a prized resource. The theoretical model leads us to expect the Commission to intervene more strongly in the name of the consumer if the initiative in question is drafted during periods of high overall EU politicisation and high public salience of the specific issues to be regulated.

Chapters Four–Six evaluate this argument by reconstructing seventeen consumer policy initiatives the Commission proposed between 1999 and 2008. The systematic case studies of these drafting processes and their outcomes generate a wealth of individual insight into consumer policy formulation inside the Commission's DGs. But to conclude finally on the nexus of EU politicisation, specific issue salience and the Commission's policy choices, this final chapter provides a bird's-eye perspective on the empirical results.

7.1 The politicisation–salience–policy nexus in comparative perspective

Starting at the most abstract level, an aggregate view across the three major subfields of European consumer policy is helpful. Despite scattered competences within the Commission and despite varying baseline public salience of the involved issues, the European regulation of contractual consumer rights, of product safety and of food safety all share a distinct commonality. In all three fields, supranational legislation had to emancipate from regulatory approaches that focused almost exclusively on market creation and efficiency.

The fall-back option for the regulation of contractual consumer rights (Chapter Four) was a sort of supranational competition policy that focused primarily on reducing governmental influence on markets. This involved traditionally state-prone sectors such as air transport or telecommunication. Here, the responsible Commission DGs had formally reached liberalisation of the sector at the beginning of the investigation period, and the consumer perspective granted a timely justification for further regulation. But the cases in this area also involved trade-inhibiting effects of variations in national consumer protection regimes. Here, European regulation had traditionally focused on the mutual recognition principle, and the idea that contractual consumer rights needed to be harmonised on the supranational level grew only slowly out of increasing cross-border consumer activities. In addition, the citizen focus of the 1992 Maastricht Treaty entailed early indications that economic consumer interests warranted further supranational regulation. This was also pushed further by the 1997 Treaty of Amsterdam, which declared the economic interest of consumers a right to be protected by supranational policy.

Similarly, European product safety regulation (Chapter Five) had initially been characterised by a strict focus on market efficiency. During the foundation of the internal market, detailed and highly technical European regulations of individual products were the major means to overcome various national product safety regimes. Such technical harmonisation measures paved the way for the free circulation of goods within Europe. Product safety regulation was then further liberalised by the 'new approach', which is based on private standardisation and total supranational harmonisation of product regulation. Two reasons turned this regulatory role model into a rather persistent fall-back option for more supranational consumer interventionism. First, that it was an economic success story breeding strong support among economic operators. Second, it resulted in a powerful enterprise policy fiefdom within the Commission that was willing to defend its vested interests. Yet in parallel to the enhanced consumer policy bases in the Maastricht and Amsterdam Treaties, a more general and consumer-oriented approach to product safety developed and was institutionalised by corresponding competences of the Commission's consumer policy DG.

Also supranational food regulation (Chapter Six) was traditionally subject to a strong emphasis on the interests of cross-nationally operating food producers. Broad sets of European laws existed and were tightly controlled by the industry and agricultural Commission DGs with their historically grown competences. Yet this changed due to a powerful external impulse. The different waves of the BSE crisis during the 1990s publicly unveiled the safety shortcomings of European food regulation and caused ruptures in the Commission's institutional set-up. Especially the incoming Prodi Commission moved all corresponding legislative competences to the health and consumer protection DG, and equipped this young DG with a legislative programme for the years to come.

In summary, all three subfields fulfilled the scope conditions of the theoretical model at the beginning of the book's investigation period. Within the Commission, the possibility of regulating more directly in the name of the consumer was mirrored by the gradual empowerment of the consumer policy service, which turned into a fully-fledged Commission DG only in 1999. And the EU treaties had equipped the Commission with competences that in principle allowed deviations from the liberal status quo. Against the book's major claim that widespread politicisation creates stronger incentives for public interest regulation, it comes as no surprise that these competences were part of the Maastricht and Amsterdam Treaties, which both met unprecedented public visibility, mobilisation and polarisation of opinions. But does the politicisation argument also hold explanatory power in the short-term? Do we find evidence that the Commission reacted to EU politicisation and public issue salience with more consumer interventionism in its day-to-day legislative initiatives?

The preceding case studies provide manifold and dense answers to these questions. To make them accessible at a glance, Table 7.1 summarises the main insights. Starting with a simple outcome perspective, the second panel of this table concentrates on the three major input and output variables of the theoretical model developed in Chapter Three.

This co-variational perspective unveils seven cases that are immediately consistent with the claim that pronounced EU politicisation in conjunction with high public salience of the specific issues incentivises the Commission to propose more interventionist consumer policies. Comparatively high values on both independent variables are associated with a redistribution of rights favourable to consumers in the initiatives on universal service (Chapter 4.1), air passenger rights (Chapter 4.3), consumer credit (Chapter 4.4), and food information (Chapter 6.5). Where high EU politicisation combined with only low public salience of specific issues, Commission initiatives, for example on sales promotions (Chapter 4.2), pyrotechnic articles (Chapter 5.2), and food supplements (Chapter 6.1) exhibited further liberalisation of the affected laws instead.

For some of the other scrutinised consumer policy initiatives, a systematic comparison of the Commission proposal's legal text with the respective regulatory status quo results in only intermediate levels on the dependent variable. In the consumer rights case (Chapter 4.6), for example, high levels of EU politicisation and issue salience occurred during drafting, but the final proposal took an interventionist position on only particularly salient key provisions concerning online trade. Other provisions in this proposal reinforced or undermined the status quo, for instance, with regard to guarantee periods. Similarly, mixed results on the consumer interventionism variable abound for 'new approach' overhaul (Chapter 5.3), the toy safety proposal (Chapter 5.4) and the food additives initiative (Chapter 6.5).

From the perspective of the book's major theoretical argument, the four cases with intermediate values on the EU politicisation variable are more challenging. The classification presented in Table 7.1 simply assesses whether the mean of the politicisation index developed in Chapter Two during each policy drafting process differs significantly from the average politicisation levels observed in earlier periods. From this perspective, EU politicisation is a moving target over time, which arguably sets the bar very high for each individual drafting process. More generally, this points to a conceptual threshold challenge in analysing the policy effects of EU politicisation. So far, we lack an absolute benchmark that could tell us at what level of public visibility, polarisation and mobilisation we could consider European integration as an issue of mass politics.[1] While EU politicisation has unquestionably increased, it is unclear how much is sufficient to create the theorised Commission incentives and whether this level had been

---

1. Future research could tackle this challenge by more systematically comparing the politicisation of European integration with respective measures for other political issues (e.g. Hoeglinger 2016) or other international organisations (e.g. Rauh and Bödeker 2016).

Table 7.1: Summary of the main case study results

	Chapter	Issue	Lead DG	Drafting period	Outcome perspective			Process perspective			
					EU politicisation	Issue salience	Consumer interventionism	Politicisation mode	Salience mode	Co-varying choices	Complementary explanations
Contractual consumer rights	4.1	Universal service	INFSO	Dec 1998–Apr 2000	+	+	+	middle	late	yes	Political feasibility (Council)
	4.2	Sales promotions	MARKT	May 1998–Oct 2001	+	–	–	late	–	no	–
	4.3	Air passenger rights	TREN	Dec 1999–Dec 2001	+	+	+	late	constant	yes	Political feasibility (Council/EP)
	4.4	Consumer credit	SANCO	Jun 2000–Sep 2002	+	+	+	early	constant	yes	–
	4.5	Unfair commercial practices	SANCO	Dec 2000–Jun 2003	o	+	–	early	constant	yes	Political feasibility (Council)
	4.6	Consumer rights	SANCO	Dec 2003–Oct 2008	+	+	o	early	late	insuff.	Political feasibility (Council/EP)
	4.7	Bus/maritime passenger rights	TREN	Jan 2006–Dec 2008	+	–	+	early	–	no	Political feasibility (Council)

Table 7.1 (continued)

	Chapter	Issue	Lead DG	Drafting period	Outcome perspective			Process perspective			Complementary explanations
					EU politicisation	Issue salience	Consumer interventionism	Politicisation mode	Salience mode	Co-varying choices	
Product safety	5.1	General product safety	SANCO	Dec 1997–Mar 2000	o	+	+	middle	constant	no	Political feasibility (Council) Productionist view
	5.2	Pyrotechnic articles	ENTR	Dec 2002–Oct 2005	+	–	–	late	–	no	Political feasibility (Council) Productionist view
	5.3	'New approach' overhaul	ENTR	Dec 2003–Feb 2007	+	–	o	early	–	yes	Commissioner nationality
	5.4	Toy safety	ENTR	Jan 2003–Jan 2008	+	+	o	middle	late	yes	Political feasibility (Council) Productionist view
Food safety	6.1	Food supplements	SANCO	Apr 1997–May 2000	+	–	–	early	–	no	Political feasibility (Council)
	6.2	Health claims	SANCO	Jul 2001–Jul 2003	o	+	+	early	constant	yes	Political feasibility (Council/EP)

Table 7.1 *(continued)*

Chapter	Issue	Lead DG	Drafting period	Outcome perspective				Process perspective			
				EU politici-sation	Issue salience	Consumer interven-tionism	Politicisation mode	Salience mode	Co-varying choices	Comple-mentary explanations	
6.3	Addition of vitamins and minerals	SANCO	Jun 2001–Nov 2003	o	–	–	early	–	yes	Political feasibility (Council)
6.4	Food additives	SANCO	Jul 2001–Jul 2006	+	–	o	middle	–	yes	–
6.5	Food information	SANCO	Jan 2005–Jan 2008	+	+	+	early	late	yes	Political feasibility (Council)

reached by the start of the period covered here. The power of the simple input/ output perspective is thus to some extent limited, but short-term policy adaptations to swings in general EU politicisation provide empirical leverage in this regard (see below).

However, the cross-case comparison is indeed telling with regard to public issue salience. Of the eight cases that indicate interventionist deviations from the regulatory status quo, six were drafted under comparatively high levels of media attention on the issues covered by the respective proposal. Only the two DG TREN cases on bus and maritime passenger rights (Chapter 4.7) drop out. The four cases with intermediate consumer interventionism are also roughly in line with a link between issue salience and Commission policy. The two cases with intermediate interventionism and low public attention – the 'new approach' revision and the food additives proposal – merely re-codified the regulatory status quo (cf. Chapters 5.3 and 6.4). The other two cases of intermediate consumer interventionism – the consumer rights and the toy safety proposal (Chapters 4.6 and 5.4) – contained some liberalising but also some rather interventionist key provisions on specific issues that were on the public agenda at the time of drafting. In these cases, the Commission's policy choices were at least partly responsive to contemporaneous public debate, although this did not tip the aggregate judgement on the overall substance of these proposals.

Arguably, one could also make these observations if salience exhibits an independent effect in the absence of wider EU politicisation. While this does not seem plausible from a theoretical point of view, the input/output perspective cannot rule out this possibility as the sample unfortunately yields no cases with consistently substandard politicisation levels and constantly high public issue salience. The only hint in this direction is the unfair commercial practices proposal. Due to strongly growing online consumer trade across borders, the regulated issues were increasingly salient to the contemporaneous public as reflected in intense media reporting, but DG SANCO nevertheless proposed a liberalising proposal when the overall politicisation of European integration declined significantly during 2002–3.

In sum, a purely co-variational perspective yields seven cases that are fully consistent with the theoretical model, six cases where it is neither confirmed nor falsified, and only two cases where the high level of consumer interventionism cannot be explained by a combination of EU politicisation and public issue salience. Against the non-deterministic nature of the argument in Chapter Three and against alternative explanations discussed below, this appears as a reasonable 'error term' for a medium-N case comparison.

Let us then turn to the procedural perspective. Panel three of Table 7.1 provides a rough indication as to the drafting stage at which general EU politicisation and specific public issue salience reached their mode. It notes whether the temporal reconstruction of policy making in the Commission revealed meaningful co-variation of the independent variables and consumer interventionism during drafting efforts.

This perspective initially reinforces the role of public issue salience. For example, in the toy safety case (Chapter 5.4), DG ENTR foresaw rather liberal rules during more than five years of drafting, but once huge recalls of Chinese toys hit the European market and were widely mediatised in 2007, it suddenly adopted more interventionist provisions on essential safety requirements, on chemical regulation and on labelling. The soaring public salience of the issue put DG ENTR under pressure at the final stages of drafting because 'people wanted to have immediate results' (COM25:234). The late inclusion of a social review clause in the universal service proposal (Chapter 4.1) – when media attention to widespread internet access rose in late 1999 – serves as a similar example.

More importantly, process tracing reveals policy adaptations in the short-term swings in the politicisation index. The health claims proposal (Chapter 6.2) provides a neat example where general EU politicisation, public attention to food safety and Commission interventionism appear almost collinear. The idea of limiting marketing claims only to foods with healthy nutritional profiles was proposed with a range of other interventionist positions in summer 2001 when both EU politicisation and food safety salience had reached local peaks. Yet it was removed from a 2002 draft proposal when both politicisation and issue salience had declined, and it recurred in the legal text only when both independent variables had set to rise again during the final drafting stages.

Process tracing also reveals cases where issue salience remained stable and the Commission adapted its position along independent swings in EU politicisation. The 2001 air passenger rights proposal provides an example (Chapter 4.3). Commission officials were aware that bad customer treatment by airline companies 'was all the time in the media' (COM33:136). But DG TREN only committed to a legislative initiative when the general politicisation of European integration started to rise again. In this context, the drafting officials argued that the EU-induced air transport liberalisation had been about 'advantages for the industry' while it was now time to 'refocus transport policy on the demands and needs of its citizens' (COM33:140). Against outright industry opposition, officials announced the highly interventionist rules on delayed and cancelled flights only when politicisation reached its local 2001 peak in the wake of the Nice negotiations and widespread public protests against the EU and its policies.

The same peak was exploited by DG SANCO in drafting the proposal on consumer credit (Chapter 4.4). In contrast to what was previously communicated internally, SANCO publicly committed to some very interventionist positions on the inclusion of mortgages and especially on the principle of responsible lending. Knowing that this was 'a very political file […] with big public appeal' (COM119:171), officials tried 'to create a very comprehensive, very exhaustive consumer credit regulation that would be burdensome for industry' (COM89:46). Also during that summer, SANCO's initial preparations for the unfair commercial practices proposal entailed a general producer obligation of fair trading (Chapter 4.5). However, this interventionist position was scaled down to a neatly circumscribed set of prohibited producer practices during the substandard levels of politicisation in the years 2002 and 2003. This change of the Commission's policy position occurred despite constant public attention on unfair commercial practices, particularly in cross-border online trade.

Likewise, high politicisation phases in 2004 and 2005 and their later decline were mirrored in Commission positions. Despite its status quo bias, the proposed 'new approach' overhaul also provides some evidence in this regard (Chapter 5.3). Here, major consumer-oriented enhancements of market surveillance, such as centralisation of the notification system, were contemplated by DG ENTR during 2004. This was later cut back to a mere re-codification of the existing rules during the final drafting stages in 2006 and 2007, when the overall level of EU politicisation had declined significantly. The other 'neutral' case in the sample showed a parallel decline in Commission interventionism. When formulating the policy on food additives (Chapter 6.4), DG SANCO considered the inclusion of processing aids and a time-limited authorisation of additives during the high politicisation phase of 2005, but dropped these ideas in the face of producer opposition when politicisation reverted during the final stages of drafting. Lastly, even in the ultimately rather interventionist 2008 Commission proposal on food information (Chapter 6.5), we saw some concessions to producers on alcoholic beverages and origin labelling in parallel with declining EU politicisation in the last half-year of position formation. Again, this happened despite a rising public salience of food policy issues.

All these examples concern only specific provisions in the Commission's policy proposals, and they reversed the judgement on the final outcome only for some. But given the probabilistic nature of the model and given that the process-tracing efforts explicitly control for alternative explanations, these swings in Commission interventionism provide tangible evidence in support of the theoretical claims. Not only was the Commission sensitive to varying salience of the issues in question, but where salience remained stable the Commission also responded to major upsurges and declines in the general public politicisation of the EU. Co-variation across and within the scrutinised policy-making processes is by and large consistent with the argument that issue salience moderates a link between the general politicisation of European integration and consumer policy interventionism of the European Commission.

7.2 The effects of EU politicisation and issue salience on the internal drafting process

Beyond co-variation of the major input and output variables, the process hypotheses developed in Chapter 3.3 allow us to be more specific on how EU politicisation and issue salience affect policy formulation processes inside the Commission. A comparative perspective on the seventeen case studies is consistent with the hypothesis that salient initiatives in a politicised context involve the administrative and especially the *political* hierarchies to a greater extent. For example, either rising levels of EU politicisation as in the consumer credit case (Chapter 4.4), or increasing public issue salience as in the toy safety case (Chapter 5.4), made lower-level administrators proactively seek the political backing of their hierarchies.

However, the case studies also indicate the rather strong dominance of lower Commission echelons when it comes to fixing policy choices. The responsible Commissioners often appeared as gatekeepers only while the possible routes a legislative proposal could take were essentially set by the administrators. As one official put it: '[W]e have a larger view, which allows us to choose at every moment, depending on the political momentum, the kind of proposal we would like to boost at that time' (COM33:164). Here the proposals on bus and maritime passenger rights (Chapter 4.7) appear to be an extreme example: an outgoing Commissioner opposed more interventionism, but the administrative level seems to have merely paused drafting until a change in the political leadership allowed their original ideas to make progress. Also on the general product safety proposal, the lower echelons of SANCO and ENTR tried to avoid too much cabinet involvement. They preferred to hammer out conflictive issues themselves because political conflict at the time was quite unpredictable (Chapter 5.1). In almost all low salience cases, in addition, the case studies hardly detect any direct involvement of the line hierarchies in specifying policy content. Here, the desk officials' original impulses and their networks within and across their DG, proved more influential (cf. Kassim *et al.* 2013: chapter 3; Suvarierol 2009). For the book's broader argument, it should thus be noted that the policy effects of public EU politicisation matter even at the purely administrative stages of policy formulation inside the Commission.

Yet the case studies above also provide some examples where the hierarchy had a much stronger steer on process and policy content. The food information proposal, which involved the Director-General to a great extent, is a case in point (Chapter 6.5). Also the Commissioners are far from superfluous to the link between politicisation and the Commission's consumer interventionism. For example, on air passenger rights (Chapter 4.3), consumer credit (Chapter 4.4) or health claims (Chapter 6.2), the political leadership locked itself into more interventionist policy positions by making early public commitments at times of high politicisation and high salience. But as the case of the 'new approach' overhaul and its rhetorical link to Verheugen's better regulation agenda show (Chapter 5.3), such public commitments by responsible Commissioners may also lock in more liberal policy choices. These findings bode well with more recent arguments that consider Commissioners as pivotal to the public accountability of Europe's central executive (Wille 2013: especially chapter 3).

A second process hypothesis in Chapter 3.3 focuses on *process duration*. Indeed, the preceding chapters have identified a range of cases where the Commission accelerated drafting so as to meet public expectations emerging from either general EU politicisation or the specific issue salience. For example, intriguing evidence for the accelerating effect of politicisation is found in the consumer rights proposal (Chapter 4.6) while public issue salience sped up the drafting of the toy safety regulation (Chapter 5.4). Yet in an aggregate perspective, this effect is not fully robust. While the average drafting time for non-salient proposals is forty-one months, reduces to thirty-seven months for salient cases, this difference is hardly meaningful against a sample standard deviation of sixteen months. Some case studies also suggest that politicisation and issue salience might prolong drafting time: the consumer rights unit in particular but also the food unit in DG SANCO engaged in rather encompassing and time-consuming consultation processes when they anticipated that their pre-set and rather interventionist positions might stir political conflict. The cases on unfair commercial practices (Chapter 4.5) as well as on food information (Chapter 6.5) provide evidence in this regard.

This points to the patterns of *stakeholder consultation*. As expected in Chapter 3.3, neither EU politicisation nor issue salience determines which external actors are invited to give their opinions. While DGs sometimes engage in encompassing consultations to shield themselves against allegations of partisanship, the preceding chapters also unveil cases where access for either the producer or for the consumer side was severely limited. Policy formulation on consumer credit (Chapter 4.4) or on the 'new approach' (Chapter 5.3) provide respective examples. Yet in contrast to the patterns of access, the comparative conclusion on responsiveness to stakeholder demands is rather clear. Where the Commission face high public EU politicisation and issue salience, the proposal's key provisions often very closely resemble the demands documented in the position papers from consumer NGOs. Where a DG shifted towards more interventionist policy choices in the preceding cases, this often occurred by almost literally taking those consumer demands on board that had been declined earlier. This finding implies that an active representation of diffuse interests remains necessary in Brussels, even if politicisation raises the Commission's incentives to appeal to widespread public interests on its own (cf. Klüver 2011). Input from organised public interest groups serves as a transmission belt that provides the Commission with readily available policy templates, which it can assume will be attractive to the public.

A fourth and final process hypothesis derived in Chapter 3.3 deals with *internal conflict* among Commission DGs. It was hypothesised that rising consumer interventionism induced by higher levels of public salience leads to opposition from more traditional DGs in the Commission. Yet if salience rises further, such opposition should decline again because all DGs share a common interest in appealing to the wider public if the initiative in question is likely to influence the overall evaluation of supranational decision making. Accordingly, this curvilinear relationship is moderated by general EU politicisation: The more supranational decision making is contested in general, the more weight the common interest of all DGs should gain, so that internal opposition declines earlier under higher levels of general EU politicisation.

The case studies have shown that the sensitive measurement of internal conflict is hampered by poor access to respective information from within the Commission. But the few process observations available do support the hypothesised relationships. One initial example on the effect of salience is present in the toy safety case (Chapter 5.4). DG SANCO had been pressing DG ENTR on a clear reference to the general product safety directive in 'new approach' instruments for years, but ENTR refused any cooperation on the matter. However, once public issue salience increased in late 2007 while ENTR was drafting a 'new approach' instrument on toy safety, SANCO's demands suddenly became assertive and cooperation across DG borders ensued.

We also find observations highlighting the moderating effect of politicisation. One example is the consumer credit case (Chapter 4.4). DG SANCO's interventionist positions met fierce internal opposition from DG MARKT, formerly the main actor on financial service regulation and a close collaborator of DG SANCO on these issues. But once politicisation peaked in 2001 in view of the constantly high public salience of consumer credit, DG SANCO publicly committed to some of the most contested provisions and managed to assert some of them until the proposal was adopted. Likewise, the temporal pattern of internal conflict was theoretically consistent in the consumer rights case (Chapter 4.6). The proposal met internal opposition from DG MARKT and DG ENTR when politicisation declined in 2007, but SANCO asserted most of its ideas in the final negotiations at the political level in late 2008, when both EU politicisation and public issue salience were on the rise again.

Note, however, that the hypothesis on internal conflict hinges on a status quo of liberalisation against which more interventionist positions must be asserted. This does not necessarily hold, as the 'new approach' case underlines (Chapter 5.3). By adopting the general product safety directive in 2001, the EU had created a more interventionist status quo of consumer product safety regulation. When ENTR tried to reinforce a more liberal model in 2007, DG SANCO could build its defence around this status quo and blocked a common Commission decision for more than five months. ENTR finally had to give in on some issues. The case shows not only that more interventionist proposals increase internal conflict, but also that more liberal positions will find internal opponents if more interventionist EU law already exists. This insight may appear trivial at first, but it suggests that if EU politicisation ultimately increases, so will conflict potential within the European Commission in the long term.

The observed drafting processes furthermore suggest that such internal conflict is dependent on how strongly internal competences overlap. Where the relatively young DG SANCO fought for more interventionism, turf conflicts with the old bulls in the respective policy field ensued. This was most pronounced in the area of product safety, which had previously been solely the responsibility of DG ENTR (Chapter Five). But it was also visible in the area of contractual consumer rights, which had been handled by DG MARKT (Chapter Four). It even occurred in food policy, where almost all respective competences had already been transferred to DG SANCO, while DG ENTR and DG AGRI were not prepared to fully give up their traditional dominance (Chapter Five). In contrast, where interventionist positions were pushed by DGs with a longer history in regulating the respective sectors alone – DG INFSO for electronic communications (Chapter 4.1) and DG TREN for transport (Chapters 4.3 and 4.7) – we observe less internal dispute. Their clear-cut responsibilities seem to grant some insulation against demands from other DGs. More evidence is needed in this regard, but interventionist policies seem to be more easily asserted if fuzzy organisational competences are settled for good. The regulation of food policy might thus provide a particularly valuable area for future studies of intra-Commission conflict.

More generally, conflict within the Commission highlights that extending the competence-seeking assumption to individual DGs carries weight in explaining the substance of legislative Commission proposals. The 2008 passenger rights proposals (Chapter 4.7) highlight that 'empire-building' behaviour around a DG's extant legislation can result in interventionist policies even where contemporaneous public salience is lacking. And the unfair commercial practices case (Chapter 4.5), the chosen harmonisation approach on consumer rights (Chapter 4.6) and the food additives case (Chapter 6.4) show that consumer interventionism might also be attenuated if it serves the expansion of a DG's own regulatory competences. Explanations of Commission policy choices should thus take the organisational and sectoral self-interest of internal actors into account (cf. Cram 1997; Wonka 2008a). Under rising levels of EU politicisation and the Commission's transformation into a 'normal' executive (Wille 2013), turf conflicts might become more pronounced, exerting even stronger demand on the coordination capacities of the central services and the Commission president (cf. Kassim *et al.* 2013: chapter 6; Hartlapp *et al.* 2013; Kassim 2006).

A perspective on competence-seeking behaviour also reminds us that individual DGs can manipulate public issue salience during drafting if more attention serves their organisational goals. The timely public commitments of Commissioners discussed earlier prove that this strategy can be quite successful. DG TREN and DG SANCO in particular employed it to garner external political support for their regulatory plans, by publishing and promoting studies and by naming and shaming producer practices. Glaring evidence also abounded during the drafting processes on air passenger rights (Chapter 4.3) where DG TREN pushed airlines into a voluntary agreement, only to override it with even stronger regulation later. Likewise, frequent newspaper appearances and public speeches by Commissioner Kuneva shielded the consumer rights proposal against concessions during the final negotiations with DG MARKT (Chapter 4.6). Similarly, widely circulated consultations, the publication of studies and a range of soft-law measures on obesity in Europe prepared the ground for the encompassing food information proposal (Chapter 6.5). But also on toy safety (Chapter 5.4), where DG SANCO was not in the lead itself, it used the publication of its RAPEX data on toy recalls as well as public speaking tours by the Commissioner to increase pressure on DG ENTR. These incidences highlight that public politicisation and issue salience are not only factors that are forced upon the Commission, but they rather also serve as welcomed opportunity structures for those Commission actors who pursue more interventionist policies with a broader public appeal.

7.3 Complementary and alternative explanations

The individual case studies have controlled a range of complementary and alternative explanations for the European Commission's policy choices (cf. Chapter 3.4 and panel four in Table 7.1).

First is the view that policy choices are driven by *Commissioners* responsible for the legislative initiative in question. Following the logic of delegation or socialisation, it is often assumed that policy content is determined either by a Commissioner's nationality or by his or her party membership. As we have seen above, individual Commissioners have often supported internal drafting measures of their DGs by publicly justifying policy choices or by committing to specific templates. But with the exception of Verheugen's pressure on publishing the 'new approach' overhaul on time (Chapter 5.3), no systematic accordance between actual policy choices and the nationality or the partisanship of the responsible Commissioners can be detected.

The comparison of the consumer interventionism across the seventeen case studies shows strong variation under the responsibility of individual Commissioners. For example, both the comparatively liberal proposal on unfair commercial practices and the highly interventionist proposal on consumer credit were adopted under the political responsibility of Commissioner David Byrne. Similarly, a pattern of varying interventionism despite stable political leadership is visible if one compares the strongly intervening health claims proposal with the liberalising food fortification initiative, or the food information case with the proposed food additives regulation. Furthermore, ten of the seventeen cases provide natural experiments, as they experienced a change in political leadership during drafting. This happened with the incoming Prodi Commission in late 1999, the shift to the Barroso Commission in 2004, or the split of DG SANCO's political leadership in 2007. However, the temporal reconstruction of these individual drafting processes does not reveal any substantial policy adaptations in response. This evidence is clearly at odds with approaches deriving Commission policy from the nationality or the party membership of the responsible Commissioners.

Second, another prominent explanation particularly for consumer interventionism is the *productionist* view (Trumbull 2006: 167). In line with the idea of 'baptist and bootlegger coalitions' striving for a 'trading up' (Vogel 1995), arguments in this vein hold that high consumer standards may also be produced by industry lobbying in the hope to protect domestic markets against international competition. Indeed, the Commission had external trade implications in mind when devising product safety regulations, especially where the affected industries were subject to import competition (especially Chapters 5.1, 5.2, and 5.4). However, the process analyses do not reveal explicit producer demands for such a 'trading up'. In contrast, especially in product safety but also in the other two subfields, more interventionist Commission positions were consistently associated with outright opposition from the major umbrella organisations representing the affected industries. Thus, the productionist view also provides little additional explanatory power for the observed variations in the Commission's political choices in consumer policy.

Third, various strands of the literature maintain that the Commission first and foremost drafts initiatives that are *politically feasible* in the EP and especially in the Council of Ministers. Contact with EP members before proposal adoption, however, could be detected in only three of the seventeen case studies in this book – probably so because the parliament is often seen as a 'champion of diffuse interests' in consumer policy, among others (Pollack 1997b). But in contrast, fourteen out of the seventeen cases underline that the set of member state preferences is highly relevant even at the drafting stage. The various Commission DGs engage heavily in uncovering which particular policy choices are likely to survive negotiations in the Council. Respective strategies include communications requiring formal Council responses, public consultations where national governments provide their opinions on specific key provisions, and working groups in which the lead DG pre-negotiates consecutive draft proposals with national representatives.

The voiced national preferences also provided real constraints, as their comparison to the final Commission position highlights in the various cases. Member state preferences provided upper bounds for the Commission's consumer interventionism, for example, on the scope of the general product safety directive (Chapter 5.1) or on colour-coded nutrient information for foods (Chapter 6.5). But member state preferences sometimes also provided lower bounds and limited envisaged liberalisation, for example, on sales promotions (Chapter 4.2) or age and trade restrictions on fireworks (Chapter 5.2). In these and other examples, new information about national positions during drafting trimmed the lead DG's ideal positions without, however, determining them fully. Against these results, political feasibility in the Council of Ministers defines the leeway with which the Commission's policy reactions to EU politicisation and issue salience can unfold. One Commission official summarises this succinctly:

> We have looked at an issue and we are trying to move forward in line with the common European interest. But then there are two considerations. One is: can we get this through? You know, if you propose something that has no chance of getting through the Parliament and the Council it makes us look politically impotent and it doesn't help Europeans. And the other side is that we would hope that everything we do is something that can be explained to the citizens because it is in their interest. But obviously sometimes the easier it is to make that case, the more we like the dossier. (COM113:98)

7.4 The book's major findings in a nutshell

Beyond other factors that may impinge on legislative agenda setting by the European Commission (see Hartlapp *et al.* 2014), this book primarily shows that policy making in Europe's central agenda setter responds to the changing political context of European integration. To put it in a nutshell, comparing the Commission's policy choices on the distribution of consumer and producer rights in seventeen policy initiatives between 1999 and 2008 yields the following results:

- The European Commission is aware of the immediate distributional consequences of its regulatory initiatives and is willing to adapt them to the general public politicisation of supranational decision making in Europe. The more the legitimacy of the EU is challenged by the wider public, the stronger are Commission incentives to produce legislative proposals that generate widely dispersed political benefits.

- This sensitivity to EU politicisation is moderated by the contemporaneous public salience of the substantial issues covered by the respective policy decision. The more the substantial topics of a Commission initiative are discussed among the wider public at the time of drafting, the more the Commission will accommodate the incentives created by the overall EU politicisation.

- The will to produce widespread regulatory benefits results in increased responsiveness to public interest groups, and is often expressed by literally taking over the policy templates these groups offer.

- More market intervention in the name of the diffuse mass of European consumers, however, often meets opposing preferences inside the European Commission. The internal coordination processes matter; and where a specific area is already covered by extant European law, pronounced turf conflicts within the Commission ensue. But EU politicisation creates an enabling context for internal actors pursuing more interventionist policies: Respective DGs can actively raise the salience of the issues in question by various publication strategies before proposal adoption.

- Finally, anticipating national preferences and Council majorities remains an important constraint. It confines the room for manoeuvre, but it does not forestall the intrinsically political choices of the European Commission when setting the legislative agenda of the European Union.

7.5 Normative implications: An enhanced scope for public interest regulation in Europe?

These empirical results speak directly to the fundamental question whether supranational decision making becomes more responsive to an increasingly involved European public. They help to hammer out how far public politicisation enhances the scope for a European legislative agenda that deviates from elite-driven models and takes public interests beyond mere market efficiency into account.

Critics of a more politicised integration process mainly fear that short-term political pressures undermine efficient decision making and credible commitments to time-consistent solutions for transnational problems (e.g. Majone 2005). But the results uncovered here lend only partial support to this view. On the one hand, we have seen that the Commission still invests heavily in forging compromise among national governments even where it deviates strongly from a lowest common denominator solution. Given that the set of governmental preferences defines the Commission's leeway, as it did before even more interventionist positions, do not systematically forestall intergovernmental agreement and political progress in Europe. On the other hand, some of the scrutinised cases highlight that public politicisation and issue salience can lead the Commission to challenge deeply entrenched regulatory solutions. Such challenges have resulted in partly contradictory European law and often translated into pronounced turf conflicts within the Commission. In this view, politicisation may indeed decrease decision-making efficiency. But this loss of efficiency may be the price to pay for an expanding supranational authority that by all normative standards has to somehow balance the various, and sometimes contending, societal interests that its activities affect.

Yet the results presented here will also not fully gratify those proponents of a more politicised integration process whose benchmark is a procedural model of popular democracy geared towards creating societal legitimacy on the input side (e.g. Hix 2006). The mechanism scrutinised in this book still firmly rests on the output legitimacy of European decision making. Nevertheless, the Commission's sensitivity to a politicised context and the public salience of regulatory issues can be seen as an improvement in the societal acceptance of supranational authority. Where public and elite preferences systematically differ (cf. Dehousse and Monceau 2009; Hooghe 2003), enhanced responsiveness on the output side should help to convince European citizens that EU policies are not fundamentally biased against public preferences – even if they may be flawed at times. In this view, the Commission's engagement in demonstrating the immediate public benefits of the policies it devises may create a highly valuable precondition for enhancing input legitimacy in the future. If citizens become aware that Europe can do something for them also in the short term, then elections to the already rather powerful European Parliament would not only be contested on *whether* voters care about Europe at all but would involve a decision on *what kind of* Europe citizens actually want (Rauh 2009).

Citizens will arguably more readily accept supranational authority if they have the periodical chance to select among competing political courses of European integration by directly holding responsible actors accountable. From that perspective, the enhanced parliamentary investiture procedure for incoming Commissioners (Wille 2013: 85–7; 2012; Judge and Earnshaw 2002) and the more recent coupling of the choice of a Commission President and the outcome of EP elections (Schmitt *et al.* 2015; Hobolt 2014; Corbett 2014) provide promising institutional complements to the politicisation–salience–policy nexus uncovered in this book. Where these procedures force incoming political leaders to early public commitments with regard to specific content of the upcoming and often rather predictable legislative programme of a new Commission, they institutionalise the Commission's incentives for appealing to the wider public. Respective political mandates would also help in rebalancing the observed administrative dominance in legislative agenda setting and could provide orientation in the ensuing turf conflicts among different Commission DGs.

But as long as the final verdict on these rather recent institutional developments is out, we should also not too hastily generalise the Commission's responsiveness this book observes in the field of consumer policy. Besides the manifold constraints on Commission policy highlighted in the individual case studies, reference to majority decisions reminds us that the European agenda setter might face much more heterogeneous public interests in other issue areas. Recall that an initiative's public salience mediates only *whether* the Commission considers the public's reception of a particular initiative in a politicised climate, while the question of *which policy choices* it proposes in response is subject to the distribution of societal interests on the regulatory issue in question. In this regard, consumer policy – a typical valence issue – is an easy case for the Commission. Here it can readily identify narrowly concentrated and widely dispersed interests among its more organised and more diffuse stakeholders. But in other issue areas, such as social security, migration or fiscal policy, the diffuse European public is often split along class lines, along identity considerations, or even along national borders (Hooghe and Marks 2009; Kriesi *et al*. 2008; Scharpf 2010). In such contexts, the logic presented here may also drive a competence-seeking Commission to blame avoidance strategies, letting it shy away from decisions on salient but much more controversial issues in which no unequivocal societal winners can be identified. This should be analysed in future research, for example, by comparing the mechanism proposed here across different policy domains (cf. Hartlapp *et al*. 2014: chapter 9) or by more systematically testing the argument along the congruence of public opinion and aggregate EU policy output (Toshkov 2011; Arnold and Toshkov 2010; Dehousse *et al*. 2009). But it again reinforces the need to equip the Commission with clear-cut, but also reversible, political mandates tied to the preferences of European voters.

Taken together, public politicisation is both a risk and an opportunity for further political integration in Europe. Insights into the nexus of EU politicisation, issue salience and Commission consumer policy indicate some decline in decision-making efficiency, but they also provide good news for democracy in Europe, particularly so because the underlying theoretical mechanism is manipulable by societal actors. In the elite-driven mode of supranational regulation, direct *access* to policy makers is the most successful lobbying strategy, enhancing the risk of regulatory capture. But since politicisation creates Commission incentives for appealing to public interest, especially in contemporaneously salient issue areas, *voice* also becomes a promising strategy for various interest groups (cf. Beyers 2004; Klüver 2011). NGOs representing diffuse societal interests, unions, political parties or even grassroots movements can gain influence over the content of European policy by raising the salience of their requests and by publicly identifying the supranational level as the relevant locus of power. In this way, the public politicisation of the European integration process can realign supranational policy making with political preferences held among the wider European public.

Appendix A: Additional Analyses of the Politicisation Index

Table A1 compares the basic time trend in the politicisation index (Model 1, cf. Figure 2.4) on dummies marking major integration events (models 2 and 3). Due to the multi-dimensional nature of the politicisation index, the effects of these dummies should not be interpreted in a causal manner. They are meant to check whether the long-term politicisation trend is leveraged only by individual events. The results are derived by OLS relying on the more conservative Newey–West standard errors, based on a maximum lag of four months to account for serial correlation in the data (Greene 1993: 378, 422).

Model 2 distinguishes Treaty preparation (time between the first mention of the respective Treaty revision on the Council agenda to final adoption) the adoption month, and the ratification phase (time between adoption and entry into force or failure). In addition it includes the EP elections as well as one preceding month. Model 3 takes a more idiosyncratic view and focuses on the respective individual integration events during the period 1990–2009.

Figure A1, in addition, plots the predictions of model 3 against the actual values of the composite politicisation index to check exactly when politicisation beyond the time trend and individual integration events occurred.

A few immediate implications are important for the present purposes (*see* Chapter Two in this volume):

- The positive time trend in the composite indicator is not driven or leveraged by individual events of European integration. Rather, the slope becomes even more pronounced once we control for individual events.
- The politicisation index exhibits higher values particularly during Treaty ratification periods and EP elections.
- This overall finding is however not robust across all individual events in this category, some of them do not exhibit politicisation levels that exceed the long-term trend.
- The Lisbon Treaty, in particular, exhibits politicisation levels below the overall long-term trend – probably due to the pronounced elite efforts to de-politicise this treaty revision after the failure of the Constitution. Yet these efforts were only temporarily successful (cf. De Wilde and Zürn 2012).

244 | A Responsive Technocracy?

Table A1: Regression models of the composite politicisation index

	Model 1 0.003*** (0.001)	Model 2 0.003*** (0.001)	Model 3 0.005*** (0.001)
Treaty negotiations		0.008	
		(0.101)	
Treaty adoption		0.231	
		(0.306)	
Treaty ratification		0.230**	
		(0.104)	
EP elections		0.453*	
		(0.230)	
Maastricht			
Negotiations			0.289**
			(0.141)
Adoption			−0.102
			(0.098)
Ratification			0.877***
			(0.137)
Amsterdam			
Negotiations			0.287**
			(0.123)
Adoption			1.388***
			(0.069)
Ratification			0.168
			(0.116)
Nice			
Negotiations			0.130
			(0.087)
Adoption			0.044
			(0.274)
Ratification			−0.680**
			(0.317)
Constitution			
Negotiations			0.082
			(0.226)
Adoption			0.235***
			(0.085)

Table A1 *(continued)*

	Model 1 0.003*** (0.001)	Model 2 0.003*** (0.001)	Model 3 0.005*** (0.001)
Ratification			0.315*
			(0.178)
Lisbon			
Negotiations			−0.550***
			(0.152)
Adoption			−0.864***
			(0.107)
Ratification			−0.023
			(0.193)
EP Elections			
1994			0.674***
			(0.126)
1999			−0.039
			(0.067)
2004			0.955***
			(0.234)
2009			0.375**
			(0.172)
Constant	−0.430***	−0.501***	−0.785***
	(0.127)	0.117	(0.115)
Adj. R–squared	0.26	0.28	0.47
Obs.	240	240	240

Notes: Newey–West standard errors based on four lags in parentheses, significant at *10%; **5%; ***1%.

Figure A1: Politicisation index and fitted values (model 3)

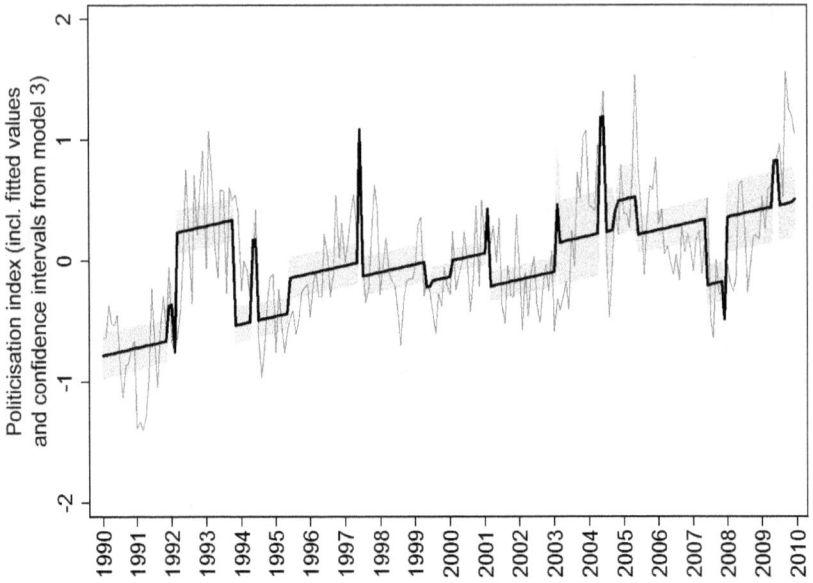

Notes: The grey line presents the monthly values of the politicisation index, the black line the fitted values from model 3 in Table A1. The shaded area indicates the 95 per cent confidence interval of the fitted values.

Appendix B: Sampling Consumer Policy Initiatives

Chapter Three identifies a Commission drafting process for an individual European consumer policy proposal between 1999 and 2008 as the relevant *unit of analysis*. Consumer policy covers all policy measures that aim at protecting the end user of products or services against risks and disadvantages in economic life. This definition is rendered operational by the respective directory codes in the EUR-Lex database (Düro 2009), taking only proposals for binding EU law (directives, regulations, and decisions) into account. Directory codes are the only non-exclusive and hierarchical descriptors in EUR-Lex, the European Union's major legislative database, and the sampling procedure relies on 'general consumer policies' (15.20.10), 'consumer information, education and representation' (15.20.20), 'protection of consumer health and safety (15.20.30)', as well as 'protection of economic interests' (15.20.40).[1] This identifies a population of 247 Commission proposals.

The explorative nature of the endeavour as well as the lack of reliable data made me refrain from analysing this whole sample with large-N inferential statistics for now. First, the theoretical argument does not allow a deduction of the exact point in drafting time at which we would expect EU politicisation and public salience to matter. Drafting processes often last several years, migrate through different hierarchical levels and involve different DGs at varying points in time (Hartlapp *et al.* 2013). A statistical analysis, in contrast, would have to rely on a uniform assumption on when to measure independent and dependent variables in drafting time, which entails the significant risk of a wrongly specified lag-structure. Second, the theory implies that the scope of the drafted legal instruments, broadly understood as the number of real-life instances affected by the respective regulation, needs to be controlled. The amount of political benefit the Commission can distribute arguably depends on the scope of the initiative in question. For a uniform statistical analysis, then, we would require a valid and reliable measure of legal scope to model such an interaction effect. Third and fourth, the operationalisation of the dependent variable requires much contextual information (cf. Chapter Three) and we often lack data access with regard to internal drafting of the Commission,[2] which renders a purely co-variational large-N approach too much of an investment.

---

1. See: http://eur-lex.europa.eu/RECH_repertoire.do, for an overview of all available codes (accessed 28 July 2010).

2. Both the principle of collegiality and strategic advantages in inter-institutional negotiations incentivise the Commission as a whole to restrict systematic access to such information (Wonka 2008a, see also the 'transparency' regulation (EC) 1049/2001.

Against these obstacles, a fair analysis of the theoretical expectations needs to allow for some within-case variation (cf. Hall 2008), should be based on cases with a roughly comparable legal scope, and should allow for some generalisable conclusions by relying on a 'structured focused comparison' along the derived hypotheses (George 1979; Hartlapp *et al.* 2014: chapter 3). Accordingly, a reasonable number of drafting processes had to be selected from all 247 cases. The major constraint is the scarcity of *ex ante* information on the theoretically relevant variables that is needed for the construction of an of an ideal-type case study design (Eckstein 1975; see also Seawright and Gerring 2008; Plümper *et al.* 2009). Noting that the book does not seek encompassing explanations of interventionism in European consumer policy but is primarily interested in whether politicisation and salience exert the hypothesised effects, I refrained from a potentially biased selection on the dependent variable (Geddes 2003). Rather, I concentrated on variation in the independent variables. Regarding politicisation and salience, this has been ensured by a sufficiently long investigation period that allowed scattering cases across differing levels of these primary concepts (cf. Chapters Two, Four, Five and Six). Regarding the characteristics of Commissioners and Commission presidents as a prime source of alternative explanations, the case selection also ensured analytical control over respective variation in the final sample.

To achieve this, the 247 proposals were cross-tabled along both Commission terms and along the internal decision mode where I distinguish oral and written procedures. While written procedures apply only if there is no formal opposition from the Commission services, oral procedures imply discussion of a proposal in the Commission's College and are either scheduled as such or apply in the case of enduring internal conflict (Hartlapp *et al.* 2013; Wonka 2008b: 65–82). In other words, the universe of cases was stratified according to changes in political leadership between the Commission terms and formal involvement of the Commission's political level. Within each of the four resulting cross-table cells, proposals were then sorted by their scope as indicated by the subject matter in the title.[3] Based on this, I purposely selected the broadest proposals from each cell while ensuring that different DGs of the Commission acted as the formally responsible lead department. Limiting myself to a sample size that is both tractable by qualitative analysis and sufficiently large for comparison, Table 3.3 in Chapter Three lists the seventeen finally selected cases.

---

3. While the judgement on scope is inherently subjective in nature, replication of the procedure is likely to result in a very similar result since many of the proposals in the original consumer policy sample come with very limited scope. For example while the original sample contains a range of regulations on individual chemical substances in foods, it contains only one proposal for a general framework on the regulation of food additives in the Union. In other words, there was a very clear line dividing broad and specific proposals. Spreadsheets documenting the individual steps of case selection are available upon request.

Appendix C: Operationalising Issue Salience

C1: Newspaper samples

As discussed in Chapter 3.6, the salience measures in this book rely on the frequency with which the issues figure in public media. Given that digital access to newspaper archives is still rather restricted and given that the data collection had to rely on manual search routines and coding procedures in the available databases, the analyses are limited to a snapshot of the European print media landscape. More specifically, the analyses rely on the newspaper sample in Table C1.

Note again that the comparative approach pursued here first and foremost requires a measure that is consistent over time. Rather than the 'true' mean of salience, we want to reliably estimate the variation in the salience of consumer rights and risks related to market transactions, product safety or food safety over time. An aggregated measure based on leading quality newspapers from some of the largest member states should pick up the sought-after variation in the public salience of consumer policy issues reliably beyond particular national debates. This is also underlined by rather stable cross-national standard deviations in the data derived below.

C2: Aggregate salience measures for the three consumer policy subfields

As highlighted in Chapter Three, the aim is to identify the presence of issues related to the economic risks of consumers in market transactions, the risks related to the safety of consumer products and the health risks related to the consumption of food in public debates. A time-consistent identification of newspaper reports that refer to these issue sets should be (1) independent of the political positions

Table C1: Newspaper sample underlying the public issue salience indicators

Newspaper	Nationality	Political alignment	Approx. daily circulation	Content accessed via
Financial Times	UK	Liberal	336,590 (2011)	Gale Infotrac
Frankfurter Allgemeine Zeitung	Germany	Centre-right	366,844 (2008)	Genios
Le Figaro	France	Centre-right	330,237 (2010)	LexisNexis
El País	Spain	Centre-left	425,927 (2007)	LexisNexis

Notes: Directly comparable circulation data let alone country rankings are only available at prohibitively high costs. The indicative figures are taken from Wikipedia instead.

of particular actors, (2) broad enough to capture also more specific issues of each policy field and (3) specific enough to attribute variation only to actual changes of salience in this particular policy subfield.

Respective media search algorithms were constructed inductively. The approach treats the English texts of all Commission proposals in the sample as well as all related stakeholder position papers I could access during case study research as relevant input data. For each of the three policy fields – contractual consumer rights, product safety and food safety – these documents were transformed into term-frequency matrices. The most common English stop words, certain peculiarities of legal speech, as well as nouns referring to political actors such as the European institutions, member state governments or interest groups were removed before all remaining terms were reduced to their common root.[1]

Uncovering those word stems that most adequately circumscribe the respective consumer policy subfield followed the idea that a term is more relevant to the policy subfield (1) if it appears in the majority of all texts regardless who authored them and (2) the more frequently the different authors use the respective words in each of these texts. Expressed differently, I assume that a word stem is more relevant to describe a consumer policy area the more often it is used both across and within all respective policy papers during the investigation period.

Only those word stems appearing in at least three-quarters of all texts per policy area were kept. This ensures a high frequency across policy papers. The remaining terms were then sorted by their relative frequency within policy papers. I refrained from using the mean share in this regard as this measure is sensitive to outliers, meaning that if a given word is used extensively by only one political actor we may wrongly judge it to be relevant for the issue area as a whole. In this light, word stems were sorted by their median share across policy papers from different political actors. In order to deal with the non-English newspapers, I translated all inflected and derived words of the top five English word stems to French, German and Spanish and stemmed them again in the respective language. Table C2 summarises the results.

The word stem 'consum*' encompassing mainly the terms 'consumer' and 'consumption' unsurprisingly exhibits a high frequency within and across policy papers in each of the three subfields. For the issue area of economic and contractual consumer rights, additional terms such as 'information', 'protection', 'right' and 'provider' as well as their inflections and derivatives figure prominently in the policy documentation – independent of the particular political position, the

---

1.   The 166 publically available documents from various sources are individually referenced in the case studies in Chapters Four–Six. Creation of the word-frequency matrixes including stop word removal and stemming was achieved by Will Lowe's *JFreq* tool (see: http://www.williamlowe. net/software/; accessed 10 June 2011). The list of the most common English stop words was retrieved from the Textfixer website (http://www.textfixer.com/resources/common-english-words.txt; accessed 10 June 2011). The full stop word list as well as the sample of input texts is available from the author upon request.

Table C2: Most relevant word stems across the consumer policy subfields

Rank	Issue area: Market transactions (T)			Issue area: Product safety (P)			Issue area: Food safety (F)		
	Wordstem	% of mentioning docs (N=79)	Median share per document	Wordstem	% of mentioning docs (N=21)	Median share per document	Wordstem	% of mentioning docs (N=66)	Median share per document
1	**consum*** *consomm** *verbrauch** *consum**	91.14	3.19	**product*** *produ** *produck** *produc**	95.24	1.61	**food*** *aliment** *nahrung** *aliment**	98.48	2.29
2	**inform*** *inform** *inform** *inform**	96.20	0.50	**safet*** *securit** *sicherheit** *seguridad*	90.48	1.49	**consum*** *consomm** *verbrauch** *consum**	92.42	1.71

252 | A Responsive Technocracy?

Table C2 *(continued)*

Rank	Issue area: Market transactions (T) Wordstem	% of mentioning docs (N=79)	Median share per document	Issue area: Product safety (P) Wordstem	% of mentioning docs (N=21)	Median share per document	Issue area: Food safety (F) Wordstem	% of mentioning docs (N=66)	Median share per document
3	**protect*** *prote* * *schutz* * *prote* *	84.81	0.65	**consum*** *consomm* * *verbrauch* * *consum* *	90.48	1.40	**nutrit*** *nutrit* * *ernährung* * *nutri* *	87.88	1.32
4	**right*** *droit* * *recht* * *derecho* *	81.01	0.62	**market*** *marche* * *markt* * *merca* *	95.23	0.92	**product*** *produ* * *produk* * *produc* *	90.91	1.30

Table C2 (continued)

Rank	Issue area: Market transactions (T)			Issue area: Product safety (P)			Issue area: Food safety (F)		
	Wordstem	% of mentioning docs (N=79)	Median share per document	Wordstem	% of mentioning docs (N=21)	Median share per document	Wordstem	% of mentioning docs (N=66)	Median share per document
5	**provid***	77.22	0.49	**standard***	76.19	0.61	**label***	84.85	0.91
	*offr**								
	*ambiet**			*standard**					
	*ofer**			*standard**			*etiquet**		
				*norma**			*kennzeichn**		
							*etiquet**		

particular proposal that is addressed, or the particular point in time the source document was authored. For the second issue area, terms like 'products' and 'safety' or 'marketing' and 'standardisation' are both broad enough and specific enough to identify respective policy issues. Lastly, the issue area of food safety can be paraphrased in an unbiased manner by terms such as 'foodstuffs', and 'nutrition' but also 'production' and 'labelling'.

On this basis, the search algorithms for the quality newspapers were derived. Initially, I employed the condition that a respective article needs to contain derivations from each of the top three word stems to count for in a respective issue area. Using fewer terms would have been too broad to identify the policy areas while employing more would have been too specific as most explicit policy papers do not fulfil such a strong condition themselves. Qualitative analyses of the results from the different newspapers during different phases of the investigation period revealed the need for some refinements within each issue area.

For economic and contractual consumer rights, the top three terms appeared to be too broad as the results contained a comparatively high number of more general articles on economic issues. Accordingly, I added the condition that beyond 'consum*', 'inform*', and 'protect*', relevant articles must also contain either 'right*' or 'provid*' or both. Low specificity was also a problem for the issue area of product safety. The qualitative analysis showed that the initial algorithm picked up many articles that actually dealt with the issue area of food safety. This was hardly surprising and I enhanced the specificity of the results by ensuring that both 'food*' and 'nutrition*' were excluded from the results. Finally, for the issue area of food safety, initial searches produced many zero results and were thus too specific rather than too broad. After closer qualitative analysis this could be traced to a linguistic problem. Especially in French and Spanish, and to a lesser extent also in English and German, words from the roots of 'aliment*' and 'nutrit*' are used as synonyms. The condition that a relevant article contains both terms was thus relaxed, demanding only the presence of either one or the other stem. This, of course, broadened the results but could be targeted by requiring the additional presence of the fourth most relevant terms derived from the stem 'produc*'.

After these refinements, the qualitative analyses indicated that the majority of articles dealt with issues subsumable under the consumer policy issue area in question. To finalise the comparative measures of contemporaneous issue salience, I collected the article frequencies for each month in the ten-year investigation period and stored them as shares of the overall number of published articles to account for variation in newspaper length. To summarise, the three measures, presented in the introductions of Chapters Four–Six, capture the average monthly prominence of consumer risks either related to market transactions, product safety or food safety relative to all other issues covered by four leading quality newspapers in Europe.

C3: Specific salience measures for each consumer policy proposal under analysis

However, as also highlighted in Chapter Three, looking only at these aggregate measures risks missing instances in which the broad issue field was not publicly salient while specific issues the Commission proposals cover attract high public attention (compare, e.g. the issues of 'product safety', 'toy safety' or 'chemicals in toys'). Thus each case study was complemented with newspaper searches directed at the more specific issues covered by each Commission proposal under analysis. Table C3 provides an overview of the respectively applied newspaper search logic (which had to be adapted to newspaper language and database syntax) and the number of relevant hits during the drafting period (as uncovered during the case-specific interviews). The actual content of the retrieved newspaper articles is discussed in each case study.

Table C3: Newspaper searches on the case-specific issue salience

ID	Legislative content	Boolean logic of newspaper search	Hits	Duration (months)	Average hits per month
1	General product safety	product AND safety AND NOT food*	379	14	27.07
2	Food supplements	'food supplements' OR 'nutritional supplements' OR 'dietary supplements'	1	40	0.03
3	Universal service and users' rights relating to electronic communications networks and services	('universal service') AND (telecoms OR 'electronic communications' OR telecommunications)	49	18	2.72
4	Sales promotions in the Internal Market	'sales promotions' AND consumer	10	33	0.30
5	Air passenger rights	('air travel' OR 'air transport' OR airline*) AND (passenger* OR customer*) AND (overbook* OR cancel* OR delay*)	501	35	14.31
6	Credit for consumers	'consumer credit'	687	36	19.08
7	Unfair business-to-consumer commercial practices in the Internal Market	(unfair OR misleading OR aggressive) AND consumer* AND (retailer OR seller OR advertiser)	166	29	5.72

Table C3 *(continued)*

ID	Legislative content	Boolean logic of newspaper search	Hits	Duration (months)	Average hits per month
8	Nutrition and health claims made on foods	'health claims' OR 'functional food' OR 'food marketing' OR 'food labelling'	122	30	4.07
9	Addition of vitamins and minerals and of certain other substances to foods	food* AND (enrichment OR fortification OR restoration) AND (vitamin* OR mineral* OR nutrient*)	2	58	0.03
10	Placing on the market of pyrotechnic articles	safety AND (consumer* OR health*) AND (pyrotech* OR firework*)	26	45	0.58
11	Food additives	'food additives'	40	42	0.95
12	Common framework for the marketing of products	safety AND (product OR products) AND (certification OR 'conformity assessment' or 'CE mark') AND NOT (food* OR shares OR stocks)	59	37	1.59
13	Safety of toys	toy* AND safety AND consumer* AND NOT toyota	184	59	3.12
14	Provision of food information to consumers	label* AND food* AND consumer*	148	36	4.11
15	Consumer rights	consumer* AND (purchase* OR sale* OR retail*) AND (distance* OR doorstep* OR online* OR payment* OR delivery* OR contract*) AND (withdrawal* OR return* OR warranty*) AND NOT (investment OR stock)	339	69	4.91
16	Rights of passengers when travelling by sea and inland waterway	(bus OR coach OR ferry) and (passenger* OR traveller* OR consumer*) AND (liabilit* OR delay* OR cancellation* OR complaint* OR protection) AND transport	170	46	3.70

Table C3 *(continued)*

ID	Legislative content	Boolean logic of newspaper search	Hits	Duration (months)	Average hits per month
17	Rights of passengers in bus and coach transport	(bus OR coach OR ferry) and (passenger* OR traveller* OR consumer*) AND (liabilit* OR delay* OR cancellation* OR complaint* OR protection) AND transport	170	46	3.70

Appendix D: Interviews with Commission Officials

The responsible official for each case was identified by contacting either the management units of the respective Directorate-General or, where obvious, the responsible policy unit. Building on these primary contacts, officials in the other participating DGs or at higher echelons of the lead DG were identified. The actual face-to-face interviews, lasting between thirty and ninety minutes each, were conducted in summer and autumn 2009 in Brussels within the context of a broader project on 'Position formation in the EU Commission'.[1] Each conversation followed a semi-structured interview guide and was based on solid preparation of each proposal under analysis (cf. Berry 2002; Leech 2002; see also Hartlapp *et al.* 2014: especially pp. 34–6 and 304–7). Note that anonymity was assured to interviewees so that information gained through interviews is marked only by the sequential interview number generated in the broader project context (such as COM166 or COM80, etc.). All in all, forty-one Commission officials from six different DGs and four hierarchy levels were interviewed for the legislative initiatives covered in the book (Table D1).

Unsurprisingly, interviews clustered in DG SANCO which was responsible for the majority of sampled cases and was associated with all others. The ranks of the other DGs also largely mirror actual involvement in the relevant key provisions. The cluster in the lower ranks of the Commission's hierarchy is explained by less time being available to those in leading positions but also by the fact that the relevant officials at higher echelons were often responsible for more than one case in my sample. Interviews have been completely transcribed and were made analytically accessible via a qualitative coding procedure in Atlas.ti.

---

1. See: http://www.wzb.eu/en/research/completed-research-programs/position-formation-in-the-eu-commission (accessed 3 December 2014).

Table D1: Distribution of interview sources

			Hierarchy Desk officer	Head of Unit	Director	Cabinet	Total
DG	SANCO	(Health and Consumer Protection)	7	9	2	2	20
	ENTR	(Enterprise and Industry)	4	0	0	2	6
	MARKT	(Internal Market)	4	1	0	0	5
	INFSO	(Information Society)	4	0	0	0	4
	TREN	(Transport and Energy)	3	0	0	0	3
	SG	(Secretariat-General)	2	0	1	0	3
	Total		**24**	**10**	**3**	**4**	**41**

Appendix E: Assessing Consumer Interventionism in Commission Proposals

The individual case studies in Chapters Four–Six qualitatively describe how the relative degree of consumer interventionism in each Commission policy was derived by comparing the rules of the respective proposal provisions to the regulatory status quo (cf. Chapter 3.6). To make these assessments replicable, the following tables provide the original Commission proposal, the direct references to the assessed key provision therein and the sources for the regulatory status quo for each of these instances.

Table E1: Assessing consumer interventionism in initiatives on economic and contractual consumer rights

Case/ Commission proposal	Key provisions	Articles in legal text	Regulatory status quo	Relative interventionism
Chapter 4.1 Universal service and users' rights in electronic communications COM(2000)392	General principles and scope of universal services	1, 3–7, 15	Directive 98/10/EC	+
	Rules for imposing universal service obligations on providers	3.2, 8–14	Directive 98/10/EC	+
	Retail price caps	16	Directive 98/10/EC	–
	Contractual consumer rights	17–8, 21–2, 25, 30	Directive 98/10/EC	+
Chapter 4.2 Sales promotions COM(2001)546	Ban of restrictions of sales promotion + mutual recognition	3	National rules	–
	Harmonisation of information provision and children protection	4, 5, annex	National rules	+
	Cross-border consumer redress	6	National rules	0

Table E1 *(continued)*

Case/ Commission proposal	Key provisions	Articles in legal text	Regulatory status quo	Relative interventionism
Chapter 4.3 Air passenger rights COM(2001)784	Scope of passenger protection	1–3	Reg. (EEC) 295/91	++
	Passenger rights in the case of denied boarding	5–9	Reg. (EEC) 295/91	++
	Passenger rights in the case of cancellation or delay	10–11	–	+
	Implementation and enforcement	4, 12–8	Reg. (EEC) 295/91	+
Chapter 4.4 Consumer credit COM(2002)443	Scope and extent of harmonisation	1–3, 30	Directive 87/102/EEC	+
	Creditor obligations prior to the agreement/ responsible lending	4–6, 9	Directive 87/102/EEC National rules	++
	Characteristics of consumer contracts/rate calculation	10–5	Directive 87/102/EEC	++
	Termination of agreements: Early repayment and recovery	16, 24–7	Directive 87/102/EEC National rules	++
	Consumer rights vis-à-vis third parties/joint and several liability	17, 19	Directive 87/102/EEC National rules	++
	Enforcement rules	7–8, 28, 31–3	Directive 87/102/EEC National rules	+
Chapter 4.5 Unfair commercial practices COM(2003)356	Scope and total harmonisation	3–4	Various EU directives	–
	Definition and prohibition of unfair practices	5, annex I	National rules	0

Table E1 *(continued)*

Case/ Commission proposal	Key provisions	Articles in legal text	Regulatory status quo	Relative interventionism
	Misleading and aggressive practices	6–9	Directive 97/55/EC National rules	0
	Enforcement rules	10–13, 17	Various EU directives	0
Chapter 4.6 Consumer rights COM(2008)614	Scope and total harmonisation	1–4	Various EU directives	–
	Pre-contractual information obligations for traders	5–7	National rules	+
	Trader obligations for off-premise and distance contracts	8–11	Various EU directives National rules	+
	Trader obligations after the sales contract	22–7	Various EU directives National rules	0
	Commercial guarantees	28–9	National rules	–
	Contract terms	30–9, 45	Directive 93/13/EC	+
Chapter 4.7 Rights of passengers in bus/waterway transport COM(2008)816 COM(2008)817	Contractual rights /information obligations for carrriers	4–5, 24–6 4–5, 23–5	National rules	+
	Carrier liability (bus/coach only)	6–9	National rules	+
	Passenger rights in the case of cancellation or delay	20–3, 17–22	–	+
	Rights of persons with reduced mobility	10–9, 6–16	National rules	++
	National enforcement	2, 27–30, 2, 26–9	National rules	+

Table E2: Assessing consumer interventionism in product safety initiatives

Case/ Commission proposal	Key provisions	Articles in legal text	Regulatory status quo	Relative interventionism
Chapter 5.1 General product safety COM(2000)139	Scope of the GPSD	1–2, 17	Directive 92/59/EEC	++
	Producer rights and obligations	3–5, annex II	Directive 92/59/EEC 'New approach'	+
	National implementation duties	6–12, 18	Directive 92/59/EEC	+
	Community level responses to unsafe products	13, 8	Directive 92/59/EEC	+
Chapter 5.2 Marketing pyrotechnic articles COM(2005)457	Scope and categorisation	1,3	National rules Private standards	0
	Manufacturer obligations	4, 9, 12, annex I	National rules	–
	Age limits	7	National rules	+
	National implementing obligations	5–6, 13–14, 20	National rules	–
Chapter 5.3 Common framework for the marketing of products COM(2007)53	Scope	1–2	Decision 93/465	0
	General principles	2–5, annex	'New approach' Global approach	–
	General obligations of economic operators	7–12	GPSD New approach dir.	0
	Conformity assessment bodies	22–6, 31–2	Decision 93/465	0

Table E2 *(continued)*

Case/ Commission proposal	Key provisions	Articles in legal text	Regulatory status quo	Relative interventionism
	Rights and obligations of member states	14, 18–21, 27, 29	'New approach' directives	0
	Safeguard clauses	35–8	Decision 93/465 New approach dir.	0
Chapter 5.4 Safety of toys COM(2008)9	Scope	1,51	Directive 88/378/EEC	+
	General obligations of economic operators	3–8, 14	'New approach' decision	0
	Essential safety requirements	9, annex II	Directive 88/378/EEC	+
	Labelling requirements	10, annex V	Directive 88/378/EEC	0
	Conformity assessment	25–8, 33–4	Directive 88/378/EEC	–
	National market surveillance	38–40, 47–50	'New approach' decision	0
	Safeguard procedures	41–4	'New approach' decision	0

Table E3: Assessing consumer interventionism in food safety initiatives

Case/ Commission proposal	Key provisions	Articles in legal text	Regulatory status quo	Relative interventionism
Chapter 6.1 Food supplements COM(2000)222	Scope and definitions	1–2	National rules	–
	Full harmonisation	11	National rules	–
	Allowed vitamins and minerals	4, 5, 9, 13 annex I and II	National rules	+
	Labelling requirements	6–10	National rules	0
Chapter 6.2 Nutrition and health claims made on foods COM(2003)424	General principles on the use of claims	3, 5, 6–7	National rules	++
	General restrictions on the use of claims	4	National rules	+
	Health claims	10–11, 14–9	National rules	++
Chapter 6.3 Addition of vitamins and minerals and certain other substances COM(2003)671	Purposes and foods for which fortification is allowed	3, 5	National rules	–
	Allowed substances	3–4, 6–7, 10–12 annexes I and II	National rules	0
	Labelling requirements	8, 17	National rules	0
	Remaining national powers	9, 13–15	National rules	–
Chapter 6.4 Food additives COM(2006)428	Approved substances and purposes	2–8, 10, annexes I–III	Directive 89/107/EEC	0
	General rules on additive usage	12–8, annex IV	Directive 89/107/EEC	0
	Labelling requirements	19–25	Directive 89/107/EEC	0

Table E3 *(continued)*

Case/ Commission proposal	Key provisions	Articles in legal text	Regulatory status quo	Relative interventionism
	Supranational management of food additives	9, 26–31	Directive 89/107/EEC	−
Chapter 6.5 Provision of food information to consumers COM(2008)40	General principles of food information	1–5	Directive 2000/13/ EC Directive 90/496/EEC	+
	Responsibilities of economic operators	7–8	Directive 2000/13/EC	+
	Mandatory food information	9–12, 18–41, annexes I–III	Directive 2000/13/EC	++
	Nutrition declarations	9, 31–4, 44–7, annex XI	Directive 90/496/EEC	+
	Implementation powers	42–3, 49	Directive 2000/13/ EC Directive 90/496/EEC	0

Bibliography

Aberbach, J. D. and Rockman, B. A. (2002) 'Conducting and coding elite interviews', *Political Science & Politics* 35(4): 673–6.

Adam, S. and Maier, M. (2011) 'National parties as politicizers of EU integration? Party campaign communication in the run-up to the 2009 European Parliament election', *European Union Politics* 12(3): 431–53.

Adam, S. and Pfetsch, B. (2009) 'Europa als Konflikt in nationalen Medien – Zur Politisierung der Positionen in der Integrationsdebatte', in *Politik in der Mediendemokratie, Politische Vierteljahresschrift, Sonderheft* 42: 559–84.

AE (2000) 'BEUC welcomes proposal of amending "General Product Safety Directive"', Agence Europe – *Europe Daily Bulletin*, 11 April.

—   (2003a) 'Commission prepares new legislation on nutritional content of food', Agence Europe – *Europe Daily Bulletin*, 4 February.

—   (2003b) 'Commission proposes general ban on unfair trade practices in Union so consumers can take full advantage of the Internal Market', Agence Europe – *Europe Daily Bulletin*, 19 June.

—   (2003c) 'Publishers and brewers react against proposed regulation on use of claims on nutritional properties and health benefits of foodstuffs', Agence Europe – *Europe Daily Bulletin*, 17 July.

—   (2004a) 'Proposal of Regulation on nutritional and health claims of foodstuffs is warmly welcomed in public hearing, mainly by consumers – controversy over nutritional make-up of food', Agence Europe – *Europe Daily Bulletin*, 14 January.

—   (2004b) 'UNICE and Eurocommerce call for "Internal Market" clause to be kept in the Directive on illegal commercial practices', Agence Europe – *Europe Daily Bulletin*, 15 May.

—   (2007a) 'Commission launches reform of rules applicable to free movement of (non) harmonised goods', Agence Europe – *Europe Daily Bulletin*, 14 February.

—   (2007b) 'Legislative package on free movement of goods aims to make life easier for companies in EU', Agence Europe – *Europe Daily Bulletin*, 12 February.

—   (2007c) 'MEPs want higher safety levels for authroisation and use of additives, enzymes and flavourings', Agence Europe – *Europe Daily Bulletin*, 12 July.

—   (2008a) 'BEUC says proposal on food labelling doesn't go far enough but EUROCOMMERCE says it creates red tape', Agence Europe – *Europe Daily Bulletin*, 6 February.

—   (2008b) 'Commission proposes modernised foodstuff labelling rules to ensure informed choice for consumers wanting healthy food', Agence Europe – *Europe Daily Bulletin*, 31 January.

—   (2008c) 'Commission proposes new EU-wide rights for shoppers to create genuine internal retail market', Agence Europe – *Europe Daily Bulletin*, 8 October.

Aissaoui, M. (2002) 'Le crédit facile nourrit le surendettement', *Le Figaro*, 13 May.

Aissaoui, M. and Ducros, C. (2001) 'Air France condamnée pour surbooking', *Le Figaro*, 21 May.

Akerlof, G. (1970) 'The market for "lemons": quality uncertainty and the market mechanism', *Quarterly Journal of Economics* 84(3): 488–500.

Aldrich, J., Sullivan, J. and Borgida, E. (1989) 'Foreign affairs and issue voting: do presidential candidates "waltz before a blind audience?"', *American Political Science Review* 83(1): 123–41.

Alemanno, A. (2006) 'Food safety and the Single European Market', in Ansell, C. and Vogel, D. (eds) *What's the Beef?: The contested governance of European food safety*, Boston, MA: MIT Press.

ANEC (2006) 'ANEC Position Paper on the revision of the New Approach', *Position Paper* (26 July), Brussels: European Association for the Coordination of Consumer Representation in Standardisation.

Ansell, C. and Vogel, D. (eds) (2006) *What's the Beef?: The contested governance of European food safety*, Boston, MA: MIT Press.

Appel, H., Kafsack, H. and Stabenow, M. (2008) 'Im Gespräch: Meglena Kuneva–"Ich will automatisch gesetzte Kreuze im Internet verbieten"' *Frankfurter Allgemeine Zeitung*, 23 September: p. 14.

Arnold, C. and Toshkov, D. (2010) 'Is the European Commission responsive to public opinion?', paper presented at the *5th ECPR Pan-European Conference on EU Politics,* 24–6 June, Porto, Portugal.

Azumendi, E. (2001) 'Las quejas de los usarios llevan a consumo a inspeccionar las academias privadas de ensenanza – El gobierno condiera que muchos centros imponen condiciones abusivas a sus clientes', *El País*, 16 September: p. 3.

Bailer, S. (2006) 'The European Commission and its legislative activity – not as integrationist and autonomous as believed', *CIS Working Paper* 2006(24).

Bär-Bouyssière, B. (1999) 'Neuer Rahmen für Telekommunikation: Brüssel setzt auf einheitliche Regeln', *Frankfurter Allgemeine Zeitung*, 3 December: p. 23.

Bartolini, S. (2006a) 'Mass Politics in Brussels: how benign could it be?', *Zeitschrift für Staats- und Europawissenschaften* 4(1): 28–56.

—   (2006b) 'Should the Union be "politicised"? Prospects and risks', *Notre Europe, Policy Paper* 19.

Bauer, M. (2012) 'Tolerant, if personal goals remain unharmed: explaining supranational bureaucrats' attitudes to organizational change', *Governance* 25(3): 485–510.

Bembaron, E. (2001a) 'Consommation: Pour éviter les pièges et choisir le meilleur prêt – Le crédit décrypté', *Le Figaro*, 5 February.

—   (2001b) 'Paiements; Visa sécurise le Net', *Le Figaro*, 15 March.

Berkhout, J. and Lowery, D. (2010) 'The changing demography of the EU interest system since 1990', *European Union Politics* 11(3): 447–61.

Berry, J. M. (2002) 'Validity and reliability issues in elite interviewing', *Political Science & Politics* 35(4): 679–82.

Bes, B. J. (2014) 'Europe's executive in stormy weather: how does politicization affect Commission officials' attitudes?', Paper presented at the *UACES 44th Annual Conference*, 1–3 September, Cork.

Betts, P. (1999) 'Italian phone users have never had it so good', *Financial Times*, 8 October: p. 27.

BEUC (2000a) 'BEUC's paper on food supplements', *Position Paper* (16 May), Brussels: Bureau Européen des Unions de Consommateurs.

— (2000b) 'BEUC comments on the DG Information Society working documents on the framework of the 1999 telecoms review', *Position Paper* (19 May), Brussels: Bureau Européen des Unions de Consommateurs.

— (2000c) 'BEUC comments on the proposal for a Directive of the European Parliament and of the Council on universal service and users' rights relating to electronic communication networks and services', *Position Paper* (20 October), Brussels: Bureau Européen des Unions de Consommateurs.

— (2000d) 'BEUC's position on the Revision of the General Product Safety Directive Com(2000)139 – final/2', *Position Paper* (14 November), Brussels: Bureau Européen des Unions de Consommateurs.

— (2000e) 'Final BEUC Position on the use of health related claims for foodstuffs', *Position Paper* (9 August), Brussels: Bureau Européen des Unions de Consommateurs.

— (2002a) 'BEUC comments on the proposed Regulation on denied boarding and of cancellation or long delay of flights', *Position Paper* (14 May), Brussels: Bureau Européen des Unions de Consommateurs.

— (2002b) 'Credit for consumers: BEUC position', *Position Paper* (19 November), Brussels: Bureau Européen des Unions de Consommateurs.

— (2002c) 'Position on the proposed regulation on sales promotions', *Position Paper* (14 February), Brussels: Bureau Européen des Unions de Consommateurs.

— (2003a) 'BEUC Position Paper: Comments on the proposal for a Regulation of the European Parliament and the Council on nutrition and health claims – COM(2003424(01)', *Position Paper* (30 October), Brussels: Bureau Européen des Unions de Consommateurs.

— (2003b) 'General thoughts on fortification of food: BEUC's consideration for the stakeholder meeting on 24 February', *Position Paper* (5 March), Brussels: Bureau Européen des Unions de Consommateurs.

— (2004a) 'Addition of vitamins and minerals and of certain other substances to foods: BEUC comments', *Position Paper* (1 March), Brussels: Bureau Européen des Unions de Consommateurs.

— (2004b) 'Unfair commercial practices – BEUC comments', *Position Paper* (15 January), Brussels: Bureau Européen des Unions de Consommateurs.

— (2006) 'BEUC position paper on the Commission proposals for a Regulation on food additives, food enzymes and food flavourings', *Position Paper* (6 November), Brussels: Bureau Européen des Unions de Consommateurs.

— (2008) 'Food information to consumers – Summary of the BEUC position on the Commission proposal', *Position Paper* (22 May), Brussels: Bureau Européen des Unions de Consommateurs.

— (2009) 'The future of European Consumers' rights: BEUC's reaction to the fundamental issues raised by the Proposal for a Directive of the European Parlimament and of the Council on consumers rights', *Position Paper* (14 March), Brussels: Bureau Européen des Unions de Consommateurs.

BEUC and ANEC (2008) 'Revision of the Toy Safety Directive: how can we make toys safer?', *Position Paper* (25 March), Brussels: Bureau Européen des Unions de Consommateurs and European Association for the Co-ordination of Consumer Representation in Standardisation.

Beyers, J. (2004) 'Voice and access: political practices of European interest associations', *European Union Politics* 5(2): 211–40.

— (2008) 'Policy issues, organisational format and the political strategies of interest organisations', *West European Politics* 31(6): 1188–211.

Biesenbender, J. (2011) 'The dynamics of treaty change: measuring the distribution of power in the European Union', *European Integration online Papers (EIoP)* 15(5): 1–24.

Boomgaarden, H., Vliegenthart, R., De Vreese, C. and Schuck, A. (2010) 'News on the move: exogenous events and news coverage of the European Union', *Journal of European Public Policy* 17(4): 506–26.

Börzel, T. (2005) 'Europäische Integrationstheorie – nicht obsolet, aber reformbedürftig', *Zeitschrift für Internationale Beziehungen* 12(2): 345–51.

Bounds, A. (2007) 'Call for online shopper rights', *Financial Times*, 9 February: p. 4.

Bounds, A., Tait, N. and Wiggins, J. (2008) 'EU proposes food label rules', *Financial Times*, 31 January: p. 4.

Bray, R. (1999) 'Cancelling can be so costly', *Financial Times*, 16 January: p. 3.

Bream, R. (2004) 'Food for thought over nutrition claims', *Financial Times*, 9 February.

Broscheid, A. and Coen, D. (2003) 'Insider and outsider lobbying of the European Commission: an informational model of forum politics', *European Union Politics* 4(2): 165–89.

Buchanan, J. M. and Vanberg, V. J. (1988) 'The politicization of market failure', *Public Choice* 57(2): 101–13.

Buck, T. (2003a) 'Brussels gets teeth into food groups' "misleading" claims: consumer protection crackdown on labelling', *Financial Times*, 1 February: p. 7.

— (2003b) 'Plan to ban "misleading" food labels: companies would have to drop "meaningless" claims of health benefits', *Financial Times*, 31 January: p. 1.

Buckley, N. (1999) 'Toymakers' softener falls foul of Brussels' hardline on safety: EU "precautionary principle" has prompted a ban on some phthalates used in PVC toys and dummies', *Financial Times*, 16 December: p. 6.

Bünder, H. (2004) 'Kaufen bis zum Umfallen: Die EU-Kommission wünscht schönen Urlaub', *Frankfurter Allgemeine Zeitung*, 27 July: p. 14.

Burstein, P. (2003) 'The impact of public opinion on public policy: a review and an agenda', *Political Research Quarterly* 56(1): 29–40.

Callan, E. and Dyer, G. (2007) 'China tries to defend goods after renewed safety alert', *Financial Times*, 3 August: p. 8.

Carbajosa, A. (2005) 'Cada ano hay 400.000 ninos mas con sobrepeso en la Union Europea', *El País*, 9 December: p. 23.

— (2007) 'Revolución de compradores', *El País*, 4 March: p. 53.

Centre de Droit de la Consommation (2000) *The Practical Application of Council Directive 92/59/EEC on General Product Safety*, http://ec.europa.eu/dgs/health_consumer/library/surveys/sur13_en.html (accessed 3 February 2010).

Centre for European Policy Studies (2006) 'Impact of selected topics of the proposed directive on pyrotechnic articles: briefing note', *IPOL/A/IMCO/2006–11*, Brussels: August.

Chayet, D. (2008) 'En Grande-Bretagne, un vendredi noir pour des milliers de voyageurs', *Le Figaro*, 13 September: p. 8.

Christiansen, T. (1997) 'Tensions of European governance: politicized bureaucracy and multiple accountability in the European Commission', *Journal of European Public Policy* 4(1): 73–90.

— (2001) 'Intra-institutional politics and inter-institutional relations in the EU: towards coherent governance?', *Journal of European Public Policy* 8(5): 747–69.

CIAA (2003) 'Positions – Nutrition and Health claims: proposal for a Regulation of EP and of the Council on Nutrition and Health claims made on foods', *Position Paper* (7 November), Brussels: Confédération des Industries Agro-Alimentaires de l'UE.

— (2006) 'CIAA recommendation for a common nutrition labelling scheme', *Position Paper* (30 June). Brussels: Confédération des Industries Agro-Alimentaires de l'UE.

— (2008) 'CIAA statement on the European Commission proposal on the provisions of food information to consumers', *Position Paper* (30 January), Brussels: Confédération des Industries Agro-Alimentaires de l'UE.

— (2011) *Data & Trends of the European Food and Drink Industry 2010*, Brussels: Confédération des Industries Agro-Alimentaires de l'UE.

Clergeau, C. (2005) 'European food safety policies: between a single market and a political crisis', in Steffen, M. (ed.) *Health Governance in Europe: Issues, challenges, and theories*, London: Routledge.

Cohen, A. (1999) 'Clipping the airlines' wings', *Financial Times*, 4 October: p. 16.

Collet, V. (2006) 'Le commerce en ligne a conquis les Français', *Le Figaro*, 23 January.

Commission of the European Communities (1985) 'Completing the internal market: White Paper from the Commission to the European Council (Milan, 28–9 June 1985)', *COM(85)310*, Brussels: 14 June.

— (1995) 'Manual of operational procedures: seventh updating', Brussels.

— (1996) 'Commission staff working paper. The 1996 Single Market Review: background information for the Report to the Council and European Parliament', *SEC(96)2378*, Brussels: 16 December.

— (1997) 'Financial services: enhancing consumer confidence', *COM(97)309*, Brussels: 26 June.

— (1998) 'Services: Commission decides to send Germany reasoned opinion on restrictions on direct marketing of CDs', *IP/98/653*, Luxembourg: 16 July.

— (1999) 'Services: Commission decides to refer Germany to the European Court of Justice over restrictions on direct marketing of CDs', *IP/99/440*, Luxembourg: 2 July.

— (2000a) 'Commission proposes better protection for air passengers', *IP/00/639*, Brussels: 21 June.

— (2000b) 'Commission proposes overhaul of rules for electronic communication', *IP/00/749*, Brussels: 12 July.

— (2000c) 'Commission Staff Working Document: air passenger rights in the European Union', *SEC(2000)535*, Brussels: 24 March.

— (2000d) 'Communication from the Commission: the results of the public consultation on the 1999 Communications Review and Orientations for the new Regulatory Framework', *COM(2000)239*, Brussels: 26 April.

— (2000e) 'Communication from the Commission to the European Parliament and the Council: protection of air passengers in the European Union', *COM(2000)365*, Brussels: 22 July.

— (2000f) 'Preliminary draft proposal for a Directive of the European Parliament and of the Council on the approximation of the laws of the Member States relating to the addition of nutrients to foods', *SANCO/1478/00*, Brussels: 6 June.

— (2000g) 'Proposal for a Directive of the European Parliament and of the Council on the approximation of the laws of the Member States relating to food supplements', *COM(2000)222*, Brussels: 8 May.

— (2000h) 'Proposal for a Directive of the European Parliament and of the Council on universal service and users' rights relating to electronic communications networks and services', *COM(2000)392*, Brussels: 12 July.

— (2000i) 'Proposal for a Directive of the European Parliament and the European Council on general product safety', *COM(2000)139*, Brussels: 29 March.

— (2000j) 'White Paper on food safety', *COM(1999)719*, Brussels: 20 January.

— (2001a) 'Proposal for a European Parliament and Council regulation concerning sales promotions in the Internal Market', *COM(2001)546*, Brussels: 2 October.

— (2001b) 'Proposal for a Regulation of the European Parliament and of the Council establishing common rules on compensation and assistance to air passengers in the event of denied boarding and of cancellation or long delay of flights', *COM(2001)784*, Brussels: 21 December.

— (2002a) 'Follow-up Communication to the Green Paper on EU consumer protection', *COM(2002)289*, Brussels: 11 June.

— (2002b) 'Proposal for a Directive of the European Parliament and of the Council on the harmonisation of the laws, regulations and administrative provisions of the Member States concerning credit for consumers', *COM(2002)443*, Brussels: 11 September.

— (2003a) 'Commission staff working paper: Extended impact assessment on the Directive of the European Parliament and of the Council concerning unfair business-to-consumer commercial practices in the Internal Market and amending directives 84/450/EEC, 97/7/EC and 98/27/EC', *SEC(2003)724*, Brussels: 18 June.

— (2003b) 'Proposal for a Directive of the European Parliament and of the Council concerning unfair business-to-consumer commercial practices in the Internal Market and amending directives 84/450/EEC, 97/7/EC and 98/27/EC', *COM(2003)356*, Brussels: 18 June.

— (2003c) 'Proposal for a Regulation of the European Parliament and of the Council on nutrition and health claims made on foods', *COM(2003)424*, Brussels: 16 July.

— (2003d) 'Proposal for a Regulation of the European Parliament and of the Council on the addition of vitamins and minerals and of certain other substances to foods', *COM(2003)671*, Brussels: 10 November.

— (2004) 'Communication from the Commission to the European Parliament and the Council on the operation and prospects of the Community framework for passenger transport by coach and bus: access to international transport and cabotage markets, safety and rights of passengers', *COM(2004)527*, Brussels: 29 July.

— (2005a) 'Better regulation: improved safety for fireworks and air bags', *IP/05/1278*, Brussels: 14 October.

— (2005b) 'Communication from the Commission to the Council and the European Parliament: better regulation for growth and jobs in the European Union', *COM(2005)97*, Brussels: 16 March.

— (2005c) 'Communication from the Commission to the European Parliament and the Council: strengthening passenger rights within the European Union', *COM(2005)46*, Brussels: 16 February.

— (2005d) 'Proposal for a Directive of the European Parliament and of the Council on the placing on the market of pyrotechnic articles', *COM(2005)457*, Brussels: 11 October.

— (2006a) 'Communication from the Commission to the Council, the European Parliament, the European Social and Economic Committee and the Committe of the Regions: a strategic review of better regulation in the European Union', *COM(2006)689*, Brussels: 14 November.

— (2006b) 'Proposal for a Regulation of the European Parliament and of the Council on food additives', *COM(2006)428*, Brussels: 28 July.

— (2007a) 'Commission Staff Working Document: executive summary of the Impact Assessment – accompanying document to the proposal for a Decison of the European Parliament and of the Council on a common framework for the marketing of products', *SEC(2007)174*, Brussels: 14 February.

— (2007b) 'Green Paper on the review of the consumer acquis', *COM(2006)744*, Brussels: 8 February.

— (2007c) 'Proposal for a Decision of the European Parliament and of the Council on a common framework for the marketing of products', *COM(2007)53*, Brussels: 14 February.

— (2007d) 'Proposal for a Regulation of the European Parliament and of the Council setting out the requirements for accreditation and market surveillance relating to the marketing of products', *COM(2007)37*, Brussels: 14 February.

— (2007e) 'Toy safety: EU Consumer Commissioner warns Member States and companies to "raise their game on enforcement of consumer safety law"', *IP/07/1318*, Brussels: 12 September.

— (2008a) 'Commission staff working document accompanying document to the proposal for a Regulation of the European Parliament and of the Council on the rights of passengers in bus and coach transport and amending Regulation (EC) No 2006/2004 on cooperation between national authorities responsible for the enforcement of consumer protection laws: Summary of the Impact Assessment', *SEC(2008)2954*: 4 December.

— (2008b) 'Commission staff working document accompanying the proposal for a Regulation of the European Parliament and of the Council concerning the rights of passengers when travelling by sea and inland waterway and amending Regulation (EC) No 2006/2004 on cooperation between national authorities responsible for the enforcement of consumer protection laws: Summary of the Impact Assessment', *SEC(2008)2951*: 4 December.

— (2008c) 'Executive Summary of the Impact Assessment – Commission staff working document accompanying the proposal for a Directive on consumer rights', Brussels: 30 July.

— (2008d) 'Proposal for a Directive of the European Parliament and of the Council on consumer rights', *COM(2008)614*, Brussels: 8 October.

— (2008e) 'Proposal for a Directive of the European Parliament and of the Council on the safety of toys', *COM(2008)9*, Brussels: 25 January.

— (2008f) 'Proposal for a Regulation of the European Parliament and of the Council concerning the rights of passengers when travelling by sea and inland waterway and amending Regulation (EC) No 2006/2004 on cooperation between national authorities responsible for the enforcement of consumer protection laws', *COM(2008)816*, Brussels: 4 December.

—   (2008g) 'Proposal for a Regulation of the European Parliament and of the Council on the provision of food information to consumers', *COM(2008)40*, Brussels: 30 January.

—   (2008h) 'Proposal for a Regulation of the European Parliament and of the Council on the rights of passengers in bus and coach transport and amending Regulation (EC) No 2006/2004 on cooperation between national authorities responsible for the enforcement of consumer protection laws', *COM(2008)817*, Brussels: 4 December.

—   (2008i) 'Questions and answers on food labelling', *MEMO/08/64*, Luxembourg: 30 January.

—   (2008j) 'Safety first: Commission proposes new strict rules for toys', *IP/08/91*, Luxembourg: 25 January.

Corbett, R. (2014) '"European elections are second-order elections": Is received wisdom changing?', *Journal of Common Market Studies* 52(6): 1194–8.

Council of the European Union (2000) 'Council resolution of 2 October 2000 on the rights of air passengers', *2000/C 293/01*, Luxembourg: 2 October.

Cram, L. (1997) *Policy-Making in the European Union: Conceptual Lenses and the Integration Process*, London: Routledge.

Croft, J. (2003) 'Move to crack down on credit lenders', *Financial Times*, 31 January: p. 2.

Cseres, K. (2005) *Competition Law and Consumer Protection*, The Hague: Kluwer Law International.

De Vreese, C. (2003) *Framing Europe: Television News and European Integration*, Amsterdam: Aksant.

De Vreese, C., Banducci, S., Semetko, H. and Boomgaarden, H. (2006) 'The news coverage of the 2004 European Parliamentary Election campaign in 25 countries', *European Union Politics* 7(4): 477–504.

De Wilde, P. (2011) 'No polity for old politics? A framework for analyzing the politicization of European integration', *Journal of European Integration* 33(5): 559–75.

—   (2014) 'The operating logics of national parliaments and mass media in the politicisation of Europe', *Journal of Legislative Studies* 20(1): 46–61.

De Wilde, P. and Zürn, M. (2012) 'Can the politicization of European integration be reversed?', *Journal of Common Market Studies* 50(S1): 137–53.

Dehousse, R. and Monceau, N. (2009) 'Are EU policies meeting Europeans' expectations?', in Dehousse, R., Deloche-Gaudez, F. and Jacquot, S. (ed.) *What is Europe up to?* Paris: Presses de Sciences Po.

Dehousse, R., Deloche-Gaudez, F. and Jacquot, S. (eds) (2009) *What is Europe up to?* Paris: Presses de Sciences Po.

Della Porta, D. and Caiani, M. (2007) 'Europeanization from below? Social movements and Europe', *Mobilization: An International Quarterly* 12(1): 1–20.

DG Enterprise (2001) 'Consultation document prepared by the Directorate General for Enterprise on the review of the New Approach', Brussels: 13 December.

DG Health and Consumer Protection (2007) 'Preparatory work for the Impact Assessment on the Review of the Consumer Acquis: analytical report on the Green Paper on the Review of the Consumer Acquis submitted by the Consumer Policy Evaluation Consortium', Brussels: 6 November.

DG III of the European Commission (1997) 'Addition of vitamins and minerals to foods and food supplements: a discussion paper', *DGIII/5934/97*, Brussels.

DG XXIV of the European Commission (1999) 'Review and revision of directive 92/59/EEC (General Product Safety): discussion paper', Brussels: 24 June.

Dickie, M. (2007) 'Beijing promises to address EU fears about dangerous products', *Financial Times*, 25 July: p. 6.

DiMaggio, P., Evans, J. and Bryson, B. (1996) 'Have American's social attitudes become more polarized?', *American Journal of Sociology* 102(3): 690–755.

Directorate-General for Health and Consumer Protection (2006) 'Labelling: competitiveness, consumer information and better regulation for the EU: A DG SANCO Consultative Document', Brussels: February 2006.

— (2001) 'Discussion paper on nutrition claims and functional claims', *SANCO/1341/2001*, Brussels: July 2001.

— (2002) 'Draft proposal for a Regulation of the European Parliament and of the Council on nutrition, functional and health claims made on foods – working document', *SANCO/1832/2002*, Brussels.

— (2005) 'Draft working paper – Regulation of the European Parliament and of the Council on food additives', *WGA/004/03 rev10*, Brussels: 2 February.

— (2006) 'Summary of results for the consultation document on: "Labelling: competitiveness, consumer information and better regulation for the EU"', Brussels: December.

Done, K. (2000) 'Surge in Europe air traffic brings delays', *Financial Times*, 8 February: p. 14.

Döring, H. (2007) 'The composition of the College of Commissioners: patterns of delegation', *European Union Politics* 8(2): 207–28.

Down, I. and Wilson, C. (2008) 'From permissive consensus to constraining dissensus: a polarizing union?', *Acta Politica* 43(1): 26–49.

Downs, A. (1966/1967) *Inside Bureaucracy*, Boston: Little, Brown.

— (1972) 'Up and down with ecology – the "issue attention cycle"', *Public Interest* 28(Summer): 38–50.

Dunleavy, P. (2000) 'Explaining centralization of the European Union: a public choice analysis', in Moser, P., Schneider, G. and Kirchgässner, G. (ed.) *Decision Rules in the European Union*, Houndmills: Macmillan Press.

Dür, A. (2008) 'Interest groups in the European Union: how powerful are they?', *West European Politics* 31(6): 1212–30.

Düro, M. (2009) *Crosswalking EUR-Lex: a proposal for a metadata mapping to improve access to EU documents*, Luxembourg: Office for Official Publications of the European Communities.

Eaglesham, J. (2005) 'Conservatives target "top 10" business red tape burdens', *Financial Times*, 5 July: p. 4.

Easton, D. (1975) 'A re-assessment of the concept of political support', *British Journal of Political Science* 5(4): 435–57.

Eberhardie, C. (2007) 'Nutritional supplements and the EU: is anyone happy?', *Proceedings of the Nutrition Society* 66(4): 508–11.

Ecker-Ehrhardt, M. (2012) 'Cosmopolitan politicization: how perceptions of interdependence foster citizens' expectations in international institutions', *European Journal of International Relations* 18(3): 481–508.

Ecker-Ehrhardt, M. and Weßels, B. (2010) 'Input- oder Output-Politisierung internationaler Organisationen? Der kritische Blick der Bürger auf Demokratie und Leistung', in Zürn, M. and Ecker-Ehrhardt, M. (eds.) *Gesellschaftliche Politisierung und internationale Institutionen*, Berlin: Suhrkamp.

Eckstein, H. (1975) 'Case study and theory in political science', in Greenstein, F. I. and Polsby, N. W. (eds.) *Handbook of Political Science*, Reading, MA: Addison-Wesley.

ECTAA (2009) 'European travel industry agrees on EU passenger rights rules', *Position Paper* (20 January), Brussels: European Travel Agents' and Tour Operators' Associations.

Eichenberg, R. C. and Dalton, R. J. (2007) 'Post-Maastricht blues: the transformation of citizen support for European integration, 1973–2004', *Acta Politica* 42(2–3): 128–52.

Eising, R. (2007) 'Institutional context, organizational resources and strategic choices – explaining interest group access in the European Union', *European Union Politics* 8(3): 329–62.

El País (1999a) 'La Union Europea prohibe la fabricacion de mordedores con PVC', *El País*, 2 December: p. 40.

— (1999b) 'Los consumidores advierten del riesgo de los "teletubbies" falsificados', *El País*, 24 September: p. 4.

— (2001) 'La UCE alerta al consumidor de la picaresca en epoca des rebajas', *El País*, 7 January: p. 3.

— (2002) 'Consumo Retira del mercado 1.750 juguetes por su peligrosidad para los ninos mas pequenos: La mayoria contienen peqeunas piezas que se pueden desprender y ocasionar asfixia', *El País*, 11 June: p. 3.

— (2008) 'Los usuarios de los autobuses viven la huelga resignados y enfadados', *El País*, 4 March: p. 3.

Enterprise and Industry Directorate-General (2005a) 'Designation of notified bodies (Part 1): common requirements for notified bodies', *Draft CERTIF 2005-3*, Brussels: 30 March.

— (2005b) 'Revision of Directive 88/378/EEC – 5th draft', *ENTR/TOYS/2005/50*, Brussels: 11 July.

— (2005c) 'The role and significance of the CE marking', *Draft Certif Doc 2005–11*, Brussels: 30 March.

— (2005d) 'Safeguard clauses and information procedure', *C1/RLA D(2005) SOGS N523 EN*, Brussels: 14 September.

— (2007) 'Revision of Directive 88/378/EEC – 7th draft', *ENTR/ TOYS/2007/43*, Brussels: 22 June.

— (2002) 'Discussion paper on the revision of the Safety of Toys Directive', *ENTR/TOYS/2002/017*, Brussels: 4 March.

Epstein, L. and Segal, J. (2000) 'Measuring issue salience', *American Journal of Political Science* 44(1): 66–83.

EPTO (2009) 'EPTO – The EU Commission proposal for a Regulation on the rights of passengers in international bus and coach transport: overview and comments', *Position Paper* (20 January), Brussels: European Passenger Transport Operators.

ESBG (2003) 'On the Commission's proposal for a Directive of the European Parliament and of the Council on the harmonisation of laws, regulations and administrative provisions of the Member States concerning credit for consumers: COM (2002) 443 Final', *Position Paper* (7 March), Brussels: European Savings Banks Group.

EURO COOP (1997) 'EURO COOP's comments on the Commission's discussion paper on the addition of vitamins and minerals to food and food supplements', *Position Paper* (30 October), Brussels: European Community of Consumer Cooperatives.

— (2003a) 'EURO COOP Comments to the Proposal for a Directive of the European Parliament and of the Council Concerning unfair business-to-consumer commercial practices in the Internal Market (COM (2003) 356 final)', *Position Paper* (31 October), Brussels: European Community of Consumer Cooperatives.

— (2003b) 'EURO COOP position paper on the revision of the consumer credit Directive– COM(2002)443', *Position Paper* (31 October), Brussels: European Community of Consumer Cooperatives.

— (2003c) 'Why and how can European consumers benefit from strict regulation claims?', *Position Paper* (27 October), Brussels: European Community of Consumer Cooperatives.

EuroCommerce (2003a) 'Position Paper: proposal for a Directive of the European Parliament and of the Council on the harmonisation of laws, regulations and administrative provisions of the Member States concerning credit for consumers', *Position Paper* (March 2003), Brussels: EuroCommerce a.i.b.s.

— (2003b) 'Position Paper: proposal for a Regulation of the European Parliament and of the Council on nutrition and health claims made on foods, COM(2003)424', *Position Paper* (September 2003), Brussels: EuroCommerce a.i.b.s.

— (2007) 'Initiative of the Commission in favour of the free movement of goods', *Position Paper* (14 July), Brussels: EuroCommerce a.i.b.s.

— (2008) 'Commission proposal for a Regulation on food information to consumers', *Position Paper* (July 2008), Brussels: EuroCommerce a.i.b.s.

Europe Information Service (1992) 'Pharmaceuticals: AESGP criticises EEC Commission's paper on food supplements', *European Report*, 18 March.

— (1997a) 'Food supplements: Commission opens debate on harmonisation', *European Report*, 20 June.

— (1997b) 'Food supplements: EU legislation expected soon', *European Report*, 18 April.

— (1999) 'Agri-foods: infringement procedures against France, Germany and Greece for barriers to trade', *European Report*, 14 July.

— (2000) 'Single market: Commission pursues action against seven Member States', *European Report*, 15 January.

European Commission (1996) 'Commercial communications in the Internal Market: Green Paper from the Commission', *COM(96)192*, Brussels: 8 April.

— (1998) 'Communication from the Commission to the Council, the European Parliament and the Social Committee: the follow-up to the Green Paper on commercial communications in the Internal Market', *COM(98)121*, Brussels: 4 March.

— (2000) 'Guide to the implementation of directives based on the New Approach and the Global Approach', Luxembourg: September 2000.

— (2001a) 'Analytical report: sales promotions in the Internal Market', *Internal working paper–DG MARKT*, Brussels.

— (2001b) 'Discussion paper for the ammendment of Directive 87/102/EEC concerning consumer credit', Brussels.

— (2001c) 'Green Paper on European consumer protection', *COM(2001)531*, Brussels: 2 October.

— (2003) 'Minutes of the 1621st meeting of the Commission', *PV(2003) 1621 final*, Brussels: 16 July.

— (2005a) 'Commission staff working paper: rights of passengers in international bus and coach transport. A consulation document by the Services of the Directorate General for Energy and Transport', Brussels: 14 July.

— (2005b) 'Communication from the Commission to the Council and the European Parliament: outcome of the screening of legislative proposals pending before the legislator', *COM(2005)462*, Brussels: 27 September.

— (2005c) 'Proposal for a Directive of the European Parliament and of the Council on the placing on the market of pyrotechnic articles: impact assessment', Brussels: 11 October.

— (2006a) 'Commission staff working paper: strengthening the protection of the rights of passengers travelling by sea or inland waterway in the European Union: Public consultation document of the Directorate-General for Energy and Transport', Brussels: 13 January.

— (2006b) 'Summary of contributions received by the Commission in response to the Commission staff working paper "Rights of passengers in international bus and coach transport"', Brussels: 30 January.

— (2006c) 'Summary of contributions received by the Commission in response to the Commission staff working paper "Strengthening the protection of the rights of passengers travelling by sea or inland waterway in the European Union"', Brussels: 30 January.

— (2007) 'Flying together: EU air transport policy'. Luxembourg.

European Council (2000) 'Presidency conclusions: Lisbon European Council, 23 and 24 March', *Nr. 100/1/00*, Lisbon: 24 March.

European Court of Justice (1991) 'Collectieve Antennevoorziening Gouda – Judgement of the Court', *C-288/89*, Luxembourg: 25 July.

— (1995) 'Alpine Investments – Judgement of the Court', *C-384/93*, Luxembourg: 10 May.

— (2001) 'Opinion of Advocate General Mischo', *Commission of the European Communities v French Republic, Case C-24/00, C-24/00,* Luxembourg: 26 June.

— (2002) 'Opinion of Advocate General Mischo', *Commission of the European Communities v. Kingdom of Denmark,* Case C-192/01, *C-192/01,* Luxembourg: 12 December.

— (2004) 'Opinion of Advocate General Poiares Maduro', *Commission of the European Communities v. Kingdom of the Netherlands,* Case C-41/02, *C-41/02,* Luxembourg: 14 September.

European Evaluation Consortium (2003) 'Evaluation of the food labelling legislation: final report', *Framework Contract No. BUDG-02–01 L2; Request for Services by DG SANCO*, Tickenham, UK: 18 October.

European Parliament (2001) 'Report on the Commission communication to the European Parliament and the Council on the protection of air passengers in the European Union', *A5–0249/2001*. Brussels: 29 June.

Falke, J. and Joerges, C. (2010) 'The "traditional" law approximation policy approaches to removing technical barriers to trade and efforts at a "horizontal" European product safety policy', *Hanse Law Review* 6(2): 237–85.

FAZ (1999a) 'EU-Kommission verbietet Weichmacher in Spielzeug', *Frankfurter Allgemeine Zeitung*, 2 December: p. 18.

— (1999b) 'Verbraucherpolitik erfordert Regeln', *Frankfurter Allgemeine Zeitung*, 29 May: p. 22.

— (2000a) 'Die amerikanischen Verbraucher im Konsumrausch auf Pump: Aktienmarkt vermittelt Wohlstandsgefühle/Hohe private Verschuldung/ Warnung vor Gefahr für die Konjunktur', *Frankfurter Allgemeine Zeitung*, 24 January: p. 18.

— (2000b) 'EU will mehr Rechte und Service für die Fluggäste', *Frankfurter Allgemeine Zeitung*, 23 June: p. 15.

— (2000c) 'Klage gegen französischen Telekom-Universaldienst', *Frankfurter Allgemeine Zeitung*, 28 April: p. 16.

—   (2000d) 'Konsumentenkredite sind wieder lebhaft gefragt', *Frankfurter Allgemeine Zeitung*, 30 June: p. 17.

—   (2000e) 'Neues EU-Verfahren gegen Deutschland: Gebühren für "letzte Meile" überhöht/Verstoß gegen Marktliberalisierung', *Frankfurter Allgemeine Zeitung*, 27 April: p. 21.

—   (2001a) 'Besserer Schutz von Flugpassagieren', *Frankfurter Allgemeine Zeitung*, 22 March: p. R12.

—   (2001b) 'Fluggäste müssen geduldig sein: Seit 1993 hat es in Europa nicht mehr so lange Wartezeiten gegeben', *Frankfurter Allgemeine Zeitung*, 17 May: p. 13.

—   (2001c) 'Hände weg vom Preisvergleich', *Frankfurter Allgemeine Zeitung*, 9 May: p. 29.

—   (2001d) 'Mehr Service für Fluggäste', *Frankfurter Allgemeine Zeitung*, 23 May: p. R2.

—   (2002a) 'EU dämmt Haustür-Kredite ein', *Frankfurter Allgemeine Zeitung*, 31 July: p. 11.

—   (2002b) 'Neue Richtlinie über Verbraucherkredit: Die Überschuldung soll eingedämmt werden', *Frankfurter Allgemeine Zeitung*, 8 January: p. 21.

—   (2002c) 'Wettbewerbsrecht gerät unter Druck aus Brüssel: Geplante EU-Verordnung könnte Sonderverkaufsverbot kippen/Mehr Informationspflichten für Händler', *Frankfurter Allgemeine Zeitung*, 12 January: p. 19.

—   (2003a) 'EU plant Verbot zahlreicher Werbeslogans', *Frankfurter Allgemeine Zeitung*, 11 July: p. 11.

—   (2003b) 'EU will aggressives Marketing verbieten: Verbraucher nicht unter Druck setzen/Richtlinienentwurf', *Frankfurter Allgemeine Zeitung*, 8 April: p. 14.

—   (2003c) 'EU will irreführende Werbung verbannen', *Frankfurter Allgemeine Zeitung*, 10 April: p. 16.

—   (2003d) 'Schutz vor Irreführung', *Frankfurter Allgemeine Zeitung*, 1 February: p. 12.

—   (2004a) 'Besserer Verbraucherschutz im europäischen Binnenmarkt: Gemeinsame Mindestvorschriften gegen unlautere Geschäftspraktiken/Vernetzung der Verbraucherorganisationen', *Frankfurter Allgemeine Zeitung*, 25 May: p. 23.

—   (2004b) 'Explosive und verblüffende Zutaten aus der Gesetzesküche', *Frankfurter Allgemeine Zeitung*, 28 December: p. 16.

—   (2004c) 'Kunden haben in Internetauktionen ein Rücktrittsrecht–Bundesgerichtshof: Verbraucher können professionellen Händlern Ware zurückgeben', *Frankfurter Allgemeine Zeitung*, 4 November: p. 13.

—   (2005a) 'Geld zurück bei Verspätungen: Gutachter schlagen gesetzliche Regelung für Bus und Bahn vor', *Frankfurter Allgemeine Zeitung*, 11 June: p. 10.

—   (2005b) 'Rechte beim Internet-Kauf', *Frankfurter Allgemeine Zeitung*, 7 December: p. 21.

—   (2006) 'Mehr gefährliche Produkte', *Frankfurter Allgemeine Zeitung*, 7 March: p. 19.

—   (2007a) 'Der Nährwert der Limo soll vorne auf die Packung: Konzerne versprechen mehr Informationen zu Lebensmitteln – Furcht vor der "Roten Ampel"', *Frankfurter Allgemeine Zeitung*, 30 May: p. 13.

—   (2007b) 'EU-Vertragsgesetz könnte bald verbindlich werden – Abgeordneter Lehne: Von 2014 an vorstellbar/Kritiker warnen vor jahrzehntelanger Rechtsunsicherheit', *Frankfurter Allgemeine Zeitung*, 23 May: p. 14.

—   (2007c) 'EU will Nährwertangaben zur Pflicht machen', *Frankfurter Allgemeine Zeitung*, 19 November: p. 13.

—   (2007d) 'Giftiges Spielzeug in Deutschland', *Frankfurter Allgemeine Zeitung*, 6 August: p. 14.

—   (2007e) 'Glos für sicheres Spielzeug', *Frankfurter Allgemeine Zeitung*, 3 September: p. 13.

—   (2007f) 'Mattel ruft zum dritten Mal Spielzeug zurück: Vorzeigemarke "Barbie" betroffen/Verbraucherverbände fordern Politik zum Handeln auf', *Frankfurter Allgemeine Zeitung*, 6 September: p. 13.

—   (2007g) 'Neues EU-Regelwerk für die Produktsicherheit: Die Skandale um gesundheitsgefährdende Konsumgüter führen zu einem Umdenken in Brüssel', *Frankfurter Allgemeine Zeitung*, 11 September: p. 21.

—   (2007h) 'Schärfere Auflagen für Spielzeug', *Frankfurter Allgemeine Zeitung*, 18 September: p. 21.

—   (2007i) 'Schon wieder Bleifarbe in Spielzeug aus China: Mattel ruft auch Millionen Magnetprodukte zurück/Hongkonger Zulieferer begeht Selbstmord', *Frankfurter Allgemeine Zeitung*, 15 August: p. 11.

—   (2007j) 'Widerruf möglich', *Frankfurter Allgemeine Zeitung*, 5 December: p. 27.

—   (2008) 'Wir brauchen automatische Brandmeldesysteme in Bussen', *Frankfurter Allgemeine Zeitung*, 6 November: p. 11.

Featherstone, K. (1994) 'Jean Monnet and the "democratic deficit" in the European Union', *JCMS: Journal of Common Market Studies* 32(2): 149–70.

Fellsted, A. (2005) 'Big rise in recalls of faulty consumer goods', *Financial Times*, 22 August: p. 2.

Ferrara, F. and Weishaupt, T. (2004) 'Get your act together: party performance in European parliament elections', *European Union Politics* 5(3): 283–306.

Financial Times (1999) 'Passenger rights', *Financial Times*, 11 June: p. 21.

Follesdal, A. and Hix, S. (2006) 'Why there is a democratic deficit in the EU: a response to Majone and Moravcsik', *Journal of Common Market Studies* 44(3): 533–62.

Foster, L. (2004) 'Tail of Batmobile is no joke: Mattel', *Financial Times*, 15 April: p. 27.

Franchino, F. (2007) *The Powers of the Union: Delegation in the EU*, Cambridge: Cambridge University Press.

Franklin, M. and Wlezien, C. (1997) 'The responsive public: issue salience, policy change, and preferences for European unification', *Journal of Theoretical Politics* 9(3): 347–63.

Friedrich, H. (2004) 'Zwischen EU-Gesetzgebung und Wirtschaft klafft eine Lücke: Von Nikoläusen, Zeitungen und Allianzen/Der künftige BDZV-Hauptgeschäftsführer Dietmar Wolff zieht Bilanz', *Frankfurter Allgemeine Zeitung*, 6 July: p. 17.

— (2007) 'Mehr Verbraucherschutz soll das Vertrauen erhöhen: Grünbuch der EU-Kommission/28 Vorschläge für bessere Kaufverträge', *Frankfurter Allgemeine Zeitung*, 13 February: p. 17.

Frohlich, N., Oppenheimer, J. A. and Young, O. R. (1971) *Political Leadership and Collective Goods*, Princeton, NJ: Princeton University Press.

Gadea, L. (2004) 'Aiju investiga la posible toxicidad de un juguete que emite malos olores', *El País*, 1 June: p. 6.

Gadhoum, F. (2005) 'Le père Noël remplit sa hotte en Asie', *Le Figaro*, 12 December.

Garry, J., Marsh, M. and Sinnott, R. (2005) '"Second-order" versus "issue-voting" effects in EU referendums: evidence from the Irish Nice Treaty referendums', *European Union Politics* 6(2): 201–21.

Geddes, B. (2003) 'How the cases you choose affect the answers you get: selection bias and related issues', in Geddes, B. (ed.) *Paradigms and Sandcastles. Theory Building and Research Design in Comparative Politics*, Ann Arbor, MI: Michigan University Press.

George, A. L. (1979) 'Case studies and theory development: the method of structured, focused comparison', in P. G. Lauren (ed.) *Diplomacy. New Approaches in History, Theory, and Policy*, London: Collier Macmillan.

George, A. L. and Bennett, A. (2005) *Case Studies and Theory Development in the Social Sciences*, Cambridge, MA: MIT Press.

Gerhards, J., Offerhaus, A. and Roose, J. (2009) 'Wer ist verantwortlich? Die Europäische Union, ihre Nationalstaaten und die massenmediale Attribution von Verantwortung für Erfolge und Misserfolge', *Politische Vierteljahresschrift Sonderhefte* Band 42 "Politik in der Mediendemokratie": 529–58.

Goldstein, K. (2002) 'Getting in the door: sampling and completing elite interviews', *PS: Political Science and Politics* 35(4): 669–72.

Gormley, W. T. (1986) 'Regulatory issue networks in a federal system', *Polity* 18(4): 595–620.

Grande, C. (2005) 'Product recalls rise sharply: EU directive', *Financial Times*, 21 March: p. 3.

Greene, W. H. (1993) *Econometric Analysis*, 2nd edn. New York: Macmillan.

Guerrera, F. (2002a) 'Brussels plan for common loan rules', *Financial Times*, 24 June: p. 6.

— (2002b) 'EU Bargains over sales promotions', *Financial Times*, 22 August: p. 6.

—   (2003) 'Business angry at "unfair practices" proposal', *Financial Times*, 5 April: p. 12.

Guigner, S. (2004) 'Institutionalizing public health in the European Commission: the thrills and spills of politicization', in A. Smith (ed.) *Politics and the European Commission: actors, interdependence, legitimacy*, London: Routledge.

Haas, E. B. (1958/1968) 'The high authority: independent federal executive?', in E. B. Haas (ed.) *The Uniting of Europe: Political, Social, and Economic Forces 1950–1957*, Stanford, CA: Stanford University Press.

Hagenmeyer, M. (2006) 'The food additives revival', *European Food and Feed Law Review* (5): 295–301.

—   (2008) 'The regulation overkill: food information', *European Food and Feed Law Review* 2008(3): 165–71.

Hall, P. A. (2008) 'Systematic process analysis: when and how to use it', *European Political Science* 7(3): 304–17.

Harcourt, A. J. (1998) 'EU media ownership regulation: conflict over the definition of alternatives', *Journal of Common Market Studies* 36(3): 369–89.

Hargreaves, D. (1999) 'Brussels plans to ease telecoms curbs', *Financial Times*, 9 November: p. 10.

—   (2001) 'Business group opposes Commission's plan', *Financial Times*, 1 April: p. 6.

Hartlapp, M., Metz, J. and Rauh, C. (2010) 'The agenda set by the EU Commission: the result of balanced or biased aggregation of positions?', *LEQS Paper No. 21*, April, London School of Economics.

—   (2013) 'Linking agenda setting to coordination structures: bureaucratic politics inside the European Commission', *Journal of European Integration* 35(4): 425–41.

—   (2014) *Which Policy for Europe? Power and conflict inside the European Commission*, Oxford: Oxford University Press.

Hauer, C. (2006) 'The regulation on nutrition and health claims', *European Food and Feed Law Review* 2006(6): 355–61.

Hix, S. (2006) 'Why the EU needs (left–right) politics: policy reform and accountability are impossible without it', *Notre Europe, Policy Paper* 19.

Hix, S. and Bartolini, S. (2006) 'Politics: the right or the wrong sort of medicine for the EU', *Notre Europe, Policy Paper* 19.

Hobolt, S. (2014) 'A vote for the President? The role of Spitzenkandidaten in the 2014 European Parliament elections', *Journal of European Public Policy* 21(10): 1528–40.

Hobolt, S. B. and Høyland, B. (2011) 'Selection and sanctioning in European Parliamentary elections', *British Journal of Political Science* 41(3): 477–98.

Hoeglinger, D. (2016) 'The politicization of Europe in domestic election campaigns', *West European Politics* 39(1): 44–63.

Holzhacker, R. (2007) 'Democratic legitimacy and the European Union', *Journal of European Integration* 29(3): 257–69.

Hood, C., Rothstein, H. and Baldwin, R. (2004) *The Government of Risk: Understanding risk regulation regimes*, Oxford: Oxford University Press.

Hooghe, L. (2003) 'Europe divided?: Elites vs public opinion on European integration', *European Union Politics* 4(3): 281–304.

Hooghe, L. and Marks, G. (1999) 'The making of a polity: the struggle over European integration', in Kitschelt, H., Lange, P., Marks, G. and Stephens, J. D. (eds.) *Continuity and Change in Contemporary Capitalism*, Cambridge: Cambridge University Press.

Hooghe, L. and Marks, G. (2006a) 'Europe's blues: theoretical soul-searching after the rejection of the European constitution', *PS: Political Science & Politics* 39(2): 247–50.

— (2006b) 'The neo-functionalists were (almost) right: politicization and European integration', in Crouch, C. and Streeck, W. (eds.) *The Diversity of Democracy: A tribute to Philippe C. Schmitter*, London: Edward Elgar.

— (2009) 'A postfunctionalist theory of European integration: from permissive consensus to constraining dissensus', *British Journal of Political Science* 39(1): 1–23.

Hurrelmann, A. (2007) 'European democracy, the permissive consensus and the collapse of the EU constitution', *European Law Journal* 13(3): 343–59.

Hurrelmann, A., Gora, A. and Wagner, A. (2015) 'The politicization of European integration: more than an elite affair?', *Political Studies* 63(1): 43–59.

Hutter, S. and Grande, E. (2014) 'Politicizing Europe in the national electoral arena: a comparative analysis of five West European countries, 1970–2010', *Journal of Common Market Studies* 52(5): 1002–18.

Imig, D. and Tarrow, S. (2001) *Contentious Europeans: Protest and Politics in an Integrating Europe*, Lanham, MD: Rowman & Littlefield.

Iskandar, S. (1998a) 'Brussels again ducks decision on toxic toys', *Financial Times*, 24 June: p. 6.

— (1998b) 'Brussels under fire over toy safety delay', *Financial Times*, 11 June: p. 5.

— (2000) 'France balks at UK-style phone auction', *Financial Times*, 12 May: p. 8.

Jabko, N. (2006) *Playing the Market: A political strategy for uniting Europe, 1985–2005* Ithaca, NY: Cornell University Press.

Janning, F. (2004) 'Der Staat der Konsumenten. Plädoyer für eine politische Theorie des Verbraucherschutzes', in Czada, R. and Zint, R. (eds.) *Politik und Markt*, Wiesbaden: VS Verlag.

Jenkins, P. (2003) 'Consumers' champion takes on a big burden', *Financial Times*, 6 May: p. 30.

Joerges, C. and Neyer, J. (1997) 'Transforming strategic interaction into deliberative problem-solving: European comitology in the foodstuffs sector', *Journal of European Public Policy* 4(4): 609–25.

Jolley, R. (2000) 'Plotting a route to more passengers' rights', *Financial Times*, 19 June: p. 22.

Jolly, M. (2007) *The European Union and the People*, Oxford: Oxford University Press.

Judge, D. and Earnshaw, D. (2002) 'The European Parliament and the Commission crisis: a new assertiveness?', *Governance* 15(3): 345–74.

Karsten, J. (2007) 'Passengers, consumers, and travellers: the rise of passenger rights in EC transport law and its repercussions for Community consumer law and policy', *Journal of Consumer Policy* 30(2): 117–36.

Kassim, H. (2006) 'The Secretariat General of the European Commission, 1958–2003: a singular institution', in Smith, A. (ed.) *Politics and the European Commission. Actors, Interdependence, Legitimacy*. London: Routledge.

Kassim, H., Peterson, J., Bauer, M., Connolly, S., Dehousse, R., Hooghe, L. and Thompson, A. (2013) *The European Commission of the Twenty-First Century*, Oxford: Oxford University Press.

Katan, M. and Roos, N. d. (2003) 'Nutrition: Pour une réglementation claire des "alicaments"', *Le Figaro*, 27 March.

Kemp, K. (1984) 'Accidents, scandals, and political support for regulatory agencies', *Journal of Politics* 46(2): 401–27.

Kiessling, T. and Blondel, Y. (1998) 'The EU regulatory framework in telecommunications: a critical analysis', *Telecommunications Policy* 22(7): 571–92.

Kingdon, J. W. (1984) *Agendas, Alternatives, and Public Policies*, Vol. 1, Boston, Toronto: Little, Brown.

Kiousis, S. (2004) 'Explicating media salience: a factor analysis of New York Times issue coverage during the 2000 US Presidential Election', *Journal of Communication* 54(1): 71–87.

Klüver, H. (2010) 'Lobbying coalitions and policy-making: how interest groups can shape policy formulation in the European Union', paper presented at the *5th ECPR Pan-European Conference on EU Politics*, 24–6 June, Porto, Portugal.

—   (2011) 'The contextual nature of lobbying: explaining lobbying success in the European Union', *European Union Politics* 12(4): 483–506.

Koepke, J. and Ringe, N. (2006) 'The second-order election model in an enlarged Europe', *European Union Politics* 7(3): 321–46.

Koopmans, R. (2007) 'Who inhabits the European public sphere? Winners and losers, supporters and opponents in Europeanised political debates', *European Journal of Political Research* 46(2): 183–210.

Koopmans, R. and Erbe, J. (2004) 'Towards a European public sphere?', *Innovation: The European Journal of Social Sciences* 17(2): 97–118.

Krapohl, S. (2007) 'Input or Output? How to Legitimise supranational risk regulation', paper presented at the *4th ECPR General Conference*, 6–8 September, Pisa, Italy.

Kriesi, H. (2007) 'The role of European integration in national election campaigns', *European Union Politics* 8(1): 83–108.

Kriesi, H., Grande, E., Dolezal, M., Helbling, M., Höglinger, D., Hutter, S. and Wüest, B. (2012) *Political Conflict in Western Europe*, Cambridge, MA: Cambridge University Press.

Kriesi, H., Grande, E., Lachat, R., Dolezal, M., Bornschier, S. and Frey, T. (2008) *West European Politics in the Age of Globalization*, Cambridge: Cambridge University Press.

Kuneva, M. (2007) 'Does the European Union's ability to act erode? Speech held at the Strategy Group on the Future of Europe', *SPEECH/07/102*. Berlin: 26 February.

— (2008a) 'Contract Rights Directive – Press Conference speaking points', *SPEECH/08/507*. Brussels: 8 October.

— (2008b) 'European culture boosting society, politics and economy: speech held at the conference "A Soul for Europe"', Berlin: 15 November.

Kurpas, S., Gron, C. and Kaczynski, P. (2008) 'The European Commission after enlargement: does more add up to less?', *Centre for European Policy Studies Brussels: Special Report*, February.

Kutschke, T. (2007) 'Online-Händler sind verunsichert: Gericht schafft keine Klarheit bei Verkauf über das Internet', *Frankfurter Allgemeine Zeitung*, 8 August: p. 12.

Kwong, R. and Mitchell, T. (2007) 'Toymakers pressed to sign pledge on product safety', *Financial Times*, 16 August: p. 5.

Le Figaro (2007a) 'Bruxelles veut durcir la directive sur les jouets', *Le Figaro*, 17 August.

— (2007b) 'Le "made in China" à nouveau sur la sellette', *Le Figaro*, 10 August.

— (2007c) 'Mattel est prêt à poursuivre les rappels de jouets', *Le Figaro*, 16 August.

Le Gales, Y. and Renault, M.-C. (1999) 'Télécommunications: bilan d'un an de concurrence', *Le Figaro*, 8 January.

Leech, B. L. (2002) 'Asking questions: techniques for semistructured interviews', *PS: Political Science and Politics* 35(4): 665–8.

Lerner, D. (2000) 'US in line for cheaper calls', *Financial Times*, 1 June: p. 4.

Lewis, J. and Strom, B. (2002) 'Balancing safety of dietary supplements with the free market', *Annals of Internal Medicine* 136(8): 616–18.

Lindberg, L. and Scheingold, S. (1970) *Europe's Would-be Polity: Patterns of change on the European Community*, Englewood Cliffs, NJ: Prentice-Hall.

Littig, B. (2008) 'Interviews mit Eliten – Interviews mit ExpertInnen: Gibt es Unterschiede?', *Forum: Qualitative Research (FQS)* 9(3).

Lobe, A. (2004) 'Un colorant allergisant dans des potions Harry Potter; Toxicologie: La tartrazine, interdite en Autriche et en Norvège, est vendue en France dans un jeu pour les enfants', *Le Figaro*, 27 March: p. 16.

Lodge, M. (2011) 'Risk, regulation and crisis: comparing national responses in food safety regulation', *Journal of Public Policy* 31(1): 25–50.

Lowi, T. J. (1964) 'Review: American business, public policy, case-studies, and political theory', *World Politics* 16(4): 677–715.

Lubbers, M. (2008) 'Regarding the Dutch "nee" to the European constitution: a test of the identity, utilitarian and political approaches to voting "no"', *European Union Politics* 9(1): 59–86.

Lubbers, M. and Scheepers, P. (2005) 'Political versus instrumental Euroscepticism: mapping scepticism in European countries and regions', *European Union Politics* 6(2): 223–42.

Mabbett, D. (2010) 'Pursuing social policy ends by regulatory means in the EU: what scope beyond the labour market?', paper presented at the Conference 'Never waste a good crisis: the social policy dimension of regulatory crisis management in the EU & the US', 19–20 November, WZB Berlin Social Science Center.

MacMaoláin, C. (2007) *EU Food Law: Protecting consumers and health in a common market*, Oxford, UK: Hart Publishing.

Magnette, P. (2001a) 'Appointing and censuring the European Commission: the adaptation of parliamentary institutions to the community context', *European Law Journal* 7(3): 292–310.

Magnette, P. (2001b) 'European governance and civic participation: can the European Union be politicised?', in *Symposium: Mountain or Molehill? A Critical Appraisal of the Commission White Paper on Governance (Jean Monnet Working Paper 06/01)*, New York: Jean Monnet Center for International and Regional Economic Law and Justice.

Mahoney, C. (2007) 'Lobbying success in the United States and the European Union', *Journal of Public Policy* 27(1): 35–56.

— (2008) *Brussels vs the Beltway: Advocacy in the United States and the European Union*, Washington, D.C.: Georgetown University Press.

Mair, P. (2005) 'Popular democracy and the European Union polity', *European Governance Papers* No. C-05-03.

Majone, G. (1996) *Regulating Europe*, London: Routledge.

— (2000) 'The credibility crisis of Community regulation', *JCMS: Journal of Common Market Studies* 38(2): 273–302.

— (2002) 'The European Commission: the limits of centralization and the perils of parliamentarization', *Governance* 15(3): 375–92.

— (2005) *Dilemmas of European Integration: The ambiguities and pitfalls of integration by stealth*, Oxford: Oxford University Press.

Marks, G., Hooghe, L., Steenbergen, M. R. and Bakker, R. (2007) 'Crossvalidating data on party positioning on European integration', *Electoral Studies* 26(1): 23–38.

Marsh, P. (1999) 'China pulls plug on counterfeit kettles', *Financial Times*, 14 December: p. 14.

Maslow, A. H. (1943) 'A theory of human motivation', *Psychological Review* 50: 370–96.

Mason, J. and Parker, G. (2005) 'Brussels warns on junk food: industry given year to stop targeting children', *Financial Times*, 20 January: p. 1.

Mattli, W. and Woods, N. (2009) 'In whose benefit? Explaining regulatory change in global politics', in W. Mattli and N. Woods (ed.) *The Politics of Global Regulation*, Princeton, NJ: Princeton University Press.

McCartney, N. (2003) 'Special report: getting the message across', *Financial Times*, 15 January: p. III.

McVea, H. (2005) 'Financial services regulation under the Financial Services Authority: a reassertion of the market failure thesis?', *Cambridge Law Journal* 64(2): 413–48.

Meier, K. J. (1989) 'Bureaucratic leadership in public organizations', in B. D. Jones (ed.) *Leadership and Politics: New perspectives in political science*, Lawrence, KS: University of Kansas Press.

Menéndez, M. (2008) 'Baleària cancela el ferry de Palma a Barcelona pese a que ha vendido miles de billetes', *El País*, 29 August: p. 27.

Menon, A. and Weatherill, S. (2002) 'Legitimacy, accountability, and delegation in the European Union', in A. Arnull and D. Wincott (ed.) *Accountability and Legitimacy in the European Union*, Oxford: Oxford University Press.

Meyer, C. (2009) 'Does European Union politics become mediatized? The case of the European Commission', *Journal of European Public Policy* 16(7): 1047–64.

Micklitz, H. W. and Weatherill, S. (1993) 'Consumer policy in the European Community: before and after Maastricht', *Journal of Consumer Policy* 16(3): 285–321.

Micklitz, H., Reich, N. and Weatherill, S. (2004) 'EU Treaty revision and consumer protection', *Journal of Consumer Policy* 27(4): 367–99.

Mitropoulos, S. (1997) *Verbraucherpolitik in der Marktwirtschaft. Konzeptionen und internationale Erfahrungen*, Berlin: Duncker & Humblot.

Molina, M. (2008) 'Las telecomunicaciones acaparan el 27% de las reclamaciones de los consumidores', *El País*, 24 January: p. 5.

Moravcsik, A. (1998) *The Choice for Europe: Social purpose and state power from Messina to Maastricht*, Ithaca, NY: Cornell University Press.

—— (1999) 'A new statecraft? Supranational entrepreneurs and international cooperation', *International Organization* 53(2): 267–306.

—— (2002) 'In defence of the "democratic deficit": reassessing legitimacy in the European Union', *Journal of Common Market Studies* 40(4): 603–24.

—— (2004) 'Is there a democratic deficit in world politics? A framework for analysis', *Government and Opposition* 39(2): 336–63.

—— (2006) 'What can we learn from the collapse of the European constitutional project?', *Politische Vierteljahresschrift* 47(2): 219–41.

Morrell, P. (1998) 'Air transport liberalization in Europe: the progress so far', *Journal of Air Transportation World Wide* 3(1): 42–61.

Netjes, C. E. and Binnema, H. A. (2007) 'The salience of the European integration issue: three data sources compared', *Electoral Studies* 26(1): 39–49.

Noiville, C. (2006) 'Compatibility or clash? EU food safety and the WTO', in C. Ansell and D. Vogel (ed.) *What's the Beef?: The contested governance of European food safety*, Boston, MA: MIT Press.

Norman, P. (2002) 'Push on financial services market', *Financial Times*, 25 February: p. 8.

Nugent, N. (ed.) (2000) *At the Heart of the Union: Studies of the European Commission*, Houndmills: Macmillan.

Odell, M. (2000) 'Brussels seeking to boost air travellers' rights', *Financial Times*, 16 June: p. 2.

Olson, M. (1965/1971) *The Logic of Collective Action: Public goods and the theory of groups*, 2nd edn. Harvard, MA: Harvard University Press.

Oppermann, K. (2010) 'The concept of issue salience in foreign policy analysis: delineating the scope conditions of theoretical approaches in the field', paper presented at the *SGIR 7th Pan-European Conference on IR*, 9–11 September 2010, Stockholm, Sweden.

Oppermann, K. and Viehrig, H. (2008) 'Issue salience and the domestic legitimacy demands of european integration: the cases of Britain and Germany', *European Integration Online Papers (EIOP)* 12(2).

Ortiz, D., Myers, D., Walls, E. and Diaz, M.-E. (2005) 'Where do we stand with newspaper data?', *Mobilization: An International Quarterly* 10(3): 397–419.

O'Rourke, R. (2008) 'Food Information or is it really Food Labelling? – the Commission's legislative proposal for a new regulation', *European Food and Feed Law Review* 2008(5): 300–8.

Oualalou, L. (2000) 'Le recours au crédit s'est considérablement accru depuis 1960; Les vertus de l'endettement', *Le Figaro*, 26 January.

Owen, D. (2000) 'State faces a telephonic tug of war: the rapidly expanding industry has been at the heart of battles between pro-market voices and those who remain reluctant to relinquish ultimate state control', *Financial Times*, 14 June: p. 6.

Pahre, R. (2005) 'Formal theory and case-study methods in EU Studies', *European Union Politics* 6(1): 113–45.

Pardellas, J. M. (2005) 'Tres muertos y 28 heridos al volcar un autobus con turistas suecos en Tenerife', *El País*, 31 October: p. 24.

Parker, G. (2005) 'Brussels moves to slay image of "bureaucratic monster"', *Financial Times*, 26 October: p. 8.

Parker, G. and Buck, T. (2005) 'Bonfire of red tape aims to signal new era in Brussels', *Financial Times*, 25 April: p. 8.

Paul, K. T. (2008) 'Thought for food (safety) in the EU: a discourse-analytical approach', *GARNET Working Paper* 2008(08).

Pelkmans, J. (1987) 'The new approach to technical harmonization and standardization', *JCMS: Journal of Common Market Studies* 25(3): 249–69.

Pérez Gil, L. (2007) 'Mattel retira del mercado español juguetes con pintura tóxica de China', *El País*, 3 August: p. 33.

Pérez Gil, L. and Pozzi, S. (2007) 'Mattel retira 18,2 millones de juguetes', *El País*, 15 August: p. 31.

Perez, J. (1999) 'Las grandes marcas piden a la administracion que intensifique la lucha contra las imitaciones', *El País*, 16 December: p. 8.

Perez, M. (2005) 'Étiquetage des aliments: les eurodéputés divisés', *Le Figaro*, 27 May: p. 14.

Peter, F. (2010) 'Political legitimacy', in Zalta, E. N. (ed.) *The Stanford Encyclopedia of Philosophy*. Stanford, CA, http://plato.stanford.edu/archives/sum2010/entries/legitimacy (accessed 27 January 2011).

Peters, B., Sifft, S., Wimmel, A., Brüggemann, M. and Kleinen-von Königslöw, K. (2005) 'National and transnational public spheres: the case of the EU', in Leibfried, S. and Zürn, M. (ed.) *Transformations of the State?*, Cambridge: Cambridge University Press.

Petitnicolas, C. (2007) 'Cinq millions d'enfants trop gros en Europe', *Le Figaro*, 21 April.

Pfetsch, B., Adam, S. and Eschner, B. (2008) 'The contribution of the press to Europeanization of public debates: a comparative study of issue salience and conflict lines of European integration', *Journalism* 9(4): 465–92.

Plümper, T., Troeger, V. and Neumayer, E. (2009) 'Case selection and causal inference in qualitative research', *Social Science Research Network Working Paper Series*.

Pollack, M. (1997a) 'Delegation, agency, and agenda setting in the European Community', *International Organization* 51(1): 99–134.

Pollack, M. A. (1997b) 'Representing diffuse interests in EC policy-making', *Journal of European Public Policy* 4(4): 572–90.

Posner, R. (1974) 'Theories of economic regulation', *Bell Journal of Economics and Management Science* 5(2): 335–58.

Pozzi, S. (2000) 'Bruselas propone que se devuelva el importe del billete al viajero cuando su vuelo se retrase el plan que impulsa Loyola De Palacio descarta de momento el cobro de indemnizaciones', *El País*, 17 June: p. 32.

—— (2007) 'Una nueva retirada masiva de juguetes fuerza a la UE a revisar sus controles', *El País*, 6 September: p. 35.

Prades, J. (1999) 'Espana bloquea la nueva legislacion anti-"Overbooking" por un conflicto diplomatico: Las companias aereas admiten pagar hasta 830.00 pesetas por la demora de los vuelos', *El País*, 17 October: p. 35.

Princen, S. (2009) *Agenda-Setting in the European Union*, Houndmills: Palgrave.

Prosser, T. (2006) 'Regulation and social solidarity', *Journal of Law and Society* 33(3): 364–87.

Quioc, G. (2001) 'Surendettement: Le nombre de ménages en situation précaire augmente de 10% par an; Les crédits renouvelables sur la sellette', *Le Figaro*, 13 December.

Rabinovich, L., Tiessen, J., Tsang, F. and Stolk, C. v. (2008) *Technical report: Assessing the impact of revisions to the EU nutrition labelling legislation – prepared for the European Commission*, Cambridge, UK: RAND Cooperation.

Radaelli, C. M. (1999a) 'The public policy of the European Union: whither politics of expertise?', *Journal of European Public Policy* 6: 757–74.

— (1999b) *Technocracy in the European Union: Political Dynamics of the European Union*, London: Longman.

Rauh, C. (2009) 'The repeatedly low turnout in EP elections: political elites fail in politicising citizens', *A Different View – IAPSS Monthly News Magazine* (31): 3–5.

— (2012) *Politicisation, issue salience, and consumer policies of the European Commission: Does public awareness and contestation of supranational matters increase the responsiveness of Europe's central agenda-setter?* PhD Thesis, Department of Political and Social Sciences, Freie Universität, Berlin.

— (2015) 'Communicating supranational governance? The salience of EU affairs in the German Bundestag, 1991–2013', *European Union Politics* 16(1): 116–38.

Rauh, C. and Bödeker, S. (2016) 'Internationale Organisationen in der deutschen Öffentlichkeit – ein Text Mining Ansatz', in M. Lemke and G. Wiedemann (ed.) *Text-Mining in den Sozialwissenschaften. Grundlagen und Anwendungen zwischen qualitativer und quantitativer Diskursanalyse*, Wiesbaden: Springer VS.

Rauh, C. and Schneider, G. (2013) 'There is no such thing as a free open sky: financial markets and the struggle over European competences in international air transport', *Journal of Common Market Studies* 51(6): 1124–40.

Rauh, C. and Zürn, M. (2014) 'Zur Politisierung der EU in der Krise', in M. Heidenreich (ed.) *Krise der europäischen Vergesellschaftung? Soziologische Perspektiven*. Wiesbaden: Springer VS.

Ray, L. (2007) 'Validity of measured party positions on European integration: assumptions, approaches, and a comparison of alternative measures', *Electoral Studies* 26(1): 11–22.

Reagan, M. (1987) *Regulation: The Politics of Policy*, Boston, MA: Little, Brown.

Reif, K. and Schmitt, H. (1980) 'Nine second-order national elections – a conceptual framework for the analysis of European election results', *European Journal of Political Research* 8(1): 3–44.

Rischkowsky, F. (2007) *Europäische Verbraucherpolitik: Theoretische Grundlagen und neue Probleme am Beispiel des Internet*, Marburg: Metropolis.

Risse, T. (ed.) (2014) *European Public Spheres: Politics is back*, Cambridge: Cambridge University Press.

Sanz, D. (2007) 'Comment profiter des soldes sur le Web?', *Le Figaro*, 10 January.

Scharpf, F. (1999a) *Governing in Europe: Effective and democratic?* Oxford: Oxford University Press.

— (1999b) *Regieren in Europa. Effektiv und demokratisch?* Frankfurt: Campus Fachbuch.

Scharpf, F. W. (2009) 'The double asymmetry of European integration. Or: Why the EU cannot be a social market economy', *MPIfG Working Paper 09/12*.

—— (2010) 'The asymmetry of European integration, or why the EU cannot be a "social market economy"', *Socio-Economic Review* 8(2): 211–50.

Schelkle, W. and Mabett, D. (2010) 'Consumer protection in the EU's financial regulatory agenda: window of opportunity or uphill struggle?', paper presented at the Conference 'Crisis as opportunity: states, markets and communities in turbulent times', 4–5 November, 2010, Hertie School of Governance, Berlin.

Scherer, B. (1999) 'Fliegen 2000: voll, eng, verspätet', *Frankfurter Allgemeine Zeitung*, 6 May: p. R1.

Schmedes, H.-J. (2007) *Wirtschafts- und Verbraucherschutzverbände im Mehrebenensystem: Lobbyingaktivitäten britischer, deutscher und europäischer Verbände*, Wiesbaden: VS Verlag.

Schmidt, M. (2004) *Wörterbuch zur Politik*. Stuttgart: Kroener Alfred Verlag.

Schmidt, S. K. (2000) 'Only an agenda setter?: The European Commission's power over the Council of Ministers', *European Union Politics* 1(1): 37–61.

Schmitt, H., Hobolt, S. and Popa, S. (2015) 'Does personalization increase turnout? Spitzenkandidaten in the 2014 European Parliament elections', *European Union Politics*: Advance access.

Schmitter, P. (1969) 'Three neo-functional hypotheses about international integration', *International Organization* 23(1): 161–6.

Schulze, R. and Schulte-Nölke, H. (2003). *Analysis of National Fairness Laws Aimed at Protecting Consumers in Relation to Commercial Practices*, http://ec.europa.eu/consumers/cons_int/safe_shop/fair_bus_pract/green_pap_comm/studies/unfair_practices_en.pdf (accessed 29 August 2011).

Schwenn, K. (2005) 'Gutscheine als Trost für verpaßte Gelegenheiten: Bahn und Verbraucherschützer streiten über das rechte Maß an Fahrgastrechten', *Frankfurter Allgemeine Zeitung*, 1 October: p. 22.

Seawright, J. and Gerring, J. (2008) 'Case selection techniques in case study research: a menu of qualitative and quantitative options', *Political Research Quarterly* 61(2): 294–308.

Secretariat-General (2001) 'Minutes of the 1538th meeting of the Commission held in Strasbourg (Winston Churchill Building) on Tuesday 2 October 2001 (afternoon)', *PV(2001)1538 final*.

Shapiro, S. (2008) 'Does the amount of participation matter? Public comments, agency responses and the time to finalize a regulation', *Policy Sciences* 41(1): 33–49.

Sifft, S., Brüggeman, M., Kleinen-von Königslow, K., Peters, B. and Wimmel, A. (2007) 'Segmented Europeanization: exploring the legitimacy of the European Union from a public discourse perspective', *JCMS: Journal of Common Market Studies* 45(1): 127–55.

Sigaud, M. (2002) 'La chasse aux labels', *Le Figaro*, 5 February.

—   (2003) 'Les e-consommateurs européens mieux protégés', *Le Figaro*, 27 March.

Simpson, S. (2000) 'Intra-institutional rivalry and policy entrepreneurship in the European Union: the politics of information and communications technology convergence', *New Media Society* 2(4): 445–66.

Skapinker, M. (1999) 'We regret to announce the flight is full', *Financial Times*, 8 May: p. 15.

Smith, A. (2003) 'Why European Commissioners matter', *Journal of Common Market Studies* 41(1): 137–55.

Smith, M. (2000a) 'Brussels plans upgrade for air passengers' rights', *Financial Times*, 21 June: p. 8.

—   (2000b) 'Brussels to take France to court over telecoms', *Financial Times*, 28 April: p. 8.

Soroka, S. (2003) 'Media, public opinion, and foreign policy', *International Journal of Press/Politics* 8(1): 27–48.

Spence, D. (2006) 'The Directorates General and the services: structures, functions and procedures', in Spence, D. and Edwards, G. (ed.) *European Commission*, London: John Harper.

Stabenow, M. (2006) 'Europa läßt es kräftig krachen–Die unendliche Geschichte einer "Richtlinie über die Inverkehrbringung pyrotechnischer Gegenstände"', *Frankfurter Allgemeine Zeitung*, 30 December: p. 16.

Statham, P. and Trenz, H.-J. (2012) *The Politicization of Europe: Contesting the constitution in the mass media*, Abingdon, Oxon: Routledge.

Steenbergen, M. R., Edwards, E. E. and de Vries, C. E. (2007) 'Who's cueing whom?: Mass-elite linkages and the future of European integration', *European Union Politics* 8(1): 13–35.

Stigler, G. (1971) 'The theory of Economic Regulation', *Bell Journal of Economics and Management Science* 2(1): 3–21.

Stimson, J. (1999) *Public Opinion In America: Moods, cycles, and swings*, 2nd edn., Boulder, Colorado: Westview Press.

Stoeckel, F. (2013) 'Ambivalent or indifferent? Reconsidering the structure of EU public opinion', *European Union Politics* 14(1): 23–45.

Strünck, C. (2006) *Die Macht des Risikos: Interessenvermittlung in der amerikanischen und europäischen Verbraucherpolitik*, Baden-Baden: Nomos.

Stuyck, J. (2000) 'European consumer law after the Treaty of Amsterdam: consumer policy in or beyond the internal market', *Common Market Law Review* 37(2): 367–400.

Suvarierol, S. (2009) 'Networking in Brussels: nationality over a glass of wine', *JCMS: Journal of Common Market Studies* 47(2): 411–35.

Taggart, P. and Szczerbiak, A. (2002) 'The party politics of Euroscepticism in EU member and candidate states', *SEI Working Paper* 51.

Tait, N. (2006) 'Dangerous product recalls hit record', *Financial Times*, 2 October: p. 4.

—   (2008a) 'Brussels plans onslaught on online retailing', *Financial Times*, 19 June.

—   (2008b) 'Brussels to harmonise rights for consumers', *Financial Times*, 6 October: p. 5.

Tallberg, J. (2002) 'Delegation to supranational institutions: why, how, and with what consequences?', *West European Politics* 25(1): 23–46.

Tallberg, J. and Johansson, K. (2008) 'Party politics in the European Council', *Journal of European Public Policy* 15(8): 1222–42.

Tansey, O. (2007) 'Process tracing and elite interviewing: a case for non-probability sampling', *Political Science & Politics* 40(4): 765–72.

Taylor, G. and Millar, M. (2002) 'The appliance of science: the politics of European food regulation and reform', *Public Policy and Administration* 17(2): 125–46.

Teney, C., Lacewell, O. and De Wilde, P. (2014) 'Winners and losers of globalization in Europe: attitudes and ideologies', *European Political Science Review* 6: 575–95.

Tholoniat, L. (2009) 'The temporal constitution of the European Commission: a timely investigation', *Journal of European Public Policy* 16(2): 221–38.

Thomson, R. (2008) 'National actors in international organizations: the case of the European Commission', *Comparative Political Studies* 41(2): 169–92.

TIE (2008) 'Position statement on the revision of the Toy Safety Directive', *Position Paper* (25 January), Brussels: Toy Industries of Europe.

Tillman, E. (2004) 'The European Union at the ballot box?: European integration and voting behavior in the new member states', *Comparative Political Studies* 37(5): 590–610.

Tod, P. (2006) 'Co-ordinated EU action over obesity makes sense', *Financial Times*, 27 January: p. 10.

Toshkov, D. (2011) 'Public opinion and policy output in the European Union: a lost relationship', *European Union Politics* 12(2): 169–91.

Trumbull, G. (2006) *Consumer Capitalism: Politics, product markets, and firm strategy in France and Germany*, Ithaca, NY: Cornell University Press.

Tsakatika, M. (2005) 'Claims to legitimacy: the European Commission between continuity and change', *JCMS: Journal of Common Market Studies* 43(1): 193–220.

Tsebelis, G. and Garrett, G. (2000) 'Legislative politics in the European Union', *European Union Politics* 1(1): 9–36.

Tucker, E. (1998) 'Plastic toy quandary that EU cannot duck', *Financial Times*, 9 December: p. 3.

Tullock, G. (1987) *The Politics of Bureaucracy*, Lanham, MD: University Press of America.

Uba, K. and Uggla, F. (2011) 'Protest actions against the European Union, 1992–2007', *West European Politics* 34(2): 384–93.

UEAPME (2000) 'Position paper on the Draft Directive replacing Council Directive 92/59/|EEC of 29 June 1992 on general product safety', *Position Paper* (January 2000), Brussels: Union Européenne de l'Artisanat et des Petites et Moyennes Entreprises.

— (2008) 'Updated UEAPME position on the Proposal for a Regulation of the European Parliament and of the Council on the provision of food information to consumers, COM(2008) 40 final', *Position Paper* (5 August), Brussels: Union Européenne de l'Artisanat et des Petites et Moyennes Entreprises.

UITP (2005) 'European Commission staff working paper on "Passenger rights in international coach and bus services" – Position of the UITP European Union Committee', *Position Paper* (11 October), Brussels: Union Internationale de Transportes Public.

— (2006) 'European Commission Staff Working Paper on "Strengthening the protection of the rights of passengers travelling by sea or inland waterway in the European Union" – UITP Draft Response', *Position Paper* (17 May), Brussels: Union Internationale de Transportes Public.

UNICE (2001) 'Revision of Directive 92/59/EEC on general product safety – lobbying letter to the parliament', *Position Paper* (15 March), Brussels: Union of Industrial and Employers' Confederations of Europe.

— (2003) 'Position paper – Proposal for a directive concerning unfair business-to-consumer commercial practices in the Internal Market (COM (2003) 356 final)', *Position Paper* (17 November), Brussels: Union of Industrial and Employers' Confederations of Europe.

Van Belle, D. A., Rioux, J.-S. and Potter, D. M. (2004) *Media, Bureaucracies, and Foreign Aid: A comparative analysis of United States, the United Kingdom, Canada, France and Japan*, New York: Palgrave Macmillan.

Van Ingelgom, V. (2013) *Integrating Indifference: A comparative, qualitative, and quantitative approach to the legitimacy of European integration*, Colchester, UK: ECPR Press.

Van Noije, L., Kleinnijenhuis, J. and Oegema, D. (2008) 'Loss of parliamentary control due to mediatization and Europeanization: a longitudinal and cross-sectional analysis of agenda building in the United Kingdom and the Netherlands', *British Journal of Political Science* 38(3): 455–78.

Vaqué, L. G. and Melchor Romero, S. (2008) 'Wine labelling: future perspectives', *European Food and Feed Law Review* 2008(1).

Visseyrias, M. (2007) 'Nouveau rappel de jouets chinois par Mattel', *Le Figaro*, 6 September.

Vogel, D. (1995) *Trading Up: Consumer and environmental regulation in a global economy*, Cambridge, MA: Harvard University Press.

Vos, E. (1999) *Institutional Frameworks of Community Health and Safety Regulations: Health and safety regulation committees, agencies and private bodies*, Oxford: Hart Publishing.

— (2000) 'EU food safety regulation in the aftermath of the BSE crisis', *Journal of Consumer Policy* 23(3): 227–55.

Waarden, F. (2006) 'Taste, traditions, transactions, and trust: the public and private regulation of food', in Ansell, C. and Vogel, D. (ed.) *What's the Beef?: The contested governance of european food safety*, Boston, MA: MIT Press.

Wagner, R. (1966) 'Pressure groups and political entrepreneurs: a review article', *Public Choice* 1(1): 161–70.

Waverman, L. and Sirel, E. (1997) 'European telecommunications markets on the verge of full liberalization', *Journal of Economic Perspectives* 11(4): 113–26.

Weatherill, S. (2005) *EU Consumer Law and Policy*, Cheltenham, UK: Edward Elgar.

Weber, M. (1925/1978) *Economy and Society. An outline of interpretative sociology*, Vol. 1. Berkeley: University of California.

Wendler, F. (2013) 'Challenging domestic politics? European debates of national parliaments in France, Germany and the UK', *Journal of European Integration* 35(7): 801–17.

Weßels, B. (2007) 'Discontent and European identity: three types of Euroscepticism', *Acta Politica* 42(2–3): 287–306.

Wiggins, J. (2005) 'Watchdog to test food labelling schemes on consumers', *Financial Times*, 20 May: p. 5.

Wiggins, J. (2007) 'Food groups shape up for action', *Financial Times*, 17 October: p. 4.

Wille, A. (2012) 'The politicization of the EU Commission: democratic control and the dynamics of executive selection', *International Review of Administrative Sciences* 78(3): 383–402.

— (2013) *The Normalization of the European Commission: Politics and bureaucracy in the EU executive*, Oxford: Oxford University Press.

Williams, B. and Matheny, A. (1984) 'Testing theories of social regulation: hazardous waste regulation in the American states', *Journal of Politics* 46(2): 428–58.

Wilson, J. (1980) *The Politics of Regulation*, New York: Basic Books.

Wlezien, C. (2005) 'On the salience of political issues: the problem with "most important problem"', *Electoral Studies* 24(4): 555–79.

Wonka, A. (2007) 'Technocratic and independent? The appointment of European Commissioners and its policy implications', *Journal of European Public Policy* 14(2): 169–89.

— (2008a) 'Decision-making dynamics in the European Commission: partisan, national or sectoral?', *Journal of European Public Policy* 15(8): 1145–63.

— (2008b) *Die Europäische Kommission. Supranationale Bürokratie oder Agent der Mitgliedstaaten?* Baden-Baden: Nomos.

Young, A. R. (1997) 'European consumer groups: Multiple levels of governance and multiple logics of collective action', in Greenwood, J. and Aspinwall, M. (ed.) *Collective Action in the European Union: Interests and the New Politics of Associability*, London: Routledge.

Young, A. R. and Holmes, P. (2006) 'Protection or protectionism? EU food safety and the WTO', in Ansell, C. and Vogel, D. (ed.) *What's the Beef?: The contested governance of European food safety*, Boston, MA: MIT Press.

Zafra, J. M. (1999) 'La OECD insta a Espana a acelerar la creacion de nuevas redes telefonicas', *El País*, 1 July: p. 70.

Zaller, J. (1992) *The Nature and Origins of Mass Opinion*. Cambridge: Cambridge University Press.

Zürn, M. (2004) 'Global governance and legitimacy problems', *Government and Opposition* 39(2): 260–87.

— (2006) 'Zur Politisierung der Europäischen Union', *Politische Vierteljahresschrift* 47(2): 242–51.

— (2013) 'Politisierung als Konzept der Internationalen Beziehungen', in Zürn, M. and Ecker-Ehrhardt, M. (ed.) *Gesellschaftliche Politisierung und internationale Institutionen*, Berlin: Suhrkamp.

Zürn, M., Binder, M. and Ecker-Ehrhardt, M. (2012) 'International authority and its politicization', *International Theory* 4(1): 69–106.

Zürn, M., Binder, M., Ecker-Ehrhardt, M. and Radtke, K. (2007) 'Politische Ordnungsbildung wider Willen', *Zeitschrift für Internationale Beziehungen* 14(1): 129–64.

Index

italics - material in figures and tables

www.ingramcontent.com/pod-product-compliance
Lightning Source LLC
Chambersburg PA
CBHW072051020426
42334CB00017B/1471